"Had Jonathan Weinkle shared the depth of his Jewish insights about the Passover Haggadah we might say *dayenu* (it would have been enough). Had he applied those insights to the healing work of the medical profession, we might also have said *dayenu*. Had he compassionately reminded us that we all are on journeys from illness to recovery, we might also have said *dayenu*. That he instead followed the wisdom of the book of proverbs that a braided threefold chord (in this instance of healing, knowledge, and applied medical ethics) is of greatest value accounts for why we are the beneficiaries of this remarkable book *From Illness to Exodus*. The 'dance' of these three sources moving in and about one another is dazzling."

—Jeffrey Schein, senior consultant for Jewish education, The Mordecai Kaplan Center for Jewish Peoplehood

"Jonathan Weinkle describes his Haggadah as a 'Passover Meditation on Empathy, Health, and Healing.' In actuality, Dr. Weinkle offers reassuring and insightful 'Passover Medication' for the souls of all those who are (or will be) patients, as well as for caregivers, and for our social fabric. This significant work provides a powerful illumination of the seder journey from degradation to dignity and shows how its lessons are directly applicable to each of our lives as we strive for wholeness within the reality of our mortality."

—Danny Schiff, Gefsky Community Scholar, Jewish Federation of Greater Pittsburgh

"Dr. Jonathan Weinkle shares deeply of himself in this profoundly personal reflection on the meaning of the Haggadah. While this collection is framed through the lens of a medical provider (and dare I say healer), even non-clinicians will find plenty of food for thought. After all, sooner or later we are all touched in some way by illness and the healthcare system, whether it be personally or vicariously. I am sure that the thoughts collected here will provide ample fodder for hours of discussion around the seder table, to be enjoyed by all!"

—Elisha Waldman, MD, attending physician, Great Ormond Street Hospital for Children, NHS Foundation Trust

"Dr. Jonathan Weinkle is an incredibly well-read, thoughtful and reflective physician who brings to life the seder in an engaging, interactive book that the reader will pick up again and again, finding new gems and learning more about oneself each time."

—Lynne Williams, MD, executive director, Southwest PA Area Health Education Center

FROM ILLNESS TO EXODUS

FROM ILLNESS TO EXODUS

A Passover Meditation on Empathy, Health, and Healing

JONATHAN WEINKLE

RESOURCE *Publications* • Eugene, Oregon

FROM ILLNESS TO EXODUS
A Passover Meditation on Empathy, Health, and Healing

Copyright © 2025 Jonathan Weinkle. All rights reserved. Except for brief quotations in critical publications or reviews, no part of this book may be reproduced in any manner without prior written permission from the publisher. Write: Permissions, Wipf and Stock Publishers, 199 W. 8th Ave., Suite 3, Eugene, OR 97401.

Resource Publications
An Imprint of Wipf and Stock Publishers
199 W. 8th Ave., Suite 3
Eugene, OR 97401

www.wipfandstock.com

PAPERBACK ISBN: 979-8-3852-2208-7
HARDCOVER ISBN: 979-8-3852-2209-4
EBOOK ISBN: 979-8-3852-2210-0

01/30/25

This is a work of non-fiction. However, all descriptions of interactions that took place during the author's medical practice have had significant personal details ("unique identifiers") altered or omitted, or represent composite descriptions of multiple individuals, in order to prevent release of any protected health information.

[Front cover image by Mara Cohen.
Illustrations by Mara Cohen.]

Author's website: www.healerswholisten.com

In memory of Elinor and Ed Goodman, my maternal grandparents (aka Nana and Gramp). At their seder table, I learned that Passover is a holiday of joy and celebration, and the birthplace of memories.

In memory of Walter and Eva Vogel. At *their* seder table, I learned that the seder can be eternal, in the best sense of that word. Their seders contained one delight after another—another dish, another song, another moment with people I love, another bit of wisdom. They were their own world.

I called to you, God, from the narrow place.
Answer me from the wide-open space.
Psalm 118:5

Contents

Preface		ix
Acknowledgments		xi
Note on Biblical Names and Traditional Jewish Sources		xv
Introduction		xvii
1	We Could All Use a Seder	1
2	Searching for Hametz	13
3	Signposts	23
4	Sanctifying the Moment	32
5	Waldman on Washing, Part 1	43
6	Of Spring and Salt	48
7	Breaking Points	52
8	Poor Bread	56
9	So What Else Is New?	60
10	We Were Slaves	67
11	Insomniac Rabbis	76
12	Four Feelings	81
13	Where Shall I Begin?	91
14	From the Beginning	99
15	Promises that Stand the Test of Time	110
16	Go and Learn	122
17	An Aramean Told My Father to Get Lost . . .	124
18	Brought Down to the Narrow Place	132
19	Wicked Wisdom	138
20	Broken Backs	141
21	Idioms of Distress	151
22	The Outstretched Arm of the Healer	159

23	A Missing Midrash	170
24	Blood in the Water	177
25	The Danger of *Dayenu*	*184*
26	The Pesa<u>h</u> Sacrifice	195
27	Matzah (again?)	200
28	Biting Bitter Herbs	204
29	In Every Generation	209
30	A Happy Mother of Children	219
31	Taunting the Sea	222
32	Four Cups of Coffee	226
33	A Clean Break?	230
34	Breakable Bread	235
35	Soup's On	239
36	The Missing Piece	246
37	Satisfaction	249
38	A Cup of Survival	254
39	Eliyahus, Every One	257
40	Neither In Your Name Nor Mine?	259
41	Nerves of Silver	270
42	How Can I Repay You for Disappointing Me?	273
43	*Hesed* Forever!	277
44	Psalm 118—The Narrow and the Wide	281
45	*Hesed* Forever—For Everyone?	290
46	Body and Soul and Spirit	294
47	A Cup of Kindness	297
48	Get Up and Do It Again	299
49	I Love to Count	302
50	The House of Hashem	306
51	Who *Really* Knows One?	309
52	Priceless at Any Price	314
Appendix: Not Quite 100 Gates—Themes and Recurring Stories		321
Bibliography		325

Preface

I'm a doctor and I'm a Jew. Here on the pages of this book, I'm both at once.

Healing people who are suffering is fundamental to my identity as a doctor. I wrote my first book about this idea, hoping to recapture the human being that's lost behind the label, "patient." That's not easy to do. For all the noise people make about "patient-centered care," it rarely succeeds in being *person*-centered care. That's because all the effort goes into promoting it, and very little goes into practicing it, teaching it, or perfecting it. At the end of my first book, I suggested that modern medicine could use some rituals that inculcate both the idea and the practice of person-centered care.

Passover, and the Passover seder especially, is fundamental to my identity as a Jew. The holiday commemorates the Israelite Exodus from enslavement in Egypt more than 3,000 years ago. The Bible tells us it's meant to help children in future generations identify with those who experienced that Exodus. But the story is evergreen. The seder ritual and its text (the Passover Haggadah) has so many nuances, digressions, and insights. They teach us that the experience of Exodus applies in all times, in all places, to all sorts of situations—if we just allow them to speak to the moment. The seder not only builds identity, but also builds empathy with those who are "strangers" to us as much as the Israelites were strangers in the land of Egypt.

At the end of Passover in 2019, the seder and Haggadah suggested, "Use us to create those rituals you were talking about." These rituals address how someone experiencing illness identifies themselves in that "narrow space" of Egypt. But they equally speak to how someone with the responsibility of healing or helping that person can build thick empathy for them—and learn concrete, compassionate behaviors through the lessons of this amazing narrative. In our lives, each of us will be in both of those roles. We'll need both identity and empathy. I hope I've brought you a book that provides these things.

Acknowledgments

> "And you shall be satisfied, and you shall bless."
> Deuteronomy 8:10

After more than five years of working on this book, I'm satisfied. Here are my blessings:

May the One who blessed our ancestors Avraham, Yitzhak, Ya'akov, Sarah, Rivkah, Rachel, and Leah, bless the wonderful souls whose love, friendship, dedication, insight, critical thinking, cooking, humor, and tolerance enabled me to write this book. Among them:

My sons Eitan, Akiva, and Adi. If the seder is about conveying the essence of what it is to be a righteous Jew to one's children, then I've succeeded. My greatest joy has been knowing that each of you is awake, engaged, and challenging me to think deeper every time we sit at the seder together, play music together, discuss politics together, or watch sports together. I'm so proud of you.

My wife Vita, my true companion for thirty years. You have put up with me now through two book-writing odysseys, because you know best of all what it means to me. I couldn't have grown so much in understanding and in compassion without you at my side, sometimes pushing, sometimes holding me back, and always holding my hand.

My parents, Phyllis and Joe Weinkle, for making sure I had a solid Jewish foundation—and a seder to attend every year. As much joy as I get from the kids, it's a special pleasure to have had my parents at my seder and Shabbat tables for so much of the last fifteen years.

My in-laws, Lia and Natan Nemirovsky, for your warmth, your stories, and your different perspectives on life, immigration, America, medicine . . . you get the idea.

ACKNOWLEDGMENTS

My dear friend Rabbi Michael Werbow and the whole Werbow clan. The cushions on the floor, the *seder lo b'seder*, and so many other staples of my table would not be possible without you.

My rabbis and teachers: Seth Adelson, Mark Asher Goodman, Kara Tav, Jamie Gibson, Danny Schiff, Cousin Rabbi Jeffrey Schein, Steven Steindel, Aaron Mackler, Mark Staitman, Larry Heimer, Eli Seidman, Amy Bardack, Ron Symons, Erica Brown, Lawrence Hoffman, Yaffa Epstein, Aliza Sperling, Avi Weiss, and David Ingber. I've learned with some of you every week for years, and some of you only once, but your wisdom is woven throughout this book regardless.

Speaking of learning, my *havruta* group who have learned with me for the last three and a half years as I've been writing: Ira Rothstein, Brian Primack, Daniel Levine, and David Finkler. And to Geoff Camp and Peter Unger—may we learn with you again soon.

The Squirrel Hill Health Center, the only real job I've ever held, for being a shining example of how to lead people from illness to exodus. Thank you to Susan Kalson and Andrea Fox for your years of leadership, and to all the wonderful physicians, advanced practice providers, nurses, medical assistants, therapists, social workers, dental staff and front office folks who make the place run.

This magical community of Squirrel Hill. The time we've endured together since my last book was published in September 2018 could have ripped a lesser place to shreds—but we've endured together and I can still walk down the street and feel that the neighborhood is giving me a hug.

The "framily." Not only for enriching my seders with memorable tag lines like "bench germs" and "use the tongs," but for being the anchor of every Shabbat, every simcha, and every holiday, and allowing a parent of three to co-parent nearly a dozen kids altogether.

Debi Gilboa, owner of the other half of my brain, my sister-from-another-mister, for . . . well, just about everything. The arm punches have stopped since we don't sit at adjoining desks anymore, but she still pushes her "kid brother" to aim high with his crazy ideas like writing books about medicine.

Ilana Schwarcz, my amazing editor. You've been a friend for over 20 years, and you did a great job on the first book, but this took it to a whole new level of dedication. Thank you for treating this book more like a baby you were helping to deliver than like a manuscript. The loving care shows in the final product. Thank you also to Dan and David Schwarcz for letting you be that dedicated.

Susan Showalter-Bucher, for coming in to help turn Ilana's keen edits into a single Word document in the 11th hour, just because you're an amazing friend to her.

Mara Cohen, for the wonderful illustrations. They create a sense of warmth, of home, of a place where it's safe to be sad, broken, or unsure and it'll still be okay—exactly the tone I wanted to convey with this book. Thanks for "getting it."

Matthew Wimer and Resource Publications, for agreeing to publish this book. I'm honored.

And finally, the people who seek my care as their physician. I only exist as a healer because you entrust me with caring for you—a humbling and awesome responsibility. In doing so, you teach me courage, resilience, humor, and vulnerability. I cannot honor you enough.

Note on Biblical Names and Traditional Jewish Sources

Throughout this work, I've used transliterated Hebrew names for Biblical persons, rather than their Anglicized equivalents. Thus, Avraham instead of Abraham, Moshe instead of Moses, and so on.

However, in my citations of Biblical text, I've used the English names of the books to enable readers to easily find those citations in an English language Bible. I've followed a simple, standard format of the book name, chapter and verse (e.g. Exodus 12:1).

Talmudic citations begin with either "Mishna," followed by the tractate, chapter, and verse; or "Talmud," followed by the tractate and folio page number. All Talmudic citations are from the Babylonian Talmud.

Commentary on Biblical text is cited by the commentator's commonly known name (Rashi, Sforno, Malbim), followed by "on _____" and the book, chapter, and verse on which they are commenting.

All Biblical, Talmudic, and Bible commentary citations appear in the footnotes only.

All text and translation of the Passover Haggadah is taken from the online free Jewish library Sefaria. Sefaria hosts an enormous collection of Jewish texts including Bible, Talmud, commentaries, philosophy, prayerbooks, and mystical texts, many translated into English and many of those with multiple translations. The Haggadah translation used here is the 2013 Koren translation. The full Hebrew text can be found at https://www.sefaria.org/Pesach_Haggadah%2C_Kadesh?lang=he, and the Koren translation can be found at https://www.sefaria.org/Pesach_Haggadah%2C_Kadesh?lang=en.

In checking the Biblical, Talmudic, and commentator citations, I've also relied heavily on Sefaria. To see the full collection, visit https://www.sefaria.org/texts.

Commentary on the Haggadah, as it's less widely known, is cited by the author's last name, title of the commentary, and the section from which the comment is taken. Likewise, these works are listed in the Bibliography, along with hyperlinks to their Sefaria electronic editions.

Introduction

More than three thousand years ago, the Israelite people were enslaved in Egypt. Jewish tradition holds that despite their enslavement, these people held onto some key elements of their identity: Belief in one God, use of their own ancestral names, and the Hebrew language. In that language, they had a different name for the land they were in: *Mitzrayim*, the narrow straits. I've been a physician for twenty years—which is admittedly less than three thousand—but still long enough to know that illness, whether critical or chronic, mental or physical, is a narrow strait. People suffering through an illness often feel as trapped as the Israelites must have felt during their time in Egypt.

If this were the whole story, it wouldn't be worth writing a book about. Enslaved Israelites suffered and you're suffering through your cancer. Why am I burdening you with stories about how other people were miserable just like you?

The story is worth telling, even for people who are in the midst of serious health crises, because the Israelites got *out* of Egypt. It's a story of hope, of possibility, of recognizing that while suffering may be a natural occurrence in our world, we don't have to accept it as unending or deserved—we can fight it. It's such a good story that Jews throughout history have been retelling it every year. In fact, the Biblical account of the moment of the Exodus, in Chapter 13 of the book of the same name, insists, "And you shall tell your child on that day . . . It's because of that which God did for me when I came forth out of Egypt."[1] They haven't even left enslavement yet, and Moses is already commanding them to retell the story to future generations.

That commandment, and three others like it, were originally attached to a Passover sacrifice of a lamb to be offered in the Temple in Jerusalem. The first of these Temples was built by King Solomon and

---

1. Exodus 13:8

later destroyed by the Babylonian king Nebuchadnezzar in 586 BCE. The second was rebuilt roughly seventy years later, and stood until it was destroyed by the Roman General Titus, in 70 CE.

In Titus' time, there was already a growing movement of Jews[2] engaged in discussing and codifying the oral law of daily Jewish life beyond the Temple service. One of those Jews, Rabban Yohanan ben Zakkai, recognized that the end was near for the Temple, and that the oral law might be the only hope that the Jewish people would survive the Roman destruction. With the help of his disciples, he faked his own death so that he could be carried out of the city in a coffin to be buried. Once outside, ben Zakkai emerged from the coffin and went to Vespasian, Titus' predecessor, to make a request: Give me the town of Yavneh and the lives of the other scholars, so that I can start an academy there and preserve Judaism for future generations. He set Judaism on the road to becoming a portable way of life (Jewish law is known as *halakha*, going or walking, because it is the "way" of going through the world).

The oral law these scholars compiled eventually became known as the Mishna. It was organized into six orders covering major divisions—Agriculture, Sacred Times, Family Law, Tort Law, Holy Rituals (like kosher slaughter, among other things), and Ritual Purity. These orders were further subdivided into tractates, each dealing with a more focused topic. One key thing the Mishna had to deal with was the question of "what now?" What were the Jews to do without the Temple that had been the center of religious life to that point? During the Babylonian exile, they'd experienced the same phenomenon—and many Jews had simply forgotten what to do. The rabbis had to make sure that didn't happen again.

One element of Jewish life that was especially vulnerable were the holidays, since most were celebrated with Temple sacrifices, Levitical priests singing and playing instruments, and pilgrims gathering in Jerusalem from all over the country. No holiday was more widely celebrated than Passover,[3] with its unique paschal sacrifice on the eve of the holiday

---

2. Jews? What happened to the Israelites? After King Solomon, the unified kingdom of Israel split into two—with the southern kingdom including only the tribes of Judah and Benjamin, but retaining the capital of Jerusalem and the national name of Judah. The northern ten tribes kept the name "Israel," and moved their capital to Samaria. Israel was destroyed by Assyria in 722 BCE, and the tribes were "lost" to Assyria's policy of scattering its conquered people throughout the empire. This left the people of Judah—*Yehudah*—who became known as *Yehudim*—Jews.

3. I'll go back and forth freely between the words Pesach (the Hebrew name of the holiday) and Passover in this text. The Hebrew word *pasach* means "passed over" and is

INTRODUCTION

to remember the lamb the Israelites slaughtered while awaiting their moment of deliverance from Egypt. Legend held that so many people used to pack Jerusalem for the holiday of Passover that the Temple courtyard had to magically expand to accommodate them all. My friend Chris Hall once taught a class about trying to make the mathematics of this gigantic pilgrimage work out; it was the first time I've ever had to use the phrase, "suspend disbelief" in conjunction with a math lesson.

The rabbis answered this challenge in Tractate Pesachim, literally "Passovers," Chapter 10. They go step by step through a ritual based not in the Temple, but at every family's own dinner table. Many of the stages of the Passover ritual I describe below, and many of the texts we will discuss, are already laid out in this chapter, written down at least 1,800 years ago. The stages are: Four cups of wine, dipping vegetables, children asking questions, expounding on a Bible passage, explaining the symbolic foods, reciting Psalms of praise, eating a festive meal, and the rules about concluding the Seder. Pesachim 10 even mentions people falling asleep at the seder table! More on that later...

What does all of this have to do with that poor person going through chemo? OK, so the Israelites got out of Egypt. Hooray for them. Why do I not only need to hear about their misery, but get a lesson on the origins of the Mishna? I'm a little busy here.

Imagine for a minute one of those dinner tables: Somewhere in the Galilee, maybe fifty or a hundred years after the Temple was destroyed. Imagine, after a cup or so of wine, a precocious child of seven or eight beginning to "ask" the prepared text of questions, then stopping to ask a real question of their own.

"Abba (Daddy), I have my own question."

"Yes, my child?"

"Why did Hashem (that's what Jews often call God in conversation, rather than risk using any of the "real" divine names that should only be pronounced in prayer) destroy the Temple? Did we do something bad?"

Now imagine people dropping their wine cups in surprise.

When you tell a story about hope and redemption in an un-redeemed world, people are going to have questions. When you gather a group of thinking people, especially thinking children, around a table to tell such a story, they're going to want to know what it all means. And when a human being finds out they're sick with a disease that could kill

---

the verb used for God skipping over the houses of the Israelites during the final plague on Egypt. Passover is therefore an exact translation of the Hebrew.

them, they're going to struggle to make sense of it. They're in a narrow place—trying to figure out how and why they got there, and how to get *out*. They're having the same conversation that has been continued at every seder table for the last 1,800 years. This book is for them, and for the people who care about and for them.

The seder has grown a lot since the days of the Mishna, even though the skeleton in Pesachim Chapter 10 survives almost intact (the questions are a little different, since the original ones reflect a time when many Jews still held out hope that, just like the first Temple, the second would be rebuilt within a few decades). But after hundreds of years of a book-happy people arguing about the same story over dinner every year, there have been a few—many—additions to the evening. Let's get oriented for a minute.

Passover falls sometime in the early spring. The holiday begins, like all Jewish days, at sundown as the 14th of the month of Nissan passes into the 15th. Since the Hebrew calendar uses lunar months but is keyed to agriculture in the land of Israel, it uses a leap month every couple of years to keep the months in season. As a result, Passover can begin as early as late March and end as late as May 1. The seder meal takes place on the first night of the holiday, and among more traditional Jews outside the land of Israel, on the second night as well (Reform Jews in the diaspora and all Jews in Israel celebrate a single seder).

Seder is the Hebrew word for "order," and there's a detailed, prescribed order to both the ritual and the meal. In practice, however, every seder is a unique experience, both because of additions and omissions, and because of the uniqueness of the participants, the setting, and the circumstances. In this book, I ask myself, and you, "How does the seder change when the circumstances include a serious illness—or when the participants include people who are weary from caring for those who are suffering? What does it all mean *then*?"

Speaking of books, as the seder has grown, a single chapter of Mishna was no longer enough to contain all of the instructions. Eventually, as more texts and practices were added, a book was needed to pull it all together. We call that book the Haggadah—Hebrew for "telling," since it's the book that facilitates the telling of the story—and that's exactly what the Israelites were commanded to do while the thing was still happening.

The Haggadah is not a prayer book *per se*. We have those in Judaism, and they even share a root with "seder." A Jewish prayer book is a *siddur*. But the siddur contains prayers meant to be recited as-is, and at

INTRODUCTION   xxi

least in theory is not to be interrupted with talking and questions (don't tell the friends and family I sit with in synagogue). The Haggadah is, well, different.

Think of it as the script of a play, but one where the director is offset, and the actors are free to mess around with the lines however they want. A play where all the actors are Robin Williams in *Good Morning, Vietnam*, continuously ad-libbing but getting the point across perfectly every time. A play where the audience is free to interrupt and demand to know, "Why did you just do that?" Like *Rocky Horror Picture Show*, but without throwing toast.[4] Because, you know, toast is bread, and bread is not permitted on Passover.

That last part was serious, by the way. In the process of leaving Egypt, the Torah[5] tells us that the Israelites' bread dough didn't have time to rise, and they ended up baking it into flat cakes called matzah.[6] Therefore, Jews are commanded not to eat any risen, leavened food during the whole seven (or eight, in the diaspora) day holiday.[7] Weirdly enough, this commandment comes *before* the detail about the dough not rising. Seder may mean order, but the story is definitely not told linearly, either in the Torah or the Haggadah.

The different material gathered in the Haggadah represents all the layers of the Jewish bookshelf. Some texts come from the Torah or the other parts of the Hebrew Bible (the Prophets and Writings, including several of the Psalms). Some come, as we've seen, from the Mishna, and some from the next layer of oral law, the Gemara, which was compiled during the three hundred years after the Mishna was completed (around 200 CE). You may hear me use the word "Talmud," which refers to the Mishna and Gemara together. The Talmud follows the same divisions as the Mishna, described above.

The Haggadah doesn't stop with the oral law. There's plenty of other material. The oldest is the Midrash—homiletical stories that try to fill in the gaps in the Biblical texts, from around the same time as the Talmud.

---

4. But, at least in some traditions, they *do* throw things at the Seder! I attended one seder where the hosts had scattered spring-loaded frogs on the table so people could aim them at each other throughout the meal.

5. Torah means "teaching." It can either refer to the first five books of the Hebrew Bible (the "Five Books of Moses"), as it does here, or the whole body of Jewish learning. You'll be able to tell the difference. If I say, "the Torah" then I mean the five books; if I say "Torah," I mean the whole shebang.

6. Exodus 12:34 and 12:39.

7. Exodus 12:15–20.

Later come the commentaries, hundreds of years of insights from rabbis in countries as diverse as Babylonia/Iraq, Spain, France, Germany, Egypt, Morocco, Poland, and Lithuania. These rabbis looked at the Bible and perpetually asked, "Yes, but what *else* can I learn from this?" even after studying all that came before.

Many also wrote commentaries on the Haggadah itself. I've included many of those insights here, often with a historical note placing that commentator in their context, because it helps to know what they were going through when they said what they said. Some are quite old, and some are writers whom I've met and studied with.

One of my favorite teachings about medicine is that disease and illness are not the same thing. We can explain disease in the language of science, but each person has a unique illness that requires understanding the context and meaning. Just the same, commentaries are not just dry observations about a word, but observations about living people who have dynamic insights on how to apply the text to their world.

Which brings us to my project that you hold in your hands. Think of me, if you think I deserve it, as the latest in a line of Haggadah commentators—but the first, so far as I know, to write a Haggadah commentary about the parallels between illness and the Exodus. This is undoubtedly a Jewish book—written by a Jew, using Jewish material about a very Jewish subject, and following the structure of a Jewish book that has seen nearly six thousand different versions. But it's not only a book for Jews, because it's equally about a very universal subject—sickness and health. For those who have picked this book up because they need some help dealing with that universal subject, let me help you find your way through this strange landscape.

Section One will get you oriented to the basics. You'll hear a longer explanation of how I came to believe that a Passover seder and the text of the Haggadah are relevant to illness and wellness. I'll explain a little about the concept of *hametz* (leavening) that's forbidden to eat on Passover, and what that might mean for our parallel. Finally, we'll talk about the signposts of the seder; steps that tell us where we are on the journey.

Section Two begins the seder ritual itself. Like all Jewish ritual meals, it begins with a kiddush, a sanctification prayer over wine. The next three steps involve ritually washing the hands, eating a spring vegetable dipped in salt water, and symbolically breaking a piece of matzah in half. I'll use these four chapters to consider what concrete behaviors these actions are supposed to teach us, because religious rituals aren't just about how well we can follow arbitrary rules. They're experiential education, exercises in linking a muscle memory with an emotional or intellectual one.

The central part of the seder is the Magid or "telling" section (from the same root word as "Haggadah"). It tells the story of the Exodus, but in a manner that literally begs the question, "What happened there—and what's going on here?" Section Three of the book deals with the first part of Magid, focused on perhaps the most well-known text of the seder, the Four Questions, which ask, "why is this night different from all other nights?"

Prior to the questions, we'll consider what the opening invitation, "Let all who are hungry come and eat," means for modern healthcare. Likewise, the questions themselves prompt a discussion of how to make each healing encounter a "different night." We then proceed to the purported answers to the questions. The first answer (that the seder is about telling the story of being freed from slavery), calls to mind how we heal from experiences of tragedy and trauma. The second, that the seder is about the Israelites moving from idolatry to knowing God, is a sobering reminder of the "idolatry" that has plagued medicine throughout its history. In between, we see what the seder has to say about a group of rabbis staying up all night—not unlike medical residents, or parents of newborns. We apply the seder's lessons about teaching different types of children to how health professionals interact with people who vex, challenge, and bring out the worst in us. We end by contemplating what we promise to do for people—and how to make those promises stick.

Section Four continues with the middle part of Magid, the text from Deuteronomy known as the First Fruits Declaration, a five-line text that tells the shortest complete version of the Exodus we have. Sometimes in medicine we need to get right to the point: There's an emergency, and we don't have much time to lose. Other times, the idol of "productivity" forces us to rush through our day, and we need to hear the story as fast as possible. In an ideal world, however, each word of that story is a world of its own, and excellent care demands understanding them all. In this section we look at the short, direct stories people tell of their illnesses, then dive deep into what some of the little details reveal. We proceed to an examination of the Ten Plagues of the seder, and the countless newer plagues that afflict our attempts to heal people in the 2020s. Then, we conclude by looking at the song Dayenu: "It Would Have Been Enough for Us," and questioning its message, especially for those who are still in the throes of suffering.

Section Five covers the end of Magid, which contains the central message of the seder, "*Have empathy for others who are going through what you once suffered yourself.*" Visible, tangible symbols help to drive home this point, in this case the Passover sacrifice (a lamb shank), the matzah, and bitter herbs. Music further reinforces the message, with Psalms 113 celebrating the miracle of a barren woman becoming a happy mother of children, and Psalm 114 celebrating the miracle of crossing the Sea of Reeds. Even in the midst of pain and suffering, there are moments of joy that we shouldn't miss.[8] In recognition of those moments, we wrap up Magid with the second of four blessings over wine (or, in my case, coffee).

Section Six covers the festive seder meal. One might think that there's nothing to say except, "Let's eat," but starting a meal in Jewish tradition requires washing again, and we take a different angle on what washing might mean in the healing encounter. We also need to bless the symbolic foods of matzah, bitter herbs, and a sandwich of the two together—before we get to the good stuff (which I've included my family recipes for, as a reward for making it that far). We learn lessons of humility, hope, and healing from the Birkat HaMazon (Grace after Meals). A third cup of wine teaches us to give thanks for surviving. With the taste of that thanks still on our tongues, we consider the lessons in kindness from Eliyahu (Elijah) the prophet, and the dangerous emotions of anger and revenge. How might we reconcile the two, especially when we feel the anger is righteous?

Section Seven is all about the songs. Psalms 115 raises serious questions about idolatry, immortality, and what constitutes a meaningful life. Psalm 116 asks us to praise and think about the gifts we receive and whether we've earned them. Psalms 117, 118, and 136 praise what many people consider the quintessential virtue of Judaism, and of medicine—*hesed*, lovingkindness. I use this opportunity to call out some people whose extreme *hesed* is often overlooked, and to recognize that what seems like *hesed* to one person may seem like tragedy to another. Psalm 118 also suggests to me that perhaps the seder was about healing all along, if we look at it in context. Next, in the spirit of the rabbis who stay up all night, we recite the first part of the morning prayers—including one beautiful meditation on the ideas of body, soul, and spirit.

---

8. These Psalms are the beginning of the collection of six Psalms known as Hallel, which are sung on all the joyous holidays of the Jewish year during the daytime. Only at the seder are they recited at night.

Section Eight is the conclusion of the seder. It opens with the last cup of wine, the one I call the "cup of kindness." The ending of the seder doesn't send the message, "we've arrived," but rather, "let's get up tomorrow morning and do it all over again," and let us count the days toward the next phase of our healing work. Our work is never done. The concluding songs that follow, at least for me, sharpen that point. It is *human beings* that matter in our healing work. The people, not the grandiose buildings, are the most important thing in medicine. Each of them is unique, and even the "least of them," like the tiny baby goat in the final song Had Gadya, may turn out to be worth the entire universe.

In Chapter 10, I reference the physician Rita Charon and her seminal book *Narrative Medicine*, which became the founding document of an entire field of study and practice. She contends that narrative medicine's goal is to teach health professionals to guide patients through telling their stories so expertly that the patient eventually says, "Thank you, now I understand what I was trying to say."[9] This is my work of narrative medicine. I hope that whether you personally are grappling with illness or are a healing professional considering those you care for, this book helps you tell your story better—to heal and to be healed more fully.

Every seder concludes, "Next Year in Jerusalem." The Hebrew name *Yerushalayim* shares three key letters, *shin-lamed-mem*, with the words *shalom* (peace) and *shalem*, whole or complete. I wish you a coming year that is more peaceful, more whole, more complete. A year where you can step out of a narrow place into a wide-open space—or to help another person do the same.

---

9. Charon, *Narrative Medicine*. 58.

1

We Could All Use a Seder

What is a Passover seder and what is it good for?

I love Passover. Specifically, I love the Passover Seder, the ritual that careens between dinner theater, an unleavened Thanksgiving feast, airing of family grievances, and intense exploration of serious religious texts and themes. I keep a running list in my head of the best sedarim I've ever attended the way some people keep track of the GOAT (greatest of all time) player in their favorite sport (Mario Lemieux) or their favorite movie ever (Princess Bride).

In 2019, I was cleaning up from a particularly memorable Pesach (the Hebrew word for "Passover") when an idea struck me. I dashed off a quick blog post declaring my intention to write a Healer's Haggadah. I was inspired by that year's latest addition to my collection, The (Unofficial) Hogwarts Haggadah by Rabbi Moshe Rosenberg, to realize anew how universally relevant the messages of the Exodus were. If there were parallels to Harry Potter, there must certainly be some to medicine. After that flash of inspiration, I dug back into my first book, Healing People, Not Patients, which had come out eight months earlier, and realized that I had already made an offhand suggestion of creating a seder as a way of ritualizing and strengthening the little behaviors that make up the practice of whole-person, compassionate medical care.

Several months later, while staying with a host in Albuquerque, NM, for a speaking engagement, I picked up Roger Kamenetz's book,

The Jew in the Lotus, and understood why a book connecting the Exodus story with illness and healing carried such resonance for me.

In 1990, Kamenetz embedded himself with a Jewish delegation to Northern India to visit the encampment of the Dalai Lama. While he profiles several members of that group, his portrayal of Rabbis Zalman Schachter-Shalomi stuck with me.

Rabbi Zalman Schachter-Shalomi was a disciple of the last Lubavitcher Rebbe and founder of the Jewish Renewal movement. I never met Reb Zalman, but I visited his protégé, Rabbi David Ingber, who keeps an enormous photo of Reb Zalman on his office wall. While every photo of the Lubavitcher Rebbe is, for all practical purposes, a black and white photograph except for the skin tones, Reb Zalman explodes in color, wrapped in a rainbow-striped tallit.

Likewise, Kamenetz portrays Reb Zalman as an explosion of color, a burst of light, an ethereal flame. His dialogue with the Dalai Lama consumes an entire day and ranges across realms of space, time, and existence that most others in the delegation never even touch upon in their practice of Judaism. Yet his advice to the Dalai Lama on how best to ensure the survival of the Tibetan community in exile is entirely down-to-earth and rooted in the most widely observed Jewish ritual of all: The Tibetans should create a seder.

Reb Zalman reasons that the perpetual retelling of the Exodus narrative has been essential to Jewish survival. The Tibetans, at that time already into a second generation of children born without memory of Tibet itself, or of the Chinese treatment of the Tibetans, should ritualize the telling of their own history in a way that transforms the tragedy of exile into a source of focus, inspiration, and hope.[1]

The themes of the seder are timeless: Suffering, exile, redemption, divine justice. It's a ritual about transforming ordinary objects into sources of holiness, and ordinary people—debased people, in fact, who served as slaves and once worshipped idols—into carriers of a divine mission. It's also a dramatization of being stuck in dire straits and finding the way out. The Haggadah is the script for that drama. As we'll see, however, it's a script open to interpretation and inviting improvisation and ad lib. One legendary event in Bronze Age Egypt becomes the template for millennia of other dramas, aspirations, and struggles.

---

1. Kamenetz, *Jew in the Lotus.* 72–90.

The Hebrew for Egypt, Mitzrayim, is the equivalent of the English, "in dire straits." It implies being stuck in a narrow (tzar) place from which escape seems impossible. My friend Elisha Waldman cared for children with cancer at Hadassah Hospital in Jerusalem for seven years. When he wrote about it afterward, he titled the book, This Narrow Space. Elisha's title captures my feeling that illness is its own sort of Mitzrayim where we feel trapped. The whole endeavor of healing is to help a person achieve an Exodus from that Mitzrayim.[2]

Being in that narrow space creates an eternal present of suffering. The psychiatrist Bessel van der Kolk maintains that the essence of being traumatized is not in remembering traumatic events so much as reliving them constantly[3]. In the reliving, the events are fragments that appear unasked for when events outside the person's body and beyond their control trigger a memory or a feeling. The Haggadah asks us to feel as if we, too, were slaves in Egypt. The person living with trauma feels as if they're still in Egypt. A seder is a way of ritualizing memory for the purpose of moving experiences of brokenness from the realm of the eternal present to the space of the contextualized past.

Reb Zalman felt that the Tibetan people collectively needed a seder to grapple with their national tragedy and to preserve their connection with their history into an uncertain future. Other sedarim and their Haggadot have dealt with women's rights, the struggles of laborers, the push to establish the modern state of Israel and the various environmental crises. In 2023, I purchased two new Haggadot. One is called The Human Rights Haggadah, which explores themes around modern slavery and exploitation, and the other is called The Israeli Black Panther Haggadah, written amid the fight for equality for the Mizrachi (North African and Middle Eastern) Jews in Israel in the early 1970s. In 2024, there were new Haggadot and sedarim expressing solidarity with those suffering on both sides of the war between Israel and Hamas—haggadot praying for the release of the hostages, and sedarim calling attention to the plight of the homeless and starving in Gaza. And at least a few, mine included, tried to make room for both.

In much the same way, a healing seder for those who are ill, traumatized, bereft or otherwise hurt offers a chance to claim agency over how

---

2. While I highly encourage you to read *This Narrow Space*, you should definitely look at Elisha's contribution to this *Haggadah*, in Chapters 5 and 33.

3. Van Der Kolk, The Body Keeps the Score: Brain, Mind, and Body in the Healing of Trauma, 53.

they'll understand that hurt in the future. It could integrate into therapy, serve as a completion ritual for cancer treatment or even signify the final leaving of a Pharaoh in one's own life who will oppress no longer.

One of Reb Zalman's traveling companions in India was Rabbi Irving "Yitz" Greenberg. Not long before that trip, Greenberg wrote an essay entitled, "Judaism as an Exodus Religion," in which he explains that by being in bondage in "Dire Straits," the Israelites were in a state that God never intended human beings to endure. Slavery is not the natural condition of humanity. The Exodus, in turn, is proof that when humanity suffers, God hears, and God cares, and God acts.[4]

In the healing professions, humans act on behalf of God (acting in God's image) to relieve each other's suffering, including getting each other out of dire straits. The Exodus imagery is supposed to remind us that healing is possible, and that we're supposed to reach out our arms and perform some signs and wonders of our own to make it happen. Modern medicine is nothing, if not signs and wonders galore.

But in performing those signs and wonders, modern healers often forget, and are more often perceived as forgetting, the more essential message of the seder: Be'khol dor va dor hayyav ha'adam lir'ot et atzmo k'ilu hu yatza mi'Mitzrayim. "In every generation, a person is obligated to see themselves as if they personally went forth from [the narrow place]." The empathy generated in a seder connects us to our own past and our own struggles, perhaps the singular moment of grief that impelled us to choose medicine as a career, or the personal hardship we endured to reach the stage in our careers where we felt ready to do the work that we do. But it also connects us to the sufferings of those we care for, just as traditional sedarim are often used as a time to channel our thoughts to those still enslaved around the world. A Healing Seder, and a Healing Haggadah, aim to shine a light not on the miracles we're empowered to perform, but on the hearing and caring that precede the action.

A BLURRY LINE

The threads connecting the Exodus narrative to narratives of illness and health don't just apply to the healing professionals, but as much or more to people experiencing illness. Quite often, the lines separating those two groups are blurred to the point of disappearance.

---

4. Greenberg, "Judaism as an Exodus Religion," 35.

Like a lot of projects from the "before times," this one sat and gathered dust for a year until the COVID-19 pandemic. When I sat down to write, it was from a very narrow place indeed—under quarantine within my own house—diagnosed with COVID-19 infection while the rest of my family mysteriously tested negative. The doctor became the patient, and not a very "good" one at that, as I think back upon my snarky replies to my in-laws' frequent, well-meaning calls and texts offering me advice to help me get better. Given that I was entirely asymptomatic, the only advice I really needed was how to make time go by faster.

Once before in my life (during my service in the Israeli Navy) I had a very similar experience. I was on a ship, had finished the book I brought with me, and was surrounded by fifty complete strangers. As emergency medical personnel with no fixed role on the ship, I had no duties to discharge. We had no firm end-date for the voyage, the purpose of which I wasn't even cleared to know, and my days melted away from the lack of structure and the despair of not knowing when we would eventually return home. It was only five or six days, but I found them excruciating and interminable, and still remember it as a miserable experience.

By comparison, my quarantine had a feeling of safety and purpose even thirty-six hours into staring at the same four walls, knowing I had at least eight and a half more days ahead of me if I remained well. The story teaches that God calculated the end of the Israelites' enslavement *(hishav et ha ketz,* in Hebrew, a phrase we'll come back to again). Knowing that suffering has an end provides strength. It gives us the ability to cross off boxes on the calendar, count down the days, and make plans for what will happen "after." My son can finally go to school on such-and-such a date, I can be with my wife and children in the same room again, we can all go out walking down the street without fear of spreading pestilence. *Not knowing when it'll end is agonizing, almost worse than the suffering itself.*

In my COVID isolation, I had an order to the day (not a Passover *seder* but a *seder yom*) punctuated not just by meals, but by remotely attending minyan (morning and evening services, which *no one* could attend in-person in August of 2020 anyhow). I churned my way through the interminable list of "to-dos" that turned out to be quite do-able from the makeshift desk between the bed and dresser. I followed Alexander Hamilton's lead by "writing my way out" of my isolation room. Halfway through the isolation period I even "went back to work," since I would have been working remotely in any case. At that stage of the pandemic, I was only working in the office perhaps three days out of ten (and my wife is still convinced that it was one of those days that got me infected in the first place).

Work allowed me a sense of efficacy that was lacking on the ship, but it also provided connection with others, something else I lacked on the ship even as I was permitted to move freely and not under "social distancing" protocols. The Pesach story, and the rituals that come with it, are a connection, a bond between all who suffer, all who are downtrodden, all who are oppressed that says, "we have shared this narrow space even if it was not the same narrow space, and we can have hope in each other's experiences that someday it'll end, because our suffering has been seen and heard." Seeing patients over telehealth while in my own isolation effectively erased any pretense of a line that separated me from them—especially when I was doing a "virtual visit" with a patient also isolating due to COVID-19.

LET ALL WHO ARE IN NEED COME CELEBRATE THE PESACH

Building connections, creating hope, and ordering the chaos of traumatic memories is the essence of *seder*. It's a supremely Jewish ritual, yet there's a long tradition of inviting non-Jews to sit at the table with us. Indeed, Greenberg's message is that the Exodus did not just save the Israelites; it put the world on notice that they, too, could have a way out of their despair. In the text we read, "Let all who are hungry come and eat, let all who are in need come and celebrate the Pesach." Knowledge of the ritual is not a pre-requisite; elsewhere we're instructed, *at ptach lo*—you shall begin for him when your child doesn't even know enough to ask the question. Whether this is your tradition or not, whether you're steeped in its knowledge or not, there's a seat at the table for you.

One of the greatest Jewish figures of my lifetime, Natan Sharansky, celebrates two *sedarim* every year: One on the traditional date (he lives in Israel, so no second seder) and one on the anniversary of his own liberation from the *gulag*. When asked by journalist Liel Liebowitz for a way that younger generations who don't remember Sharansky's struggles firsthand can feel connected to that era, Sharansky replied, "We already have a way! We have the *seder*!"[5]

---

5. *Unorthodox* podcast, Ep. 240, "Respect Your Elders," 38:34.

There's a perception, at least partially true, among some of my patients that physicians are a privileged class, removed and sheltered from the suffering that most other people go through. While this is far from universal, the rising cost of medical education ensures that fewer and fewer people currently lift themselves out of poverty through careers as doctors. As physician assistant and nurse practitioner pathways become more lucrative and pricier, those avenues, too, have begun to privilege those who already have access to them, while only the lower rungs of the hierarchy remain truly open for people of lower SES and minority ethnic background.

In such a setting, it can be easy for the people making the decisions to seem like the generation that has forgotten Sharansky, unaware of what sacrifices people made under communism. The seder is a way of awakening that understanding—even as the seder must also question why the hierarchy is as it's, and not a more inclusive, diverse one. The seder is a subversive ritual, one invented in Roman times when the oppressed Jews adopted the aristocratic traditions of their Roman rulers for a night. It's a ritual which year after year invites us to subvert the oppressive order in our own day, in order to hasten a day when we celebrate not in our current homes, but in a rebuilt Jerusalem—the city symbolic of finally having achieved peace and justice in the world. That task, as we'll see, involves assessing our own part in that order.

Sometimes it's hard to know whether we should be identifying with the Israelites, or with the taskmasters. As a white-appearing, Ashkenazi Jew living in America, I was hesitant to write a book that spoke so extensively about analogizing a slavery experience to individual illness, especially in the polarized climate of 2023. I briefly touched on the idea in a draft of *Healing People, Not Patients*; one of the reviewers hated it so much it never saw the light of day.

I carried this hesitation with me to the 2023 Conference on Medicine and Religion in Columbus, OH, hoping to run into someone there, among the health professionals who see the synergy between their faith and their trade, who could guide me through telling my story without minimizing either the historic suffering of enslaved Africans in this country or the ongoing narrowness facing their descendants to this very moment. That someone turned out to be Rev. Anastasia Holman, Director of Chaplaincy Education for Indiana University Health System.

I met Anastasia at a session she was leading with two doctors and another chaplain representing four different faith traditions. Using the theme of "Lament," they shared text from all across the Abrahamic traditions, including several that had been written either by enslaved people or people recently liberated from slavery in America. They lead us, a group of doctors, PAs, chaplains, nurses and academics, through our own understanding of what lamentation means, what it does for us, and what we might lament in our own lives and careers.

At the end, we each composed a lament of our own. Mine started with a text from the Koran about the death of the Prophet Mohammed's son, and the role of scent. It wove in the reactions of the Christian colleagues with whom I discussed it, while ultimately coming home to a consideration of whether scent plays a role in my own religion, or in my profession. It was a most *seder*-like experience.

I sought out Anastasia afterward, knowing she would understand my dilemma. Her response to the question lifted the weight from my shoulders immediately and completely. "Speak your own truth," she told me. As long as I remained true to the text I knew and interpreted it from within my own frame of reference, I was on safe ground. After all, I wasn't attempting to analogize one person's heart surgery to an historic injustice whose repercussions are still playing out across the US. I was using an ancient text; one to which many enslaved people in this country turned to for answers, and reinterpreting it in accordance with a custom which is almost as ancient as the text and the ritual itself.

But Anastasia didn't stop with reassurance. She introduced me to NaShieka Knight, who by day works for the American Association of Medical Colleges, but in her spare time is doing a PhD thesis in theology on a radical reinterpretation of the Exodus story. It took me ten seconds to know that NaShieka and I belong at the same *seder* table.

On one foot, NaShieka's idea is that the story of the Exodus is the story of an Afro-Asiatic diasporic people. Egypt was what post-colonial theorists call a "contact zone," a place where the colonizers and the colonized intermingle and rub off on one another. While the Israelites were an immigrant people who were enslaved by the natives, rather than the more typical narrative of an outside conqueror dominating the natives that we saw in the 15th-20th centuries CE, what followed was a blurring of the lines between these refugees from the famine in Canaan and the Egyptian elite. After a couple hundred years in slavery, there couldn't help but be some overlap between the groups.

Jewish interpretation downplays this overlap, citing the Israelites' maintenance of their distinct names, language, and traditions even as the yoke of slavery got heavier and heavier.⁶ But the plain text includes several examples of people whose identity blurs the boundary of whether they're part of the oppressor class or the oppressed, beginning with Moshe (Moses, an Egyptian name rather than a Hebrew one⁷). Raised in the palace of Pharaoh, his Israelite consciousness awakens slowly, and only when he confronts the taskmaster beating a slave does he make his choice of which side he is on. Even then, his eventual wife initially calls him "that Egyptian man," and he's able to freely approach Pharaoh on his return to Egypt as if he belongs to the nobility.

Moshe isn't the only one, either. Pharaoh's own daughter, while Egyptian by birth, clearly develops sympathies for the Israelites that lead her to rescue the baby Moshe (and name him with an Egyptian name!). The midwives that are commanded to murder the Israelite boy babies on the birthstones are called *(ha)meyaldot ha'ivriyot*, which could either mean, "the Hebrew midwives" or "the ones who midwife (deliver the babies of) the Hebrew women." In other words, it's not clear whether they're Israelites themselves, or whether they're Egyptian women tasked with the birthing. It's hard to imagine Pharoah believing that Israelite women would do such a thing to their own babies, but in a post-Shoah (the Hebrew term for the Holocaust) world, we know all too well what sadistic leaders will demand of the people under their control—just to show that they can. But let us surmise that Pharaoh knew better than to ask for such a thing. Therefore, they *were* likely Egyptian midwives sent to the Hebrews. Yet they were willing to lie to Pharaoh to save the babies, playing on Pharaoh's own prejudice that the Hebrews were little better than animals. They (and perhaps a lot of the Egyptians) took the side of the Israelites.⁸

By the time of the actual Exodus, the Israelites had somewhat of a cult following. During the plague of darkness, the penultimate disaster, the benighted (literally) Egyptians give gifts of gold and jewels to the Israelites to take with them—gifts that serve both for good, as they're used to build the Tabernacle in the wilderness, and for evil, as some of them are melted down to make the molten calf. And finally, at the moment of departure, a mixed multitude of other peoples enslaved in Egypt capitalize

---

6. Leviticus Rabbah 32:5.

7. Goelet, "Moses' Egyptian Name," https://library.biblicalarchaeology.org/article/moses-egyptian-name/

8. Exodus 1:15–21.

on the widespread chaos of the Exodus to march to freedom themselves, in company with the Hebrews.

These fellow travelers are often the scapegoats for trouble in the Israelite camp in the wilderness years. At least one commentator, the Shadal, identifies them as Egyptians who left Egypt still practicing their religion, but who underwent a sincere conversion to the Israelite religion (not called Judaism yet; that didn't happen until much later) after seeing the signs and wonders of the Exodus, the crossing of the Sea of Reeds, and the giving of Torah at Sinai.[9] Just as Reb Zalman suggested to the Dalai Lama, this is one people's story, but in a sense it's everyone's story.

There's a little of each of us in all of us. Not for nothing does the central commandment of the *seder* state, "In every generation, the person (*Ha-Adam* in Hebrew) is obligated to see themselves as if they went forth from Egypt." Not "the Jew." Not "the Israelite." The person. And if the line between Israelite and Egyptian, oppressor and oppressed, is so easily blurred, how much more so is it blurred between the healing professional and the person experiencing illness. Sooner or later, nearly all of us will play each of those roles in turn. A seder, and the Haggadah that guides us through it, is meant to generate empathy for the person currently oppressed, currently struggling, by reminding a person, "Hey, you've been there, too."

USING THIS BOOK

This book is built around the structure of a traditional seder and brings in sections of the traditional Haggadah text, in Hebrew (and some Aramaic) with English translation taken from the indispensable website Sefaria. Interspersed is a start-to-finish commentary which is my own work, exploring the myriad connections between the healing process and the Exodus narrative; the Hebrew text that's included is from the sections that I've chosen to focus on. There exist countless other commentaries and Haggadot, but I've resisted the temptation to import readings, songs, or illustrations from them. Each of those works is important for what it is; this is my own addition to the genre. The bibliography at the end includes my personal favorites, and Rabbi Vanessa Ochs wonderful "biography" of the Haggadah names many more.[10]

---

9. Luzzatto, *Shadal on Exodus*, 12:38.
10. Ochs, The Passover Haggadah: A Biography, 90–112.

I've made liberal use of the Hebrew (in transliteration but with the relevant sections highlighted in the traditional Hebrew Haggadah text) because much of the depth and nuance comes from understanding the language—as we've already seen, it's knowing the connection between *Mitzrayim* and narrowness that makes this book possible. Where needed, I get a little pedantic and teach some grammar (Chapter 17 has a quick primer on how Hebrew verbs and root words work). Avoid the temptation to skip this stuff; sometimes the greatest "Eureka!" moments of studying a text and trying to apply it to real-world issues come from sudden understandings of little grammatical points.[11] Likewise, I retain the Hebrew pronunciation of the names (like Moshe and Aharon instead of Moses and Aaron) when rendering them in English. This is how I speak, so you should read and feel like you're sitting at my table with me.

What truly makes this a Haggadah, though, and not a book *about* the Passover Haggadah, is the presence of the questions and prompts that I've written into each section. One of my favorite teachers and Jewish authors, Dr. Erica Brown, titled her own Haggadah *Seder Talk*, because it has commentary like cable news crawl running across the bottom of each page that's packed with questions, thought experiments, and challenges to the reader/participant to see old texts in a new light. In that spirit, I want this Haggadah to be a springboard to *your* narrative of illness and recovery.

I've written this Haggadah to be "of a piece," so it can be read as a book that lands somewhere between narrative non-fiction and theology. If you wish, though, you can use it at your *seder* as one of several extra resources to supplement a more standard Haggadah that includes the full text (or as much of it as you and your guests require). That's what I do with many of the works I've mentioned in this introduction; using Noam Zion's *A Night to Remember* as the book that sits at every place on the table, and adding a copy of Erica Brown here, Seymour Rossel's *Storybook Haggadah* there, and so on. Alternatively, conduct a traditional *seder* around the theme of "healing" and use parts of this volume as supplemental readings, or use specific prompts and exercises as the jumping off points for discussion.

---

11. The most chilling example was the realization that a single dot, called a dagesh, in Ezekiel 37:34 made the difference between a word meaning "soul" and "desolate." The passage in question is the one we read in synagogue on March 14th, 2020, the last service before we shuttered the building for COVID lockdown. A single, spiky "dot" of a virus was indeed desolating our souls.

If you're looking for something more relevant to your own experience, choose a path through the text that matches what you're going through as a personal caregiver, emergency doctor, someone being treated for cancer, or a person living with chronic illness (just as a few examples). Hit as many of the stops along the path as you have time—or emotional energy—to take in. Pick a theme like the blurring of roles between sick and well, or between weak and powerful; the holiness of mundane work, the trickiness of promises, or the power of late nights and sleep deprivation. The Spanish exilic commentator Don Yitzchak Abarbanel introduced his Haggadah commentary, *Zevach Pesach*, with a section called "100 Gates." Each gate is a probing question, like the one we'll tackle in this book, "What good did it do me, living in this time of exile, that my ancestors were freed from Egypt?"[12] I didn't get all the way to 100, but I found close to 50 recurring themes, though some were just stories that I accidentally repeated in multiple places while editing this Haggadah. They're listed in the appendix titled, "Not Quite 100 Gates." Start with a few you like and follow those threads through the service or build your own service around them.

Look around your narrow place. See what it is that confines you, that oppresses you, that makes you feel unwell. Imagine what it would take for you to be able to say with your whole heart: "This year I am in bondage to these forces, but next year I will be free. This year I am in a narrow place, next year I will be able to spread my wings. This year I am ill, next year I will be well. This year has been hell, next year I will heal."

---

12. Abarbanel, *Zevach Pesach*, Tenth Gate.

2

Searching for Hametz

On Pesach, the Torah commands the Jews not to eat, or possess, even one morsel of hametz, leavened grain. How to be sure it's all gone? By conducting a search the night before.

Barukh atah Adonai eloheinu melekh ha-olam, asher kideshanu bemitzvotav vetzivanu al bi'ur hametz. Blessed are You, LORD our God, King of the universe, who sanctifies us with His commandments and commanded us regarding the removal of hametz.	בָּרוּךְ אַתָּה יהוה אֱלֹהֵינוּ מֶלֶךְ הָעוֹלָם, אֲשֶׁר קִדְּשָׁנוּ בְּמִצְוֹתָיו, וְצִוָּנוּ עַל בִּעוּר חָמֵץ.

Next, hold the lit candle and search for hametz in every room, as well as any other area of the home that may have hametz, such as the basement, attic, garage, or car. Even once a house is thoroughly cleaned, there's often still a bagel crust or a Cheerio hiding in some overlooked cranny.

When you're done, take all the hametz that was found in the search, wrap and seal it securely, and place it in a conspicuous spot. This hametz will be joined with all remaining hametz in your home and burned the next morning. (Food intended to be sold or eaten later should similarly be carefully put aside.)

When you've completed the search, recite the "Kol Chamira" declaration, nullifying all unknown hametz and relinquishing it from your ownership.

| All חָמֵץ and anything leavened that is in my possession, whether I have seen it or not, whether I have observed it or not, whether I have removed it or not, shall be considered nullified and ownerless as the dust of the earth. | כָּל־חֲמִירָא חֲמִירָא וַחֲמִיעָה דְּאִכָּא בִרְשׁוּתִי, דְּלָא חֲמִתֵּהּ וּדְלָא בְעַרְתֵּהּ וּדְלָא יְדַעְנָא לֵהּ לִבְטִיל וְלֶהֱוֵי הֶפְקֵר כְּעַפְרָא דְאַרְעָא |

The next morning, the eve of Passover, you will burn the hametz that was found during the search, and you recite the "Kol Chamira" declaration yet again culminating the end of the "hametz-free" process. This burning is often called *bi'ur hametz* (The removal of the Hametz).

| On the evening of the fourteenth (of Nissan) they search the house for hametz by the light of a lamp. Mishnah Pesachim, 1:1 | אור לארבעה עשר בודקין את החמץ לאור הנר משנה פסחים א:א |

WHERE IS IT HIDDEN?

You never know where the *hametz* is hiding. We do a thorough cleaning at my house each year, complete with the orchestrated search described above and blaming the toddler for eating bagels in the bedroom. We even hold a "Get Rid of your *Hametz*" party most years, where we hold a potluck for all our Pesach-observing friends to bring over every imaginable variety of grain-based starchy dish on the Shabbat afternoon before Pesach, stay all afternoon, and ensure there are no leftovers. One year our friends' sons and their pre-teen buddies, who had been watching the Final Four Showdown between the University of Kentucky and whomever they had just beaten, poured through our front door looking for our oldest son to come join them. Their eyes grew wide when we said, "Are you hungry?" Basketball 1, *Hametz* 0.

Yet inevitably we miss something. I was dismayed once to look around at midnight on the 14th of Nissan, the floors finally mopped, and the counters finally covered, to see that I had left the aprons hanging on the wall, some still with visible bits of flour on them from the last time we'd baked cookies. Another year I realized I'd left the whiskey on the wine rack; still another time I forgot the wooden knife block with the meat knives was hiding in plain sight like Poe's purloined letter. Decades of searching for *hametz* has taught me a truth that I could stand to remember in the rest of my life: Even when I think I'm "done" with something, I'm never done. I must keep going back, keep checking, keep picking up the pieces I missed. Only God is perfect; the rest of us need blessings like the one at the opening of this chapter to retroactively "nullify" the stuff we forgot about.

THE WRONG HIDING PLACE

None of these gaffes compared to second seder night of 2008 or 2009, though. It was an epic seder, attended by several families we love dearly, including my friend and *Rav*, Rabbi Michael Werbow and his family. We started late, the way I prefer it, and had a very festive mood going, as it fell during the week in April when both our eldest son and the eldest daughter of one of our guests had birthdays. We'd spread couch cushions, bought specifically for the purpose, on the living room floor and held our seder lounging on the cushions; eating our karpas finger foods from trays going around the room.

But the kids were young; even the oldest and most responsible in the group was only about seven or eight. They dove into hiding the *afikomen* with great zeal; their enthusiasm had waned considerably by the time the adults got up from the table to search for it. And by waned, I mean they had fallen asleep, all except for my then-youngest, now middle, child, who was not quite three at the time. Needless to say, he couldn't remember where they had hidden it.

We were stuck. Normally you bargain with the kids to get back the *afikomen* (in 2019 they decided to ask for a helicopter, and when we said no, they planned to counter by asking for a dog. We now have two dogs, so who knows what they'll ask for next). But with no one awake to bargain with, and no one who remembered where the thing was hidden, we were in for an even longer night than normal.

I searched high, and my toddler searched low. Suddenly he opened a bottom cabinet and yelled, "Here it is, Abba!" I was relieved for a moment, but my relief turned to dismay when I realized which cabinet he was in—the one that held the sold, off-limits, didn't belong to us *hametz*.

Fortunately, I had a trusted, and lenient, rabbinic authority in my living room at that exact moment to tell me what needed to be done, so we could finish our seder. But I've never forgotten the real moral of this story: If you're not continually careful, even the *afikomen* at the end of a rich and wonderful seder—for which we prepared in meticulous fashion—can become *hametz*.

SOURDOUGH, OR SOUR DOUGH? WHAT AM I MISSING?

The Hebrew word *hametz* really earns its, er, bread. In the context of Pesach, it means "leaven," whether actual bread or other items that are leavened, either on purpose or by default. According to rabbinic law, flour made from grain becomes leavened after eighteen minutes of contact with water, unless it's been thoroughly baked by that time. Once the eighteen-minute mark passes, the flour begins to rise on its own due to natural yeasts—be they airborne, on the grain itself, or on the hands of the baker.

It takes *both* yeast and a biblical grain (wheat, barley, oats, rye or spelt) to make *hametz*. The implication didn't fully dawn on me until the year I downed a very tasty bottle of *Kasher l'Pesach* date ale (which turns out to be what the Talmud means when it refers to a drink called *shekhar*, literally, "intoxicant") from a brewery in Israel that clearly listed yeast as an ingredient. Since the sugar being fermented was from dates and not from a grain, all was well. On the flip side, I, um, flipped out a little bit one Pesach when I realized my soap was made with oatmeal. I was washing my body with wet grain, the very essence of *hametz*.[1]

However, the *shoresh*, root, het-mem-tzadik, has two additional meanings. The first is an obvious connection: "Sour." Other Hebrew words with this *shoresh* include *hamutz*, sour, and *hometz*, vinegar. All relate to fermentation. The other word is more of a stretch, though: *Lehah'mitz*, to miss, as in "to miss an opportunity" or "to miss the bus." Showing up too late, being a little bit behind the curve, wasting a chance. A Hebrew teacher (whose name I don't remember, so count that as a missed opportunity to properly credit that person) once explained to me that it was because if you were a minute late in baking your *matzah*, it had gone sour, turned into *hametz* and you had to start over again. The explanation may be apocryphal, but I love it anyway.

---

1. I haven't yet gotten a clear answer to whether this counts as *hametz* or not. One the one hand, it is wet grain. The definition of food in Jewish law isn't whether a person thinks it's food, but whether a dog would eat it. My dogs would eat anything, so I am still on the hook here. On the other hand, the soap part, the part that isn't oatmeal, should stop the fermentation process by killing the yeast, right?

I learned more recently that if you keep kneading the dough continuously, that eighteen-minute clock never starts, at least according to some interpretations. It only turns sour, becomes a lost opportunity, if you walk away from it—leave it lie too long. I've experienced that more than once in writing this Haggadah. Working during and shortly after multiple cataclysmic historical events, I wrote many chapters in the heat of a moment, walked away from them, and came back not minutes but months later to find that the "fresh take" had soured in the interim, and no longer sounded new, or even intelligent.

Hametz also has symbolic meaning. Just as bread rises—inflating or puffing up as it goes, *hametz* symbolizes self-importance, haughtiness, and arrogance. *Matzah* is flat, hard, and brittle; *lehem 'oni*, the "bread of poverty." Juxtaposed with *matzah*, *hametz* is a representation of (self-indulgent) luxury. Rabbi Ethan Tucker notes the trend over the last few hundred years to distinguish *matzah* from *hametz* led to the abandonment of many forms of *matzah* that were previously permitted, like cakes of *matzah* up to the thickness of a *tefah* (handbreadth about three inches thick) instead, Ashkenazic legal codes preferred thin *matzot* that were like a *rakik*, a cracker.[2]

We can take these meanings separately or together as we look for the "spiritual *hametz*" in our lives, in our work, and in our care of our health. Individually, we can ask, "Where are the things that have soured and need to be thrown out? What opportunities have I missed? In what ways have I grown haughty and condescending, and how can I 'flatten' myself to make room for others again?" Linking the meanings together, we may think of missing the opportunity to root out bad, selfish habits that eventually take root and give us a sour disposition toward others, always being critical, cynical, and standoffish.

BY CANDLELIGHT

The opening quotation from the Mishnah tells us that in preparation for Passover, we're expected to conduct a thorough search for *hametz* a full 24 hours before the *seder* can begin, on the eve of the 14th of Nissan. We can't begin our ritual of reenacting our Exodus until we have gotten rid of the *hametz*, (whichever meaning we apply to it) that has accumulated over the past year. This is a hard stop: H*ametz* that remains in our

---

2. Liebowitz and Tucker, *Take One Podcast*, Pesachim 36 and 37.

possession during the festival is forbidden to ever be used again. We can't continue as we were before.

In preparation for our ritual—a seder focused on healing, of making an Exodus from narrow places of illness, trauma, compassion fatigue or burnout—we must make a search for *hametz*. We can't go forward unless we do. The Mishnah prescribes using a *ner*, a candle or lamp, to shine light into the cracks and dark places where *hametz* might accumulate—be it actual cracks and crawl spaces in between kitchen cabinets and under beds, or in the cracks and crevices of our bodies and souls.

Over time the ritual grew, in some communities, to include a feather with which to sweep up the crumbs and a wooden spoon in which to collect them. Spiritually, I might think of the feather as a symbol of how we might wish to gently remove these bits of *hametz*, using a light touch rather than a blunt instrument—perhaps a touch so light that it tickles, using self-deprecating humor and laughter to purge what scolding or physical affliction will only drive in deeper. As for the spoon, I always found this the most physically awkward part of the ritual, difficult to use in the first place (a dustpan is far better built for the purpose) and even more difficult to hold steady, so the crumbs don't spill right back out. But as my editor Ilana reminded me, the spoon is supposed to have high, curved sides which trap the *hametz*, so it won't fall out. It reminds me of the old tradition of shouting gossip you couldn't keep to yourself down a well. Later tradition refers to one's spouse or trusted friend as being like that well—a safe place to share your secrets so they won't go anywhere else. Undertaking this spiritual process with less than the requisite amount of caution, balance and attention to detail will only result in us finding the same *hametz* in a different location before the day is out.

Search for your *hametz* now. Light your candle: Choose a method that's most suited for shining light into the places you have usually not dared to look, for fear of what you might find. Perhaps you meditate, or journal, or use creative canvases like music or art, or seek feedback from others who know you better than you do yourself. Find your feather; a way of sweeping it all away without causing further damage. And select your spoon, a safe receptacle where you can be sure it won't come spilling back out.

Don't be afraid of what you might find; after all, you're seeking it in order to throw it away. The search, whether it's a house search or a soul search, can be difficult. You may not be ready to do this work from scratch, not ready to ask yourself the questions that need to be asked. As the traditional *Haggadah* tells us—for the one who doesn't know how to ask, or is not prepared to do so, *at p'tah lo*—you begin for them. Try the questions that follow, the first of many such questions that I promised in Chapter 1, to guide you in looking for the leaven.

Thoughts and Discussions

- *Where is my hametz likely to be hiding? Which parts of me, of my life and my work, are likely to harbor things that need to be purged?*
- *What formerly fresh, sweet, wholesome things have become stale and sour? Where has my attitude followed a similar path?*
- *What opportunities have I missed? Which paths should I have taken that are now closed to me. How will I recognize when a similar path opens in the future so that I don't miss it again?*
- *Where have I grown arrogant, haughty, self-important and inflated? How can I humble myself again—without humiliating myself?*
- *Six months and sixty seconds—what are some minor projects that I've put off for far too long?*
- *Where are you and how do you move along the continuum of humility: Self-deprecation è humility è confidence è arrogance?*
- *Do I have a "God complex" or impostor syndrome? How do I avoid the extremes and practice with both humility and confidence?*
- *What is the "feather"—the fine line of humor vs. humiliation, educational or healthcare trauma vs. constructive critique, feedback, and teaching?*
- *What is the "spoon"—who do you tell your troubles to? What is the role of friends, therapists, colleagues, and what happens when there's no safe place to put the hametz?*

THE DUST OF THE EARTH

The search ends with a nullification formula, which declares in Aramaic that any seen or unseen *hametz* is now null and void, *k'afra d'ar'a*, like the dust of the earth. The following morning, in the last moments before the prohibition of owning *hametz* takes effect, the remaining *hametz* from the search is burned and a version of the nullification formula repeated.

I've never given much thought to the formula, but as I write this with spiritual rather than tangible *hametz* in mind, I can't help but wonder if for some people the process of nullifying and burning the *hametz* might be painful, almost to the point of not being able to complete it. Imagine that the *hametz* you identify is a lifelong dream that you're chasing, but which has led you to repeated heartbreak. Imagine that it's an abusive relationship, and that in burning you're choosing to burn the bridge it represents, and the physical tokens of that relationship. How will you declare these things into which you have poured your soul for so long to be "nullified and ownerless as the dust of the earth?"

They're not ownerless—they belong, have always belonged to you. Not having them any longer leaves a hole in your soul. Filling that hole, however, is the very essence of the Pesach seder, and of the ritual we're creating here together. What came before is not what will be in the future; the healed you is not going back to the way it was before, but into a new future. At some point in the COVID-19 pandemic, the phrase "new normal" *became* the new normal, presaging a very different reality into which we would emerge when the pandemic eventually abated. The things we have given up may never return as they were.

The Israelites leaving Egypt realized they were giving up things they had enjoyed; in Numbers 11:5 they lament the "fish we ate for free in Egypt, the cucumbers and melons and leeks and onions and garlic." Even that which they try to take with them doesn't survive the journey; their bread bakes flat on their backs as they've taken the dough in haste before it has time to rise—the origin of *matzah*. Something new, like *matzah*, and later manna, and the quail which God sends in that same chapter of Numbers (with a side dish of spite) will need to sustain them in their new life. Many will not truly succeed in nullifying that *hametz* and burning it; it'll remain with them and prevent them from ever moving through the process of healing and growing. Even in regard to actual *hametz*, I alone in my family look forward to the holiday and its unique cuisine with joy. Everyone else, and I know they're not alone, is looking simultaneously back and ahead, to the bread they ate freely in the days before we cleaned, and to the pizza and pasta they'll consume when the sun sets at the end of the holiday.

HEALTHCARE SEARCHES FOR HAMETZ

Twenty-twenty was a year of reckoning for medicine in the United States. Biases, inequities, and outright racism that have been baked (pun intended) into the system for decades, even centuries, came to light all at once as the deaths of George Floyd, Breonna Taylor, and Ahmaud Arbery in the space of just a few weeks broke a dam of silence that some within the system had already been chipping away at for years. I mentioned at the beginning of this chapter that we're never "done." When slavery ended, when Jim Crow ended, when the Civil Rights Act and the Voting Rights Act passed, when segregated institutions were finally integrated, many white-passing people thought we were done, that we'd finally achieved equality. Instead, we'd simply driven inequality into a variety of disguises; subtle biases embedded into the way most of us were taught to practice. This is exactly the type of bias that requires shining a bright light into the corners to see what we've been missing.

One physician who shines that light especially well is Dr. Bonzo Reddick, a family physician and associate dean at Mercer University School of Medicine in Georgia. If you believe that Black Americans should be treated with different blood pressure medications than White Americans, he'll show you the data as to why we shouldn't have jumped to these conclusions. If you consider kidney function differently in Blacks than in Whites, he'll demonstrate how you're potentially withholding life-saving care from the Black patients. And if you're calculating cardiovascular risk and can't figure out why the calculator says it's more dangerous to be Black than to smoke, Dr. Bonzo will set you straight. Essentially all the "truths" we have believed about racial differences in medicine, he demonstrates with great humor and a machete of hard data, have no basis in biology, and are often based on shoddy, outdated science that could never even pass Institutional Review Board muster today.

Yet when Reddick brought this data, as well as data on social determinants of health, the inequality of outcomes, and the role of intersectionality (for example, the additive burdens of being Black, female, and rural at the same time) to his institutional leadership, they fought him. They responded in disbelief. These were established norms, some of which had been taught to them very sternly as "things they must never forget," like always naming a patient's race when beginning to present their story to a more senior physician. They'd not give them up easily, any more than the

Israelites could let go of the memories of fish and leeks in Egypt, or for that matter any more easily than Pharaoh could let our people go.

It took eight years, and a spring and summer of very public deaths of Black Americans at the hands of police, to finally mobilize enough white coats for Black lives and make the changes Reddick asked for. Today, Mercer students no longer put race at the front of their presentations but learn a lot about the medical effects of racial inequality. They no longer believe that Black kidneys work differently than white ones (and no longer use the old equation that hard wires it into the lab data) but know that Black people with kidney disease have much worse outcomes than white people with the same disease, and that the old data is partially to blame.[3]

Even if we fail to purge all the *hametz*, even when we accidentally hide our *matzah* in the same cabinet where it's stored, we can grow and heal through this ritual of searching. Everything that comes afterward helps us to understand where this *hametz* came from in the first place, why we must leave it behind, which pieces of it we have missed, and what we're looking to become instead. By making a habit of looking for *hametz* we open ourselves up to the kind of change that Dr. Reddick is asking for, or the kind of change that allowed us to begin speaking openly about breast cancer years ago, or the recognition that treating food insecurity and homelessness are worth more years of life than all the diagnostic equipment we have put together. By burning it, we accept that we should be humble like a flat piece of *matzah*.

---

3. Paraphrased from Dr. Reddick's presentations at the Society for Teachers of Family Medicine Conference on Medical Student Education (held virtually), entitled "The Intersection of Racism & Race-based Medical Decision Making in Medical Education" and "Implementation of a Health Equity Curriculum Into Undergraduate and Graduate Medical Education." February 1, 2021.

3

Signposts

In many seders, the participants begin by chanting the steps of the seder, a musical road map for the evening.

I had a brief "teachable moment" with my medical student one Sunday morning while seeing patients via telehealth during the doldrums of the January 2021 wave of the COVID pandemic. After the second or third time that he asked the same person, "What brings you in this morning?" I decided to "hold him after class" so we could come up with a different approach.

"I appreciate that you're letting the patient set the agenda," I began, "but after three times of not getting a useful answer, you may need to rephrase. Also, you have to admit it sounds weird to ask someone what 'brings them in' when they haven't left their living room. How about, 'What would you like to talk about today?'"

Beginning is hard. It's hard to know what to say, and many people find themselves in a medical encounter, supposedly meant entirely for their benefit, having no idea why they're there. Many of my patients who speak little English learn the word "follow-up" early in their encounters with doctors; when I say, "What can I help you with today?" they dutifully respond, "I'm here for the follow-up." Only when I ask, "What are you following up about?" does it become clear that they never learned that one follows up about something specific, otherwise it's just a check-up. By the same token, I can complete an entire visit, discuss cancer screening, order a cholesterol check, do a complete physical exam with hearing and vision screening, and give three vaccinations, and the patient will ask, "So when is my physical check-up?"

I'm not blaming the English learners for their confusion. Our terminology is just as arcane and confusing to many natives. The healing arts in the West seem to begin in the middle, reach the end before ever addressing first principles, and often leave the patient out of the journey entirely. People miss appointments because they can't find the correct office in the labyrinthine hospitals, because they fail to complete trivial administrative requirements, or because they weren't instructed properly on how to prepare for their procedure. If they do make it to the visit, they might not be able to address their most important concern because they want to talk about their child's asthma, but this is a "well-child check-up." There are not enough signposts to show them the way.

SIGNPOSTS IN THE SEDER

The Seder has signposts galore: Fourteen of them, each denoting an important step of the ritual. In many families, the signposts make the first song sung around the table. In my family we sing them at each transition to a new step, singing all fourteen then repeating the steps until we reach the step we're about to perform. It works a little like *The Price Is Right*; you have to stop right at the correct step without going over, or you lose. What you lose is never clear; I think it's mostly your dignity because then all of the children at the table laugh at you.

Singing the signposts lays out the plan for the evening—it sets the agenda; to borrow the phrase I used with my student this morning. From medical research we know that setting an agenda that everyone agrees on leads to a much better outcome at the end of a visit. *Soliciting* an agenda is even better; when a patient is asked for their goals at the start of a visit, it leads to an 80% concordance between patient and provider goals, as opposed to only 50% when the agenda is not solicited. However, if you're from any typical Jewish family, I don't recommend *soliciting* an agenda at the beginning of the seder; many of the participants will likely say that their agenda is to skip the text and the singing and go right to dinner. Just stick with singing the signposts song:

Kadesh (sanctify), Urhatz (and wash), Karpas (greens), Yahatz (break in half), Magid (tell the story), Rahtzah (wash, but different), Motzi Matzah (bread blessing over matzah), Maror (bitter herbs), Korekh (make a sandwich), Shulhan Orekh (set the table—the meal), Tzafun (hidden), Barekh (bless after the meal), Hallel (songs of praise), Nirtzah (fulfilled).	קדש, ורחץ, כרפס, יחץ, מגיד, רחצה, מוציא מצה, מרור, כורך, שולחן עורך, צפון, ברך, הלל, נרצה.

Signposts and Symptoms

The reason signposts work is that even when the agenda is set ahead of time, it helps to set expectations when it's shared aloud, reviewed frequently, and even reflected upon. Think about the parallel signposts that exist with a serious illness—heart disease, for example. The prologue of a life of smoking, not exercising, and eating breaded, fried, salty food is followed by the initial symptoms of crushing chest pain and trouble breathing. The story may continue in an ambulance or emergency department, travel to a cath lab and eventually to the cardiac ICU. In a happier version, it can lead through the family doctor's office to an EKG and stress test, eventually to the cath lab and then home on medications, a new diet, and a supervised exercise program.

There may be other signposts—the heart attack one has struggled to avoid but which happens anyway. The medication side effect that no one warned you about. The procedure to unclog an artery, put in a pacemaker or a defibrillator or transplant a new heart when the old one finally gives out.

I can tell you all of this with my eyes closed in under a minute. It's what medical textbooks used to refer to as the "natural history" of a disease, except that modern medicine doesn't allow things to have a natural history anymore. So now we might call this the "typical course" of heart disease, and telling someone this is what is likely to happen to them is their "prognosis."

"NO OUTLET" SIGNPOSTS

Delivering prognosis is something that modern American doctors are notoriously bad at. In his book, *Death Foretold*, Nicholas Christakis shares data from several studies on end-of-life care prognosis. They revealed that physicians treating cancer patients often predicted their patients would survive two to three times as long as they actually did. Meanwhile, intensive care doctors often predicted imminent death in as many as 40% of their patients who survived and went home.[1]

I worked for several years on an end-of-life education project. One of my co-workers on that project told me about her terminally ill father, on the morning before his death, sitting in his hospital bed and declaring, "I've got to go to PT today or I'm never going to get out of this hospital!" Imagine the shock of the family members, and indeed the patient themselves, realizing that the end has arrived. They believed there was another half a year in which to tie up loose ends, check things off the bucket list, and achieve a measure of closure. The signposts were wrong, and now they've reached a literal dead end—and they can't go back the way they came.

Christakis muses on reasons why the healers of the late 1990s were so bad at prognosis. The most obvious is that they had no knowledge of how to make a prognosis. Medical textbooks in 1900 routinely included a paragraph or more on natural history and prognosis for every disease

---

1. Christakis, *Death Foretold*. 64–67.

they discussed. Therapeutics were limited, and one of the most important roles of the doctor wasn't to deliver a cure to every patient, but to prognosticate on which patients would live and which would die, and how long the death or recovery would take—and, only having done so, to *then* identify the small subset for whom medical care could sway the outcome.

Those signposts have gradually become fewer and farther between until they've disappeared entirely from many medical texts,[2] so that even the most diligent student doesn't encounter discussions of prognosis for most of the diseases they'll treat. They come to believe that there's an intervention for every illness, at every step. When the road map comes to an end, they simply make it up as they go along, because no one has marked the edge for them with "Here be Dragons!"

Thanks to the meticulous use of registries in cancer care over the last several decades, that knowledge gap has narrowed in some cases. Statistics on mortality, relapse, and the effects of treatment now exist for many of the most common cancers, and oncologists routinely use this information to inform their decisions. But many people fall outside the category for which the statistics exist: They have a different cancer, have other illnesses or have already tried the treatments that are standard. or they've a disease for which the range of prognoses is so wide that it's nearly meaningless. Outside of oncology, the data quickly becomes murkier still. There are no signposts.

SOMETIMES WRONG, NEVER IN DOUBT

Physicians hate this lack of knowledge. We don't like uncertainty, and we hate being wrong even more. As a result, many physicians-in-training receive advice from their mentors to avoid prognosticating altogether, or to be extremely vague if they must. Most have heard some version of the story that begins, "I once knew a doctor who told his patient they had six months to live. . ." and ends, "Twenty years later that patient attended their funeral."[3] Don't be that guy, warns the mentor. Don't look like an idiot. Out of fear of being wrong, and appearing less than omniscient, we often say nothing at all.

At other times, the temptation to look like we know what we're doing in the moment is too great. We must say something—yet at the

---

2. Christakis, *Death Foretold.* 4–7.
3. Christakis, *Death Foretold.* 100–102.

same time we're afraid to take away hope. Rather than offer an honest assessment, we over-promise. Avraham is singled out in the Torah for offering the mysterious guests in his tent a small morsel and delivering a great feast; modern medicine promises miracles and delivers a few extra months of misery. Our optimism, our somewhat idolatrous faith in our own efficacy, leads us to make six-month predictions on a twenty-four-hour prognosis. True, it's sometimes the patient, or the family, who are unreasonably optimistic—or all three parties who are engaged in a conspiracy of silence, speaking about hope when they should be speaking about elephants.

The Israelites in Egypt were only able to see the signs and the signposts, of the Exodus because they avoided falling into idolatrous practices. By stepping back from our self-idolizing, returning to a knowledge of natural history can help us to remember that everything is not in our control. We can begin to see the signposts of an illness.

Judaism is not a fatalistic tradition; it's a paradoxical one. It commands both belief that everything is in God's hands and that human beings have an obligation to intervene in the workings of the world to achieve healing, pursue justice, and perform acts of kindness. Healing people who are dying requires holding these two contradictory ideas in mind simultaneously and always.

LIVING IS HARDER

However, in the words of the George Washington character in *Hamilton*, "Dying is easy, son; living is harder." In terminal illness, the destination is clear even if the road is unknown and the travel time uncertain. I spend most of my time caring for living people who are grappling with limitations, suffering and challenges that don't seem to have a starting or ending point. They don't have a cause, and don't have an easy remedy.

Many of these illnesses are loosely grouped together as "functional illnesses" such as irritable bowel syndrome, fibromyalgia, or even migraine—if they have names at all. My colleagues and I continue to struggle with how to define the syndrome affecting many of the older people from Bhutan that we care for; despite the recurring themes of burning pain on the feet and in the stomach, headaches and dizziness, cramping and pinching pain in the legs, racing heartbeat and inability to sleep, it defies codification into one disease process.

With each functional illness comes the dreaded phrase, "X is a diagnosis of exclusion." Diagnosis of exclusion is a medical concept that means that there's no definitive test to say that someone *has* this disease; it's simply the last thing left standing after exhaustive testing has ruled *out* all the other diseases. With that process of ruling out comes the agony of believing that one has not a functional illness, but a fatal one. People with irritable bowel syndrome fret about having colon cancer; fibromyalgia sufferers wonder if they have lupus; migraineurs are often mistaken for having epilepsy, MS, stroke, or brain tumors.

The signposts of the seder help to give meaning to the process, to alert us to what comes next, and yes, to know how much longer until dinner. In chronic illness and in the care of the well, we need signposts to give shape to the uncertain and to ensure diligence in preserving that wellness. In the mid-20th century, pioneers like my fellow Pittsburgher Dr. Peter Safar began to create a road map for bringing people back from the dead, now known around the world as the ACLS algorithm. Airway, breathing, circulation, 30–2 compressions to breaths, place pads, shock, shock, shock, everybody shock, all shock, ladies shock, men shock. . .

But waiting until that last moment to have a clear road map of what to do uncovers exactly what is wrong with our system. We need signposts for healing much earlier. The Ages and Stages and Bright Futures frameworks from the American Academy of Pediatrics tell us what to watch for as our youngest patients pass the signposts of growth and development, and how to know if they're falling behind, failing to thrive, or facing challenges they shouldn't need to face. Lawrence Weed's record-keeping revolution in the 1940s and 50s, when he invented the soap note, the review of systems, and other taken-for-granted parts of the medical interview, helps healers enter a new relationship, or revisit an old one, with an organized mind that's prepared to take in new information. And the USPSTF (a hard initialism to say, but it stands for US Preventive Services Task Force) issues and continually revises guidelines for maintaining the health of adults of every age, gender, and propensity, in the hopes they can keep people like me from overlooking obvious dangers to the people we care for.

I AM NOWHERE

But for each of these road maps, there are countless people, like those I mentioned above, who can't follow them, for they don't even know which road they're on, nor can their healers clearly tell them. They wait for the signposts, and when they don't pass the ones they expect to see, they're lost, with no GPS signal or even an old-fashioned paper map. This Haggadah is for every person who feels, like the young refugee father I spoke to years ago, that "I'm nowhere." The Exodus narrative says, "No, you are somewhere, and there's someone standing there with you."

There's a moment when Ya'akov is about to descend to Egypt, and God appears to him in a dream;[4] the third time in his life that Ya'akov has had a nocturnal encounter with God.[5] God enjoins Ya'akov not to fear the descent into Egypt and promises to make him into a great nation while he is there. The final line of this exchange should linger with both the healers and the seekers of healing: *Anokhi ered imakh mitzrayma, v'anokhi a'alkha gam aloh, v'Yosef yashit yado al eynekha*. "I will go down with you to Mitzrayim (Egypt, but also 'the narrow place') and I will also bring you up on an ascent, and Yosef (Ya'akov's beloved, long-lost son) will stretch out his hand over your eyes (will be there to close your eyes when you die)." The narrative doesn't just say, "there is someone standing there with you," it demands, "go stand there with them and help them get out."

God provides a road map and concludes with a promise to be there both in the going down, the bad, scary times, and in the happy, hopeful times. God even reveals that the ending, whether it happens in the narrow place or in the elevated one, will happen while Ya'akov's most beloved son is by his side. He will never be alone, even in his last moments.

Healers are striving to emulate what God does for Ya'akov. A classic scene in the TV series *The West Wing* features White House Chief of Staff Leo McGarry consoling his deputy, Josh Lyman, after Josh has been meeting with a trauma psychiatrist about his slow unraveling after being shot months earlier. Leo tells the story of a man who falls into a hole, and his appeals to a doctor and a priest walking by are met with a scribbled prescription and a scribbled prayer being thrown down to him in the hole. Only when his friend (named, appropriately, Joe) walks by, do things change. Joe jumps in with him. "Our guy says, 'Are you stupid?

---

4. Genesis 46:2–4.

5. The first is the dream of the angels ascending the ladder to heaven, in Genesis 28:12. The second is when he wrestles with the mysterious stranger in Genesis 32:35.

Now we're both down here.' The friend says, 'Yeah, but I've been down here before, and I know the way out.'"[6]

Every piece of the seder encourages us to be like Joe. "Hey, Joe," it's saying, "you've been down there before. Get down in that hole and show them the way out."

---

6. Parnell and Sorkin, *The West Wing*, S2:E10, "Noel."

4

Sanctifying the Moment

The seder begins with Kiddush, a prayer that uses a glass of wine to sanctify the wine itself, the people of Israel, and the holiday. After the prayer we drink the wine while reclining, as though we are ancient royalty.

Kadesh	קדש
We pour the first cup. The matzot are covered.	בָּרוּךְ אַתָּה ה', אֱלֹהֵינוּ מֶלֶךְ הָעוֹלָם בּוֹרֵא פְּרִי הַגָּפֶן.
Blessed are You, Lord our God, King of the universe, who creates the fruit of the vine. Who has chosen us from all peoples and has raised us above all tongues and has sanctified us with His commandments	אֲשֶׁר בָּחַר בָּנוּ מִכָּל־עָם וְרוֹמְמָנוּ מִכָּל־לָשׁוֹן וְקִדְּשָׁנוּ בְּמִצְוֹ. . (לשבת: שַׁבָּתוֹת לִמְנוּחָה וּ) מוֹעֲדִים לְשִׂמְחָה, חַגִּים וּזְמַנִּים לְשָׂשׂוֹן, (לשבת: אֶת יוֹם הַשַּׁבָּת הַזֶּה וְ) אֶת יוֹם חַג הַמַּצּוֹת הַזֶּה זְמַן חֵרוּתֵנוּ, (לשבת: בְּאַהֲבָה) מִקְרָא קֹדֶשׁ זֵכֶר לִיצִיאַת מִצְרָיִם . . . .
Blessed are You, O Lord, who sanctifies [the Sabbath,] Israel, and the appointed times.	בָּרוּךְ אַתָּה ה', מְקַדֵּשׁ (לשבת: הַשַּׁבָּת וְ) יִשְׂרָאֵל וְהַזְּמַנִּים.
Drink while reclining to the left and do not recite a blessing after drinking.	שותה בהסיבת שמאל ואינו מברך ברכה אחרונה.

AT HIGH ELEVATION

My friend Rabbi Danny Schiff is a dynamic teacher. He often jokes that when he had his own congregation, he could have read aloud from the phone book and kept them riveted, thanks to his mellifluous Australian accent. But his real gift is his way of stating his point just so, to make it "sticky" in people's memory. His teaching about the root of the word *kadosh*, or in the header of this section of the seder *Kadesh*, is especially notable.

"Kuh. Duh. Shuh. Separate, in order to elevate. Kuh. Duh. Shuh."

We learned about the magical powers of Hebrew roots in the last section, including the way one root, *het—mem—tzadik*, links together the ideas of rising bread, fermentations, sourness, and missing opportunities. Danny's signature line focuses on a different root, *qoof-dalet-shin*, the root that means holiness, and the one that's front-and-center in this first section of the seder proper.

The *Kadesh* section of the seder separates the seder from the mundane day that went before it, and even from the somewhat holy time of the holiday that comes after it. The *Kiddush* prayer said in this section focuses on three things that God has separated in order to elevate them.

ART THOU A LOAF OF BREAD, OR A JUG OF WINE?

The first is wine, or more generally "fruit of the vine," which is uniquely tasked with consecrating our special occasions and gets a blessing unique among the fruits, the only one considered neither fruit of the tree nor of the earth. Ironically, given all our talk about getting rid of the fermented grain items in the last section, and how that represented a fresh start with all the missed opportunities and sour feelings removed, we now consecrate this moment with something fermented—literal "sour grapes!"

Remember what sets these two things apart, though. Like my date ale, there's a difference between fermented grain and fermented fruit. Grain swells and gets puffed up, representing self-importance. And while wine can have some disastrous consequences, when we use it to consecrate a moment, it doesn't inflate one person—it elevates everyone present.

If you have any experience in the medical system, you've encountered people who are like *hametz* and people who are like *kiddush* wine. The first group are self-important. Doctors so impressed with their own knowledge and skill that everyone else must worship at their feet. They're horrible to the nurses, the administrative staff—and to the patients. Administrators so enamored of their rules they forget that rules are there to serve the patients, not vice versa. And, sadly, patients as well, people who treat caring professionals like servants and regard their own issues as emergencies while the needs of others are merely an inconvenience to them getting what they deserve.

The second group dignify everyone they interact with. Nurses who dry people's tears and cheerlead people they know are gutting out terrible pain. Pharmacists who patiently teach the nuances of a complicated medication regimen, complete with little "tricks" for remembering how to take it. Patients who bring baklava (I dearly love baklava) and write thank-you notes. And let us not forget medical assistants who babble nonsense to babies to distract them, and their parents, while giving life-saving vaccines.

If you have any experience in the medical system, you've encountered people who are like *hametz* and people who are like *kiddush* wine. If you have enough experience with it, chances are you've *been* both of those kinds of people. Like I said, the boundary is fuzzy. "Kuh-duh-shuh" is one of the ways we try to sharpen that boundary and put ourselves on the right side of it.

WASTED TIMES

The second of the three sanctified items are the *zmanim*, "times," the three pilgrimage holidays of Pesach, Shavuot, and Sukkot. Specifically, the aspect of Pesach called *Hag HaMatzot*, the festival of *matzot*, is set aside from other, more mundane times as holy.

These holidays only come around three times a year, and in Biblical and Temple times there was no mistaking what a big deal they were. People traveled the length and breadth of the land of Israel just to get to Jerusalem, with their sacrificial animals and first fruits in tow. Right at the time of the harvests, people took weeks off from their agricultural duties to give thanks and celebrate.

Three times a year is about as frequently as most people manage to see their doctors, especially in primary care and especially with the growing shortage of providers. If you see a highly sought-after specialist, the wait may be a year, and the visits may be two or more years apart. One would think these would be as holy as bringing a Paschal lamb to the Temple, something that must be treated like gold and handled as delicately as glass.

Yet providers rush through the visits to stay on schedule and get interrupted multiple times by other patient emergencies both inside and out of the office. Staff turn people away for being ten minutes late or having the wrong paperwork or because the interpreter didn't show up. Patients forget, or ghost, or spend the appointment half-listening because their cell phones keep ringing. There's hardly enough separation to achieve any elevation.

HOLY PEOPLE

Third to be elevated are the people of Israel, who are separated and elevated not just by this prayer, but by the very act of the Exodus itself, without which this God would not be our God, nor we God's people. The act of the Exodus could be seen as a *kiddush*-in-action, and the blessing merely its commemoration; a declaration that this happened.

If you live in a city where the Susan G. Komen Foundation hosts a "Race for the Cure" on Mothers' Day, you have seen this kind of elevation in action. Just take out the words, "people of Israel," from the sentence and replace them with the words, "breast cancer survivors," and you have it. By the very act of their survival, of emerging from the narrow place of having cancer into a world where it's past yet eternally present, they've been elevated to a place of honor and respect, and to a place of gratitude and transformation.

Thoughts and Discussions

- *Bread or Wine? Think about your behavior as you've dealt with illness and suffering in your life. Have you been one to inflate yourself, or one to elevate others? What could you change—or what good behavior would you like to try to repeat?*

- *If you've been more like matzah than either of the others—flat, humble, lowly, maybe feeling like you are an impostor or someone whose suffering doesn't deserve other people's attention—how could you try to elevate yourself and recognize that you're worthy of saving?*

- *What do you do to sanctify important times in your life—especially ones that are important for your own wellness or healing, or that of someone you care about or care for? What have you done that undercuts that sanctity?*

- *Who are the people you're elevating in your own life? What are they doing that's worthy of that elevation?*

A BLESSING OVER... SCUT?

Most patients frown upon their physicians drinking wine in clinic—and *vice versa*, to be fair. But imagine if there were a *kiddush* for a medical encounter. When would we say it, and over what action? Do we say it when draping our stethoscopes around our necks? Checking in for an appointment at the reception desk? Donning our white lab coats (or embarrassing patient gowns)? Or, sadly, logging into our electronic medical records?

So much of what medical professionals do in the electronic medical record (EMR) feels thankless, pointless, and diametrically opposed to hands-on, person-centered care—the antithesis of the kind of medicine I wrote about in my first book. Again, if you've had any experience with the modern medical system, you've had a clinician turn their back on you while asking you questions, fail to make eye contact, or believe the stuff on the screen over your lived experience. Yet the EMR, carefully maintained, and used with commitment, contains vital clues to a person's health and illness, and constitutes a powerful tool to detect patterns of illness and disease across populations. It has the potential to save lives.

The pioneers of modern medicine, like William Harvey in the 16th century and Oliver Sacks in the 20th, kept meticulous written notes. Their works serve as a kind of sacred text that's foundational to medicine today. Similarly, the attention to detail and adherence to protocol in massive studies like the Framingham study, the Women's Health Initiative, and the SUPPORT trial have produced volumes of bedrock science that has radically altered how we treat heart disease, respond to the onset of menopause, and care for people approaching the ends of their lives.

However, studying a foundational sacred text doesn't automatically excite the mind. Attitude matters. Consecrating the act of learning can make a huge difference. Perhaps the time has come to sanctify our first log-in of the day, just as when Jews first study Torah on a particular day, we praise God for commanding us "to busy ourselves with the words of Torah." We're not just reading, or indulging our curiosity, or even looking up the instructions for an especially confusing ritual; we're doing what we were put on Earth to do.

Part of that sanctification is in recognizing the value of a task that seems mundane and even counterproductive. Think of hospital workers and other folks we might now call "essential workers" or even "heroes" who take a task that seems peripheral, at best, to the mission of healing and transform it into a sacred duty.

The crossing guard who stood at the corner of Shady Avenue and Douglas Street when I was in high school, who used to tell us how many A's we would get that day based on how big a smile we had, was in that category. When my youngest son was in third and fourth grade, years upended by the pandemic, our crossing guard Miss Sherry would still run down cars in the middle of the intersection to yell at the driver for not stopping at her signal, and bring a specific selection of dog treats with her every morning to feed the doggy regulars who passed her while she was on the job, including our Harry and Benny.

In every hospital there are larger-than-life characters who should remind us how to approach the drudgery of electronic charts, or whatever other "scut" work we're doing at the time.[1] For thirty-one years, Children's Hospital of Pittsburgh had such a character in Albert Lexie. Albert shined shoes, first in the Monongahela Valley steel town of Monessen, PA, and then in the hospital lobby, from 1982 through 2013. He did painstaking work, charged three dollars a shine, and donated every tip over that amount to the hospital's Free Care Fund, totaling more than $200,000 by the time he retired.[2] I remember him well from residency; his pride was contagious.

Albert Lexie's legacy also raises some painful questions. Why was this man, making poverty-level income, making such sizable donations to a hospital's free care fund? Why could the hospital afford neither to ensure Albert was better taken care of financially, nor care for all the children who came there without having to take charity from a man who donated an amount equal to more than 50% of what he earned over that same period? If we're sanctifying "scut," we ought to think about sanctifying

---

1. "Scut" is a catch-all term for the work everyone hates to do while in training, sometimes including demeaning things like fetching coffee for the attendings, but more often being the intern assigned to recheck all the bandages on a surgical service at the end of the operating schedule—and not being able to leave to go home until all of them were "clean, dry, and intact." When I was a resident, I decided SCUT was actually an initialism for Subordinates Completing Unpleasant Tasks.

2. Children's Hospital of Pittsburgh, https://www.chp.edu/about/donate/albert-lexie

the people who do the most of it. It's lip service to call someone a "hero" or "essential;" it's a lot holier to pay them a respectable living wage. I'm proud to count among my friends Rabbi Ron Symons, who put himself on the front line a few years back demanding a living wage for all workers in our flagship health system, the largest employer in Pennsylvania. As of this writing that's about to become a system-wide reality.

A FIFTEEN-MINUTE SANCTUARY IN TIME?

If we're able to find the inspiration to say praises when logging into our computer charts, then sanctifying the time we get to spend *with* our patients becomes easier. Rather than saying praise for going "up" to Jerusalem three times a year, we can separate and elevate going "in" to our face-to-face encounters with the people we care for ten, fifteen, twenty or more times each day. In the absence of a Temple, the holiest place for many Jews today is the *beit k'neset*, the synagogue, the "house of gathering." But *k'neset* is from the same root as *nikhnas*—to enter, or go in.

There's indeed a prayer for entering the synagogue, called "*Mah Tovu*." It is the biblical blessing uttered by the pagan prophet Bil'am, who meant to curse the Israelites but ended up being forced to speak words of praise against his will. He said, "How beautiful are your tents, Ya'akov, your dwelling places, Israel." Imagine a prayer we might say at the door to each exam room or hospital room, extolling the healing to take place within.

The moments with that person we "go in" to are precious. Those are the moments when the healing takes place. Even though we're doing valuable work behind the scenes, on the computer, phone or in books, the encounter is where we heal. It's where the eye contact, the carefully chosen words, the touch (if we're fortunate enough to be in the same place) all happen. It's the location of what the Catholic bioethical tradition calls the *cura personalis*, the personal cure, that which is achieved through the presence and caring of the individual healer rather than the effects of any drug or surgery.[3]

---

3. Thank you to my former student Dr. Yadhu Dhital for teaching me about this concept during his clinical rotation at our health center. As a student at Georgetown University Medical School, this concept was a part of his curriculum, and we found through our discussion that it meshed very well with my own Jewishly-centered concepts in *Healing People, Not Patients*.

THANK YOU FOR GIVING ME THIS RESPONSIBILITY

Finally, we separate and elevate *ourselves*. Not out of arrogance, but as befits the holiday of flat, humble bread—out of humble gratitude for being healers. Being a healer is not the same as any other profession. We have awesome responsibility, make great personal and family sacrifices of time, finances, and relationships, and are in a not insignificant amount of danger, a fact that was overshadowed for many until the recent pandemic.

Just as the Exodus was an essential formative event for the people of Israel and their relationship with God, the healing process is essential to forming the covenant between a healer and a person confronting illness. In the introduction, I referenced Rabbi Yitz Greenberg's concept of Judaism as an Exodus religion, which says that the lesson of the Exodus is that God did not intend for people to suffer or be enslaved. The healing professions are saying to the people they heal, "You don't need to continue suffering in the way that you have been, and it is our job to figure out how to change your reality." That overture, that "strong hand and outstretched arm" that we offer those we care for, is our Exodus gesture, the one that creates the sacred covenant of healing described by Rabbi Harold Schulweis.

One of the themes of *kiddush* in the traditional seder is that through this event of leaving Egypt, the Israelites and God became part of a unit. In our seder of healing, we acknowledge that, when it works well, the healer and the patient become part of a unit, and being part of that unit's a blessed, holy thing.

RE-SANCTIFYING THE HEALING RELATIONSHIP

There's much that desecrates the healing relationship in our society, and indeed in most societies. Several chapters of *Healing People, Not Patients*, my first book, are devoted to examining what those unholy elements are. Health disparities, lack of access, and the undue burden that caring for the sick places on those who can least afford it are at the top of that list. So, too, are the administrative burdens on healers, and the design of EMRs that are essentially billing software that attempts to add detailed record keeping as an afterthought and call it "meaningful use." It's hard, sometimes, not to feel that we're doing work that should be in service of God, but really still working for Pharaoh.

In *Healing People, Not Patients*, I related a story/joke that I first heard from Richard Joel, at the time the head of Hillel International and later president of Yeshiva University. It concerned an ancient reporter interviewing workers building Solomon's Temple, each answering questions about the specific job he did, until the reporter reached a janitor who was sweeping up after construction, who declared that his job was to build a Temple to God Almighty. It seems even then there was "scut"—and even then, there were people who knew how to rise above thinking of it as scut and recognizing the role it played in a greater mission. I recently wrote a recommendation for an aspiring med student highlighting that person's work as a patient-care technician, because they had spoken to me with genuine enthusiasm about being able to help in a patient's care by doing things like holding icepacks, or bathing after surgery.

The tasks the Israelites did in Egypt were not so different from the tasks they did in Jerusalem 400 years later. They cut stone and hauled it, built scaffolding and climbed it, and assembled it into a glorious building where people would worship someday. The only thing that changed was which Master they served.

True healing is like that. The only difference between a temple to the pharaohs and a Temple to God Almighty may be the intent of the builder. If the healer chooses to separate and elevate the work before they do it, then Pharoah's power begins to crumble. We've seen it more and more in the days of the pandemic. Frontline workers were refusing to submit any longer to unsafe or unreasonable demands like working without adequate PPE, being trained in abusive environments, or working shifts so long they needed toothpicks to prop their eyes open.

In the Exodus story, Moshe, at the time still a privileged Egyptian prince, happens upon a taskmaster mercilessly beating a Hebrew slave. The text tells us *vayifen koh va'khoh, vayar she ein ish*— "He looked this way and that, and saw that there was no one around," and then struck the taskmaster dead[4]. It seems like Moshe is checking to see if the coast is clear so no one will see him do this, but the commentator HaKtav V'HaKabbalah observes that Moshe is looking around to see if any of the other Hebrews is going to step up to protect this slave. More than a thousand years after Moshe, Hillel would say, *Bamakom she ein ish, hishtadel lihy'yot ish.* "In a place where there are no humans, try to be a human."[5]

---

4. Exodus 2:12
5. Mishna Avot 2:5

What Moshe was looking for wasn't a person who would catch him in the act—he was looking for a human being to rise to the occasion. Seeing no one was going to do so, he does it himself.

Not all civil disobedience happens in the streets with signs and megaphones. My cousin Jed Diamond shared a different definition: Civil disobedience is when someone tasked with enforcing a rule or regulation recognizes that it's an unjust rule, or that it can't justly be applied in this case and refuses to default to "just going along with things."

An example of this type of civil disobedience in the previous chapter of Exodus is that of Shifra and Puah. These two midwives are asked to commit infanticide whenever they deliver a male Hebrew baby. They don't argue, or protest—they simply don't carry out the task and allow the babies to live, telling a lie that the Egyptian establishment is only too ready to believe to cover for their actions.[6]

Of course, the ultimate goal is to throw off the yoke of Egypt altogether. But that type of change moves slowly, and at this point in the story the Israelites have been waiting hundreds of years for change, too long to ask for more patience. Jed's subversive form of civil disobedience, the Shifra and Puah variety, can happen right now—even as the Moshes of the world fight the long fight for systemic change. And the actual midwives, along with the doctors, nurses, physician assistants, nurse practitioners, technicians, therapists, receptionists, patient transporters and hospital administrators, are the ones who will be called upon to do it.

We hope for a world where the Albert Lexies don't need to sacrifice their already meager income to help children afford medical care, and where heroes saving lives from COVID-19 don't need to "heroically" endanger themselves by not having adequate protective equipment. In the meantime, acts of compassion in a system that doesn't promote compassion, acts of care in a system focused on cure, and acts of kindness in a system that values commerce will separate and elevate us. Over acts like these, we should surely make kiddush.

Every time I write in my burdensome EMR that a patient was stigmatized and received poor treatment due to a history of drug use, or document my refusal to perform preoperative testing that evidence-based guidelines find unnecessary, or call out the role that racial injustice played in causing a patient's illness, I'm reclaiming the edifice that I'm building from Pharoah, and rededicating it to a holy purpose.

---

6. Exodus 1:15–19

The system is still broken, and the cracks more visible than ever, but I would argue that it's precisely by consecrating the work, rather than drudging through it as a servant to a new Pharoah, that we'll be more likely to stand up. Brian C. Miller's 2021 book, *Reducing Secondary Traumatic Stress*, observes that it's not the deeply committed, leave-it-all-on-the-field professionals who burn out in the helping professions, but those who try to hold themselves back and remain disengaged and aloof who are most likely to burn out. He offers a comprehensive program called CE-CERT aimed at recapturing the commitment (what I would call the sanctity) of the work.

To my great delight, the CE-CERT curriculum is based in a three-act story, an epic tale of an adventurer entering the woods to find a magic elixir. In my curriculum, we begin with an ordinary elixir and separate it in order to elevate it. L'chaim.

5

Waldman on Washing, Part 1

Now everyone washes hands (Urhatz) without saying a blessing over the act.

RAISED UP WHEN WE'RE LAID LOW

In his memoir *This Narrow Space*, Elisha Waldman describes being pulled into a patient's hospital room just after their death and being asked to help wash the body. The scene so moved me and raised so many questions about the meaning and symbolism of water and washing in the healing process, that I knew I needed to hear from Elisha when it came time to discuss the washing sections of the *seder*.[1]

It turns out that Elisha had experienced a couple of impromptu washings in his time at Hadassah, but the one he spoke with me about involved a young man who died a "horrible death," from a spreading tumor with an unsettling appearance and powerful smell. Elisha described his initial emotions as the washing began as "a mixed bag of trepidation and disgust, bracing when pulling back the sheet." But then, "There was a quick shift from selfish fear, wanting to walk away, to heartbroken human sympathy for how his body was corrupted." It was an honor, he said, being allowed to minister to a human being in this way.

I recognized this feeling. I've served for several years now in one of Pittsburgh's *chevra kadisha* organizations, a volunteer society that attends

---

1. We spoke in June of 2022, more than two years into the COVID-19 pandemic, and what follows here and in the Chapter 33 are the fruits of that conversation.

to the dead before burial, preparing them through washing and dressing in shrouds according to traditional Jewish practice. I've often stood over the body of a *meit*, a deceased person, whether a stranger or a friend, and thought the exact words that Elisha spoke.

If you notice a familiar Hebrew word in *chevra kadisha*, you're correct. The same *k-d-sh* root that we explored in the last chapter is back. At the lowest time in our lives, confronted with mortality, the work of the *chevra* separates and elevates. It separates the dead from the living while elevating the soul of that *meit* for the first step of their journey into the next world. It also separates the members of the *chevra* from the rest of society for a time, as we do work known as *hesed shel emet,* the truest kindness, done with no hope of repayment.

In the worst moments, participating in the work of *hesed shel emet* provides a ritual that gives voice to the anguish and creates meaning and purpose where there was only helplessness. For some of my own *chaverim* (friends and partners in the *chevra*) these moments followed the terrorist attack on one of our synagogues. For Elisha, at that moment, in that place, washing that body—the death of that patient didn't feel like failing, as so many patient deaths do for dedicated physicians. Instead, it felt oddly like professional fulfillment.

Once, several years ago, I participated in *taharah* for a man I had cared for professionally, who died at a ripe old age. I had once gifted him the Robert Heinlein novel *Time Enough for Love*, about an immortal who has finally grown old enough to be bored with existence. There was no shock in his death, only the strange, comfortable sadness of missing someone I knew had done all he wished on this earth. The *taharah* was a way of thanking him for entrusting me with his care when he was alive, and of accompanying him to the other side.

For both Elisha and me, we were crossing a boundary. *Taharah* preparations are careful to keep certain boundaries in place, for reasons of gender and general modesty. Yet, our usual boundary between our personal and professional lives, and our spiritual and scientific lives, broke down with these ritual washings of lovingkindness that could never be repaid. Just as the border between life and death dissolves at that final moment, these boundaries of clear identity, these buckets of what belongs where, are spilled and erased by the pouring of the water, the careful cleansing, the gentle wrapping in clean cloth.

THE PARADOX OF PURITY

Ironic that our conversations should zero in on the washing of corpses. In Jewish law, a corpse is the quintessential source of ritual impurity. In contrast, the washing we do before eating is meant to *remove* impurity and allow us to eat our meal in a heightened spiritual state. It's one of the many paradoxes of faith, the consequence of worshipping a frankly paradoxical God—the work we do to purify in one realm renders us impure in another. And when we can't perform that ritual, when we're unable to purify, and so remain safe in other parts of our lives, we lose something.

During the Ebola epidemics of the 2010s, epidemiologists linked at least some of the spread to local generic burial practices involving close, hands-on contact with those who had recently died of Ebola. Western scientists and public health experts self-righteously opined that these practices needed to stop in order to stamp out the epidemic, knowing little about how vital those rituals might have been to the people performing them.

People like my *chevra*, for example. We perform *taharot* like the one I described above in small, chilly, poorly ventilated rooms in the unseen precincts of funeral parlors; three to five *chaverim* circled around the table where the *meit*, the deceased, lies modestly covered. Such circles, of necessity involving people who were not of the same household, are certainly not distant, socially or physically, enough to meet the guidelines that evolved like dividing bacteria in the early days of the COVID-19 pandemic—especially if the dread new virus had been the cause of death.

Suddenly, we were not the condescending Westerners imposing our views on the people of West Africa. It was our "quaint" practice of washing the dead by hand that was a potential disease hazard. That had to stop if we were to observe the even-more-important dictum of preserving life still being lived. Would we be so arrogant as to say, "Their way was too dangerous in that epidemic, but we enlightened folks will be just fine?" Or, alternatively, would we have to admit that we didn't recognize how critical these rituals had been to others when faced with having our own closure, our own purification practices, taken from us?

Leaders in the *chevra Kadisha* movement, including my long-distance friend Rick Light, created alternate rituals under the name *taharah ruhanit*. Following pandemic-era norms, they moved everything to video conference platforms, retaining the liturgy and the intent of the washing and dressing while eliminating the contact. Funeral home staff placed the *meit*, still enclosed in the hospital body bag to minimize contagion, on camera in the *tahara* room, while the remotely located *chaverim* read the liturgy, often pouring water symbolically from pitcher to bowl to replicate the actual washing that couldn't safely happen.

Like so many other decisions made early in the pandemic, the decision to make this shift begat two new questions that took much longer to answer: When would it be safe to return, and would the new ritual hold up as sufficient replacement for the traditional methods? Taken to its logical extreme, that second question might even lead to asking, "Do we need to do this at all? Ever?"

Strange as it might seem today, two years after the germophobic Howie Mandells of the world finally won the argument, that last question has plagued advocates of medical handwashing for years. The pioneer of hand hygiene, Ignatz Semmelweis, was ostracized by his peers. He died in disgrace and poverty because he insisted that childbed fever came from the unwashed hands of the doctors, while the spic-and-span midwives kept their delivered mothers safe and healthy. Englishman John Lister got all the credit more than 15 years later, thanks to Louis Pasteur's germ theory and a better personality, and as a result he's the guy with his name on a mouthwash bottle. Imagine washing with Semmelweisine for thirty seconds a day.

Why the struggle? Certainly, it might be mere laziness. The play *W;t*, by Margaret Edson, depicts the irritation of Doctor Jason Posner, a research-focused oncology resident, at having to wash and don protective equipment "just to look at the I&O sheets for one minute" for his patient Vivian Bearing—whose immune system has been wiped out by the experimental chemotherapy that Jason himself is delivering to her.[2] Real-world physicians often chafe at the amount of time required on rounds for an entire team of residents and medical students to wash before entering a patient's room, even if only one of them will touch the patient.

More than laziness, many decisions are driven by ego. There's a certain implication in the act of washing that there's something unclean, or impure, about me. Jewish practice teaches humility, a quality that might lead us to accept that as fact and wish to remove that impurity. In Western medicine, the hierarchy rewards confidence and even arrogance among physicians, making it very hard for us to recognize ourselves as a potential source of sickness—whether due to the toxic effects of our drugs, to our filthy hands, or to a condescending, hands-off attitude.

---

2. Edson, *W;t*, 47.

FROM RESTRICTION TO RITUAL

Not everyone struggles. Elisha shared with me that one of his colleagues uses her moment of handwashing much as we do in the context of the seder. She makes it a personal ritual, one which clears her and separates her from what came before, outside the door, and prepares her for whatever encounter is to come next, after she enters.

This ritualization of washing points to something Elisha has noticed increasingly over his career—the degree to which medical practice takes on the trappings of a religion, with dicta and fixed practices that its adherents follow dutifully. Surgeons don't complain about scrubbing in; on the contrary, there's a certain amount of indoctrination and shaming that takes place as new trainees struggle to learn the detailed process of surgical scrubbing—and screw it up as they do. If medicine is its own quasi-religious enterprise, then perhaps handwashing is an element of that religious practice that we incorporate.

Ritual has the power to shape behavior. I'm writing this book *because* rituals and religious practice of all kinds has the power to shape behavior, and because I think that studying the Exodus and engaging in seder rituals can inform how we respond in the face of illness, loss, and trauma. Yet the ritualization of medicine has an ironic effect, as Elisha sees it. The more features of a religion it takes on, the less open it's to acknowledgement of Religion, as the rest of the world sees it. The more orthodox it is in its practice of the precepts and punctilious action of Medicine as Faith, the less room there is for a person (patient or healer) to bring their own beliefs and practices to bear.

Perhaps handwashing, an act which has such valence in both general religious practices and in the Religion of Medicine, can be a common point from which to begin a reconciliation—much as it is one of the opening acts of our seder.

6

Of Spring and Salt

We pass spring greens and salt water around the table and dip the greens in the salt water.

Karpas	כרפס
Blessed are you, Lord our God, Ruler of the universe, who creates the fruit of the earth.	בָּרוּךְ אַתָּה ה', אֱלֹהֵינוּ מֶלֶךְ הָעוֹלָם, בּוֹרֵא פְּרִי הָאֲדָמָה.

THINGS THAT WON'T WASH OFF

I can't get the sunshine out of my mind.

On September 11th, 2001, I was a third-year medical student doing my pediatric clerkship at a private office in the suburbs. I have many memories of that awful day that don't really fit together. The first reports coming over the radio in the office manager's office (I only saw the TV footage later); the tearful staff meeting in the afternoon conducted by my instructor, Dr. Scott Tyson (a master class in how to shepherd people through a tragedy no one has control over) and the visit with a family who were among the last people to travel the skies over America for the next four days—who had come straight from their gate to the office.

But the one common thread to all of them is the sunshine.

Just like in New York on that morning, the skies were cloudless and blue, and the golden late-summer/early-autumn sunshine was that incredible color that you know when you see it. You can scarcely believe it actually exists in the waking world. It's the warmest, most radiant, most invigorating thing that exists, and that day of all days it filled the sky, poured in the windows, and made a mockery of our grief and shock. And the shock is still there more than 20 years later. No amount of washing will take it away.

THE PURITY PARADOX OF EMOTIONS: NO SORROW WITHOUT JOY, NO JOY WITHOUT SORROW

It's a quintessentially Jewish memory. The memory of the worst day of my life to that moment is suffused with the glow of an absolute gift from God.

Think about other terrible dates in American history. Roll September 11th in with December 7, 1941, and the attack on Pearl Harbor. Add January 28, 1986, the day the Challenger exploded, and November 22, 1963, when John F. Kennedy was assassinated. I focus deliberately on these dates in the 20th and 21st century because they occurred in the era of instantaneous media; where radio, telephone, and television (and by September 11, 2001, the internet) enabled the whole country to feel as if they were experiencing the events in real time.

Now imagine they all happened on the same date in the calendar. That the bullet struck JFK on December 7th, the O-ring on the Challenger broke on December 7th, and the hijackers boarded the planes on December 7th. Now you have a date that approaches the indelible significance of Tisha B'Av for the Jews.

Yet even on Tisha B'Av, the 9th day of the midsummer month on which both Temples were destroyed, the exile from Spain was made final, and countless other major and minor tragedies are supposed to have occurred—all is not lost. On that date (in some future year if not already) the Messiah will be born. The darkest day on the calendar will become the day when the seeds of our redemption emerge.

This admixture of sorrow and joy cuts the other way, too. On each of the days of Pesach, we recite the Hallel service praising God; a sign of rejoicing for our freedom. Yet on all but the first two days, we abbreviate the Hallel as if it were Rosh Chodesh, a less joyous day than the full Festivals. We deliberately diminish our joy because Hallel calls to mind the crossing of the Sea of Reeds—and the Sea of Reeds calls to mind the Egyptians who had to drown there for us to escape. We can't be fully joyous in the face of their deaths—we even dump out perfectly good wine at the seder to reduce our enjoyment because of the plagues our enslavers had to endure.

More well-known is the tradition of breaking the glass at the end of a wedding. My contrarian friend Chuck Diener, not content to accept the tradition that the glass recalls the destruction of the Temple, wrote in his wedding card to my wife and me that this broken glass symbolizes the imperfections of the couple. On a day when we're empowered to lie to a bride and tell her she is beautiful, the glass nevertheless uncovers the truth—both partners to the marriage have flaws, and they're enjoined to say to one another, "Your flaws, too, are holy, even these I love." Still not content, Chuck offered one further interpretation—the broken glass is a warning that if the marriage should be broken, it can no more easily be mended than the shards of glass can be reunited into a glass.

Talk about a party-pooper.

The *karpas* section of the *seder* fits right into this mode of "A Little Happy, A Little Sad," like the song from the *Addams Family* musical. Text-wise, it consists of nothing more than a one-line blessing over "fruits of the ground," like green vegetables and root crops. But like the wedding, it's not what we say but what we do in that moment that carries the intermingled sadness and joy.

A sprig of green, usually parsley, symbolizing spring and all the new life and hope that comes with it, is dipped in salt water—representing the tears that were cried by our enslaved ancestors in Egypt. The future dipped in the past. The hope dipped in despair.

Yet the taste is oddly satisfying. In fact, anyone who cooks (well, anyway) knows that salt is essential. It reveals all the other flavors in a dish, even the sweet ones. Don't believe me? Come back after you've tried a sea salt brownie and tell me you weren't transported to another dimension (unless it's Pesach right now—then you should definitely NOT try a sea salt brownie until after Pesach is over).

Tears are essential, too. The Disney/Pixar film *Inside Out* features five personified emotions living in, and trying to control, the brain of 11-year-old Riley, who has just had to move across the country with her parents. Joy, a gratingly optimistic character who's shaped like Tinkerbell but is the color of that sunshine I described on 9/11, is nominally in charge of the control center, and spends most of the movie trying to keep

Disgust, Anger, and Fear in check, but mostly trying to prevent Sadness, a blue blob with glasses in a shapeless sweater, from touching the memories. Every memory Sadness touches turns sad, revealing the disappointments that happened just out of the picture, or just shatters on the floor. It's not until Joy and Sadness must team up to save Riley from losing her sense of self and destroying her relationship with her parents that Joy can see that some of the happiest golden memories she's been protecting only happened on the heels of deep blue memories that belong to Sadness.

The trick is in knowing where to focus.

7

Breaking Points

In Yahatz, we take the stack of three matzot from the table, remove the middle piece, and break it in half. The larger piece, um, goes missing (is stolen by the children) to be rediscovered (ransomed) before the end of the seder.

We are the King's horses, we are the King's men
We cannot put Humpty Dumpty back together again.

Every Haggadah reaches this point, the Yahatz section where we break the middle matzah, and rightly speaks of brokenness—the brokenness of the world, the brokenness of people's relationships to one another, the brokenness of individual human spirits. And for some reason, my mind moves from broken worlds and broken glasses in the sad-sweet moment of Karpas to a variation of a nursery rhyme about a broken egg. Maybe because, through most of my childhood, I had a stuffed Humpty Dumpty that I repeatedly nursed through the brokenness of her face washing off so that I needed to draw it back on with magic marker.

We who busy ourselves with the brokenness of the human body and mind can relate.

We are the King's horses, we are the King's men
We cannot put Humpty Dumpty back together again.

Challenge us to repair something and we'll jump at the opportunity. In the seventy-plus years that have passed since the mid-20th century, medicine has come to believe that there's no bacteria we can't wipe out with antibiotics, no tumor we can't vanquish with chemotherapy, no imbalance of bodily chemicals we can't correct if we simply measure and titrate often and exactly enough.

We are the King's horses, we are the King's men
We cannot put Humpty Dumpty back together again.

Life is composed of catastrophes and recoveries. Unlike an electrical circuit, we're better off experiencing them in series than in parallel—one at a time, with a moment to catch our breath in between, or perhaps even feel like everything is all right sometimes. In a parallel circuit one limb can go down and the current will keep flowing. In a life experiencing tandem disasters, the damage is not additive but grows exponentially.

We are the King's horses, we are the King's men
We cannot put Humpty Dumpty back together again.

One failed organ can be repaired or replaced. Two are dicey. Three or more requires a miracle. And when the brain (or the soul) is failing, sometimes even miracles don't work

We are the King's horses, we are the King's men
We cannot put Humpty Dumpty back together again.

My favorite seder joke goes like this: An observant Jew is the lead engineer on a new supersonic aircraft project. The engines work well, the takeoffs are smooth, the plane maneuvers great, but every time the pilot pushes it past the sound barrier the wings break off from the fuselage right at the point where they were attached. Test flight after test flight ends with the pilot and copilot ejecting with their parachutes and the plane exploding in a fireball on the desert floor.

Finally, the lead engineer tells his crew, "I want you to make the next prototype with perforations where the wings are attached to the fuselage." The crew don't understand why he made the request but comply with the order. On the next test flight, the plane takes off, accelerates to Mach 3, completes all its maneuvers and lands intact on the runway.

"How did you know that would do the trick?" asks the pilot.

"I'm fifty years old," says the engineer. "In the one hundred sedarim I've attended in my life; I've never once seen a piece of matzah break on the perforations."

In my final seder before I turned fifty, the matzah broke on the perforation. Now even my joke is broken.

We are the King's horses, we are the King's men

We cannot put Humpty Dumpty back together again.

People don't break on the perforations. Or, as my teachers in medical school used to enjoy saying, "Patients don't read textbooks." We don't see "a case of heart failure." We see a person whose heart is failing, who also suffers from kidney failure and generalized anxiety, and is recently bereft of the love of their life. They've a failing heart and a broken heart all at once.

We are the King's horses, we are the King's men

We cannot put Humpty Dumpty back together again.

A clean break is easy to mend—but like the story of the broken glass in the previous section, or a piece of matzah cracking across the perforations, a jagged break doesn't go back together so easily. Yahatz reminds us that more often than not, we're trying to find ways to rejoin irregular pieces that don't wish to be mended—in our work and in our world. The leaders of our sedarim, without knowing it, are taunting us healers, who think we're omnipotent, by breaking this matzah in our face and reminding us of our inadequacy.

We are the King's horses, we are the King's men

We cannot put Humpty Dumpty back together again.

Yet in this inadequacy, a way out. Perhaps we have it all wrong, thinking that our mission as healers is to make everything whole and perfect again. What if it's as the Kotzker Rebbe taught, "There is nothing more whole than a broken heart?" Like my Ferri's Practical Guide to the Care of the Medical Patient says in the introduction, "Don't just do something, stand there." Stop fixing and appreciate that most of life is not lived in the space that Yehuda Amichai yearned for: The space between the wars, in the peaces. It's lived in the catastrophes, crises and calamities.

Lived—and relived. So many of those catastrophes, crises, and calamities happen not once, but cyclically, erupting every few months, or years, or centuries—or never quite simmering down in the first place. The decades of Troubles in Northern Ireland. The Serbs and Croats. Russia and Ukraine. India and Pakistan. Israel and Palestine. Even the treatments we use for survivors of trauma involve a sort of reliving, as we'll see in Chapter 10.

We're here, not to fix all those hearts, but to hold the pieces of the broken ones in our hands for as long as we can, because ultimately all of them will break again. It's for this reason that the central symbol of the seder, the matzah, is broken into pieces before we even begin to tell the story. What good would the story of our slavery and redemption be with whole, pristine matzah? Would we still be telling it now, more than three thousand years later, if we weren't still broken and crumbled ourselves? And yet, would we still be ourselves if we weren't broken or crumbled?

Humpty Dumpty had a great fall
So what else is new? Haven't we all?
Forget the King's horses, forget the King's men
If I tell you my story I'll feel whole again.

Thoughts and Discussions

- *Where are your breaking points? Are they clean, even breaks, jagged lines, or a pile of crumbs?*
- *Can those breaks be mended? How, or by whom?*
- *What have you tried to fix in your life, only to find that you can't—or that you've broken it even more irreparably?*

8

Poor Bread

The telling of the Pesach story, Magid, begins with the song Ha Lahma 'Anya, an Aramaic song about the matzah.

Pesach Haggadah, Magid, Ha Lachma Anya	הגדה של פסח, מגיד, הא לחמא עניא
The Recitation [of the exodus story]	מַגִּיד
The leader uncovers the matzot, raises the Seder plate, and says out loud:	מגלה את המצות, מגביה את הקערה ואומר בקול רם:
This is the bread of destitution that our ancestors ate in the land of Egypt. Anyone who is famished should come and eat, anyone who is in need should come and partake of the Pesach sacrifice. Now we are here, next year we will be in the land of Israel; this year we are slaves, next year we will be free people.	הָא לַחְמָא עַנְיָא דִּי אֲכָלוּ אַבְהָתָנָא בְּאַרְעָא דְמִצְרָיִם. כָּל דִּכְפִין יֵיתֵי וְיֵיכֹל, כָּל דִּצְרִיךְ יֵיתֵי וְיִפְסַח. הָשַׁתָּא הָכָא, לְשָׁנָה הַבָּאָה בְּאַרְעָא דְיִשְׂרָאֵל. הָשַׁתָּא עַבְדֵי, לְשָׁנָה הַבָּאָה בְּנֵי חוֹרִין.

THE DOCTOR IN THE RED DRESS

Scene 1: In a busy 21st century city, amid towering skyscrapers, transit stops, storefronts and bustling crowds, a frail, elderly man hobbles away from a hospital emergency department. His left arm is in a sling, provided for him in that emergency department—likely after a fall caused by his frailty, his poor vision, or the clutter in his cramped, lonely living quarters.

Scene 2: The man arrives home from his long journey by public transit to find he now struggles to manage his basic daily needs of feeding, clothing, and bathing himself. Tragically, he realizes he also can't do a passable job of shopping, cooking, or cleaning. Lonely and isolated, he has no one to step in and do those things on his behalf.

The Haggadah declares, "This is the bread of poverty, which our ancestors ate in *Mitzrayim*. Let all who are hungry come and eat, let all who are in need come celebrate Pesach." In their *Passover Haggadah Graphic Novel*,[1] Jordan Gorfinkel and Erez Zadok open this section with scene 1, the frail man leaving the hospital. We who know how the system works immediately imagine scene 2 to follow. Let all who are hungry," reads the lettering on the panel. We shake our heads cynically.

But Gorfinkel and Zadok defy expectations. In their scene 2, a doctor in a white coat and a red dress, possibly the same physician who treated the injured arm, follows him through the revolving door into the sunlight and calls out, "Come and eat!"

When we do things on others' behalf, it helps us to be whole. It feels almost like putting the pieces of the irreparably broken matzah "back together again," perhaps because we're serving a ruler with different priorities. And whatever your cynicism about the medical profession today, most people in the helping professions entered those fields because we thought we would be putting broken pieces back together, all day, every day.

SILOS

For most of us, though, the scope of that help, and advocacy ends up being quite limited. Access to our services—to our very caring—is constrained by insurance, transportation, cost, language and structured, systematic discrimination so baked in we don't even realize when we're perpetrating it.

Many of us are in such perfect silos. We specialize (as my friend the retina specialist says) in "one square inch at the back of the eyeball." We're protected from ever "seeing" the lonely apartment, the accumulating dirty dishes, or the fear of leaving home lest a fall or an assault turn the

---

1. Gorfinkel and Zadok, *Passover Haggadah Graphic Novel*, 13–15.

trip into a disaster. We stay insulated from the violence, the trauma, and the injustice that people face when they pass through the revolving door.

Even when we *do* see it, we're often so jaded as to be unmoved. Surgeons need to set aside the natural human aversion to causing pain to be able to cut through living skin and do their vital work. All healers learn to steel our stomachs against others' nausea and toughen our nerves against their pain, or we couldn't bear to do our jobs. But we succeed too well in this exercise when we enter the territory of eye rolls, snark, and outright dismissal of the suffering before us.

We certainly don't go looking for these problems to solve. Public health leader and podcaster Dr. Abdul El-Sayed describes trying to extend himself beyond the walls of the ER as a medical student and being met with ridicule at his suggestions of how to build a safety net for one of his patients. It so disheartened him that he never practiced medicine at the individual patient-care level, choosing a career in public health instead.[2]

We serve a system that's reactive, not proactive. The problems that come before us we solve; those that don't are not our problems. We'll go to the ends of the earth for "our patients," but not even wait until the end of the sentence for someone who's not "ours." We're beholden to that which is "medicolegal," industry jargon for right in the eyes of the law but wrong in the heart of the healer. And even for those who are in our care, when we hear something that's "outside our scope of practice" or "off topic," our usual response is "What am *I* supposed to do about that?"

That's why the doctor in the red dress is so remarkable. She steps out of her secure zone, into the wider world. She looks up from the broken arm to see the person from whom it dangles limply. She takes personal responsibility for their need, issuing a literal invitation, "Come and eat, let me feed you." Three thousand, three hundred years earlier, give or take a few decades, a similarly sheltered princess went to the river to bathe and saw a baby that was not her baby floating by in a basket of reeds. Had she not, at that moment, chosen to step out of *her* secure zone and take personal responsibility for that baby, we would not be having this discussion right now—indeed, the faith traditions of half of humanity would not exist.[3]

Let all who are hungry come and eat, and let us set the table and cook the meal. One of surgeon and author Atul Gawande's seminal articles was

---

[2]. El-Sayed. 2019 University of Michigan School of Medicine Commencement Address. https://www.youtube.com/watch?v=EQ7LnzP1QmU

[3]. Exodus 2:5–8.

called "Hotspotting,"[4] an examination of how one hospital in Camden, NJ, recognized that the "frequent flyers" in their emergency department were not coming in because they needed the care in the hospital so badly, but because their circumstances outside the hospital failed them so badly. They decided as an institution to do what Abdul El-Sayed was ridiculed for suggesting as a lone trainee.

Ha lahma 'anya holds up the matzah and forces us to look at a symbol of suffering and to remember that it symbolizes *our* suffering. "Don't blind yourself to what others are feeling—you and your ancestors suffered like this," it reminds us. That awareness calls us to action, to let all who are hungry come and eat, to let all who are in need take part in Pesach.

What's the difference between the two? Feeding meets the needs of the moment, the hunger of the hour. Pesach, the moment of redemption, is a watershed event beyond which nothing remains the same. For Hashem it's the work of an instant, but for a human and for humanity, it's the work of many lifetimes. Two hundred and ten years of slavery in Mitzrayim could end overnight, but the wound of two hundred and fifty years of slavery in America must still be dressed and debrided every day nearly one hundred and sixty years after it "ended."

The first mention of "physicians" in the Torah refers to the Egyptian "physicians" who are the professional embalmers, the ones who mummify and preserve the bodies of the Pharaohs and who tend to Joseph when he dies. The first mention of actual healers of living humans comes in Exodus, when we meet the midwives Shifrah and Puah, whom we learned about in Chapter 1. They play a critical role in allowing "those who are in need," the Israelites, to celebrate the very first Pesach. The midwives, not the embalmers, need to be our role models today. Our job is not to preserve what was, but to enable and bring about what needs to be.

As we saw, the midwives' identity is ambiguous, leaving us guessing whether these are Hebrew women protecting their own—or outsiders whose empathy compels them to deceive Pharaoh and thwart his plan. Their spiritual descendants are the doctor in the red dress, Abdul El Sayed, and the staff of that hospital in Camden. Heroes recognize that they eat the same bread and need the same redemption as the people they care for. They're not afraid to step out of their silos to provide it. May we all merit to become their spiritual descendants.

---

4. Gawande, "The Hot Spotters." *New Yorker*, January 16, 2011.

9

So What Else Is New?

One must ask questions at the seder. One way to guarantee it? Make the children ask scripted questions about things that haven't happened yet.

Pesach Haggadah, Magid, Four Questions He removes the plate from the table. We pour a second cup of wine. The son then asks: What differentiates this night from all [other] nights? On all [other] nights we eat hametz and matzah; this night, only matzah? On all [other] nights we eat other vegetables; tonight (only) maror. On all [other] nights, we don't dip [our food], even one time; tonight [we dip it] twice. On [all] other nights, we eat either sitting or reclining; tonight, we all recline.	הגדה של פסח, מגיד, מה נשתנה מסיר את הקערה מעל השולחן. מוזגין כוס שני. הבן שואל: מַה נִּשְׁתַּנָּה הַלַּיְלָה הַזֶּה מִכָּל הַלֵּילוֹת? שֶׁבְּכָל הַלֵּילוֹת אָנוּ אוֹכְלִין חָמֵץ וּמַצָּה, הַלַּיְלָה הַזֶּה—כֻּלּוֹ מַצָּה. שֶׁבְּכָל הַלֵּילוֹת אָנוּ אוֹכְלִין שְׁאָר יְרָקוֹת—הַלַּיְלָה הַזֶּה (כֻּלּוֹ) מָרוֹר. שֶׁבְּכָל הַלֵּילוֹת אֵין אָנוּ מַטְבִּילִין אֲפִילוּ פַּעַם אֶחָת—הַלַּיְלָה הַזֶּה שְׁתֵּי פְעָמִים. שֶׁבְּכָל הַלֵּילוֹת אָנוּ אוֹכְלִין בֵּין יוֹשְׁבִין וּבֵין מְסֻבִּין—הַלַּיְלָה הַזֶּה כֻּלָּנוּ מְסֻבִּין.

WHAT IS YOUR QUESTION?

Is it, "why is this night different from all other nights?" Or perhaps, "how different this night is from all other nights!" Either way, Pesach is about remarking and expounding on what makes things special and different, unlike the remainder of the year in so many ways.

At a healers' seder we might be tempted to find symbolism for the matzah, the maror, the dipping and the reclining in our healing practices. For example, should we see reclining as the expression of freedom, a regaining of dignity after healing from a distressing illness? Or is it, in fact, symbolic of illness and weakness, an inability to sit fully upright or stand?

Likewise, it might be meaningful to reflect on the things that make this *specific* seder different from others, when global or personal circumstances loom large over the table. In 2017, what was different was the absence of my Nana, Elinor Goodman. My first experience of seder was in her enormous dining room less than a block from where I currently live, and where we also celebrated our first seder without her. She was inextricably linked to Passover; she retold her birth story every year at seder. How her mother, in the pre-feminist world of 1924, had set the table with a seder she would never eat because she had to be rushed to the hospital and give birth the following morning.

Passover 2020 was a "different night" for other reasons. The global COVID-19 pandemic was still in its first full month, and our warm, boisterous gathering was reduced to faces on a screen. And even among those faces, we were missing Arlyn Gilboa, our dear friend who left us mere weeks before the pandemic would have prevented us wishing her goodbye or accompanying her to her rest. Yet that seder was also the first in my memory that, owing to not having to serve the soup to 23 people, dinner went by so efficiently that the entire assembled crew stayed on afterward to *bentsch*, sing Hallel, and sing the songs at the end.

If you're well-steeped in Jewish culture, you know that there's another understanding of *Mah nishtana ha-laila ha-zeh mikol ha leilot?* Said with just the right tone of sarcasm, it means, "So what else is new?"

I worry that as healers, we arrive at this portion of our day, when we first actually encounter a person in need, and enter with an attitude of *Mah nishtana?* "What are you going to tell me that I haven't already heard before?" It's easy to become jaded, numb, or cynical with repeated exposure—not just to a specific disease or surgical procedure, but to human suffering and tragic stories as well.

SAME ROTATION, DIFFERENT DAY?

My fourth year of medical school, I spent a month doing a fascinating rotation on inpatient rheumatology consults. Rheumatology is notorious for being a discipline that no one outside of rheumatology really understands—and that's also skillful at draining fluid out of swollen joints. As a result, my month was split between immensely satisfying hands-on procedures and *House, M.D.*—level medical mysteries like central nervous system vasculitis and Wegener's Granulomatosis.

One such medical mystery was a young woman with lupus (told you this was like *House*) who had developed a devastating complication called TTP (thrombotic thrombocytopenic purpura). TTP is a catastrophic pathological paradox, where a person's blood is so dysfunctional that they both bleed profusely and clot uncontrollably all at the same time. The only potential treatment for her at that time was plasmapheresis, a dialysis-like machine-based therapy which cleans the deadly, misguided antibodies out of the bloodstream, and which needs to be repeated daily until the patient is out of the woods.

Each day of treatment became a negotiation so pitched it should have been held at Camp David. The young woman would agree to treatment, grudgingly, angrily, and then change her mind, hesitate, and then relent again. Finally, on the third day, she decided to leave against medical advice. The news reached us on rounds and I immediately offered to excuse myself to go to her room and "talk her down" so she would stay. Our fellow waved me off.

"I trained in New York City," she said, speaking of her recently completed internal medicine residency. "We walked around the hospital with blank AMA forms in our pockets; if someone said they wanted to leave AMA we handed them the forms on the spot. No waiting. If we spent the time trying to convince every one of them to stay we'd never do anything else. If they don't want to get better that's their problem."

Mah nishtana ha laila hazeh mikol ha leilot, said the rheumatology fellow, "how is this night different from any other night?" I've seen this movie before and I'm not even going to sit through the opening credits.

One might argue that the fellow's attitude here was actually the "enlightened" one. She was respecting patient's autonomy and humbly recognizing that what we offered as medical professionals was not miraculous, but merely one option among many that the patient was free to choose, or not choose, based on their values. I, running to her room to "talk her into staying," was being paternalistic.

One might argue that, but one would be missing the larger picture to score academic points.

Seen through the lens of eighteen years later, as medicine seems finally ready to acknowledge the existence of systemic racism, this episode looks like a classic example. The young woman with TTP coded Black and spoke in a way that seemed to our fellow, who coded White, to be abrupt, rude, demanding and confrontational. When she referred to not wasting her time to "convince *every one of them to stay*," she was referring to the category of people who looked and spoke like our patient, whom she didn't feel warranted her extra effort. She wasn't being enlightened—she was being dismissive. *They* could conform to her idea of how people *like them* should behave in the hospital, or they could leave, and die, for all she cared.

I fared only slightly better. There's overt racism, like the fellow's dismissiveness, and then there's subconscious bias—paternalism, as I called it above. Surely if I, the well-meaning, White-appearing medical student, would just explain the situation again to this patient so she could finally understand, she would suddenly become grateful for all our efforts and gladly submit to another round of treatment. As if she didn't know she was in danger of dying from all the none-too-subtle bleeding and clotting in her body. As if she didn't know that what we were planning to do in the hospital couldn't happen at home. As if she didn't realize that I, and my good intentions, were subordinate to the same fellow who had referred to her as *one of them*. Both of us, ultimately, were ready to hold the system and ourselves blameless if this woman left the hospital. This didn't serve the patient whether out of belligerence, as the fellow believed, or out of pitiable ignorance, as I apparently thought.

MAKE TONIGHT DIFFERENT!

"Why is this night different?" she might have asked *us*. What made us think that we were going to behave differently than the countless doctors she had surely seen before, receiving care as she did at an academic hospital where the faces change as often as the pages of an old-school wall calendar? What made us think we weren't going to repeat the same insults and indignities she had suffered so many times before? For that matter, what made us think we were going to do better *medicine*, somehow providing her with a better physical outcome than she had been able to achieve previously?

What was this woman's goal in coming to the hospital at all? Perhaps she knew all along she was dying. At what cost would she be able to save herself? How much physical imprisonment, tethered to the plasmapheresis machine, could she endure? How much condescension could she tolerate? How closely could she sit with her fear, hearing ominous lab results read off to her every six hours, before she retreated into denying reality, as anyone might when the alternative was to lie on the railroad tracks staring down the oncoming train? Only after years more training did I acquire the knowledge and skills to allow me, maybe, to be with this woman and learn what she, not *one of* them, was experiencing so I could help her reach *her* goal, not win her over to mine.

Why is this night different from all other nights? It's not a rhetorical question, it turns out, but a genuine expression of curiosity, or a sincere appreciation of the specialness of the occasion. If we're to have a healers' seder, let our four "questions" reflect that inquisitiveness, and awe. Not toward the miracle of the Pesach, but toward the wonder of beholding

God's own likeness: The final act of God's first great miracle, the Creation of Humanity.

How different is this night from all other nights! On all other nights we're puffed full of ourselves like *hametz*. Tonight, we humble ourselves like matzah. Similarly, God withdrew at the start of Creation to make space for the universe, and for each of us. Ever since, God has sought to know us and connect with us, giving us free will instead of dictating the course of human history. Let us make space for the people we care for to share their whole stories, even if they go in directions that don't fit what is "supposed" to happen.

How different is this night from all other nights! On all other nights we hear only what we want to hear and taste the sweetness of what we want to taste. Tonight, we sit with the bitterness of others, listening to bad news, listening to anger—even if that anger is rightfully directed at us. We must learn how to validate bitterness, not deflect the blame, and learn to change ourselves.

How different is this night from all other nights! On all other nights we like things straightforward, devoid of nuance or confusion. Tonight, we recognize that, like ogres and onions, everything has layers. Bitterness is dipped in sweetness, and hope is dipped in tears. A forward step can be accompanied by two backward ones, and a victory can be more costly than a loss. We need to learn this lesson about living with uncertainty, about holding simultaneous, conflicting thoughts and emotions in our hearts, and knowing both are equally true.

How different is this night from all other nights! On all other nights we sit up straight, work slavishly, punch the clock, and move on as quickly as we can. Tonight, we may recline. Our gesture of being free aristocrats conveys to the ones we're with that tonight, we have all the time in the world, and we're spending it with them. Even the difficult conversations feel full and holy in this environment, like the earnest, late-night heart-to-hearts we had as teenagers. These are the moments that made us choose this profession in the first place.

Once we recenter ourselves this way, we can actually ask, "*Mah Nishtanah?*" Not sarcastically like my fellow, but out of the curiosity I was just describing. Why did this family who has always steadfastly declined to vaccinate their child (for complex reasons they've taken pains to explain to me many times because I wouldn't let it go) just ask for me to provide catch-up vaccinations? What has changed for them? Or why has this person with a stable, chronic, painful disease come into the emergency setting to get care for that disease? What is wrong tonight that wasn't wrong yesterday? What are they now afraid of? What do they think is happening?

This *mah nishtanah* is how we uncover the fears, the hopes and the breaking points that make all the difference. In 2017, medical students at the University of Colorado asked their own version of *Mah Nishtanah* when they began a project in their emergency department called, "What Worries You the Most?"[1] They distributed cards with that question to patients and their families and asked them to write down their answers. Not surprisingly, only some of the answers had to do with the diagnosis, but all of them clearly explained why this night, here in the ER, was not the same as other nights:

"I worry about dying too young to see my kids grow up."

"About healthcare—my Medicaid got cut last year."

"My daughter and her substance abuse."

Thoughts and Discussions

- *Every day, challenge yourself: Find out what's different about today. What do you notice?*

- *Make today different from all other days—what will you do to achieve this?*

- *Demand that someone help make your today different from yesterday. What do you need from someone that you haven't gotten?*

---

1. U of Colorado School of Medicine, "What Worries You Most?" https://www.cuanschutz.edu/centers/bioethicshumanities/arts-and-humanities/past-exhibits/what-worries-you-most.

10

We Were Slaves

There are two answers to four questions: The first is that we do these things because we were once stuck in a narrow place called Mitzrayim. With this answer, we begin telling a story that meanders into a second story, then a third story. It's not linear or chronological, but in the end it all comes together.

We Were Slaves in Egypt	עבדים היינו
We were slaves to Pharaoh in the land of Egypt. And the Lord, our God, took us out from there with a strong hand and an outstretched forearm. And if the Holy One, blessed be He, had not taken our ancestors from Egypt, behold we and our children and our children's children would [all] be enslaved to Pharaoh in Egypt. . . . anyone who adds [and spends extra time] in telling the story of the exodus from Egypt, behold he is praiseworthy.	עֲבָדִים הָיִינוּ לְפַרְעֹה בְּמִצְרָיִם, וַיּוֹצִיאֵנוּ ה' אֱלֹהֵינוּ מִשָּׁם בְּיָד חֲזָקָה וּבִזְרֹעַ נְטוּיָה. וְאִלּוּ לֹא הוֹצִיא הַקָּדוֹשׁ בָּרוּךְ הוּא אֶת אֲבוֹתֵינוּ מִמִּצְרַיִם, הֲרֵי אָנוּ וּבָנֵינוּ וּבְנֵי בָנֵינוּ מְשֻׁעְבָּדִים הָיִינוּ לְפַרְעֹה בְּמִצְרָיִם. . . וְכָל הַמַּרְבֶּה לְסַפֵּר בִּיצִיאַת מִצְרַיִם הֲרֵי זֶה מְשֻׁבָּח.

WHAT WERE THEY THINKING?

For the past dozen years or so, my family has used Noam Zion's *A Night to Remember: The Haggadah of Contemporary Voices* as the main text for our sedarim. Among the poems, songs, stories, and historical vignettes are several accounts of past sedarim that took place under unique, extraordinary or extreme circumstances.

Two of these accounts have made regular appearances in our sedarim: Natan Sharansky's seder in solitary confinement, and the seder of four captured Israeli pilots in a Syrian prison. When we read these, I always struggle with the same question: "What were they thinking when they got to *Avadim Hayyinu*?"

True enough, "We were slaves to Pharaoh in Egypt," is an historical statement regardless of who says it or under what circumstances. It's the continuation of that paragraph that troubles me in this context. "But the Lord our God took us out of there with a mighty hand and an outstretched arm. And if the Blessed Holy One had not taken our ancestors out of Egypt, then we, our children and our grandchildren would still be enslaved to Pharaoh in Egypt."

I'm not the only one who's troubled. In the introduction I referenced a Haggadah called *Zevah Pesah*, the work of Rabbi Yitzhak Abarbanel. In 1496, just recently expelled from Spain, he posed the question, "What have we gained, living in exile, from the fact that our ancestors went forth from Egypt that we should say, 'If God had not taken our ancestors out of Egypt, we, our children, and the children of our children would still be subjugated to Pharoah in Egypt?' It might have been better for us to live peacefully in Egypt than to live in exile of Edom and Ishmael (Christian Europe and the Arab lands of North Africa and the Middle East)."[1]

FREE MINDS OR FREE BODIES?

The traditional answer to that question might run somewhat like this: Sharansky and the pilots were all informed by the story of the Exodus *before* they conducted their sedarim. While their bodies were imprisoned, their minds were free. They were the inverse of the Israelites in the desert, who while physically free and material witnesses to the miracle of the Exodus, were influenced by their enslavement in Egypt far more than by the events they had just experienced. Their dependency, some might say learned helplessness, meant that their minds remained stuck in the narrow place even though their bodies were now free from the "burdens of Egypt."

---

1. Abarbanel, *Zevach Pesach*, Tenth Gate.

The day before sitting to write these words, I participated in a narrative exercise with Elizabeth J. Berger, aka The Burnout Chaplain. She shared a Facebook post from the writer Laura Lentz, who in 2019 woke up from a kidney surgery to find she couldn't feel her left leg. Without much discussion, the neurologist and later the social worker in the hospital consigned her to the narrow place of never being able to walk again. Lentz had her own narrative, though, one told through the voices of her grandparents, one of them had survived a stroke and the other an amputation of a limb ravaged by diabetes. Those voices bid her to secure a walker and to will herself out of bed and around the hospital corridors, dragging the leg stubbornly behind her, never making eye contact with other patients declining in their beds. After returning to bed and napping for a bit, Lentz awakens to feel, "Tiny bugs began dancing on the skin of my left leg. My toes yawned, my left knee said to my right knee, 'What? did you say something?'"[2]

Lentz is not Jewish, but the conclusion she draws from this experience is straight out of a seder:

"It never occurred to me then that the fate of generations before me might be passed onto me. By the time physical therapy showed up—two days later, I didn't need therapy. I walked into my new life, leaving the story of my sleeping leg behind. This was not my story, I came to understand that, and I no longer had to carry the weight of my grandparents forward—they had come to show me how. And aren't we all carrying something from generations ago? Not just the physical, but also the emotional, and sometimes when we unpack that heavy generational luggage, the content takes us by surprise."[3]

In Chapter 1, I referenced the idea that ritual can heal us from trauma by enabling us to re-enact the traumatic event as a thing that happened in the past, rather than re-experiencing it in an eternal, hellish present. For Sharansky and the pilots, having the reference point of someone else's bondage and liberation provided a window to gaze out toward a different future; for Lentz it provided a door to limp through.

Lentz' next sentence, however, really clarifies the question I asked at the beginning. She writes, "I'm not saying it's easy. I'm not saying we don't often have to find a new way to live with something and then another new way to live with something else. Physical and emotional challenges are hard."[4]

2. Lentz, https://www.facebook.com/Laura.Lentz.6/posts/10220635357142590
3. Lentz, https://www.facebook.com/Laura.Lentz.6/posts/10220635357142590
4. Lentz, https://www.facebook.com/Laura.Lentz.6/posts/10220635357142590

Lentz' story, Sharansky's story, and the pilots' story are all heroic narratives, linked by the sheer force of will it took for mind or spirit to triumph over matter. But they're heroic precisely because what they each did was extraordinary. What they faced was hard, perhaps seeming impossible. What do mere mortals who are not feeling heroic do?

DON'T YOU DARE TELL ME "IT COULD BE WORSE..."

There's a great temptation to impose an Exodus narrative on a person struggling to find hope in a dark time. At the beginning of the COVID-19 pandemic a lot of us, including me, were naively trying on the role of community morale-boosters, not imagining the downward spiral that would continue dashing our hopes for more than a year as of this writing. More than one well-meaning but hopelessly misguided celebrity wrote social media posts referencing Anne Frank, and how she had been confined to an attic for more than two years—so we should be able to survive a couple weeks in our comfy homes.

It was classic at-least-ism at its worst. At-least-ism is a word I made up to describe the category of ill-conceived words meant to comfort that begin with the phrase, "At least..." and end up making things worse by minimizing or dismissing the person's loss. Worse in what way? A false equivalency between the pandemic restrictions and the Shoah; a stark reminder that at the end of those two years Anne and her family were found, deported and murdered; and a failure to recognize that suffering is not a competitive sport. Your narrow place is your narrow place; it may feel narrow to you even when someone else might feel they can pass through it easily with room on both sides, and it may feel you'll never get out even as people all around you're emerging from "tighter" spots than the one you're in.

Avadim hayyinu could have felt like a failed promise to Sharansky, just like it did to Abarbanel—why were his ancestors freed from slavery just so he could be thrown in prison? The pilots imprisoned in Syria could have seen their situation as symbolic not of the Pesach they were celebrating, but of the destruction of the Temple and the Prophet Jeremiah fleeing back to Egypt. Laura Lentz might have heard her grandparents' voices and felt they were commiserating with her, bemoaning their common fate and not rallying her to fight it. It was the story they told themselves, the way in which each used the narrative, that made the difference. Sharansky was alone. Lentz and the pilots were surrounded by hostile voices (including, in the pilots' case, the recently imprisoned former president of Syria who had still been in power when they were shot down and captured). This gave them a very different version of how they should view events, but it was a version they chose not to accept.

LET'S DISCUSS THIS IN GREAT DETAIL FOR A LONG TIME SO GOD WILL BE PROUD OF US

The passage that begins with *avadim hayyinu* ends with the following phrase: *V'khol ha marbeh l'saper biyitziat Mitzrayim harei zeh m'shubah*. "Anyone who increases the telling of the Exodus from Egypt, indeed this is praiseworthy!" The "telling" in this statement is synonymous with "interpretation." The reason that sedarim often stretch to four, five or even six hours in length is because of the ever-growing list of interpretations—midrashic, Talmudic, medieval, Kabbalistic, and modern—of the basic story.

Repeated telling is necessary because not every interpretation leaves every person with that feeling of liberation that our heroes were able to tap into. I spend every day of my professional life in the company of people who have had a real-life exodus from the narrow place of being refugees at the mercy of plague, fire, and violence to being free in the United States. But that reading of their story, for many of them, ignores the fact that their exodus was preceded by exile from the places they consider their true homes, homes that in many cases they can never return to. Their narrative is not a Pesach story, but one that more closely resembles that of the Jews after the destruction of the Temples. They don't sing *Dayyenu* or *Adir Hu*,[5] but something akin to the *kinah*, the lament, from Tisha B'Av[6] called *B'tzeiti mi Mitzrayim/B'tzeiti mi Yerushalayim*— "On My Leaving Egypt/On My Leaving Jerusalem"—which juxtaposes the joy of the Exodus with the calamity of the exile from Jerusalem.[7]

For many of these people, the trauma of separation from home, family, and the purposeful life they lived is irreparable. America is not a *goldene medineh*, as my late 19th century Yiddish-speaking ancestors might have said, a golden country, it's a prison all its own that keeps them isolated from one another in houses too distant to have neighbors, and

---

5. Joyful songs from the end of the seder—see Chapters 25 and 50.
6. See Chapter 6.
7. Kinot for Tisha B'Av Day (Ashkenaz), 31.

dependent on their families and on strangers for food, travel, and even for communication with the outside world that's beyond their mastery.

In this case, the telling must begin again, and we can't be the ones to tell it for them. Even though we might like to tap into the healing power of the narrative, we can't begin for them. *V'khol ha marbeh* may seem like an invitation to reframe, and to discuss at length, but it's not an invitation to the healers to discuss it in the absence of the one seeking to be healed. Many institutions hold very comprehensive clinical team meetings that include pharmacy, social work, physical therapy, and chaplaincy. About the only one missing from those meetings is the patient.

The worst sedarim most of us have ever attended were the ones where the leader simply read from the Haggadah without discussion, droning on in a monotone without translation or eye contact. The best are the ones where our views are solicited, included, and even given space to change the course of the whole evening. When my youngest son was in kindergarten or first grade, he requested permission to ask a question. I eagerly encouraged him to continue; what followed was only a question in the way that a tenured professor stands up at an academic conference and "asks a question." Instead, he began, "Isn't it true that. . ." and sing-songed his way through the entire story of the Exodus, complete with baby Moshe in the basket, the Burning Bush, the plagues, and Nachshon diving into the Sea of Reeds before the waters had parted. It took fifteen minutes and was the most beautiful, perfect telling of the story I've ever heard or will ever hear again, so much so that when everyone at the table said, "Now can we eat?" I almost agreed.

ON SECOND THOUGHT, LET'S NOT TALK ABOUT THIS AT ALL

For most of those still suffering from their illness or trauma, that perfect interpretation still lies somewhere in the future, and we can't go there and find it for them. Neither is it enough to just keep rehashing the events or continue asking the same questions. Much to my disappointment, there's no magic in narrative; simply engaging in narrative for narrative's sake doesn't necessarily heal the teller.

Sometimes the time isn't right, like the story I told in my first book when I tried to delve into the emotional story of a young, HIV-positive mother from Africa who had come to the US while pregnant to ensure that her baby would get the right care to ensure he would not contract the virus at birth. The beginning and end of her narrative was, "I don't think about that."

For others the telling is a re-traumatization. The space is not safe enough, the wounds too deep, the effort too painful. The *way* the story is told matters tremendously; van der Kolk devotes several chapters of his book to different, structured methods of getting the narrative out in a way that de-fangs it and allows the teller to gain mastery at long last. Looking at family structures, using EMDR to "notice that" feeling or emotion without needing to respond to it, or enacting dramas to unleash the power of trauma responses in a safer controlled fashion are all in his toolbox. They all strongly resemble different techniques I've seen used at sedarim in the past, which have examined the family dynamics of Moshe and Miriam, drafted the children to put on Pesach skits using paper bag dramatics, and engaged Bibliodrama methods to find out how the river felt when it realized it was turning into blood.

As much as we can't tell someone's story *for* them, they can't tell it *without* us. I've elsewhere quoted Rita Charon, a founder of the discipline of narrative medicine, whose text on the subject includes the view that at the end of a narrative, a patient should be able to say to the healer they're working with, "Thank you, now I understand what I was trying to say.[8]"

This same idea has roots as far back as the Gemara. In discussing suffering and affliction, we read that Rabbi Yochanan heals Rabbi Hiyya bar Abba by extending his arm and "standing him up" to restore him to health. However, when Rabbi Yochanan falls ill himself, Rabbi Hanina comes to him and extends *his* arm and "stands up" Rabbi Yochanan. The sages are perplexed: Why can't Rabbi Yochanan, who's clearly endowed with the gift of healing others, simply heal himself? The Gemara answers, *Ein habush meitir atzmo mibeit ha-asurim*, "a prisoner does not free himself from prison.[9]"

Sharansky's solo seder did not arise *de novo* from his stout heart, but rather recalled an earlier seder with other leaders of the dissident movement many years prior.[10], It flowed outward toward other, non-Jewish prisoners in adjoining punishment cells, for whom Sharansky's story and the Exodus story resonated with their own plight. The pilot Pini Nahmani and his companions were encouraged in their seder by the Chief

---

8. Charon, *Narrative Medicine*, 58.
9. Talmud Berakhot 5b
10. Zion and Zion, A Night to Remember, 13.

Rabbi of Zurich, who ensured they could celebrate Pesach by sending them two Haggadot and some matzah[11]. They're enabled and exhorted to tell their story by others who sit with them, eager to hear.

Ruhama Weiss refers to the episode of Rabbis Yochanan, Hanina, and Hiyya bar Abba as a "Conspiracy Against Suffering".[12] None can free themselves entirely from their plight, but each in turn, or all together, can "stand the other up." This is the essence of Harold Schulweis' covenant model of the medical dyad, and it's the role that the Exodus narrative in general (and Avadim Hayyinu in particular) can play. We each help the other see that liberation is possible; that hope lives.

Weiss' conception also points to one final possibility. Wise as we believe ourselves to be, healers are often humbled to discover that *we* are the ones who are enslaved—to limited notions of what is possible or how it can be accomplished. The 21st century in the US is the age of the activated patient, or if you prefer, the liberated patient, who comes into the clinic with internet references, published journal articles from peer reviewed sources and suggestions from well-meaning friends, asking "could I possibly benefit from this?"

Sometimes their suggestions are colossal misunderstandings of the situation. At a seder years ago, I read the verse about the wicked son, *hakheh et shinav*, and missed the subtle but important difference between the Hebrew letter *kuf*, which is used in that phrase, and *kaf*. As written with a *kuf*, the verse means "blunt his teeth," meaning to defang him by calling out his arrogance. With a *kaf*, as I mistakenly thought I was reading, it means, "punch him in the teeth." When I shared this interpretation, the host blunted *my* teeth by pointing out my misreading, and I sat quietly for a good bit of the seder after that. So too, our patients often latch onto articles about therapies that are effective in a disease that bears only a passing resemblance to theirs, have only been tested in rats, or have some important limitation meaning that they themselves could never use that intervention.

At other times, however, it's that determination, the refusal to be cowed by overwhelming statistics, the belief that "I'll be the one in a hundred who survives" that leads to their miraculous recovery and uncovers the treatment that proves effective or defies the survival odds by months or even years. At such times it's the patient who's standing *us* up. They're

---

11. Zion and Zion, A Night to Remember, 37
12. Weiss, "Neither Suffering nor its Rewards," Midrash and Medicine, 107–128.

healing our pessimism, our fatalism, our defeatist approach, which the narrative of *Yetziat Mitzrayim* tells us is not the whole story. As the Torah says when your enemy's donkey falls under its burden, *azov ta'azov imo*—you should unload it *with him*.[13] Together we lift each other up, pick up the burden of suffering, and accomplish healing that neither of us could do alone. We're both trapped in our own narrowness, but we keep telling the tale over and over until an ending suggests itself that can release us. Therefore, the more we tell, the more we look, *harei zeh m'shubah*—is this not praiseworthy?

The message of *Avadim Hayyinu*, then, is not that we were irrevocably freed at some point in history. As we learned in the introduction from Rabbi Yitz Greenberg, the Exodus teaches us the *possibility* of freedom, and even more so the *necessity* of freedom, as the state we're meant to be in. While the creation story may teach us that we entered a world created in chaos and blew our one chance at paradise, the Exodus tells us that we're nevertheless meant to move to a world that rises above that humble beginning. And *that's* praiseworthy indeed.

Discussion Questions

- *What "Humble Beginnings" do you recall?*
- *How do you look back at joyous moments in your life when you're in a dark time?*
- *Are there moments, or topics, you just can't discuss at all?*

---

13. Remember this donkey. He'll be back after dinner. Exodus 23:5.

11

Insomniac Rabbis

Five Rabbis living under Roman occupation "pull an all-nighter" discussing the story of Passover.

Story of the Five Rabbis	מעשה שהיה בבני ברק
It happened once [on Pesach] that Rabbi Eliezer, Rabbi Yehoshua, Rabbi Elazar ben Azariah, Rabbi Akiva and Rabbi Tarfon were reclining in Bnei Brak and were telling the story of the exodus from Egypt that whole night, until their students came and said to them, "The time of [reciting] the morning Shema has arrived."	מַעֲשֶׂה בְּרַבִּי אֱלִיעֶזֶר וְרַבִּי יְהוֹשֻׁעַ וְרַבִּי אֶלְעָזָר בֶּן־עֲזַרְיָה וְרַבִּי עֲקִיבָא וְרַבִּי טַרְפוֹן שֶׁהָיוּ מְסֻבִּין בִּבְנֵי־בְרַק וְהָיוּ מְסַפְּרִים בִּיצִיאַת מִצְרַיִם כָּל־אוֹתוֹ הַלַּיְלָה, עַד שֶׁבָּאוּ תַלְמִידֵיהֶם וְאָמְרוּ לָהֶם רַבּוֹתֵינוּ הִגִּיעַ זְמַן קְרִיאַת שְׁמַע שֶׁל שַׁחֲרִית.

Psalm 121 teaches *hinei lo yanum v'lo yishan Shomer Yisrael*: "The Guardian of Israel (God) does not slumber or sleep."

Of all the forms of walking in God's ways, this is the one most familiar to healers and patients alike. I began my journey into medicine in the Israeli military, already accustomed to taking a shift of guard duty in the middle of the night. As a nervous recruit on watch with my friend Danny Bakalo one night, in the desert outpost where we did basic training, I nearly opened fire on a jackal sniffing for food near our trash bins. Months later I was routinely awakened at 3 a.m. by soldiers seeking to get *out* of guard duty on the pretense of a sore throat, a sore foot, and in one case a soaring hangover. That one got me reprimanded.

Twenty-five years after that, I still take overnight call by phone, and the calls still have a familiar, bittersweet ring to them. They remind me of midnight vigils in the hospital watching multicolored wavy lines scrawl across a monitor screen. They recall dimly lit hallway strolls with crying newborns who will only sleep if they're being held prone, swaddled tightly, stroked lightly on the head from vertex to forehead, and sung to. They recreate suicide watches over friends and patients who cling to life and long for death in the same breath.

Clarity dawns in the middle of the night, after the initial annoyance wears off and before the delirium takes hold. We find it in moments of excitement, in swooping into the midst of a crisis and suddenly understanding exactly what must be done. It appears in moments of calm, when everything stops and the *kol d'mama dakah*, the still small voice, can finally be heard as a last breath (or a first) passes someone's lips. And it blankets the room when, on certain rare nights, even the ICU falls silent. One Christmas, all my colleagues slipped away to the midnight feast in the breakroom. Since I was neither celebrating the holiday nor able to eat any of the pork-laden delicacies that filled the slow cookers on the side table, I put my feet up by one of the computers and discovered a mind-blowing lecture on the hidden Jewish themes in the Harry Potter universe.

THE FIRST "ALL-NIGHTER"

I imagine such a night in the story of the five Rabbis of B'nei B'rak. Their night has been a *tzimmes* of wine, argument over minutiae of the story of the Exodus, fear of the lurking Roman legionnaires, and the inexplicable energy that fills a person when they're among close friends and the juices of conversation begin to flow. Sometime around the end of the second watch, a notion grabs them that they're on to something, that another twenty or thirty minutes and they'll arrive at the essence of everything. The mystery of that night of the Exodus, the raw power of the miracle, the visceral knowledge that redemption has arrived, will reveal itself to them—and everything will make sense. The story comes on the heels of the declaration we talked about in the last chapter, *kol ha marbeh l'saper, harei zeh m'shubah*; whoever expounds greatly in the telling is praiseworthy. The five rabbis are flexing, saying, "Try and top *us*, why don't you?"

If only all the late-night vigils caused us to tingle with fascination like this. So many are just nights of torture on the rack with back pain—or of fear that falling asleep might mean slipping into a diabetic coma from which there's no waking. Fever dreams drowning in sweat, like December 2020 after I received my first COVID vaccine. Waking dreams of past traumas, like those that torture my patients who arrived here as refugees. Many prefer to remain alert rather than fall far enough into REM sleep to encounter the knife, the wild animal, or the dead grandchild yet again. Hospital rooms strewn with empty packaging, blood-stained gauze and torn linens after a "flail" trying to save someone who was already gone but whose physicians or loved ones were not ready to let go.

It helps to remember that those five were gathering, according to some interpretations, under threat of death from the Romans. This is a theory borne out by the eventual end that awaits Rabbi Akiva, whose death by torture we recall every year at Yom Kippur. They lived forever in the shadow of the great tragedy of their time, the destruction of the Temple. Yet, just as we discussed in the last section, they multiplied their tellings of the story so long that they pulled an all-nighter. Until the wisest among them, who in his acquisition of wisdom became like an old man despite his youth, learned something new that he had never understood before.

Thoughts and Discussions

- *Describe your experience of late nights, all-nighters, or sleepless nights.*
- *What do you think about when you're awake at odd times?*
- *How do you feel during those times?*
- *During those late nights, do you prefer solitude, or would you rather be among the five rabbis?*

OLD DOG, NEW TRICKS?

We're used to thinking of those old grey eminences as beyond change, too set in their ways to learn anything. A student recently shared an unsettling story about a veteran doctor, one of the leaders in their field, whose attempt at lighthearted humor in clinic ended up crushing the spirit of the patient they were talking to. The student's goal in telling the story was to ask whether there was any hope for softening the sometimes-crass approach of that generation of physicians. These five rabbis teach that there's always hope to learn, that both book knowledge and emotional intelligence can always grow, even if we appear as old as seventy—or older.

And if this is true of physicians and rabbis, usually so sure in our knowledge, how much more so of patients who are wondering, questioning, doubting? If *we*, the people wearing scrubs and stethoscopes, are willing to "expound" all night, to really dig deep into the story and pull out more interpretations, think how much they can learn with us.

Early in my career I learned an adage that smokers "quit" an average of twelve times before they sustain abstinence from tobacco. Imagine, then, that it's about to be that twelfth time. Every moment that a person is grappling with their smoking behavior, or their reluctance to take their medication, or their failure to complete the recommended exercises for their knee injury, is an opportunity for them to learn what it'll take *for them* to make a behavioral change. It's one more opportunity to understand the situation differently than they have until now. These nocturnal vigils, the retellings of the stories, the turning over and over again,[1] teach us. They teach us things we would never learn if they were told to us simply and easily. They teach us how much we care *about* the people we care *for*. They teach us how much we love our children even when they're at their worst, and how much we love our country even when it makes us stand alone in the freezing cold at night. They teach us what suffering means, and equally importantly, what it doesn't mean if we choose not to accept the meaning that others are trying to sell us. And they teach us that we can *always* be taught, even when we think we're beyond help.

And then morning comes, and we must rise, as it were, to say the morning *Shma*, or to fulfill what other responsibilities may come our way—breakfast for the children, morning rounds, shining shoes and polishing weapons, or simply getting ourselves out of bed and washed clean of the sweat that sticks to us from the night. The time has come. How we move from this night of watchfulness and endless storytelling to the day of doing will tell us whether it's all been worth it.

---

1. The delightfully named Rabbi Ben Bag Bag, in Mishna Avot 5:22, taught, "Turn it (the Torah) over and over, because everything is found there."

Thoughts and Discussions

- Describe an "aha!" moment that happened to you in conversation with another person.
- Talk about a time when you came to a new understanding of an illness, or a behavior that you needed to change. How did you reach that understanding?

12

Four Feelings

The "Four Children" section of the Haggadah discusses how to frame the story for people with differing attitudes, levels of knowledge, and learning styles.

The Four Sons	כנגד ארבעה בנים
Corresponding to four sons did the Torah speak; one [who is] wise, one [who is] evil, one who is innocent and one who doesn't know to ask.	כְּנֶגֶד אַרְבָּעָה בָנִים דִּבְּרָה תוֹרָה: אֶחָד חָכָם, וְאֶחָד רָשָׁע, וְאֶחָד תָּם, וְאֶחָד שֶׁאֵינוֹ יוֹדֵעַ לִשְׁאוֹל.
What does the wise [son] say? "'What are these testimonies, statutes and judgments that the Lord our God commanded you?' (Deuteronomy 6:20)" . . .	חָכָם מָה הוּא אוֹמֵר? מָה הָעֵדוֹת וְהַחֻקִּים וְהַמִּשְׁפָּטִים אֲשֶׁר צִוָּה ה' אֱלֹהֵינוּ אֶתְכֶם . . .

What does the evil [son] say? "'What is this worship to you?' (Exodus 12:26)" 'To you' and not 'to him.' And since he excluded himself from the collective, he denied a principle [of the Jewish faith]. And accordingly, you will blunt his teeth and say to him, "For the sake of this, did the Lord do [this] for me in my going out of Egypt' (Exodus 13:8)." 'For me' and not 'for him.' If he had been there, he would not have been saved. What does the innocent [son] say? "'What is this?' (Exodus 13:14)" . . . And [regarding] the one who doesn't know to ask, you will open [the conversation] for him.	רָשָׁע מָה הוּא אוֹמֵר? מָה הָעֲבוֹדָה הַזֹּאת לָכֶם. לָכֶם—וְלֹא לוֹ. וּלְפִי שֶׁהוֹצִיא אֶת עַצְמוֹ מִן הַכְּלָל כָּפַר בְּעִקָּר. וְאַף אַתָּה הַקְהֵה אֶת שִׁנָּיו וֶאֱמוֹר לוֹ: "בַּעֲבוּר זֶה עָשָׂה ה' לִי בְּצֵאתִי מִמִּצְרָיִם." לִי וְלֹא־לוֹ. אִלּוּ הָיָה שָׁם, לֹא הָיָה נִגְאָל: . . . תָּם מָה הוּא אוֹמֵר? מַה זֹּאת וְשֶׁאֵינוֹ יוֹדֵעַ לִשְׁאוֹל—אַתְּ פְּתַח לוֹ.

There was one perfect seder.

Before the year 2001 became the worst sort of watershed year, there was an evening in April when the entire maternal side of my family gathered for seder. Two days earlier, my Uncle Hal had wed his new wife Carla in an intimate service at my grandparents' apartment and everyone remained for seder—all four Goodman siblings and many of the Harris cousins. We gathered for a boisterous evening in the "party room" of my parents' condo, probably 35 people in total, and nearly as many different editions of the Haggadah.

Hands down, the highlight was the Four Children. This classic text about the wise child, the wicked child, the simple child, and the child who does not know how to ask was the jumping off point for an extended reminiscence about the seven Goodman and Harris cousins growing up together, and often having seder together. All I had to do as the leader was turn to my great-aunt Florence and say, "OK, I think I know what you're going to say, but who was who?"

She smiled mischievously, glared at Hal, and off she went. I won't repeat her pronouncements or the stories that went with them to protect both the innocent and the very guilty, but we have never laughed so hard in our lives.

It's a bittersweet memory. Within less than two months, my cousin Richard died suddenly of a pulmonary embolus (a blood clot to the lung). Within two years my Aunt Janet followed, after suffering for a handful of years with the bone marrow cancer called multiple myeloma. A few more years and three of the four parents that raised that noisy brood—my Gramps, Aunt Florence, and Uncle David—were gone as well. I believe this was somewhat due to heartbreak over losing their children, be they wise, wicked or simple (there was *never* a Harris or Goodman who didn't know how to ask—not know how to stop talking, maybe, but never not know how to ask).

Because of the loss that fixed that evening in my memory, I think a lot about the roles we play, the paradigms of the Four Children and what they represent. Our Haggadah, *A Night to Remember*, devotes 16 pages to different pictorial versions of the Four Children—four generations of Israeli women, four figures from the Soviet Union (including a fur-hatted officer lighting a cigar from the Yom Tov candelabra), even four Marx Brothers (the comedians, not the political philosophers).

But there's one child that we get stuck on—the *rasha* or "wicked" child, or as the old Polychrome Haggadah translated *rasha*, the "Chutzpadiger" child, the one with gall, moxie or impunity (depending, of course, on how you translate *chutzpah*). We'll return to them in a minute.

THE FIRST THREE PATIENTS

To be sure, as healers, we probably have plenty of analogies for the other three children. We look at the wise child, the one who wants to know every last law and precept and think of the "activated patients" who comb the web, join support groups, bring meticulous spreadsheets of their home glucose readings and maybe even teach us about their disease. They remind us of our own colleagues; we wish everyone were this engaged in their care.

We read of the simple child and think how simple it is for *us* to care for them. They ask basic questions, like "What's wrong with me?" and trust our answers implicitly. Even when we offer autonomy, a chance to make their own choices in care, the reply is usually, "What do *you* think I should do?" Their needs are straightforward, like knowing whether there will be pain, how long it'll take to get better, and whether they'll live or die. We get to practice our craft, make decisions from a place of authority, and receive gratitude in return.

We hear of the child who does not know how to ask and think of our colleagues in pediatrics and neonatology, whose patients have not yet acquired speech. We think about geriatrics, where many of their patients are losing their speech, about psychiatry where their speech may not make sense, about surgery and anesthesia where speech has been temporarily silenced, or about pathology where they'll never speak again. We think, too, of patients who arrive unconscious and unaccompanied in our emergency rooms, alone in the world except for us. And in my practice among people from all over this wide world, I think of the people who speak in ways that I can't understand. Those who do not know how to ask in a way that I can answer them even though they have so many questions, and who are so overwhelmed with the foreignness of everything around them that they may know *how* to ask, but they can't figure out *what* to ask. As my first boss, Barry Finestone, used to say, they don't even know what they don't know—and neither do I.

Our decisions and our answers must come either from our own initiative, or from interaction with a proxy—a parent, an adult child, or a piece of paper containing written remnants of the person who can no longer advocate for themselves. *At p'tah lo*, says the text, "You must begin for them," even when we don't know where to begin, when we don't know what they'd want, what they'll need, or what might happen.

You who serve as that proxy know that you, too, must "begin for them." You initiate the appointments, ask the questions, share the embarrassing details and bear the burden of interpreting, explaining and implementing our detailed, oppressive instructions. You're the ones who enforce the bans on Pepsi and cigarettes—the ones who experience someone who "didn't know how to ask" suddenly remembering how to ask, "why the hell can't I have my Pepsi?!?" It's no problem for us in the medical world to take care of the non-askers—we can forbid whatever we want. The caregivers are the ones who pay the price.

THE RASHA FOUR WAYS

It's the *Rasha* that ties us in knots, that takes even the most seasoned healer and makes us realize we may not have any idea what we're doing, that takes the most compassionate caregiver and awakens their demons.

In 1978 a psychiatrist named James Groves published a seminal paper called "Taking Care of the Hateful Patient."[1] It's a cringeworthy title, for sure, and the content also raises hackles in 2022. Groves describes

---

1. Groves, "The Hateful Patient," 883–887.

four (of course four) archetypes of "hateful patients," by which he means personality types that most physicians dread to treat. They're patients who bring out the worst in their caregivers, people who trigger Freudian counter-transference mechanisms that can leave a clinician wondering who's the ill one in the relationship.

Groves has labels for these people: The "clingers," the "demanders," the "help-rejecters" and the "self-destructive deniers." For each label, there's a particular feeling they evoke in the clinicians who care for them.

Clingers seek contact with their physicians at all hours, on all days, and with all haste, provoking feelings of aversion, Groves says. While the initial attention can flatter the healer, as it usually frames them as "the only one who understands me," it wears thin in a hurry. Their caregivers need to set clear boundaries around the relationship to avoid being drained of all energy.[2]

Demanders insist on every available test and frame their demands angrily, as threats of retaliation, if they're not met. Previous "failed" healers bear the brunt of their disapproval and serve notice to the current healer to toe the line, or else. They provoke either fear, or a desire to counterattack, to "cut them down to size" so they no longer feel so entitled. Their caregivers, Groves proposes, ought instead to agree they're entitled—to compassionate, competent care that conforms to the highest standards but not unreasonable demands.[3]

Help Rejecters feel they'll never get better, and revel in pessimism that every treatment is destined to fail even before it's tried. Groves posits that what worries them most is not their disease, but the possibility of losing their caregivers if they should get better. Those same caregivers play into the relationship by determining to try even harder, their fragile egos determined that they'll not be defeated by this person's vexing symptoms. According to Groves what they should be doing is acknowledging, "yes, this may not work, but you need to keep coming in so we can keep a close eye on this together." Thus, the clinician doesn't over-promise or create an impossible standard that they can only fail to reach, but they *do* allay the patient's fear of losing the relationship in the event of actual success.[4]

Self-Destructive Deniers could see a skull-and-crossbones on a bottle, shrug and say, "Bottoms up!" Unrepentant alcoholics, smokers

---

2. Groves, "The Hateful Patient," 884.
3. Groves, "The Hateful Patient," 885.
4. Groves, "The Hateful Patient," 885.

with lung cancer, diabetics eating chocolate in bed the night before their above-knee amputation are but a few of those who Groves labels as engaging in chronic suicidal behavior. Nearly a dozen years ago, I participated in a "Spirituality in Medicine" retreat, and these individuals were the ones whose behavior challenged even the enlightened souls I was working with to see their divine spark. Even the most compassionate clinician might have to fight the impulse to abandon this patient to their rock-and-roll ending, or to silently wish they won't wake from the next overdose, or that whatever disaster awaits will be mercifully fast. Groves admits that there's a limit to how much help one can provide here, other than psychiatric consultation. His final call to compassion is sobering indeed—that we must provide such people with the same compassion and loyalty that we provide to any other person *with a terminal illness*.[5]

Reading Groves ought to leave any self-aware healer feeling acutely ashamed—not for reading an article that labels people, but for having felt all the feelings Groves identifies *in the clinician*. The point of the article is not to disparage these individuals, but rather to make an important point: As my teacher Rabbi Elka Abrahamson told us, "You can only build your half of the bridge."

Of course, these individuals have their own disordered thought patterns. Show me the truly rational human being and I'll declare it a miracle that any such person exists. Groves' point is not to gawk at their strangeness, but to uncover how disordered our *reactions* to those strange behaviors can be. His suggested ways to "handle" these patients go directly back to the point of the original Four Children text—teach each person according to their learning needs. Where one person needs compassion; another needs validation, another firm boundaries, and still another steadfast presence. Groves' lesson isn't about recognizing the ways in which patients can act irrationally—it's about clinicians recognizing their own limitations in dealing with people who aren't "appropriately" grateful, respectful, cooperative or hopeful, and learning how to change those limitations.

Groves has his critics; the language he uses is dated and the labeling is undoubtedly *passe*. In 2017, Richard and Peter Gunderman published a response to the article as we neared the fortieth anniversary of its publication. Writing from a Christian perspective inspired by the work of St. Teresa of Calcutta (aka Mother Teresa) they conclude: "An appropriate

---

5. Groves, "The Hateful Patient," 886.

response is to redouble our efforts to glimpse the dignity—perhaps even the divine spark—in every patient."

MAKING AND MANAGING THE RASHA

You might think, considering I based my entire first book on the idea of doctors and patients carrying the divine spark, that this approach would be far more satisfying to me. And of course, the goal is for us to see divinity in everyone. Groves, however, makes a much more realistic point: First, we need to see *humanity*, and specifically human imperfection, in everyone, beginning with ourselves.

"Negative feelings about medical and surgical patients," writes Groves in his own conclusion, "constitute important data about the patient's psychology. When the patient creates in the doctor feelings that are disowned or denied, errors in diagnosis and treatment are more likely to occur. Disavowal of hateful feelings requires much less effort than bearing them. But such disavowal wastes clinical data that may be helpful in *treating* (italics mine) the 'hateful patient.'"

Ohhh, so much data I have. I've encountered every one of Groves' stereotypes, felt every one of the negative emotions he describes, gone home drained after visits nearly identical to the ones in his vignettes.

As a college sophomore, I took an English class called, "Making and Managing the Monster." It was a course on fantasy and romance literature, ranging from fairy tales to *Lord of the Rings* to classic horror/suspense stories. We looked at them all through the lens of the "Frankenstein myth:" How does this author create the "monster" in the story?

The sobering conclusion of the course was that every monster has a tipping point where he, she, or it could have turned out differently and never become a monster. This was all well and good when we were reading *Dr. Jekyll and Mr. Hyde* or contemplating what might have become of Gollum under other circumstances. It was downright chilling when reading Alice Miller's non-fiction work *For Your Own Good*, describing how childhood abuse "made" monsters like Adolf Hitler. To paraphrase the Rolling Stones: Taking that course, and especially reading that last book, was an exercise in being asked to have "sympathy for the devil." But it turned out to be a useful exercise.

I want to be clear that no amount of *understanding* the monster should be confused with *excusing* the monster. I've lost friends to murderers and terrorists, and don't for a moment equate empathy for the killers' past traumas with forgiveness for their terrible deeds. But for most people in the healing professions, we're not nurse Ari Mahler, encountering a murderer while he literally still has blood on his hands.[6]

We come in a day, or a week, or a year before, when there's still a faint hope of transforming that trauma into something more hopeful, something that doesn't have to lead to despair, violence, to manipulative, "hateful" behavior. We're not encountering murderers, or even thieves, just ordinary people whose lives are in chaos and whose distinguishing trait is "not nice behavior." They're people who have all experienced trauma, whether childhood abuse, racism, rape, or some other horror from a previous "monster" they were forced to interact with. We're just encountering the consequences of that trauma.

And it's here that *we* may end up inadvertently "making" the monster we dread interacting with. While there's been a wave of violence directed at hospital and clinic staff over the last few years, at least some of those events have avoidable consequences. Patients are already traumatized by the stigma of mental illness, the allostatic load of experiencing racism or experiencing yet another slight or offense before snapping. How can we moderate our behavior to avoid being that person's last straw—whether we're the doctor or the custodian cleaning that room (one recent student interviewed a man who identified a worker refusing to clean his room as the worst experience he endured in the hospital)?

By the same token, what is it that the healing professionals contribute to the making of these "hateful" patients? Did their ego, believing that they were somehow better than all the other doctors, help them mold their patients into clingy or demanding people, setting themselves up to fail and disappoint? Did their desire to appear indispensable create an expectation that would cause every other health professional to appear like a poor imitation? Did we somehow convince ourselves that, just because some of our patients had "aha!" moments like the ones I discussed in the last chapter, we had the power to make everyone "see the light" and would never lose anyone to runaway self-destructive behavior? How omnipotent did we think we were, exactly?

6. Ari Mahler is a trauma nurse at Pittsburgh's Allegheny General Hospital. He's also a rabbi's son. News reports after the Pittsburgh synagogue shooting in 2018 made frequent mention of the Jewish nurse who provided care for the wounded murderer after the police finally subdued him. After a week or so of being referred to anonymously in the media as "the Jewish nurse," Mahler broke his silence with a Facebook post entitled, "I Am the Jewish Nurse." (Facebook, November, 2018, no longer publicly available).

REDEEMING THE RASHA

The traditional Haggadah text has the Rasha as a disaffected Jew, one who no longer counts himself in the minyan, one who stands apart from his people and wishes to cast off his identity. The Haggadah would have us respond by "blunting his teeth," telling him he wouldn't have merited redemption in any case. The Haggadah, in this instance, is in league with the physician's gut instinct, telling her to say to the hateful patient, "don't bother me after hours," or "you'll get whatever tests and medications I think are appropriate and not an aspirin more" or "if you don't think I can cure you, you're welcome to go elsewhere," or even, "it would be a blessing if he didn't survive this time."

Groves is telling us not to dismiss the Rasha so quickly. He does deserve redemption—but we, the healers, are being "voluntold" to bring him slowly along to the point where he earns it, despite every obnoxious thing he says. We're not expected to get them all the way there ourselves, in spite of themselves. That's neither healing for them, nor is any of us that good. The 'hateful' patients deserve healing too. There are way more than four archetypes, and each has their own unique need for specific kinds of interaction, and it's your job—really our job—to figure out what that need is.

The Four Children passage in the Haggadah begins with a line called Barukh HaMakom—Blessed is the Omnipresent One, who gave Torah to God's people Israel. Bless him not just for giving Torah in general, but for giving Torah that fits the needs of each individual learner. Each of the four children is answered with a different passage about the Exodus according to their question and their capacity to learn.[7] What "Torah" is there to meet the needs of the endless variety of people who place their concerns in our healing hands—and their unique personalities in covenant with our equally unique ones?

Thoughts and Discussions

- *Which child are you?*
- *Which "wicked" qualities push your buttons the most? How do you reframe those to be able to interact with that person?*
- *What is the way you learn—or teach—most effectively?*

7. Proverbs 22:6, "Teach a child according to his way."

13

Where Shall I Begin?

The seder continues by asking when, where, and how we should begin recounting the story of the Exodus.

Yechol Me'rosh Chodesh	יכול מראש חודש
It could be from Rosh Chodesh (the first of the new month of Nisan) that one would have to discuss the Exodus. . . .. we learn it is stated, "on that day. . ."	יָכוֹל מֵראשׁ חֹדֶשׁ? תַּלְמוּד לוֹמַר בַּיּוֹם הַהוּא

There's a Mishnaic expression *roeh et ha-nolad*, one who can clearly see the outcome of a situation even as it's just unfolding; a literal translation would be "sees that which is born." In medicine we have doctors who are the opposite: Pathologists. If anything, they're *ro'im et ha-met*, "seeing the one who is already dead." In my preclinical years we used to refer to them as specializing in "retrospective medicine." They always seemed to know exactly what we *should have* done, and exactly what *should have* been obvious to our eyes, if only we were as all-knowing as they were. As second-year students studying cardiology, we thought it strange that the pathologists had the unfair advantage of knowing how the story had ended and only needing to figure out how the patient got there, instead of having to guess where the patient was going soon enough to change their ticket.

The whole enterprise of medical diagnosis, and much of the prestige in that enterprise, is predicated on being *roeh et ha-nolad* as often as possible. The more often you can stand at the beginning of the story, say, "this patient has sarcoidosis," and be right, the better a clinician you are. Inevitably, though, some of the diagnoses you make will be wrong. Accepted estimates are that 15% of the diagnoses made in hospitals, and 5% of those made in doctors' offices, are wrong. My gut, and perhaps my negativity bias, tells me these estimates grossly underrepresent the number of mistakes we make. This is based on the number of people I see every day who tell me of things that were missed, or who simply have no explanation for what's wrong with them. A shoulder shrug, while honest, doesn't count as a correct diagnosis. Wrapped up in those estimates are the people who receive the right diagnosis but receive it late: After a heart attack has already happened, or a cancer has already spread.

Those missed diagnoses beg an essential question in the practice of narrative medicine: When and where does the story begin? The sages compiling the *Haggadah* asked the rhetorical question, "*Yachol me-Rosh Chodesh?*" Can the story of Pesach be told beginning on Rosh Chodesh Nisan, when Moshe and Aharon are commanded that this will be the first month of the year for the Israelites from now on?[1] Is this the very point where the Talmudic sage Rabbi Yitzchak felt the entire Torah should begin?[2]

The answers to this question move in two very different directions. The *Haggadah* brings a series of scriptural references to say "no." The story can't be told on Rosh Chodesh, or even during the daytime of the 14th of Nisan, but only after dark, and only when the symbolic foods are laid in front of us. The story must be told in exactly the right moment. But what of the content of that story? While we may only tell it in the right moment, what should we tell about?

The Torah begins not with the preparations for the Exodus, but for the creation of the world. It's the story of the universe, and particularly of humanity. Only after the Flood and the Tower of Bavel does it zero in on the special relationship of one individual and his descendants to the Creator. By starting at the beginning, the Torah places all the history that comes afterward in God's Hand.[3] If we look in the *Haggadah,* we'll see all sorts of different suggested starting places: Our roots as idol worshippers and Avraham's revelation that there was something greater; the tricks

---

1. Exodus 12:1–2
2. Rashi on Genesis 1:1
3. Rashi, Genesis 1:1.

that Lavan played on Ya'akov, or our descent into slavery. Look further and we see that even among these, the story is not told in linear fashion but unfolds like an episode of the TV drama *This Is Us*; toggling between past, present and future story lines. It becomes clear that the character, namely *Us*, is what's important here, and not the plot. The plot merely reveals to us who we are, and what we're meant to be.

THE STORY OF US

Think, then, of the question, "When did I start having cancer?" as being akin to "When did the story of the Exodus start?" The moment of hearing the news seems to close all doors that were open before then, shutting out all the worlds in which there was no cancer. Yet there was a story before that, perhaps beginning the moment a partner first felt the lump in her breast, or the first time mowing the lawn caused that squeezing pain in his chest.

With a delayed diagnosis, the question of where to start the story is even more fraught. "Did the story begin," the patient asks herself, "when I knowingly chose not to make the appointment for a pap smear?" "Was chapter one when I took up smoking again?" "Was I deluding myself all those times I said, 'Don't be silly, I'm fine?'" Could I have made the difference by going in earlier? Meanwhile the doctor asks herself, "Should I have ordered that MRI two years ago, when he first lost his sense of smell?" "Why didn't I check his cholesterol last year?" "Why didn't I call and insist he come see me to refill his medication?"

In each of these "what if" scenarios, we're searching for someplace where we could have intervened and rescued ourselves or our patients from the narrow place they're in now. But these questions belie the fact that it was never as simple as just doing that thing which we can now clearly see we didn't do soon enough.

DON'T OPEN THAT BOX!

When is the right time to do cancer screening? When the children are sick with the flu, or there's a major conference coming up, or you're working two jobs to keep up with rent? Multiple times a day, I begin a "wellness visit" with a person whom I'm supposed to screen for colon cancer, or give vaccines, or test for hepatitis. Then I discover that they've much bigger fish to fry: Thinking they might be having a heart attack or actually *having* cancer of a different, unscreenable, part of their body. The preventive care goes out the window. It becomes the *hametz*, the missed opportunity, of that visit.

It happens in reverse all the time, too. A person comes in having screwed up the courage to ask me about their mammogram appointment, only to have me look at their chart and say, "Your blood pressure is *how high?!?!?*" and never return to the subject they really wanted to discuss. But let's say the screening *did* happen. If the dreaded positive result came back, how would you handle it? As medical providers, we ask ourselves this all the time. We don't do screening at all if we don't have a good treatment for the disease we're thinking about testing for. Even psycho-social interventions carry a warning. Internist Megan Gerber, an expert on trauma-informed care in the primary care setting, warns doctors not to screen for trauma if they're not prepared to deal with the stories they hear.[4] But how do patients approach the possibility of bad outcomes?

Only recently I was stricken with fear that a patient was describing telltale signs of colon cancer as I scanned their chart to see that 14 years had passed since their last colonoscopy—long-overdue by any standard. As I read further, however, I found regular orders, every 2–3 years since, for referrals to a colonoscopy, none of which were ever completed. They knew it was time but did not want to know the results. In behavior change theory, they were still in the "contemplative" stage, not yet ready to act. Still other people I care for are steadfast in the "pre-contemplative" stage, unready to even consider thinking about uncovering the "ticking time-bomb" of illness. The less they know, the better.

Another patient came to see me after being diagnosed with cervical cancer. They had been my patient before the diagnosis, so I was dismayed to see that there was no sign I had discussed Pap smear screening with them. "Oh, no," they said in response, "I had a gynecologist, but I never went to see her. I knew I needed the pap smear; I just didn't go."

The Exodus narrative has a little-known sidebar that speaks to this real fear of opening the Pandora's box of knowledge—the story of the Israelites who never left Egypt. My dear friend and colleague Dr. Deborah Gilboa, an expert in raising resilient children (I know her kids, she's an expert!) tells the tale this way:

---

4. Block, "Physician's Guide to Trauma-Informed Healthcare Approaches."

So, it turns out I can't read ANYTHING without looking for parenting advice. Many scholars have suggested that we look towards the Torah for a model on how to raise our children. In the beginning of the Torah God is a daily, active presence in the lives of God's children, as we are when our kids are small. God appears to them, speaks to them, guides and punishes them. As the books move forward God is less directly involved; sending messages and watching, letting natural consequences play out so we can learn important lessons, not unlike what we have to do for our teenagers and young adults.

[Parashat Beshalach, Exodus 13:17–17:16, in which the Israelites leave Egypt, cross the sea, watch the Egyptians drown, run out of water for the first of many times, and begin to receive manna] picks up after the 10 plagues and the first thing that struck me is how few Jews had the courage to leave slavery. Some sources say 20% left, some say 1:50, some 1:500[5]. But most agreed the majority stayed behind. Keep that in mind as we talk.]

The portion we've heard this morning is rich with wonders and miracles. We leave Egypt and head into the wilderness. We don't get lost. Why? God accompanies us, appearing as a pillar of cloud during the day and as a pillar of fire at night. Suddenly unconvinced by the devastation around him and realizing there was no one to clean up the mess and make dinner, Pharaoh again changes his mind and takes off after his former slaves. The terrified Israelites find themselves trapped between the pursuing Egyptians and the Sea of Reeds and they tell Moses in no uncertain terms what they think of this "let's get out of Egypt and go to a new land" plan. God tells Moses to hold out his rod over the sea and the sea splits. The Israelites cross on dry land then, at God's command, the sea closes, and the Egyptians drown.

So, in this we notice a structure—the Israelites have a problem, they make that problem known to God, God brings a miracle, but the miracle involves a test of faith. Head into the wilderness and THEN you'll get directions. "And the Israelites went into the sea." It's understood that they had to enter the water and then it split. There's a midrash that explains that the waters didn't part until after they were in "up to their nostrils." So, walk into the roiling sea with all your children and animals and belongings even though you don't know how to swim and THEN I'll hold back the water.

---

5. For example, Rashi on Exodus13:18, who reads the phrase "*v'chamushim alu*," which we might translate as "they went up armed," and takes it to mean "*mechumashim*," from *chamesh* for five, meaning only one out of five left, one fifth of their original number, while the other four-fifths died in the plague of darkness.

In a sense, this is a decision not to tell a narrative at all, never to sit at a seder or read one's own Haggadah of their escape from the narrow place—because the process of escaping is legitimately terrifying, possibly worse than the narrow place itself. In asking someone to see a doctor, to take a test, to change a habit or get a vaccine (painfully relevant as I write this), we're asking them to be roeh et ha-nolad and to trust that we are, too. To trust that both of us know how this is going to end and that it'll be better than where things are now. But it's all too easy to imagine that it'll be worse, to allow the remote dangers of unknown things to dwarf the real and present dangers in front of us.

I'm one of the few doctors I know to have had a literature professor write me a recommendation for medical school—Dr. Bill Coles, who taught the undergraduate seminar in Fantasy and Romance literature, subtitled, "Making and Managing the Monster," that I mentioned in the last chapter. In addition to learning about the dark traumas that created those monsters, Coles pointed out how the authors instilled the readers with a fear of the monster. In looking at most of our texts as retellings of the Frankenstein myth, we also learned how the narratives filled us with a fear of ourselves and the darkness that lurks there.

Dealing with illness, especially in the prevention and screening phase, is kind of a retelling of the Frankenstein myth as well. There's a thing we fear—and one reaction to fearing it is to hunt it down and kill it with pitchforks and torches, while the other common response is to pretend it doesn't exist. In confronting fear, we also confront the ugly truth I mentioned in discussing the rasha—the role we may have played in "creating the monster" through our behavior or our neglect.

THE WRONG MONSTER?

As healers, we have another fear: That we'll make a good faith effort to help, and it'll fall on deaf ears. In the wilderness of the Burning Bush, Moshe resists God's charge to return to Egypt to lead the people, saying, "they will not believe me and will not hear my voice." We delude ourselves if we think trust in authority suddenly evaporated in the 21st century; it was always tenuous, and those who speak words of warning and communicate risk were always least assured of a sympathetic hearing. We habitually do a lousy job of explaining risk, and how to mitigate it, and in "managing the monster" of illness we often find people afraid of the completely wrong "monster."

The enslavement in Egypt, after all, came about in part because of Pharaoh "making and managing" a "monster" called the Hebrews, creating a perception of risk to justify enslavement, oppression, and ultimately genocide. And Moshe was returning not as a Hebrew, but as a scion of Egypt's throne. How to trust that this warning could be believed after the lies that Pharaoh told? How can we know, doctor, that your treatment isn't worse than the disease you're trying to scare me about? Weren't your people responsible for Tuskegee? Thalidomide? The swine flu vaccine of '76? Why should we believe you about COVID?

REFRAMING THE STORY

Knowing when to begin the story, and knowing which details to include, is an art. The best healers know how to carry a person back to the beginning, even if there are multiple jumping off points, and to lead the detours back to the main road. As Yitz Greenberg taught us in Chapter 1, the Exodus narrative works because it shows us that being in a narrow place is not the natural order of things, and that God, often through the agency of human beings, wants to free them from that place.

For those who fear telling the story, I might choose to begin not with Creation, nor with the plagues, nor with the blood of the lamb on the doorpost. Instead, I might begin on the shores of the Sea of Reeds, at that exact moment Debi Gilboa spoke of above. Moshe turns to the people and says *ki asher r'item et Mitzrayim hayom lo tosifu lir'otam od ad olam*. The usual understanding of this line is, "For as you saw the Egyptians today, you shall not see them ever again."[6] Your troubles are about to be over.

But the word *Mitzrayim*, doesn't mean Egyptians, but Egypt itself, and the symbolic meaning of Egypt as a narrow strait. An alternate translation could be, "For you will never again see Egypt, your dire straits, in the way that you see it today." Not necessarily a promise of salvation (though the text afterward does promise that God will fight on behalf of the Israelites) instead, it's an honest assessment. "Nothing will be the same after today. It may be good or difficult, and I see that you're afraid. But choosing not to tell the story is also a choice, a choice to let the story unfold without your agency; to let the monster you fear be the main character. You can choose now that you will never see that monster with such trepidation again, and it will never have power over you."

6. Exodus 14:13.

One of the texts I studied with Bill Coles shows what we're up against when we make this statement—and how healing even a "who knows what happens next" opening can be. Midway through *The Two Towers*, the second of the *Lord of the Rings* trilogy, we meet Theoden, the wizened, cloistered King of Rohan. He's been fed palatable lies by his adviser, Wormtongue, who's been co-opted by the evil wizard Saruman to lull Theoden into not fighting for his kingdom as Saruman slowly encroaches. Wormtongue turns his fear away from the real monster to cast doubt on those who are loyal to him.[7]

When the heroes of the story arrive to counter Wormtongue's narrative, they don't offer Theoden promises of sure victory; in fact, it's clear they're encouraging him to ride into great danger. Yet the chance at agency once more, even if it ends in defeat, is invigorating. We see him stand tall again, unaided, lift a sword, mount a horse, and command his people without the whisperings of fear in his ears.[8]

We can't hope to see the end of every story we tell those we try to heal. We can't even hope to tell them the stories correctly. At the very least, we need the wisdom to begin, and the honesty to say, "This is your story, and I can't tell you whether it'll be tragedy, comedy, or farce. But if you choose to begin to tell it yourself, on your own terms, I can promise you that you'll see the world anew, forever changed."

Not all our stories are matters of life and death. A lot of the work of being a healer, or a patient, is pure drudgery. Write the note, click the boxes, ask the rote questions. Take the pill, do the PT exercises, follow the bland diet. They seem to *lack* a beginning, or an end, to the point where it doesn't matter where we begin telling them, because there's no story, no change. But the drudgery *is* the story, like "A blessing over—scut?" and the story of the janitor who chose to see his job of sweeping up as part of the building of a glorious Temple to God.

Thoughts and Discussions

- *Where—or when—does your story begin?*
- *When was the moment in that story that everything changed—the moment nothing looked the same as it had before?*

---

7. Tolkien, *Two Towers*, 148–151.
8. Tolkien, *Two Towers*, 151–155.

14

From the Beginning

The second answer to the Four Questions

| From the beginning, our ancestors were idol worshipers. . . . as it is stated (Joshua 24:2–4), "Yehoshua said to the whole people, so said the Lord, God of Israel, 'Over the river did your ancestors dwell from always, Terach the father of Avraham and the father of Nachor, and they worshiped other gods. . . | מתחילה עובדי עבודה זרה היו אבותינו מִתְּחִלָּה עוֹבְדֵי עֲבוֹדָה זָרָה הָיוּ אֲבוֹתֵינוּ. . . שֶׁנֶּאֱמַר: וַיֹּאמֶר יְהוֹשֻׁעַ אֶל־כָּל־הָעָם, כֹּה אָמַר ה' אֱלֹהֵי יִשְׂרָאֵל: בְּעֵבֶר הַנָּהָר יָשְׁבוּ אֲבוֹתֵיכֶם מֵעוֹלָם, תֶּרַח אֲבִי אַבְרָהָם וַאֲבִי נָחוֹר, וַיַּעַבְדוּ אֱלֹהִים אֲחֵרִים. . . |

In the era of *23 and Me*, there's an expectation that we be proud of where we came from. In the last chapter we talked about when a story should be told, and where we should start in the story. But the *seder* also focuses on what Hollywood likes to call an "origin story"—and in so doing, promotes two different origin stories for the Jewish people that would not traditionally have inspired such pride.

It's true that in the 21st century, there's no shame any longer in saying, "I was once a slave, or am the descendant of slaves, but now I am free." Slavery is shameful not to the slave, but to the slaveholder. But the second origin story is more curious still—the story that begins, "From the beginning, our ancestors were idol worshippers."

Idol worship is the most grievous sin in Judaism, equated with child murder and incestuous debauchery. Why would Jews, at one of their two most widely observed rituals, claim *that* distinction as the starting point of their shared history? Surely, we'd be better off focusing on all the times we *resisted* the temptation to worship idols, like the book of Esther or the story of the sons of Hannah in the Chanukah story?

On the contrary, the *Haggadah* puts this fact front and center. We don't run and hide from our past, even from the parts which were embarrassing or even sinful. We confront them.

It begs the question: Who were we, the healers, the medical profession, from the beginning? What idols did *we* worship? For that, naturally, I need to tell you a few stories. . .[1]

ICONOCLASTS

I've a lot of memories of things being blown up. As a kid in Pittsburgh, one of my earliest recollections is the TV news coverage of the Brady Street Bridge being dropped into the Monongahela River. Years later, the Greenfield Bridge, mere blocks from where I lived, started losing pieces onto the highway below. It ultimately met the same fate as the Brady Street while people watched it live over the internet. Even the home of four Super Bowl championship teams and two World Series victors (yes, there were World Series games *in Pittsburgh*. With fans in the stands. Sitting mere inches apart) couldn't escape the high explosives. Three Rivers Stadium came down in 2001 to make way for its two successors, flanking the parking lot that was poured over the old building's footprint.

Pitt Stadium couldn't be dynamited; it was too close to too many busy streets and other buildings. So, to make way for the Petersen Events Center, the old concrete bowl was painstakingly and very loudly deconstructed, its turf peeled up and cut into squares for sale, and the rubble carted away over the course of a year. I remember this one best of all, because I spent that year sitting in the building across the street, trying to study over the noise of the cranes and wrecking balls. It was my first year of medical school.

I was still holed up in that same building the following year when there was a demolition that got a lot more attention. It wasn't a decrepit bridge or an outdated stadium whose time had come, but an irreplaceable

---

1. Portions of this chapter originally appears under the titles "Don't Be an Adler," at https://healerswholisten.com/dont-be-an-adler/ and "What Goes Up When the Idols Come Down?" at https://blogs.timesofisrael.com/what-goes-up-when-the-idols-come-down/

piece of history halfway around the world from my study table—the stone Buddhas of Bamiyan, Afghanistan.

For 25 days in March 2001, the Taliban bombed away at those statues carved into the sandstone cliffs, forcing prisoners from the city to lay the explosives, until nothing remained except the stone recesses into which the statues had originally been carved[2]. The Taliban were not trying to bring the cliffs up to code, or put up newer, more modern Buddhas. They were tearing down an idol. In the years since, sites in Iraq and Syria have met the same fate, for the same reason, as the Bamiyan Buddhas. ISIS weren't much for ancient history, either, if it looked like idolatry to them.

I felt like I should be horrified—and yet there's a commandment in the Torah, one that was read during my own *aufruf*, that tells us to do exactly this sort of thing on entering the land of Israel. "You shall smash their altars, and you shall shatter their monuments, and their sacred trees you shall burn in fire, *and the idols of their gods you shall cut down and you shall eradicate their name from that place.*" (Deuteronomy 12:3, italics mine, translation from the 2018 Steinsaltz Chumash). It begged the question: Whose side was I on, the Buddha or the Taliban?

Ironically, one of the areas where Islam and Judaism are pretty much in lockstep is in vigilant opposition to the worship of objects, graven images, or any depiction of God. Islam takes it so far that Islamic art consists primarily of calligraphy, rather than risk any sort of depiction. Moderns like to praise the "iconoclast," without remembering that the word literally means, "idol smasher." And the Jews? We trace our origins to Abraham, the original iconoclast, who legend holds broke up his father's statuary store and cleverly tried to blame the mayhem on the one surviving figure, thereby also smashing his father's belief in those idols. *Night to Remember* illustrates this portion of the Haggadah with a cartoon of a jeans-and-bandana-wearing Abraham wielding a baseball bat and surrounded by broken pottery.

Surely, however, I argued in a d'var Torah I gave in 2018, the idolatry that challenges us today is more symbolic. No amount of destroying statues will suffice to "cut down" idols like the profit motive, or racial hatred, or the incessant spreading of gossip that seems to power most of the content of produced and social media. Did we really see ourselves on the same side of this—or any—issue as a group that would tear down

---

2. Behzad and Qarizadah, "The man who helped blow up the Bamiyan Buddhas."

an "idol" while at the same time treating their prisoners with the same regard for human life as the builders of the Tower of Babel?

But it was 2018. Events were already underway that should have, even then, caused me to see yet another layer of this question. A year earlier, the deadly conflict in Charlottesville, Virginia, had erupted after the city decided to move a statue of Robert E. Lee, the commanding general of the Confederate Army, out of a public park. A graven image, representing values the city no longer endorsed, had to go.[3] In 2020, Lee came under fire again. Sherman Neal II, the assistant football coach at Murray State University in Murray, Kentucky and a military veteran, became a leading voice asking that city to remove a statue of Lee from the square in front of the courthouse.[4]

Lee has company, though. Central Park in New York City has all sorts of fascinating statues, including one of Balto, the half-dog, half-wolf sled-puller that helped save the children of Nome, Alaska from a diphtheria epidemic. But one statue you will no longer see there is the statue of J. Marion Sims. Sims is known as the father of modern obstetrics and gynecology—and known for making most of his important discoveries through experimenting, without anesthesia, on enslaved women. In 2018, the city removed the statue from Central Park and deposited it next to Sims' grave in a Brooklyn cemetery.[5]

Protests in the wake of the murder of George Floyd in the spring of 2020 often targeted statues and monuments of the Confederacy, slavery, and white hegemony. These ranged from generals to segregationist politicians to former Philadelphia mayor Frank Rizzo, known for his endorsement of brutal police tactics during his tenure in the '60s. Meanwhile, the last few years have seen movements to knock even US presidents from their proverbial pedestals for their roles in slaveholding, segregation, and the slow genocide of the First Nations: Woodrow Wilson, Andrew Jackson, and inevitably Washington and Jefferson.

All of which led my decidedly secular friend in Herzliya to share the following with me in the summer of 2020:

"...I gained a deeper understanding for the wisdom of the ['make no graven images'] commandment. Don't make statues of your great leaders, for they're doomed to eventually disappoint. Heroes often don't age well,

---

3. Fortin, "The Statue at the Center of Charlottesville's Storm."
4. Rogers, "Murray State Coach Asks for Lee Statue to be Removed."
5. Lockhart, "New York just removed a statue of a surgeon who experimented on enslaved women."

no human is perfect, and if we intend to improve ourselves, far better to be inspired by the best of their ideals . . . than to venerate (or worse, deify) their flawed humanity."

HEARTS OF STONE?

The Torah doesn't tell us to smash the idols of our enemies to erect new ones of our own. It tells us to smash idols *because there shouldn't be statues we set up to worship in the first place.* I think it's safe to say most in my parents' generation cheered when statues of Josef Stalin were pulled down during rebellions in Hungary and Czechoslovakia. Certainly, many in my generation celebrated the fall of Saddam Hussein's likeness in Baghdad in 2003 (which, come to think of it, was hard to distinguish from Stalin's). But how worthwhile is it if we replace a Louis XVI statue with a Napoleon, a czar with a Stalin, or a Lee with a civil rights leader who later turns out to have committed fraud, domestic violence, or worse? A person we lionize for years can be laid low by one misdeed—or even by the failure to prevent someone else's hateful act, as in the case of the late Penn State football coach Joe Paterno. Our likenesses may be made of stone—our reputations are not.

Which brings me back to that noisy room overlooking Terrace Street. It's in a building named Scaife Hall. The Scaife in question is Alan Magee Scaife, notable mostly for being wealthy and related by marriage to the Mellon family. Yet the 2018 Racial Justice Report Card commissioned by White Coats for Black Lives identifies Scaife as a building with a racist legacy. Scaife's daughter, Cordelia May Scaife, believed in eugenics, and was a strong supporter of anti-immigrant policies in the US. It's not clear whether her father held the same views in his lifetime, but the association was enough that WC4BL thought it was time for a change.[6,7]

My alma mater has had to ditch a building name already in the past decade, removing the name of Thomas Parran from the school of public health in 2018 after it became painfully clear that, as surgeon general of the US from 1938–1948, he had not only participated in the infamous Tuskegee syphilis study (and a less well-known study done in Guatemala)

---

6. White Coats 4 Black Lives, *Racial Justice Report Card, 2019,* 33.

7. Ultimately Pitt's review determined that Alan Scaife was not connected with his daughter's activities; people I know who were personally involved in the process felt a name change would have been a visible, symbolic move that served little purpose compared to the much harder changes that needed to be made.

but was likely its designer.[8] Parran also perpetuated the "American Plan," under which women underwent harmful treatment and forced sterilization under suspicion of being "promiscuous," whether or not they actually had any sexually transmitted diseases.[9]

But whose name goes up in place of Parran and Scaife? Just a few blocks from those two buildings is an empty plinth, once occupied by a troubling statue of the songwriter Stephen Collins Foster standing over a Black man playing the banjo and looking up at him adoringly. Foster took leave of his post just a few months before Parran vacated his nameplate; the plinth still sits alone.[10]

After I read the report card, I did a little thought experiment: Whose name would I put in Scaife's place? I thought of the recently deceased Dr. Morris Turner, a legend among Pittsburgh OB/GYN physicians, whose hands brought thousands of babies into the world. A deserving honoree, but perhaps not a public enough figure. Former Pitt pathologist Bennet Omalu, the Nigerian physician whose work on chronic traumatic encephalopathy led to the sea-change in rules around head injury in 21st century sports, also came to mind. Yet Omalu, perhaps because of the people he chose to challenge with his findings, fights a constant battle to preserve his reputation as a scientist.[11] I pondered Rebecca Skloot, a Pitt-associated author whose book on Henrietta Lacks was a major contribution to understanding the way in which Lacks' cell line helped to catapult researcher after researcher to fame while her legacy and her family were forgotten in obscurity.[12] But wouldn't honoring Skloot, a White woman, just perpetuate the same indignity that had been done to Lacks repeatedly *before* Skloot's book came out?

Even when the statues don't offend, they sometimes memorialize the wrong person. I've spent many vacations in the Niagara region of Canada. In Queenston, partway between Niagara Falls and Niagara-on-the-Lake, a large tower topped with a statue of General Isaac Brock commemorates the battle that kept the American invasion of Canada at bay

---

8. "Parran Hall Name Disappears After Board of Trustees Agrees with Chancellor's Recommendation."

9. Drzymalski. "Scott Stern discusses American Plan legacy."

10. For a fuller discussion of Foster's legacy and *why* that statue was so troubling, I suggest Emily Bingham's 2022 book, *My Old Kentucky Home: The Astonishing Life and Reckoning of an Iconic American Song.*

11. Laskas, *Concussion.*

12. Skloot, Immortal Life of Henrietta Lacks.

in the War of 1812. But as Canadian folksinger Stan Rogers reminded his fans in his song, "McDonnell on the Heights," Brock fell in battle, and it was a low-ranking officer named John McDonnell who led the troops to victory.[13] Brock got the top of the tower, while McDonnell's plaque hangs at ground level, just to the right of the door to the staircase.

At the time the song was released, Stan was probably right when he sang of McDonnell's name being lost to history (his song brought McDonnell some measure of delayed renown).[14] Decades later, the Government of Canada chose to belatedly recognize others who fought that battle and had remained unknown in the shadows of the Brock Monument for years. The members of eight First Nations now have an intricate memorial strategically placed on the grounds of the park, so that one must pass next to or through it before reaching Brock.

An old Israeli pop song about the Western Wall, called "HaKotel," speculates that the stones of that wall may have more human emotions than some stone-hearted people.[15] In the end, the statues, and the plaques, are human beings turned to stone. Ossified in that stone are all the deeds, good and bad, hidden and revealed, of the people whose likenesses are carved there. As my Herzliya friend pointed out, they don't age well.

1950 years later, the Kotel still stands with the power to make us weep. So, too, the civil rights memorial, Maya Lin's Vietnam War memorial, and countless other structures which carry not a name, but a message; they're stones with human hearts. It's not just a statue of Dr. King, but enduring words that he spoke from the Bible: "Let justice roll down like waters, righteousness like a mighty stream."

Words, not statues. A very Jewish memorial. The legend is told of Shimon haTzadik, a sage from the era of Alexander the Great, meeting the emperor to address his demand that a statue of him be built in Jerusalem. Rather than engage in open rebellion, as happened some 160 years later under the Hasmoneans, Shimon haTzadik called Alexander's bluff. "We cannot agree to your statue. However, surely you know that we Jews value nothing so much as our children. Let our tribute to you be that every boy born in a Jewish family for the next year will bear the name Alexander." To this day there are Jewish Alexanders (including one rabbi who honored me with a speaking invitation to his shul) but no statues of Alexander the Great in Israel.

13. Rogers, "McDonnell on the Heights."
14. Rogers, "McDonnell on the Heights."
15. Haza, "HaKotel."

Words, not statues. The greatest legacies left by many Jewish luminaries are their books, and while some books are indeed known by their author's names (the old blue Chumash is the Hertz, the heavy Talmudical dictionary the Jastrow) Jewish culture is curious in that many times, the authors become known by the titles of their books: The Chofetz Chaim, the Ben Ish Chai, the Netivot Shalom.

If we're going to knock down these idols, let's put something different in their place when the dust and rubble settle: Sites of inspiration. Memorials not to one "great" individual, but to the thousands who can finally be named by name, whose memories have been suppressed and covered up by the people who used to sit on that pedestal. Words of comfort and encouragement, poems and prose and preaching. Living monuments, like that year of the Alexanders—people who resolve never to oppress, never to experiment on their fellow human beings without consent or compassion, never to settle for an unjust arrangement. People with the humility to know that no matter what they achieve, a new generation will someday come and say, "you don't deserve to be on that pedestal, we will not worship your image anymore."

IDOLS OF OUR OWN

Even these living monuments can become idols to be worshipped. In the 20th century, in supposedly "enlightened" Europe, the Nazi ideology arose that worshipped the idealized, "perfect" human form of the Aryan race, and smashed all others they deemed imperfect. And in this evil, too, our "ancestors," the "healers" of Nazi Germany, were no better than rank-and-file idol worshippers.

I know what real-life Nazi doctors like Jozef Mengele did in Auschwitz, but that doesn't make it any easier to stomach Dr. Gerhard Adler. Adler is the "kindly" old physician in the Amazon series *The Man in the High Castle*, the disturbing alternate reality drama in which the Nazis and Japan won World War II and divided the United States between them. Season 2, Episode 3 finds Adler in a well-appointed study on Long Island, pronouncing a death sentence.

"You don't need me to tell you. Withholding his diagnosis is a crime against the state," he reminds Obergruppenfuhrer John Smith (talk about the banality of evil—a Nazi officer named John Smith). Smith's son, Thomas, the perfect specimen of the Hitler Youth, is not so perfect, after all. He has inherited the crippling neuromuscular disease that put Smith's brother in a wheelchair before the war, when America was still the America those of us in this version of reality would recognize. In other words, Thomas is "defective," and must be removed from the gene pool before he becomes a burden to society—or worse, before he reproduces and makes more defectives.

"I'm sorry, John," sighs Adler, "but if you don't take care of this today, I'll have to do it tomorrow."[16] "Take care of this," as in "euthanize your son."

Bizarrely, I watched this episode on Holocaust Remembrance Day.[17] It was a perverse reminder of how much worse the already unfathomable tragedy could have been. Yet I was strangely able to turn it off and go to sleep without nightmare visions. It was chilling but reassuringly distant.

Adler's character, however, undoes me. He hides a monster, the medical arm of Hitler's killing machine, under impeccable bedside manner. The Reich was replete with Adlers. They packed "defectives" into woodsheds and piped in car exhaust until carbon monoxide poisoning did its service to the "Master Race." They measured skulls with calipers to suss out "Aryans" from "Slavs" or "Semites." They infamously tortured one twin to find out if the other would experience the pain.

What unsettles me is that Nazi Germany did not have a monopoly on co-opting healers to do harm. The Nazi eugenic program was Made in the USA, from the same intellectual origins as the work that Parran was doing at the very same time, and Mengele's experiments did not differ much from Sims'. It's no consolation to know that doctors in China may support the harvest of organs from unwilling donors, or that doctors in Myanmar have helped to dehumanize the Rohingya minority by denying them medical care. The same system that grew me into the doctor I am, nurtured, supported, and even celebrated them.

Toward the end of the episode, Smith takes Thomas and the euthanasia meds to the lake for a fishing trip. Thomas is blissfully unaware and begins to soften his father up to get permission to go on a camping trip—a trip where there will be a bunch of friends, but especially a girl

---

16. *Man in the High Castle*, Season 2, Episode 3, "Travelers."

17. Holocaust Remembrance Day in the US is January 27, the anniversary of the liberation of Auschwitz. On the Jewish calendar, however, we observe Yom HaZikaron LaShoah v'LaGvurah, Holocaust and Heroism Remembrance Day on the 27th of the month of Nisan, 5 days after the conclusion of Passover.

he likes . . . Smith's eyes glaze over and the viewer dreads what we think is coming next.

The scene shifts. Smith, back in the suburbs, in the ruthless officer's most redeeming moment of the series to that point, lures Adler into a car and plunges the syringe into the doctor's thigh instead of Thomas's.

We may have begun life, and even our medical careers, as idol worshippers, whether idols of stone or idolized human perfection. The inclusion of this story in the seder is a reminder that it's time to dispense with that idol worship, to kill our inner Adlers and tear down our statues. That means removing racial prejudice from our treatment of pain and our assessment of kidney disease, refusing to have terrorists set up their headquarters in the basement of our hospital, and breaking ranks with the military to insist that religious and ethnic minorities in our country still get equal care. We as a profession have work to do the world over, regardless of faith or nationality.

SMASH YOUR OWN IDOLS FIRST

We can see now why the Haggadah insists on these dubious origin stories. They're not meant to humiliate us, but they *are* meant to *humble* us. Humility is essential to the practice of the healing arts—recognition that we're being entrusted with other people's lives, gratitude for that trust, vigilance against letting our egos trick us into cavalierly thinking we know what's best for those people without extreme care and caution. Most of all, humility leads us to judge other people favorably[18] when we encounter them struggling to break free of their own idols.

Whether you're a healer or a person seeking healing, you know what I'm speaking about. The experience of illness often begins in idol worship of one sort or another: Idolization of work, of an addictive substance, of food, of thrill-seeking, or of a person who makes our hearts race with desire while making our spines tingle with fear. For years, medicine spoke in the language of "bad habits" and the "willpower" needed to break those habits, as if the only reason people couldn't smash those idols was a weakness of resolve.

The humility of recognizing that we, too, come from a background of idol worship, and that we slide back into it all too easily, can help us

---

18. Mishna Avot 1:6, the maxim of Yehoshua ben Perahiya to "judge every human favorably," literally, "On the pan (of a balance scale) of merit."

recognize both what true addictions and dependent behaviors feel like, and how difficult it's to break free of them. My Christian friends would say that it encourages us to give the other person a little "grace." Humility like this can lead us to approach the business of smashing those idols as a covenant, a holy partnership, instead of a scolding lecture.

And speaking of smashing idols, if anyone lays a finger on the Fred Rogers statue on Pittsburgh's North Shore, you and I are going to have words.

Thoughts and Discussions

- *Who—or what—are your idols?*
- *What idols do you want to see torn down—and which ones are you still worshipping? Is there a way you could smash those as well? What would that do to you?*

15

Promises that Stand the Test of Time

The seder participants thank God for keeping the promise of liberation made to Avraham—and for saving the Israelites time and again from disaster

Blessed be the One who keeps God's promise to Israel, blessed be God; since the Holy One, blessed be, calculated the end [of the exile,] to do as God said to Avraham, our father, in the Covenant between the Pieces, as it is stated (Genesis 15:13–14), "And God said to Avram, 'you should surely know that your seed will be a stranger in a land that is not theirs, and they will enslave them and afflict them four hundred years. And also that nation for which they shall toil will I judge, and afterwards they will go out with much property.'"	בָּרוּךְ שׁוֹמֵר הַבְטָחָתוֹ לְיִשְׂרָאֵל, בָּרוּךְ הוּא. שֶׁהַקָּדוֹשׁ בָּרוּךְ הוּא חִשַּׁב אֶת־הַקֵּץ, לַעֲשׂוֹת כְּמוֹ שֶׁאָמַר לְאַבְרָהָם אָבִינוּ בִּבְרִית בֵּין הַבְּתָרִים, שֶׁנֶּאֱמַר: וַיֹּאמֶר לְאַבְרָם, יָדֹעַ תֵּדַע כִּי־גֵר יִהְיֶה זַרְעֲךָ בְּאֶרֶץ לֹא לָהֶם, וַעֲבָדוּם וְעִנּוּ אֹתָם אַרְבַּע מֵאוֹת שָׁנָה. וְגַם אֶת־הַגּוֹי אֲשֶׁר יַעֲבֹדוּ דָּן אָנֹכִי וְאַחֲרֵי־כֵן יֵצְאוּ בִּרְכֻשׁ גָּדוֹל. מכסה המצה ומגביה את הכוס בידו, וְאוֹמֵר: וְהִיא שֶׁעָמְדָה לַאֲבוֹתֵינוּ וְלָנוּ. שֶׁלֹּא אֶחָד בִּלְבַד עָמַד עָלֵינוּ לְכַלּוֹתֵנוּ, אֶלָּא שֶׁבְּכָל דּוֹר וָדוֹר עוֹמְדִים עָלֵינוּ לְכַלּוֹתֵנוּ, וְהַקָּדוֹשׁ בָּרוּךְ הוּא מַצִּילֵנוּ מִיָּדָם.

> Cover the matzah, and lift up the cup and say: And it is this that has stood for our ancestors and for us; since it is not [only] one [person or nation] that has stood [against] us to destroy us, but rather in each generation, they stand [against] us to destroy us, but the Holy One, blessed be, rescues us from their hand.

I WANT YOU TO PROMISE ME

"I want you to promise me," said the interpreter for the third time, adding his own emphasis to leave no doubt that he had accurately conveyed the woman's demand for my sworn word the first two times he used those words.

She wanted a guarantee that the letter I was submitting on her behalf to a government agency, detailing her medical and psychiatric condition, would succeed in getting her the benefits she desperately needed to keep supporting her family—a family she had brought here at the invitation of that same government, to escape the threat of genocide and raise her children in peace and freedom.

In the *Haggadah* we read:

Baruch shomer havtachato l'Yisrael, Baruch hu. She-ha-Kadosh Baruch Hu hishav et ha ketz, la'asot k'mo she amar l'Avraham bivrit bein ha-Betarim...

"Blessed is the One who keeps the Divine promise to Israel, Blessed be God. For the Blessed Holy One calculated the end, to do what God said to Avraham at the covenant between the pieces..."

God makes and keeps promises, even when they take centuries to unfold. The message of Torah, of ritual, and of prayer is that sooner or later, if you're paying attention and reading things correctly, God will come through for you.

Human beings, including healers, make and *break* promises. The story in the *Haggadah* begins, or at least one version of it begins, with the bait-and-switch of broken and bent promises Lavan makes to Ya'akov. But we don't need to intend deceit for our promises to break. Healers especially are good at over-promising and under-delivering. Each day I open my Outlook task list to see forwarded action items that I *promised* would be completed the day, or the week, or even the month before, when I believed myself more efficient, more persevering, or less over-committed than I was. Each day I receive messages from the people to whom I promised those things, wondering what happened. If we're meant to be emulating God, this is an area where we're hopelessly behind.

BLIND TO THE FUTURE

God can "calculate the end," to foresee how history will unfold in both the short and long term. We lack that vision. We're utterly blind to what will happen five minutes into the future, as I learned when I came down to dinner one night in June 2021 to a sudden burst of rain that dropped a massive tree branch into my yard and plunged my neighborhood into darkness. I'd promised friends we would learn together at 8:30 that night; instead, without internet service or power to keep my laptop on, I was out in the backyard with a hand saw and a hatchet. God didn't give me lemons, God gave me lumber, so instead of lemonade I made firewood.

As little control as we have over the elements, it sometimes seems we have even less control over the actions of our fellow human beings. We can prepare for natural disasters, buying backup generators and batteries, stocking our pantries with dry goods and keeping alternate fuel and light sources that are "off the grid." Human reactions are so capricious and unpredictable that no amount of foresight can reassure me that I know what another person might do.

Hence the interpreter repeated the phrase about promising three times. Each of the first two times, I'd refused. "I can't make that promise," I told her, "I don't have any control over what will happen when that document leaves my hand."

Just before I sat to write this chapter, I heard a talk from Rabbi Adina Lewittes, recounting one of the first times in her rabbinate that she was called to the bedside of a person who had just died.[1] Distressed to learn that the deceased had made very clear her wishes to be cremated, at odds with Jewish tradition, Rabbi Lewittes nonetheless spoke lovingly of other traditions that the family might still embrace, especially *taharah*, the washing of the body with clean water. To her great joy, the family agreed. To her great dismay, when she called the *chevra Kadisha* in her town to perform the

---

1. Lewittes, "Smashing the Tablets: Disassembling and Reassembling the Torah for a New Generation."

taharah, they hung up on her when she shared that the deceased wished to be cremated, forcing her to walk back her entire sales pitch.

I've been burned in similar ways, not once before but many times. Burned sending people to the emergency room with the promise they'll be admitted to a hospital where I don't have privileges. Burned referring people with trauma histories to specialists who re-traumatize them by insulting or mistreating them. Burned by promising a social service or a government benefit which the agency in charge decides they don't deserve. I can no longer make promises on behalf of others whom I can't control.

This inability to guarantee results often leaves us feeling impotent as healers. The more integrated and mechanized the healthcare system becomes, and the more hands touching each person's care, the more room exists for promises made in good faith by one healer to be broken by someone else whose face they never see, and whose identity they'll never know. I'll never find out the name of the receptionist who erroneously tells my patient that they don't have an appointment at the cardiologist that day, merely because the receptionist didn't understand what the patient was telling them. I'll never know the identity of the nurse who dismissed my patient's symptoms in the neurology ICU and ruined her rapport with the entire team as a result. And I'll never find out which interviewer in the citizenship office made the decision that an 87-year-old woman with dementia had to sit for the oral examination because there was a comma out of place on my medical exemption.

THE PROMISE OF UNCERTAINTY

I could argue that even my own skills shouldn't be subject to my promises. It's one of the few areas where I break with my mentor-from-afar, the late Bernard Lown. In his book *The Lost Art of Healing*, Lown argues for a physician to convey certainty when providing a prognosis or a plan to a patient.[2] Even if there's doubt, he reasons, the confidence generated when a physician simply says "yes" or "no" to a question, or states clearly, "this is what will happen," is worth the chance of being wrong.

When I first read this, I was a pre-clinical medical student, still believing in the limitless power of medicine. Lown's charge to exhibit confidence made perfect sense. After thirteen years of practicing medicine myself, I've held space with too many people betrayed by promises of

2. Lown, *Lost Art of Healing*, 106–120.

recovery or cure that never came to be. False hope, or even real hope that's ultimately disappointed, is more painful than anticipated suffering. Better honest uncertainty, in my opinion, than unwarranted conviction.

Yet clearly, we can't get through our careers without making promises, without some measure of confidence. The contemporary teacher of *mussar*, Alan Morinis, cautions that one who goes to the extreme of the soul trait of *anavah*, humility, is not humble but humiliated, so self-effacing that they've lost all belief in their own worth.[3] Imagine a healer so humble that they could only say, "I'm going to give you advice, but I can't promise it'll be right; I'll treat you but I can't promise it'll help." Who could turn to that person for healing? Instead, Morinis explains, *anavah*, and most of the *middot*, soul traits, are a continuum where we should aim for the middle, as if trying to land between two foci of an ellipse, rather than at the extreme poles. The opposite extreme of *anavah* from self-effacement is arrogance. The two foci are: True humility and confidence. Taking no more than one's space, and accepting no less than one's place. Confidence befits the healer; we've all trained and disciplined ourselves to be able to serve those we heal, even as we ought to take care not to over-inflate our abilities or claim credit for what isn't rightly ours. No more than my space, no less than my place.

What, then, are the promises we *can* make, in keeping with our place of expertise, of striving to learn the ways of healing and the skills of repairing bodies and souls, while not claiming space of certainty that we have no right to?

In the previous chapter, we recalled the shameful origin story of the Israelites as idol worshippers, and its parallel to all the times and places where the healing professions have paid tributes to idols of our own. Surely, we can begin by promising not to follow the paths of J. Marion Sims, or of Thomas Parran, or of the fictional Dr. Adler, not to build our careers on the bodies and bones of those deemed "less than" or perpetuate the inequalities and injustices in our system?

It hardly seems sufficient. Is all that we can manage a negative promise? A just, equitable system is something most people feel they've a right to *expect*. Part of what makes the experience of marginalized people in the medical system so traumatic is precisely the fact that the doctor's office, hospital, or nursing home is supposed to be a safe place. The difference between injury and trauma is precisely that violation of presumed

---

3. Morinis, Everyday Holiness, 50.

trust, that betrayal of assumed safety, that shock at having been taken in by false promises.

Imagine a spouse promising their partner at the altar, "I promise not to abuse you." Imagine a taxi driver reassuring a new fare, "Don't worry, I promise not to kidnap you." Imagine a lawyer handing a client a letter of retainer that says, "I, the undersigned do hereby state my intention not to deliberately commit legal malpractice and in so doing cause my client, hereafter referred to as 'Client,' to be held civilly or criminally liable for their actions and thereby incur such penalties as the law may provide while I, hereafter referred to as 'Attorney,' suffer no legal or professional consequences."

OK, that last one is easier to imagine. . .

WHERE THERE'S A PROMISE, THERE'S A WAY

The miracle of God keeping the promise described in this passage of the *Haggadah* is precisely that God must go out on a limb to do so. Rabbi Barukh HaLevi Epstein, the "Barukh SheAmar," wrote in his 1930 commentary on the Haggadah that God made this promise of redemption at a time when it wasn't clear how it would be fulfilled. God makes a promise of inheriting the land to Avraham that's contingent upon Avraham's children—and, in fact, on a specific line of succession, at a time when Avraham doesn't have children.

Barukh Sheamar goes on to say, however, that God nevertheless keeps the promise as it's stated. While the prayer from which Epstein takes his pen name has already told us that God speaks and brings the world into being, we should still be amazed that God keeps this promise *exactly as outlined*. "Human promises," on the other hand, "are dependent on fate and luck. For instance, if a king places a man in prison and promises him that he will be there for three years, he cannot know if he'll survive the entire three years. Certainly, it wouldn't make much sense to keep him there after he died just to fulfill his promise of three years of incarceration. Human promises are often fickle and based on circumstances beyond our control."[4]

Epstein's example, however, makes clear that human life still requires that we *make* promises; there could be no justice, no commerce,

---

4. Epstein, *Barukh SheAmar on Haggadah*, "In the Beginning our Fathers Were Idol Worshippers" paragraph 3.

no healing without them. We must simply acknowledge that since we're not God, our promises depend on forces that we don't command. We affirm, not swear; we avoid vowing, and if we have vowed, we annul those vows each year on Yom Kippur. Our very humanity is an ever-present escape clause, but it can't be an excuse not to try.

PROMISING TO BE HUMAN

At the end of the paragraph of Barukh shomer havtachato, we read "And I will also judge the nation that will enslave them." The first salvo of that judgement is not fired by God directly, but by Moshe. In Exodus 2:11–12, we read:

Sometime after that, when Moshe had grown up, he went out to his kinsfolk and witnessed their labors. He saw an Egyptian beating a Hebrew, one of his kinsmen. He turned this way and that, and seeing no one about, he struck down the Egyptian and laid him in the sand.

I wrote about this passage in late 2018, still reeling from the trauma of the Tree of Life synagogue shooting. The essay was called "Try to Be a Man."[5] It focused on the phrase that above is translated as "seeing no one about."

The Hebrew in that place is *va-yar ki ein ish*, "He saw that there was no man."[6] One might think that Moshe, having decided to kill the taskmaster to save his kinsman, is checking to see that the coast is clear so that no one catches him in the act. It would have been a simple act of vengeance, an anonymous warning—something that I fantasized about doing to the evil person who killed my friends and neighbors.

Not so, says Rabbi Yaakov Tzvi Mecklenberg, known as HaKtav VeHaKabalah for his early 19th century commentary. "He saw that there was no man of courage; not one of them took his brother's travail to heart to try and save him."[7] It was Moses, or no one. Mecklenberg's observation calls to mind Hillel's statement in Pirke Avot, *Bamakom she ein anashim, hishtadel li'h'yot ish*. "In the place where there are no humans, strive to be human."[8] The taskmaster was behaving inhumanly, and none of the bystanders had

---

5. Weinkle, "Try to Be a Man."
6. Exodus 2:12.
7. HaKtav VeHaKabalah on Exodus 2:12.
8. Mishna Avot, 2:5.

enough humanity left, after years of enslavement, to see the humanity of their brother who was about to be killed. No one except Moshe.

Promise, then, that you will never stop striving to be human—and to see humans, where others see dollar signs, criminals, mouths to feed or burdens to care for. Promise to be human, a promise that should be always within the grasp of anyone who chose to heal for a living.

For such promises to be fulfilled we don't need to see how the future will unfold; we can act in the moment. Moshe didn't know what would happen after he stepped into the breach; indeed, if he were to forsee what was coming next, he might never have acted. Mocked by his own people when he attempted to intervene in an internal quarrel, his bloody defense of his kinsman now public knowledge, Moshe must flee Mitzrayim for 40 years. Many of my most fiercely human colleagues are the ones who've been fired, demoted, passed over, ridiculed, marginalized and labeled for their troubles.

But it's only after Moshe strikes that we read that "God heard their moaning."[9] It's only after the midwives rescue countless babies in Exodus 1, when we read that "God dealt favorably with them," that we read that "God remembered (God's) covenant with Avraham, Yitzchak and Ya'akov."[10] A human act must precede divine intervention. We must pledge to stand up when everyone else is sitting, to advocate for the people that no one else will speak for, and to notice the things that everyone else is ignoring. Our promise to be human is an integral part of God keeping the Divine promise. We have to walk into the Nile up to our noses.

In a way, this promise, and many of the others we make in the healing professions, do mirror the Divine promise as Epstein understands it. There's an implied promise of treating someone when we don't know their diagnosis, agreeing to take on their care without the path being clear. I can't see how I'm going to help you, but I'm committing myself to finding a way. Going back to the episode of the taskmaster, I'm committing myself *even if everyone else seems to have given up on you.*

SEE THE HUMAN, BE THE HUMAN

There's one consequence we *can* see: The long-term outcome of *failing* to keep these promises. If we won't promise, won't commit, won't pledge or take oaths or affirm our intentions, there will be no healing.

9. Exodus 2:23
10. Exodus 2:23

Oaths as promises are tricky. As a Jew I'm forbidden to swear to God, for if I fail (and I'm humble enough to know that I'll fail) my failure diminishes God. *Kal va-chomer,* so much the more so, am I forbidden to swear to anything other than God, like the oath such as the original one Hippocrates swore to "Apollo the Healer," a pagan deity. Such an oath is itself *avodah zarah,* idol worship, the very thing the Pesach story is leading us away from. Even the much looser, "We swear by whatever each of us holds most sacred," authored by the delightfully named Louis Lasagna in 1964, gets us into hot water.

In place of swearing oaths, we can promise to pray. Whenever I'm called upon to lead an oath as I was at the graduates' luncheon at the end of my medical school training, I substitute the Physician's Prayer by Dr. Marcus Hertz, often misattributed to Maimonides. I pray for the vision to see the *ish*, the human being, and to be the *ish*, in places where no one else can, just as Moshe did. If I'm going to be a keeper of any promise, then let it be a promise to pray for God's help; in whatever language is meaningful to the patient that we can authentically share. This was ultimately the promise I made to the patient whose story begins this chapter, a Muslim woman who heard me loud and clear when I said, "I promise to write the letter, and to pray with you to Allah that everything else will happen as it needs to. I'll be praying for you often, until everything is well."

"THIS" WILL STAND

Candy apples, several trays of baklava, a crafted Santa Claus with a Hershey kiss in his mouth, multiple shirts and countless pairs of funky socks, donations in my honor to the health center where I work, a library of Elie Wiesel's books and a pile of greeting cards and thank you notes marking Rosh HaShanah, Chanukah, Christmas and secular New Year's.

This treasure trove is the collective expression of thanks I've received from people over the years for the care I've given them as their physician. It's, in some ways, the raising of a glass in my name, a toast, "To the curly-haired doctor!" as one patient who couldn't remember my name once called me to our receptionist.

After reciting *Baruch shomer havtachato,* participants in the seder also raise a glass as we sing, *V'hee she amdah la'avoteinu v'lanu.* "And it's this that has stood for our ancestors and for us; since it's not [only] one [person or nation] (*she lo echad bilvad,* in Hebrew) that has stood [against] us to destroy us, but rather in each generation, they stand [against] us to destroy us, but the Holy One, blessed be He, rescues us from their hand."[11]

The Hebrew translated here as "this" is the word *hee*, the word for "her" but also the pronoun "it" "this," or "that" when the item being referenced has a female gender. This one word, *hee*, is interpreted in a different way by nearly every commentary I consulted. For example, it may refer to the promise, *havtacha* (feminine nouns typically end in the letter *heh* and an "ah" sound).[12]

But perhaps *hee* refers to the Divine Presence, the *Shechinah*.[13][14] We're not alone; God doesn't just promise but accompanies us along a difficult journey. For all we've said about being human where no one else is acting that way, and all we'll say about "going into battle" for the people we care for, just the knowledge that someone is with us, thinking about us, by our side, as we experience trying times is sustaining. I've learned from many mentors and colleagues over the years, too many to credit them all here, that the most valuable thing one can say after delivering a difficult diagnosis or a dim prognosis is, "I'll be with you every step of the way."

Hee may also mean the previous line, "And afterwards they will go out with great property." The Maarechet Heidenheim, R. Tevele Bondi, says that in leaving Egypt, the Israelites did indeed carry out much property, as they were given gold and jewels and much else from the Egyptians during the Plague of Darkness.[15] In Bondi's day, 19th century Germany, that fortune was a distant memory. All that remained was the heritage of Torah, and the word *v'hee* is an acrostic, each letter of which is a numeric hint to part of that heritage: *Vav* (6) to the six orders of Mishna, the foundation of the Oral Law, *heh* (5) to the five books of the Torah, *yud* (10) to the Ten Commandments, and *aleph* (1) to the oneness of God. This "property," the valuable lessons and relationships learned and formed at that climactic moment, are the things that kept people going in future times of crisis. I'm reminded of a distant relative who lived 36 years (yes,

11. https://www.sefaria.org/Pesach_Haggadah%2C_Magid%2C_In_the_Beginning_Our_Fathers_Were_Idol_Worshipers.5?lang=bi&vside=Sefaria_Edition|en&with=Translation%20Open&lang2=en but seven other English translations housed on the site from the UK and US all translate as "And it is this *same promise*."

12. Rosenberg, *Divrei Negidim*, "In the Beginning Our Fathers Were Idol Worshippers."
13. Azulay, *Geulat Olam*, "In the Beginning Our Fathers Were Idol Worshippers."
14. Weil, *Marbeh Lesaper*, " In the Beginning Our Fathers Were Idol Worshippers."
15. Bondi, *Maarechet Heidenheim on Haggadah*, " In the Beginning Our Fathers Were Idol Worshippers."

that's double *chai*, twice the Hebrew numeric value for the word "life") after her initial diagnosis of breast cancer. I didn't know her well when she got that first bad news, but when future setbacks occurred, she met them with determination, wry humor, and a belief that she knew how to beat it this time.

Finally, *hee* might mean the story of the Exodus, the *Haggadah* and the seder themselves. The act of telling the story, the very act in which we're engaged when we say these words, is what sustains us—just as Reb Zalman suggested to the Dalai Lama. Rabbi Benjamin David Rabinowitz, in his 1872 commentary *Ephod Bad*, writes, "This story has strengthened our faith in God throughout the ages. 'They have risen to destroy us,' the word destroy has the connotation 'to make us forget our faith in God.' By recalling the miracles in Egypt and the greatness of God, it's as if God has performed these miracles anew each time and has saved us from the hands of our enemies."[16]

A hundred years before Rita Charon invented the term, Rabinowitz describes the power of narrative medicine, the ability of storytelling to effect healing. More importantly for me, Rabinowitz shows us the power of *this* story, and *this* ritual—my very reason for writing this book so that others might experience its sustaining force.

NOT JUST ONE THING

Years ago, I saw an ad run by the American Academy of Family Physicians, touting the versatility and dependability of family physicians. It was a photo of a boy, probably teetering on the edge of his teens, wearing a soccer uniform. All around him were lines and labels detailing all the things his family doc had either already done for him (deliver him from his mother's womb) or would eventually do for him in the future (prevent his looming heart attack by diagnosing his angina and putting him on the right medicine).

She lo echad bilvad—more than one thing goes wrong in the life of a human being, like my relative with her breast cancer recurrences. The medical life of a person bears a strong resemblance to the succession of persecutors depicted in *A Night to Remember*. Pharaohs followed by Romans followed by Crusaders followed by Cossacks followed by Nazis, one

---

16. Rabinowitz, *Ephod Bad*, Magid," In the Beginning Our Fathers Were Idol Worshippers," 5.

thing after another, a blight followed by a curse followed by a plague.[17] A healer with the right relationship keeps on showing up in the moment, because that healer is not on the scene for one moment, or one skill, but for the long haul—helping you out of the frying pan today and the fire tomorrow.

PROMISES UNFULFILLED?

There are days when I get one of these gifts and it feels like a validation of every ounce of sweat I exude. There are other days when I feel mocked and undeserving and think of all the times I didn't keep a promise, whether to the gift-giver or to someone else who has far less reason to be grateful to me. I'm hesitant to wear, or to nibble or to treat myself when I wonder if I've earned the reward that lies in my hand.

When we sing *V'hee she-amdah* at the seder, we stand, with wine glass in hand, like a toast. However, we set our cups down untasted at the end of the song, not yet ready to drink to the redemption. It's a curious move, but one which recalls my feeling when I get a gift, especially when it's from someone who's still in limbo, for whom I've "not yet" come through." My hesitation, it seems, is justified. So how will I know if I've indeed "stood for them" in the end? By hearing the multivocal interpretations of *v'hee*.

We stand by our patients when we make a promise to them, even though we discussed in the last section how tentative those promises must necessarily be. We stand by them when we share in their story and aid them in its telling. We stand by them when we're present with them, providing sheltering wings in the way the *Shekhinah* is often depicted. We stand by them not by all the "wealth" of medicine, the devices and pills and fancy hospitals, but rather when all of that's gone, when we're available to them as people of wisdom and integrity. We stand by them when we learn, together, the hard but valuable lessons that their illness has taught both the sufferer and the healer. And God willing, we'll still be standing by them when their redemption from the narrow place of their illness and suffering finally arrives.

---

17. Zion and Zion, 69.

Thoughts and Discussions

- *What promises have people made to you, and kept, during your illness? What did that mean to you?*
- *Which promises have people made and broken?*
- *What promises have you made and kept as a healer? Which have you broken?*
- *Which promises have you refused to make or refrained from making? Why?*
- *Which promises have you wanted to hear but no one will make?*

16

Go and Learn

The seder is an experience for learning...

| Go out and learn what Lavan the Aramean sought to do to Ya'akov, our father... | צֵא וּלְמַד מַה בִּקֵּשׁ לָבָן הָאֲרַמִּי לַעֲשׂוֹת לְיַעֲקֹב אָבִינוּ |

There's a line in every evaluation I complete for my students which asks me to assess whether the student in question is a "self-directed learner." The administration of the medical school and the physician assistant training program where these students are enrolled are interested in whether, confronted with a disease they don't know about or a medicine they've never heard of, the student will, of their own accord, look up the information, share it with me unsolicited, and integrate it into the plan for the patient.

Self-directed learners take ownership of their situation. Not only do they begin to regard the patients that they care for as "theirs," meaning they're responsible for the person's well-being, but they take ownership of their own knowledge. If there's something they don't know, they don't sit and complain about the curriculum not teaching them adequately. They dig up the information they need and take responsibility for their own deficits, constantly looking to improve.

When the *Haggadah* commands, "Go and learn," it's not talking about finding a topic review on UpToDate™. "Go and learn what Lavan the Aramean tried to do to Ya'akov our father," reads the text. Hear this story, this formative story that explains so much about how we got to this place. No, it didn't happen in Egypt, and it doesn't involve Pharaoh, but you can't understand Pharaoh without understanding Lavan.

This is the self-directed learning I would like *my* students to engage in. "Go and learn" what an abusive parent, a biased society, a raging hurricane tried to do to the woman we're about to see about high blood pressure that won't respond to medicine. "Go and learn" why the person we ordered a test for three months ago still hasn't completed it. "Go and learn" how hard it's to follow the diet and exercise advice you gave in your last visit.

The *Haggadah* is about the narrative of a people as it grows out of a few individuals in a single family to become the Nation of Israel. Medicine, as I laid out in my first book, is the illness narrative of the individual before us. *Tze u'l'mad*, go and learn, binds the two together as an imperative to get those stories straight. Otherwise everything else we do is merely meaningless ritual, disconnected facts in a textbook.

Let us indeed go and learn what Lavan, and Pharoah, sought to do to Ya'akov and his descendants, and how God intervened, and what that might tell us about the people we care for and our own humble endeavors to help them.

17

An Aramean Told My Father to Get Lost

... or Something Like That ...

With special guest David May

The "First Fruits Declaration" in Deuteronomy 26:5–9 tells the whole story of the Exodus, from before Ya'akov went down to Egypt until the Israelites entered the land of Canaan. The seder then breaks that passage apart to consider each word and phrase to great depths.

Deuteronomy 26:5–9	דברים כ״ו:ה׳-ט׳
(5) You shall then recite as follows before Hashem your God: "My father was a fugitive Aramean. He went down to Egypt with meager numbers and sojourned there; but there he became a great and very populous nation. (6) The Egyptians dealt harshly with us and oppressed us; they imposed heavy labor upon us.	ה) וְעָנִיתָ וְאָמַרְתָּ לִפְנֵי ׀ יְהֹוָה אֱלֹהֶיךָ אֲרַמִּי אֹבֵד אָבִי וַיֵּרֶד מִצְרַיְמָה וַיָּגָר שָׁם בִּמְתֵי מְעָט וַיְהִי־שָׁם לְגוֹי גָּדוֹל עָצוּם וָרָב: (ו) וַיָּרֵעוּ אֹתָנוּ הַמִּצְרִים וַיְעַנּוּנוּ וַיִּתְּנוּ עָלֵינוּ עֲבֹדָה קָשָׁה:

(7) We cried to Hashem, the God of our ancestors, and Hashem heard our plea and saw our plight, our misery, and our oppression. (8) Hashem freed us from Egypt by a mighty hand, by an outstretched arm and awesome power, and by signs and portents, (9) bringing us to this place and giving us this land, a land flowing with milk and honey.	(ז) וַנִּצְעַק אֶל־יְהוָה אֱלֹהֵי אֲבֹתֵינוּ וַיִּשְׁמַע יְהוָה אֶת־קֹלֵנוּ וַיַּרְא אֶת־עָנְיֵנוּ וְאֶת־עֲמָלֵנוּ וְאֶת־לַחֲצֵנוּ: (ח) וַיּוֹצִאֵנוּ יְהוָה מִמִּצְרַיִם בְּיָד חֲזָקָה וּבִזְרֹעַ נְטוּיָה וּבְמֹרָא גָּדֹל וּבְאֹתוֹת וּבְמֹפְתִים: (ט) וַיְבִאֵנוּ אֶל־הַמָּקוֹם הַזֶּה וַיִּתֶּן־לָנוּ אֶת־הָאָרֶץ הַזֹּאת אֶרֶץ זָבַת חָלָב וּדְבָשׁ:

NOT SO FAST

Emergency medicine prizes speed over all other skills except medical knowledge (and cynics would say, not even that). The art of being a student or resident in emergency medicine is being able to "present" a patient to the attending physician as fast as possible while leaving out none of the critical information. "This is a 19-year-old first year college student who presents from a party where she was engaged in under-age drinking and complains of lower abdominal pain and being unable to urinate for the past 12 hours."

The central passage of the seder is like an emergency medicine resident presentation of the Exodus. Found in Deuteronomy 26:5–8, it's the declaration a person makes in the Temple in Jerusalem when they bring the first fruits offering from their land. In four lines, it's meant to cover the whole arc of history from humble beginnings to great blessings, hundreds of years in a handful of words. This passage is the most succinct such summary that exists;[1] indeed, the whole book of Deuteronomy is itself supposed to be a "summary" of the travels of the Israelites, yet it stretches to 34 chapters. Apparently, Moshe was not a man of so few words after all...

However, when we get such a succinct summary, our job as healers is not to be satisfied with it. There's a logical fallacy prey called "premature closure:" The belief that we've found the answer after reviewing a few neatly organized pieces of evidence, without scratching the surface to see the far more complicated picture beneath it. The opening words of the first fruits declaration provide a perfect example of "premature closure" and the need to scratch beneath the surface.

---

1. Kulp, Joshua. *The Schechter Haggadah*,. 215.

TRIGGER WARNING: THIS IS A GRAMMAR LESSON

Most *haggadot* translate the words *Arami oved avi* as, "An Aramean (namely, Lavan) tried to destroy my father (namely, Ya'akov)." The passage becomes, like the preceding lines about "go and learn what Lavan tried to do to my father Ya'akov," about the attempts to destroy us and our ancestors that outstripped even what Pharaoh tried to do. But what if that understanding of the word leads to a misdiagnosis of what the whole passage is about? Some translations read, "My father was a wandering (or fugitive) Aramean." Some include both interpretations.

Grammatically, this is the correct way to read it. Hebrew uses the same three-letter roots, called *shorashim*, to mean multiple different things, usually closely tied shades of the same concept.[2] The root *alef-bet-daled* or just *a-b-d*, which is the root of *oved* in this sentence, refers to losing something. However, the roots are conjugated in different *binyanim*, literally "buildings," which impart additional meaning on top of the *shoresh* itself. Like turning chocolate into candy, cake, or mole sauce, they take the same raw materials and achieve disparate results. Some *binyanim*, like the *hiph'il*, are causative (making a thing happen to someone else), others, like *niph'al*, are passive (someone else making a thing happen to you), and the "easy" *binyan*, also called *pa'al*, is subtly different from the *pi-el*—both are active voice, but *pi-el* can sometimes also be causative. There's even a reflexive *binyan*, *hit'pa'el* (doing something to yourself).

In the "easy" form, *oved* (or *avad* in past tense) means "lost" as in "hopeless" or "dead." Queen Esther, realizing she must go before the king to plead for her people whether he had invited her or not, finally steels herself to do what needs to be done, and tells Mordechai, *"Ka'asher avad'ti, avad'ti."* "If I'm lost (i.e. if I die), then I'll be lost (i.e. I'll die if that's what is meant to happen)."[3] In contrast, the *pi'el* form would be *ibed* in the past tense, or *m'abed* in the present, and means "lost" as in "I can't find the #@$(Y&@# thing! I must have lost it!" However, because *pi-el* is sometimes causative, it can also mean to destroy, or as I think of it, "make something get lost permanently." This is the form we see in the

---

2. My favorite tie-in is that the root *s-p-r* is the root for "to tell," "book," "story," and "barber," because of course barbers tell stories while cutting hair. My hairstylist through medical school, residency, and into my medical career, Andrew Leo, exemplified this so completely I often had to remind him to continue cutting hair, because he would start gesticulating with the comb and scissors during his tales.

3. Esther 4:16

instructions Moses gives to the Israelites about how to deal with pagan altars they'll encounter: *Abed toveidun*,[4] "you shall surely destroy."

HOMELESS, HOMELESS

The phrase in the Haggadah, taken from Deuteronomy 26:5, is *Arami oved avi*, my father was a hopelessly lost Aramean, or something in that vein. Remember that Ya'akov was adrift, running from a brother who wanted to kill him for stealing the birthright. He was homeless, having crossed over the boundary of the land where he was born back into the land his grandfather had been told to leave. He was a duped, indentured servant to a man who kept pulling a bait-and-switch on him, first with his bride and later with the end of his term of service. Ya'akov was lost, unmoored, a wanderer. Toward the end of his life, he arrives in Egypt and tells the Pharaoh of his time, "The years of my sojourning are 130."[5] Rashi explains that this means Ya'akov has been a wanderer his entire life, even when in the land that's supposed to be his home.[6]

Prior to becoming one of the most recognizable doctors in America during the COVID-19 pandemic, Leana Wen co-authored a book called *When Doctors Don't Listen*, which took on premature closure and a host of other cognitive errors that lead to misdiagnosis, mistreatment, and harm. The book was formative to my thinking about how to ask questions, listen more attentively, and frame my thinking about what's happening to the people I care for.

Wen and her co-author Joshua Kosowsky take aim at the practice of emergency rooms writing down a 1–2 word "chief complaint," usually not in the patient's exact words (it's very rare that someone comes to the ER and only says 2 words when asked why they're there) and then embarks on a "pathway" for working up and treating that chief complaint.[7] If you're unfortunate enough to reach the end of that pathway without a clear diagnosis, you end up getting sent home not knowing what's wrong, only knowing, "well, it's not my heart." If you're really unfortunate, something

---

4. Deuteronomy 17:2, and see Chapter 14, From the Beginning, for where that passage figures into our story.
5. Genesis 47:9
6. Rashi on Genesis 47:9
7. Wen and Kosowsky, *When Doctors Don't Listen*, loc.166.

major gets missed. And some of those misses may hinge on how someone interprets a single word, just like our understanding of the passage above.

Thirty percent of my patients speak Nepali as their first language. I don't speak Nepali as any of my three languages where I could successfully order a meal or diagnose a patient, but I've learned a few words. One of them is *chhati dukhcha*, which means, "chest hurts." So, naturally, when one of these folks goes to an emergency room and says, *chhati dukhcha*, and their daughter-in-law translates it as "My mom's chest hurts," they're on the pathway to rule out a heart attack.

However, if you *watch* the person as they're saying this, they'll often be pointing to the pit of their stomach with the tip of their index finger, meaning that we don't actually have the same definition of the word "chest," regardless of whether we call it a chest or a *chhati*. They're on the wrong pathway. We need to ask an idiotic question, "What do you mean by chest?"[8]

At every seder, as we learned earlier discussing the four children, there are people who need the four-line version of the story, and those who need to dive deeper and expand on every word—to know, as it were, what we really mean by "chest."

Thoughts and Discussions

- *Think of the most compelling story you know about someone you were privileged to care for, or about your own journey through illness or healing. Tell the story in only four lines.*

My example would be the following story, told by then 13-year-old David May in his Bar Mitzvah d'var Torah on September 5, 2020. It runs a little longer than four lines (ten, to be exact) but it subsumes years of his life, a spectrum of emotions and an astonishingly mature amount of perspective in that space. I've numbered it as if it were a biblical text, so the "verses" stand out.

1. "My reading today was Deuteronomy Chapter 26, verses 1–13, which is (in) Parashat Ki Tavo.

---

8. Given that I spent half of a recent chapter discussing the meaning of the word, "this," you shouldn't be surprised that "chest" can cause me confusion.

2. In this passage, the Israelites are instructed to give the first fruits of their harvest to the priest in a basket as an offering to God. As they made the offering, they said, "my father was a wandering Aramean." He went to Egypt, became a nation, and was treated harshly by the Egyptians. Why did they say this?

3. Our ancestors began their ritual of thanksgiving by remembering the whole story of their journey, beginning with Jacob and Joseph's time in Egypt. They said these words to remind themselves of where they've been, how far they've gotten, and to express gratitude for the entire journey.

4. These same words are part of the Passover seder. In other words, we remind ourselves of where we have been. We tell the whole story.

5. We celebrate Passover to celebrate our release from slavery and oppression. When we retell the story, we remind ourselves of our oppression. We remind ourselves of that to remember that people who are oppressed today are in a situation we were in, and so we have an obligation to help them.

6. When I'm asked about my hearing aids, I retell the story of my cancer treatment. I was diagnosed with kidney cancer shortly before my first birthday. Radiation and chemotherapy were two of the main treatments used to resolve my cancer, which made it possible for me to grow into young adulthood and be here today. The side effect of one of my cancer medicines was hearing loss.

7. While I don't remember my days of being sick or my time in the hospital (just as the Israelites didn't remember being in Egypt themselves), I do know the story, including the fact that I was in and out of the hospital a lot. I spent most of my toddler years either in the hospital or too compromised to go out. I was diagnosed in June of 2008, and April of 2010 was when my treatment stopped.

8. I can understand what it means to be in the hospital because I've been in a position of those in the hospital. I can only imagine what it's like to be there now, when a potentially life-threatening disease is making everything worse. No one can visit and people can't bring their own comfort objects in. This is why I'm making pillows and blankets for the kids in the hospital. We've also collected donations for Children's Hospital of Pittsburgh.

9. I can now tell the whole story of my cancer beginning with my own diagnosis, describing my treatments and my hearing loss, remembering and celebrating April 1 as the day I was released from the hospital, and now ending with the giving of these gifts to the children in the hospital.

10. My cancer story is an exact parallel of the story of the Israelites' offering of the first fruits: First we describe how it started, we talk about the journey, and we celebrate our freedom. . .and then we offer thanks for where we are now."

Thoughts and Discussions

- *Now think of a story someone told you that was terse and yet complete and break that story down bit by bit to share what you discovered as you dug deeper. What lessons did you learn as these details were coming to light?*

See what different skills and sensibilities you need to complete this second exercise compared to the first one. One of the great paradoxes of medicine is our ability to lose the forest for the trees, a problem that stereotypically plagues internal medicine and its subspecialties, while simultaneously being able to rescue the forest while killing all the trees, a problem we more commonly attribute to surgeons and oncologists. Neither stereotype is true, but it's eminently true that we can be both bogged down in details and missing crucial details. These skills of narrative medicine are meant to train our minds to simultaneously synthesize a big picture and pinpoint the tiniest truth.

Attend to how the story changes with something as subtle as the placement of punctuation. In the song *Take a Break*, from Lin-Manuel Miranda's *Hamilton*, Angelica Schuyler obsesses over the meaning of a stray comma at the beginning of one of Hamilton's letters to her. Does that single scratch of ink in between change a formal greeting into a forbidden flirtation?[9]

My hero, Dr. Bernard Lown, shares a story of a man who saw him for heart disease for many years. Every time Lown did his review of systems and asked about sexual function, the man responded emphatically,

---

9. Miranda, "Take a Break."

"Sex no problem!" Only when the man's wife accompanied him on the visit for the first time did Lown notice the doubtful expression on her face when the man made his declaration. Sensing the story was about to change, Lown asked the man to punctuate the sentence. Sheepishly, he replied, "Sex, no! Problem!"[10]

Lown's subtle question seems like a stroke of genius, but rabbis have been interpreting Jewish text that way for Millenia. We'll follow in that tradition as we dismantle the rest of these four succinct lines of text. We'll turn to grammar, punctuation, intertextual comparison, homiletics, allegory and numerology to see what this capsule narrative of the Exodus can teach us about understanding our own and others' journeys of suffering and healing, and the stories we hear from others. The position of a period and the distinctions between arm and hand, chest and belly, neck and throat will open us up to seeing familiar stories in a new light.

---

10. Lown, The Lost Art of Healing, 19.

18

Brought Down to the Narrow Place

Sometimes, both in the Bible and today, people make choices that aren't really choices.

First Fruits Declaration 3	ארמי אבד אבי ג׳
"And he went down to Egypt"— helpless on account of the word [in which God told Avraham that his descendants would have to go into exile].	וַיֵּרֶד מִצְרַיְמָה—אָנוּס עַל פִּי הַדִּבּוּר.

BROUGHT DOWN

Arami oved avi vayered Mitzrayimah. "My father was a lost Aramean, and he descended to Egypt."

Why did Ya'akov descend to Egypt? The Haggadah tells us he was *anous al pi ha dibur*, "Forced to do so because of the word." Ya'akov had no desire to go to Egypt. He was aware of God's promise to Avraham his grandfather, that Avraham's (and therefore Ya'akov's) descendants were to be enslaved in Egypt and not return to the land until 400 years from the time the promise was made. But God's promise is a historical force that can't be resisted; it'll fulfill itself even if Ya'akov wants to resist it.

The key word in the sentence is *'anous*, forced. The related word in modern Hebrew, *'oness*, is the word for rape. The root *aleph-nun-samech* implies external forces beyond a person's control, compelling them to enter situations not of their choosing, situations that may seem for the best at that moment, but are ultimately dangerous and destructive. The descent into Egypt occurred under *'oness*, duress, one by one until the entire family of Avraham's descendents were there.

First Yosef descended to Egypt, as the Torah says, "*V'Yosef* hurad *Mitzraymah vayiknehu Potiphar*."[1] In our grammar lesson last chapter, we learned about the *hiph'il*, the causative verbs. *Va-yered*, "descended," as in the verse at the beginning of the chapter, is a regular action verb. *Hurad*, is a *hiph'il*, a causative. "Yosef was *brought down* to Egypt and Potiphar bought him."[2] Yosef was under *oness*, so much so that he didn't *descend*, but was *brought down*.

However, this is still an example of a turn of events that seemed like the lesser of two evils at the time. Yosef's brothers had planned to kill him. Reuven planned an ill-fated rescue attempt that never happened. When that failed, he suggested the brothers leave him in the pit rather than actively murdering him.[3] Consequently, Yehudah urges them to sell Yosef as a slave rather than letting him die. It's these brave actions that save Yosef.

Ya'akov descends next, not yet to Egypt, but metaphorically to "Sheol," telling his sons, *Ered el-b'ni avel Sheolah*. "*I will go down* to my son in mourning to Sheol (a word for the afterlife or underworld, the pit of despair and death)."[4] He chooses to descend, not because he is forced to do so, but because he can imagine no possible comfort in the world for the loss of his most beloved son—due to the *oness* of grief and bereavement.

Next, the brothers descend, not once but twice, due to the *oness* of the famine which sweeps the entire known world. Unbeknownst to them, Yosef has risen again, after being brought down, and now stands second in command to Pharaoh. Yosef's genius and foresight are the only thing standing between Egypt and the starvation that grips the other nations. Ya'akov sends the brothers to descend to get food, keeping Binyamin, Yosef's only full brother, the youngest and favorite remaining son, behind in Canaan so that nothing disastrous will happen to him.

The gambit fails. Under Yosef's knowing stare, the brothers reveal that another brother remained behind, and he demands that they return and bring the boy to him. Ya'akov strenuously objects, castigating the

---

1. Genesis 37:36
2. Genesis 39:1
3. Genesis 37:22–27
4. Genesis 37:35

brothers for spilling their secrets to "the man who is lord of the land."[5] He responds, "My son must not go down with you, for his brother is dead and he alone is left. If he meets with disaster on the journey you are taking, *you will send* (*v'horad'tem*, causative voice) my white head down to Sheol in grief." Now it's no longer Ya'akov's choice to plummet into sorrow, but his sons who will bring it upon him.[6]

Ultimately the brothers prevail; if they don't, they and their families will starve, and their brother Shimon, left as a captive in Egypt until they return to prove their honesty, will remain in prison. Now Binyamin must go down to Egypt *'anous al pi ha dibur*, forced not by the word of God, but by the words his brothers have spoken to one another. However, his descent to Egypt with his older brothers is very different than Yosef's. When Yosef goes, the brothers literally wash their hands of him, presenting in their clean hands a blood-stained coat as "proof" that a wild animal tore him to bits. When Binyamin goes, Yehudah takes an oath to defend Binyamin with his own life if need be. Binyamin's descent to Egypt, and Yehudah's promises, are willing sacrifices in the duress of dire circumstances to save the family from doom.

Finally, the masks are removed, after Yosef's plan to test his brothers' change of heart leads to Yehudah's heartfelt plea on Binyamin's behalf. Now it's Ya'akov who must go down to Egypt, to reunite with his sons. Yosef is *'anous*, forced by his responsibilities to remain in Egypt, and he places *'oness*, the burden or compulsion of longing, on his father to come down to him.[7]

Thoughts and Discussions

- *What "brought you down" to your narrow place?*

---

5. Notice the blurring of lines between Egyptian and Israelite even here, even before the enslavement, just like we discussed in Chapter 1.

6. Genesis 42:38

7. Genesis 45:28 and commentary to this verse by Rabbi Adin Steinsaltz. According to Steinsaltz, Yosef wasn't permitted to travel to Canaan, so Ya'akov came immediately to him on learning that Yosef was still alive.

FORCED INTO OUR CHOICES

The *dibur*, the words, of four consecutive American presidents created the *oness*, the duress, that brought a family here from Afghanistan; I welcomed them to America with three plastic storage bins full of dishes and cookie cutters. The words of the King of Bhutan that we'll discuss at length in the next chapter displaced nearly a quarter of the people in my practice from their homes and possessions. Add to them the children and grandchildren born in the camps and since their immigration to America and it's more like a third, including a group of teens and twenty-somethings who created an online presence as "The Children of Shangri-Lost."[8]

Like Yosef, like his family, and indeed, like the ancestors of most people who populate the United States, these people were pushed (or dragged) rather than pulled to their new homes by a forces not of their making: Poverty, war, famine, disease, torture, domestic strife. My old friend Rachel Tiven spent a decade of her life documenting the *'oness* (sometimes in the literal, modern Hebrew sense of rape) experienced by LGBTQ individuals from developing nations, especially those with powerful religious establishments. Her goal was to make persecution based on sexual orientation an officially recognized cause to grant a person asylum or refugee status in the US. The effort succeeded,[9] and I've taken advantage of that criterion more than once in my thirteen years of practice to help a person remain safely here rather than return home to a family waiting to kill them.

Not everyone I care for is a refugee; they're simply the ones whose story most obviously parallels that of the Israelites in Egypt. But I can see the effects of other kinds of duress in many narratives, individual as well as global. I see a person who seeks shelter in a relationship, or comfort from a drink of whiskey, or calm from a cigarette, and by inches and degrees finds themselves abused, or addicted, or unable to breathe. Medicine traditionally looked at these moments of decision as choices, but so often these individuals, too, are *'anousim*. They're under the duress of circumstances they don't control. And yet these forced decisions sometimes seem to work out quite well at the outset: The relationship has

---

8. https://www.shangri-lost.org/; the site is no longer active but the videos, photos and writings detailing their mixed blessing of immigrating to the US are still up from roughly 2015–17. Fittingly, several of the students involved in the project are now young adults beginning careers in healthcare.

9. This should surprise no one. Rachel's birthday is August 9, 1974, the day Nixon resigned. She steadfastly maintains that she scared him out of office just by being born.

a "honeymoon period," the alcohol helps them sleep better, the cigarette allows them some mental clarity and relaxation. Like the Israelites newly arrived in Egypt, they feel like they're flourishing—until that new king arises...[10]

A relationship may offer the only guard against poverty in youth, vulnerability in a war, or loneliness in old age, yet hide the seeds of violence later. A bottle or a smoke may provide the only equanimity in a sixteen-hour workday and a houseful of people screaming, crying, or hurting. They're less choices than moves of desperation, last resorts when there seems nowhere else to turn. What, really, can I say to a person who has prediabetes, but depends on a food bank where the most plentiful items are bags of rice and boxes of pasta? The prisoner, says Talmud Berachot, can't free himself from prison.[11] And we have allowed our society to build a lot of prisons, both physical and metaphorical.

In clinical medicine, we encounter one person at a time in their individual narrow places. If the Haggadah has a message for us, it's that God didn't free one enslaved Israelite at a time—and as the American experience tells us, even an enslaved person who did earn their freedom was often one *oness* away from returning to that narrowest of places. God brought about systemic change in Egypt to bring the Israelites to freedom, and the bloody tragedy of the Civil War was only the first step on what Mandela called the "Long Walk to Freedom" that's still not over here in America.

We're free from the duress of smallpox because of two centuries of efforts to develop the vaccine and spread it to every corner of the world. We're free from the dread that every wound could be fatal because of the development of reliable antiseptics, clean water sources, and antibiotics. To be free from the duress of drug addiction, despair, discrimination, and environmental hazards will take the work of a whole lot more people like my friend Rachel, and a whole lot more time. If someone has "calculated the end" of these narrow places,[12] they've not told me about it. But as the *Ephod Bad* taught,[13] knowing the story, knowing that even as

---

10. Exodus 1:8, "A new king arose over Egypt who did not know Joseph." This is the point in the story where the new Pharaoh begins to legislate the changes that lead to enslavement, which we'll discuss in the next chapter.

11. Talmud Berachot 5b.

12. See my discussion of this idea in Chapter 1.

13. See Chapter 15.

we're headed down into the depths there's the promise of coming back up someday, has to be enough to let me carry on one small Exodus at a time.

Thoughts and Discussions

- *What "choices" have you made that weren't really choices, just the best you could do under the circumstances?*

19

Wicked Wisdom

Pharoah begins to afflict the Israelites, or as he puts it, "deal wisely" with them.

First Fruits Declaration 7	ארמי אבד אבי ז׳
"And the Egyptians did bad to us" (Deuteronomy 26:6)—as it is stated (Exodus 1:10), "Let us be wise towards him, lest he multiply and it will be that when war is called, he too will join with our enemies and fight against us and go up from the land."	וַיָּרֵעוּ אֹתָנוּ הַמִּצְרִים וַיְעַנּוּנוּ, וַיִּתְּנוּ עָלֵינוּ עֲבֹדָה קָשָׁה. וַיָּרֵעוּ אֹתָנוּ הַמִּצְרִים—כְּמָה שֶׁנֶּאֱמַר: הָבָה נִתְחַכְּמָה לוֹ פֶּן יִרְבֶּה, וְהָיָה כִּי תִקְרֶאנָה מִלְחָמָה וְנוֹסַף גַּם הוּא עַל שֹׂנְאֵינוּ וְנִלְחַם־בָּנוּ, וְעָלָה מִן־הָאָרֶץ.

THE "WISDOM" OF TYRANTS

"I never told you this before because I thought, 'I'm still healthy, I can work,'" he told me the other day.

"This" was the fact that he was imprisoned and tortured for three years, then separated from his family, and unceremoniously dumped in India, on the other side of a border he would never be allowed to re-cross, stranding them apart from each other to this day.

The Bhutanese refugees, Nepali-speaking Hindus, came to Bhutan a hundred or more years ago seeking economic prosperity only a short distance from where they set out—not unlike Ya'akov and his family descending to Egypt. They thrived in Bhutan until, quite literally, a new king arose and decided that they posed a threat, a potential fifth column that might break off a part of Bhutan and unite it with Nepali-speaking parts of India and Nepal to form their own country. Suddenly they were no longer welcome in the land of Goshen. . .

Havah nithakmah lo, said the Egyptian Pharaoh about the Israelites. "Let us deal wisely with this (nation)," lest some nation make war on us, and they join with our enemies."[1] How very shrewd of Pharaoh—and how often his "wisdom" has been taken up by tyrant after dictator after despot to justify maltreatment of people who are different.

There's a tendency in a post-*Shoah* world to see the Holocaust in World War II Europe as a singular experience, a horror that befell the Jews which is unequaled in the history of humanity. How wrong this is. The election of the Jews in the Torah, the imperative to Avraham to be *l'or goyim*, as a light of nations, is precisely because our story is *not* unique—not in human history and not even in Jewish history. Rather, it's archetypal. The Jewish story is the paradigm of the triumphs and tragedies that befall human beings of all nations. Our role in history, *apropos* "light," is to shine the light of our story on the stories of others. To say, "Hey, that happened to us, and it was wrong then, and it's wrong now that it's happening to you."

PRISONERS OF PARADIGM

As healers, our response to those stories may be simply to listen and to validate them. It may be to bind the wounds that they've left festering. And as we saw in the last chapter, occasionally, it must be to pick up where Moshe left off, to stand before Pharaoh and say, "Let my people go"—because if we don't, the suffering will never end.

The challenge is knowing which of those responses a given situation demands. Our Exodus narrative is archetypal, but its individual iterations are distinct from one another, if not totally unique. They're equivalent to the distinction between "illness" and "disease." A disease is a biological entity, one that has the same cause, mechanisms, and treatment in everyone who contracts it. An illness is the way a single individual experiences that disease, which is different from all other individual experiences of that disease.[2]

---

1. Exodus 1:10
2. Kleinman, *The Illness Narratives: Suffering, Healing, and the Human Condition.*

This dichotomy between illness and disease places healers in a narrow place of our own. If we operate exclusively on the disease paradigm, we often respond in a way that doesn't help the person. If we operate exclusively on the illness model, we can fail to recognize obvious patterns of disease, respond to urgent clues or learn from prior experiences with the same disease.

Those same refugees from Bhutan I spoke about a moment ago seem to suffer from a very specific pattern of physical symptoms and cognitive decline, leading to dependency on family and social supports. In caring for them I'm constantly struggling not to lean too far in the direction of over-psychologizing their illness, and missing serious physical illness like stomach cancer, ulcers, traumatic brain injury, or stroke. At the same time, when we and our hospital-based colleagues focus too much on the physical symptoms, these people suffer through unnecessary procedures that don't address the grief and loss that are at the core of their anguish.[3]

Sadly, in caring for individuals like this who've been through trauma, we often begin to act like Pharaohs ourselves, trying to "deal shrewdly" with them by entrapping them. We convince ourselves that they're "gaming the system," or that patients with chronic pain are "drug-seeking," or that people with work injuries are "malingering," and design entire treatment protocols with the sole purpose of catching them in the act, instead of understanding how they ended up in this mess in the first place.[4]

As we build our interpretive framework for understanding the narrow place, and our escape from that place, as a metaphor for illness and recovery, we must also build a capacity to *frame-shift*, back and forth as the situation demands, in and out of that metaphor to serve the needs of the person in front of us at that moment. To turn Pharaoh's words on their heads, "let us deal wisely with them" in finding the right path to healing.

Thoughts and Discussions

- *Talk about a piece of "wicked wisdom" you've encountered—a policy or ideology that's rational on its face but viciously cruel in its heart.*

This concept is the central thesis of Kleinman's book.

3. Fox, Gurung, Kurek, Thompson, and Weinkle, "Meeting the psychiatric challenges facing the Bhutanese refugee community in Pittsburgh: How one Community Health Center is doing it."

4. Chapter 8 of my previous book, *Healing People, Not Patients*, details some experiences I'd rather forget with this sort of "care," if you can call it that.

20

Broken Backs

We learn about the various kinds of hard labor the Israelites performed during their enslavement.

First Fruits Declaration 9	ארמי אבד אבי ט׳
"And put upon us hard work"—as it is stated (Exodus 1:11), "And they enslaved the children of Israel with back-breaking work."	וַיִּתְּנוּ עָלֵינוּ עֲבֹדָה קָשָׁה. כְּמָה שֶׁנֶּאֱמַר: וַיַּעֲבִדוּ מִצְרַיִם אֶת־בְּנֵי יִשְׂרָאֵל בְּפָרֶךְ.

LIVING IS KILLING US

"Ain't nothing but blue skies, and the sun always shines.

But blue sky and sunshine are bad for the bottom line. . ."

I wrote those words ten years ago, the opening lines of a song I call, "Living is Killing Us." The tag line of the chorus, as you might guess, is, "Even though the way that we make a living is killing us." One of my colleagues regularly visits an area of town that inspired those first few lines, the river valley that sits under the clouds of the US Steel Clairton Coke Works and Edgar Thompson Works, two of the last remaining major industrial polluters in the area. His job? Running a pediatric asthma clinic.

The economy in this region was devastated by the collapse of the steel industry, and the people who continue to work in those plants are incredibly fortunate to still have work. The children who live nearby?

They've the highest rates of asthma in the county. My grandmother used to reminisce about the "gray-collar" workers—office workers in Downtown Pittsburgh who used to take spare white shirts to work because the soot would stain their first shirts gray by lunchtime. In my first-year anatomy lab in 1999, we learned that their lungs looked a lot worse than their laundry.

I took care of one resident of Homestead, formerly one of the most famous steel towns (as much for the infamous Pinkerton strike-breaking that took place there as for the steel itself) long after the mill there had been turned into a strip mall.[1] He wasn't a steelworker; he delivered large appliances for a major distributor. By the time I met him, twenty years into his delivery career, his rotator cuffs were all but shredded. He couldn't even raise his arms in surrender.

KILLING US WITH KINDNESS

When the Haggadah tells us about the Egyptians forcing the Israelites into slave labor, it says they made them work *b'farekh*,[2] translated variously as "backbreaking" or "with brutality" among other things. One widespread interpretation of the word is that it's a contraction of *b'feh rakh*, "with a soft mouth," meaning with gentle words.[3,4] This interpretation holds that Pharaoh originally cajoled the Israelites into working voluntarily, even doing some of the work himself to show they were "pitching in," doing their part in a collective enterprise, and only later, when they were accustomed to the labor, locking them into it under progressively worse conditions.

A few chapters ago, we talked about the "descent" into situations of duress, where people make what they perceive as necessary sacrifices in the moment, only to find themselves locked into making those sacrifices without end. Here, we see that sometimes, people find themselves entrapped in no-exit situations that begin not as sacrifices, but as enticing

---

1. I'd be remiss if I mentioned Homestead in this book and didn't mention my friend Tammy Hepps. She's a direct descendant of one of the founders of Homestead's synagogue, and has single-handedly compiled the history of the Jewish community of that town—including this 2015 article on the Jewish history of that steel strike. https://homesteadhebrews.com/articles/the-jews-of-homestead-and-the-1892-strike/

2. Exodus 1:11

3. Weil, *Marbeh Lesaper*, "First Fruits Declaration."

4. Treves, *Kimcha DAvshuna*, "First Fruits Declaration."

invitations. In his 2023 *Human Rights Haggadah*, Shlomo Levin points out that this is how modern sex trafficking works, often luring young women with promises of high-paying jobs overseas, fame and fortune, or friendship and shelter.[5] The practice isn't new, however. Levin quotes Midrash Rabbah on Exodus 1:22 as saying that the Egyptians decided to spare the baby girls among the Israelites figuring that they'd grow up and become sex slaves.[6]

FROM FARM TO FACTORY TO FIRESIDE

Not everyone sees the word *b'farekh* this way, however. The 18th century Haggadah commentary *Ma'aseh Nissim* sees mystical hints in the text that show that *b'farekh* implies that Pharaoh afflicted the Israelites with every different type of labor, numbering 39 in all. These correspond to the type of work that would eventually be needed to build the *mishkan*, the traveling sanctuary, once the Israelites were on their own in the desert—the same 39 kinds of work that were in turn *forbidden* to be done on Shabbat. We started our journey through the seder with Kadesh (Chapter 4), with the prayer that blesses the wine and sanctifies the holiday, but our *Shabbat* kiddush prayer also includes the phrase, "a reminder of the Exodus from Egypt." Celebrating Shabbat is a repudiation of the enslavement by the Egyptians, every single week.

Recently I learned the story of the building of Duquesne University, a Spiritan Catholic University just a few miles from my house in Pittsburgh. We learn in Exodus that the Israelites continued to thrive physically despite their enslavement, therefore Pharaoh upped the ante and required them to make their own bricks to build with—and to gather the straw to do so.[7] But in willing service to a different ruler, the Spiritans baked bricks in their own foundry, from clay dug on that very hillside, to build the first structure of the university now known as Old Main.[8] Call them the Ma'aseh Nissim of the Monongahela River.

Indeed, many commentaries believe that the next verse, which says that God heard the Israelites' cry *vayar' et 'anyenu v'et 'amalenu v'et*

---

5. Levin, Shlomo, The Human Rights Haggadah,39.
6. Levin, Shlomo, Human Rights Haggadah, 38.
7. Exodus 5:7–8
8. Gormley, Public remarks at the ribbon-cutting of the Duquesne University College of Medicine.

lahatzenu—"and saw our affliction and our toil and our duress"—uses three different nouns to refer to many different types of labor, both agricultural and construction, that were imposed on them.

The way that we make a living is, indeed, killing us. Few trades, professions, or unskilled jobs are free of "occupational hazards;" in the song I opine that "occupational hazard is only a buzz-word for putting our lives on the line." Working in high finance or corporate sales can rob us of our basic human decency and ruin our relationships, even if it doesn't break our backs. Creating "better living through chemistry" can leave behind poisons in our air, toxins in our water, and cancer in our own bones. Living the pastoral life of herding cattle in rural Bhutan came with an alarmingly high rate of people falling headfirst out of trees as they cut vegetation for the cattle to graze on in an area that was more jungle than pasture.

Healers are not exempt from this phenomenon of *avodah b'farekh*. Oregon family physician Pamela Wible spends her non-clinical time advocating for awareness and prevention of physician suicide, an alarmingly common tragedy.[9] Physicians in emergency medicine, I've written elsewhere, have a career "life expectancy" only about twice as long as that of an NFL football player, roughly 7 years, due to burnout. Retail pharmacies, once able to maintain multiple 24-hour locations in most cities, are progressively cutting hours, closing for lunch to catch up, and yet still saw their retail pharmacists go on a strike in early 2023 that was so crippling to the system people called it Pharmageddon. One billboard I saw during 2022 warned that 93% of healthcare workers were considering leaving their jobs within the coming year, and 50% were considering leaving the profession.

Thoughts and Discussions

- *What parts of your profession or occupation feel like they're making you sick or killing you?*
- *When you get out of your narrow place, how will you "repudiate" the way you had to live when you were in it? What will you do even while you're still not quite free, to show you can't be defined by it?*

---

9. Wible, "What I've Learned from 547 Doctor Suicides." https://www.idealmedicalcare.org/

LIVING IS BURNING US TO A CRISP

The phenomenon of physician burnout, especially during training, is so common that I once taught a Torah study comparing medical interns to the doomed sons of Aaron, Nadav and Avihu, who were burnt from the inside for bringing strange fire before God. Both the interns and Aaron's sons struck me as wet-behind-the-ears neophytes tasked with an awesome responsibility but lacking the tools and knowledge to carry it out safely. In doing their *avodah b'farekh*, they end up *parikh*—(burnt to a) crisp. And even when the outcome is not as shocking and dramatic as a suicide or inhaling the fire of God through one's nostrils, physicians, nurses, advance practice providers and all manner of other health professionals inexorably wear down under the strain of their job.

In the first week of January 2021, which was both arguably the worst week of the coronavirus pandemic and a cataclysmic week in American society, we read from Parashat Sh'mot, which early on contains the line I alluded to in chapter 18, "There arose a new king over Mitzrayim that did not know Yosef."[10] I imagine that in Yosef's time, you could stroll down a street in Egypt during the famine years and see crudely chiseled stones and hastily written papyri on people's front stoops that said, "Thank you to Yosef, our administrative hero!" People stood on their balconies as his chariot passed and played reed flute music or banged on pots and pans to salute him. After all, they weren't starving thanks to him. Right?

At that point in the pandemic, my colleagues and I in all phases of the healthcare system had been hearing for 10 months about what heroes we were. People in other fields like law-enforcement and public safety, agriculture, food service and Amazon delivery had suddenly become "essential workers," recognized as important for doing the tasks they've always done that keep our society from grinding to a halt. Our "kings," meaning our elected officials, media outlets, and corporate leaders, lauded these folks for their invaluable contributions during the pandemic, the papyri have given way to video displays and posterboard with markers, and the reed flutes to Italian opera and *"Ehad Mi Yodea,"* but it was a heroes' salute all the same.

Yet already by that stage of the pandemic, I felt that a "new king" had arisen who did not know these modern-day Yosefs—or worse, that even in the very beginning, when the outpouring of support was greatest, that the "king," and his people, never really knew these Josephs to begin with.

10. Exodus 1:8

Front-facing healthcare workers and students, as well as all those presumably "essential" workers, were initially unable to get vaccines—but still had to see patients. Whistle-blowers cried out about *still* inadequate supplies of personal protective equipment despite months of efforts to improve the situation. Doctors were accused of padding the numbers of dead and hospitalized from COVID-19 because it somehow, perversely, must have been benefiting us. Clearly, whoever these kings and their people are never knew Joseph and wouldn't have bothered to pluck him out of prison given their choice. They were indifferent to his advice, averse to his knowledge, resentful of his caring.

Some commentators on this verse suggest that it was the same king, at least the same as one of several who knew Joseph personally, who pretended he didn't know Joseph after he died. And indeed, many of the same people who put the signs on their lawns and banged the pots and pans still had 20-person Thanksgiving dinners in the pre-vaccine era of November 2020, ate in restaurants, went to worship unmasked, and lobbied their elective officials to open the country back up even though we were *losing* ground to the virus. Hospitals reached the point that all earlier mitigation efforts had been designed to avoid—turning away patients, running out of supplies, and unable to provide adequate care due to lack of personnel and resources.

The trend only continued through 2021. Unvaccinated patients and their families called their doctors liars and conspirators because they wouldn't play along with the ruse that "this couldn't be COVID, that's not real." Lawyers and state governments tried to dictate medical practice and force those same doctors to prescribe debunked treatments against their own clinical judgment. Public health officials, already under threat of death over daring to try to keep the public safe, were removed from their posts for promoting vaccination among teens.

Toward the end of Parashat Exodus, Moshe is on the road from Midian back to Egypt and stops at an inn. A very confusing passage states that he met God there *vayivakesh hamito*, "and he tried to kill him." Why on Earth would God try to kill Moshe just as he is headed to do a task that God sent him to do? My friend Brian Primack, a family doc and dean of a college at University of Arkansas that includes their school of public health, taught me this interpretation from Richard Elliot Friedman: God isn't trying to kill Moshe. Moshe is *asking God to kill him* rather than face the gargantuan task before him. It's too much. And indeed, all those disturbing trends we saw above grew worse as practicing in a pandemic took its inevitable toll on the healthcare workforce.

At the same time, we can hope that the experience generated empathy between healthcare workers and the rest of the frontline workforce. Doctors and cashiers suddenly faced the same risks; nurses and taxi drivers the same vulnerability; pharmacists and meat packers the same indifference from society. All received lip service, and little else, for being heroes. But one shouldn't need to be a hero to go to work. It should be enough to be good at one's job, to be responsible, without having to put in super-human effort and risk one's life. Yet that's the reality—making a living is often killing us.

If the role of the seder is to generate empathy, to ritualize Greenberg's assertion that the world was not meant to be this way, then viscerally understanding the feeling of *avodah b'farekh* is essential to that goal. Let us who work in the health professions not forget this experience or be so embittered by it that we forget to learn this lesson: Humanity is not destined to always work *b'farekh*, but rather *lifroah*—to blossom.

Thoughts and Discussions

- *Have you ever experienced the feeling of doing the right thing and being hated or punished for it?*
- *What makes you feel like quitting—or has made you wish, like Moshe, that God would strike you down so you didn't have to put up with it anymore? How did you get out of that place to go on?*

LEAVE THE LIGHT ON

Brian Miller sees this empathy, this identification between the healer and the patient, as a key to *avoiding* burnout. In *Reducing Secondary Traumatic Stress: Skills for Sustaining a Career in the Helping Professions,* Miller commits blasphemy. Three times, actually. His first blasphemy against the conventional wisdom of the burnout literature is that burnout is a myth. People don't become chronically depleted of energy over their careers; they feel the most burnt out early and either stay there or get less burnt-out as they mature. The second is that "compassion fatigue," thought to be a key feature of burnout, is a misnomer. The act of behaving compassionately toward someone is *rewarding*, not draining, and if burnout makes us less compassionate, then it's robbing us of a benefit that could reinvigorate us.

Miller's book is structured around a mythical narrative designed to give helpers tools to thrive in the stress of caring for others, so it's no surprise that he taps directly into the power of the empathetic imperative of the seder. It's uncomfortable to talk about sex trafficking and other forms of modern enslavement over dinner, but leaning into it, and committing to doing compassionate acts for others as a result, makes us feel more human, not less. Miller's third blasphemy drives this point home—traumatic stress doesn't come from overexposure to intense feelings; it comes from freezing *before* we allow ourselves to experience those intense feelings, cutting ourselves off from the chance at compassion, and from the chance to ride those feelings to a peak and then let them dissipate. It takes way more energy to keep our shields up all the time.[11]

Thoughts and Discussions

- *What part of your work drains you the most?*
- *What would it feel like to "lean in" to the work, rather than lean out?*
- *How much does context matter—can the same task be invigorating in one setting and demoralizing in another?*

---

11. Miller, Reducing Secondary Traumatic Stress, 13–15.

LIVING IS KILLING US

Ain't nothing but blue skies, and the sun always shines
But blue skies and sunshine are bad for the bottom line
Without the smokestacks, without the furnace, without the freight train and the heat
How in the hell is a family supposed to eat?
So we all bear a burden and it's breaking our backs
We bend over backward so we won't have to pay any tax
If we're making a killing and it keeps us alive then we don't make a fuss
Even if the way that we make a living is killing us

He's the face of the city for the things that he does on the ice
But he's not very pretty, he's been punched in the mouth once or twice
His dad was a miner, not a designer, spent his time down in the ground
Where the insides of his lungs turned as black as the coal that he found
His sister loves mysteries, and devotes her life to achieve
Better living through chemistry and give us plastics and products that clean
And once she delivers they dump in the river the waste products and the surplus
And then the way that she makes her living is killing us

Get out of our backyard, this is where we make our stand
No one is willing to let you go drilling so get the frack off of our land
But we grew so refractory they closed down the factory and hired a crew in Pakistan

So now the drilling isn't making a killing or pouring out smoke
But we've got nowhere to earn our living and it's making us broke

The candle is burning at both of its ends
You count up the earnings and watch what you spend
You got a promotion but showed no emotion because you're an ocean away from home
If you're such a company man why do you always feel so alone?
So pour another cup of coffee, 'cause no one is going to sleep
The axe keeps falling but no one has time to weep
Over friends that were lost while cutting our costs and betraying the public trust
While the way that we make a living was killing us

They call me a hero and say that I'm saving lives
But the stress and the strain of healing their pain is killing me from inside
"Occupational hazard" is only a buzzword for putting our lives on the line
Somehow we might still survive if we see it in time
To provide for the people we love we all do what we must
Even if the way that we make a living is killing us

21

Idioms of Distress

The Israelites express their distress by crying out to God.

| Pesach Haggadah, Magid, First Fruits Declaration

"And we cried out to the Lord, the God of our ancestors, and the Lord heard our voice, and He saw our affliction, and our toil and our duress" (Deuteronomy 26:7). | הגדה של פסח, מגיד, ארמי אבד אבי

וַנִּצְעַק אֶל־ה׳ אֱלֹהֵי אֲבֹתֵינוּ, וַיִּשְׁמַע ה׳ אֶת־קֹלֵנוּ, וַיַּרְא אֶת־עָנְיֵנוּ וְאֶת עֲמָלֵנוּ וְאֶת לַחֲצֵנוּ. |

IDIOMS

My father-in-law loves idioms. A native Russian speaker, he didn't really learn English until he was in his late twenties and burning the candle at both ends (yes, that's an idiom) trying to earn a living while also studying for both the US Medical Licensing Exam and the Test of English as a Foreign Language that were his entry ticket to a residency in the US.

Thanks to his friends, I know that during this period he slept like a log (again, an idiom) and that these same friends used to have to call him repeatedly to awaken him after all his alarm clocks had rung to no avail. However, after seven years with his shoulder to the wheel (you guessed it, another idiom), he successfully completed the exams and entered his psychiatry residency. At some later time, my wife gifted her father a

Dictionary of Idioms, which he thoroughly enjoyed. Each time he hears me use a new American idiom that he doesn't know, he mulls it over for several minutes to make sure he has the sense of it. My wife, on the other hand, deprived of these same idioms growing up since her father didn't know them, accuses me of making them up as I go along. Regarding the origins of the Russian idioms they both teach me, I won't speculate...

Some idioms are less fun. We call these "idioms of distress," and they are expressions of illness and dis-ease that have special valence to the person expressing them. A person going through heroin withdrawal doesn't need to describe to another person who has themselves experienced withdrawal that they're nauseous, drooling, sweating, shivering, and having loose bowels. They just need to say, "I'm dope sick," and everyone who's been there knows what they mean. A person experiencing crushing substernal chest pain doesn't even search for the words; they instinctively signal their agony by holding a closed fist directly over the heart, a gesture millennia old but described in the medical literature of the 1940s by S. A. Levine and named, "the Levine sign" in his honor.

An infographic I keep handy describes specific idioms of distress commonly used among Nepali-speaking Bhutanese refugees. This would be a mere curiosity if more than half the people I care for, and 30% of the people who receive care at our health center, didn't come from this community. It groups the different types of distress into those affecting the Ijjat (social status), Dimaag (brain-mind), Man (heart-mind), Jiu or Saarir (body), and Saato (spirit or soul). Contained in this graphic are many of the idioms of distress that I hear people express to me daily: Gastrik (dyspepsia), jham-jham (tingling or burning pain, especially in the feet), and ringata lageko (dizziness). Some fall into the body category, but many, like nightmares, aggressive behavior, psychosis, and "heaviness" (which when it's relieved is replaced with "feeling light") are in the brain-mind, soul or other categories.[1]

Recognizing these idioms requires far more than a dictionary. I've spent more than a dozen years working daily with members of the Bhutanese community, including my friend and frequent translator Pancham Tamang, and my former student Dr. Yadhu Dhital. Yadhu studied medicine at Georgetown, and as a student taught me about the Catholic tradition of cura personalis, the ability of the physician to cure just by their personal touch and involvement, rather than their prescriptions of

---

1. Kohrt and Hruschka. "Nepali Concepts of Psychological Trauma, " 25.

medicine. But it was on the language of suffering in his native culture where he really gave me an education, where I'm still in the remedial class. Part of the challenge is that understanding the words, the simple translation of Nepali terms into English, is barely enough to begin with. I mention Pancham and Yadhu because of their ability to "code switch," telling me what they hear as insiders in the culture in terms that will make sense to me as a Western medical professional.

AN IDIOMATIC CRY FOR HELP

The Israelites' redemption begins with a cry—an idiom of their distress:

> The Israelites were groaning under the bondage and cried out; and their cry for help from the bondage rose up to God. God heard their moaning, and God remembered His covenant with Abraham and Isaac and Jacob. God looked upon the Israelites, and God took notice of them.[2]

2. Exodus 2:23–25

The 13th century Italian kabbalist Menahem Recanati remarks on these verses, "Why four times? It would have been enough one time, 'And God heard their moaning.'"[3] Recanati is alluding to the fact that there are four verbs applied to God's actions in verses 24 and 25: Heard, remembered, looked (saw) and took notice (knew, in the intimate sense v'yeda'). These are four idioms for God paying attention, and the Torah uses each verb because each idiom hints at some other aspect of the Israelites' suffering. Together, they're a road map for recognizing and responding to a person's cry for help.

The Torah and the Haggadah begin with two verbs attributed to the Israelites: Vayeanhu v'nei Yisrael min ha'avodah va-yiz'aku. "The Children of Israel were groaning from their labor and cried out." The groan is the day-to-day distress, the cry, the moment when they're finally unable to bear it alone anymore and reach out for help. The cry may take any number of forms, and may include multiple idioms of distress, not just one.

The literature on suicide often notes a "cry for help" in the days or weeks preceding a death by suicide. The text of this verse continues, "and their cry for help rose up to God," but we know that many of those cries never make it to their destination. Stephen Trzeciak and Anthony Mazzarelli, in their 2019 book Compassionomics, tell the story of a man who died by suicide by jumping from a bridge. His note read, "I'm going to walk to the bridge. If one person smiles at me, I will not jump." Not one person triggered the escape clause. The man jumped.[4]

RESPONDING TO THE CRY

God's response to the cry models four distinct phases. First, God listens. There are three layers of listening, going from the obedient (usually sh-m-'a in Hebrew, meaning "whatever you say!") to the reflective (a-z-n, from the word for ear, meaning "what you said is") to the attentive (k-sh-v, meaning "what I understand you are saying is"). Recanati also notes that God goes through a process that begins with simple hearing, proceeds through an expression of mercy, and ends with attending to the answer. The cry goes up; we may or may not understand what we're hearing. Often, we ask questions or simply express empathy when we don't know what else to say. The key to the hearing phase is to keep listening so

---

3. Recanati on Exodus 2:24-25.
4. Trzeciak and Mazzarelli, *Compassionomics*, 14–15.

that we can get to the next phases, and not to tune out cries that can be irritating, unpleasant, or even overwhelming.

The second phase is remembrance, as Recanati says, "remembrance with mercy." For God, the remembrance is of a promise made long ago—to Avraham, Yitzhak and Ya'aqov. God recognizes the cry as a sign that the time has come to fulfill God's promise. It's time to have mercy on the suffering Israelites.

In a hectic day, a person in the healing professions may hear dozens of cries for help. We learned earlier about the work of Brian Miller, who contends that many professionals, guarding themselves against "compassion fatigue," filter out many of these cries—and make a grave mistake in doing so. Miller describes a day where, "I was in survival mode . . . this wasn't compassion fatigue, because I hadn't touched compassion once that day."[5] It's not hard to imagine that someone in that mindset would miss many of these cries. But as we've already learned, the healing professions make a promise no less critical, and no less enduring, than when God promised Abraham descendants as numerous of the stars of the sky who would move from slavery to freedom, to great wealth, and ultimately to dwell safely in their own land.[6] We advertise ourselves as the ones who can cure disease, lengthen life, and heal hurt. We get to hear those cries because we have promised people that we are the ones who can answer them.

There's a challenge here to both the healer and the patient. For the person suffering, the verses above remind us that it's not enough to keep groaning about the everyday burdens of life. There needs to be a cry. A person needs to feel empowered to say just how distressed they are, and why today is not just another day but a real crisis. They need, if it comes to that, to grab the healer by the collar and say, "Listen, you, I need your help now!" And the healer needs to give them that power and pay enough attention that there's no need for the patient to rough them up to get their attention. The physician needs, in Miller's words, to "lean in" to hear those cries, from those who still feel embarrassed to shout them out. They need to center themselves on the promise at the start of each visit; not to forget.

The practice of healing depends heavily on memory—not just remembering our promise but remembering endless details. Whether one

---

5. Miller, Reducing Secondary Traumatic Stress, 5.
6. See Chapter 15.

studies nursing, goes to PA school, gets an MD or learns pharmacy, the years of medical education are a torrent of facts, processes, concepts and encounters with people in the throes of illness, with the "pearls" and "take-home points" often circled with laser pointers or sage nods from senior lecturers and clinical mentors. "Remember this," they might say. "You'll need this information one day, and you'll thank me for it." When the cry goes up, years later, we have a dull sense of recognition that sends us scrambling for the book, the website, the color-coded page of notes that holds the factoid, diagram or anecdote that will bring today's challenge into sharper resolution. We remember with mercy the suffering of the patient with glowing jaundice, with gasping breathing or with massively edematous legs that we met years ago, and we recognize that same suffering in the "ill person who lies before us" today.

Occasionally the memory involves us directly, especially in primary care. A "spurious" abnormal lab value from five years ago suddenly takes on real significance; an odd physical finding finally turns sinister. Like a carefully planned Hollywood epic, we need to be paying close attention to every episode, using sleuth-like powers of perception, to see the clues and recall them at this moment.

Thus, remembering leads to the third phase, seeing. Recanati explains, "Seeing with understanding." Hearing, linked with memories that deepen our knowledge, allows us to see clearly. It's no accident that Sherlock Holmes was created by a physician; Doyle modeled him after a professor who was undoubtedly like legendary diagnosticians everywhere, able to watch a man take his dinner and recite not only his medical history but his entire life story. But in many renditions of the Holmes stories, the great detective with all his insight is nevertheless blind to humanity. Benedict Cummerbatch's Holmes can enter a "mind palace" where everything he's ever learned is archived according to a system that allows him to access it almost instantly. Yet he's also a sociopath, callous to those who care about him, painfully arrogant and entirely obtuse regarding emotion. He is, in short, a perfect portrayal of the tragic shortcomings as well as the monumental skills of those physicians of yore.

Seeing with understanding goes beyond deciphering clues and flaunting amazing powers of deduction. Our heuristic reasoning often leads us to the conclusion that "everything's fine"—everything, of course, except that the person's still ill, and we have no explanation to offer. We can see, hear, remember, and put all of that together to decide that a suffering person isn't really sick. So-called functional illnesses debilitate people even as parts of the medical community debate whether they "really exist"—including the spreading secondary plague of long COVID.

Hence the final verb, "took notice," the Hebrew root y-d-'a, know. This is not factual knowledge, but intimate knowledge—among people, the euphemistic term for physical intimacy, but between God and humanity the term for God seeing into the hidden spaces. These are the spaces in the other four domains on my graphic—the heart-mind, brain-mind, soul-spirit, and social status. Seeing allowed God to recognize what the Egyptians were doing to the Israelites that everyone could see. Knowing showed God what was happening to them in secret. This included (according to the interpretation of the Chizkuni) how the Egyptians prevent them from being physically intimate with one another, and according to the text of the Haggadah itself, the drowning of the baby boys and the "crushing" of the Israelites in body and spirit.[7]

THE BODY CRIES FOR HELP

During the week I was writing this chapter, I met a woman at work who hadn't been to see me in more than a year. Her average blood sugar had risen by more than 50% over that period, she had lost weight unintentionally, and while she wasn't reporting any other symptoms of uncontrolled diabetes, the labs and the scale didn't lie. I could see the problem very clearly. What wasn't obvious was the context in which her once-controlled diabetes had spiraled out of control.

I remembered and I knew: Her mother-in-law, who lived with her and was often in her care when she was home from work, was declining precipitously, in and out of the hospital for lung and heart problems while complaining bitterly about how she suffered when she was home and had to go to dialysis. At wit's end, my patient was unable to sleep without a glass of wine before bed, which then made her hesitate to take her evening meds because she had heard you shouldn't take medicine with alcohol. Between the half-dose of medicine and the extra liquid sugar and alcohol it wasn't hard to really see how her disease got worse—and to know that her disease of diabetes was a symptom of a larger illness, one she was experiencing together with her whole household.

That same day I saw another person who'd been in my care for a dozen years. After doggedly remaining independent through two shoulder

---

7. Chizkuni on Exodus 2:25.

surgeries, knee pain, and a stiff neck, they had finally reached the point of bringing me the form for nursing home level care in their home so they can qualify for a state subsidy to hire someone.

The form is short, a single page which asks me to check two boxes and list the person's diagnoses. Yet it's fraught; the Pennsylvania Department of Justice periodically investigates the agencies that provide home-based services because they're certain there's rampant fraud perpetrated by people faking their disabilities. Like insurance companies, they see their job as protecting the funding for the program from going to anyone who doesn't truly need it, even if that means some people in serious need have their care delayed or denied. Much like those who are suffering from functional illnesses, they end up in a situation where the healer can either become the enemy, or risk being considered complicit in the fraud.

After a dozen years, I wasn't falling into that trap with this person. I know to ask for what's going on beyond what I see: Who else is in the home? What is showering like? Can you get dressed in the morning on your own? I know to recognize that when this person (who never brings anyone to their visits) comes with an adult son, that's a sign of losing independence. And I know enough about this extended family that even though this person has never once complained about their anxiety, anger, or depression, there's a heavy weight around their neck due to another adult child's chronic illness and family stress, a weight that's always foremost in their mind and wearing away at their resolve to continue resisting disability.

Knowing and seeing these hidden truths, also means trusting and believing. The Sforno reads the verb va-yed'a as God believing that the cry of the Israelites was genuine.[8] Practicing the healing arts in the 21st century virtually guarantees we'll face forces that either try to convince us our patients are deceiving us, or try to convince our patients that we're frauds. This passage in the Haggadah stands as a reminder to resist these forces trying to drive a wedge into the middle of our covenant with one another, and to use all our ways of acquiring knowledge—our senses, our memories, and our trusting hearts—to make that covenant stronger.

---

8. Sforno on Exodus 2:25.

22

The Outstretched Arm of the Healer

God leads the Israelites out of Egypt with a strong hand and an outstretched arm—but if God has no body, what do those terms mean?

Pesach Haggadah, Magid, First Fruits Declaration "And the Lord took us out of Egypt with a strong hand and with an outstretched forearm and with great awe and with signs and with wonders" (Deuteronomy 26:8)...	הגדה של פסח, מגיד, ארמי אבד אבי וַיּוֹצִאֵנוּ ה׳ מִמִּצְרַיִם בְּיָד חֲזָקָה, וּבִזְרֹעַ נְטוּיָה, וּבְמֹרָא גָּדֹל, וּבְאֹתוֹת וּבְמֹפְתִים.
"With a strong hand"—this [refers to] the pestilence, as it is stated (Exodus 9:3); "Behold the hand of the Lord is upon your herds that are in the field, upon the horses, upon the donkeys, upon the camels, upon the cattle and upon the flocks, [there will be] a very heavy pestilence."	בְּיָד חֲזָקָה. זוֹ הַדֶּבֶר, כְּמָה שֶׁנֶּאֱמַר: הִנֵּה יַד־ה׳ הוֹיָה בְּמִקְנְךָ אֲשֶׁר בַּשָּׂדֶה, בַּסּוּסִים, בַּחֲמֹרִים, בַּגְּמַלִּים, בַּבָּקָר וּבַצֹּאן, דֶּבֶר כָּבֵד מְאֹד.
"And with an outstretched forearm"—this [refers to] the sword, as it is stated (I Chronicles 21:16); "And his sword was drawn in his hand, leaning over Jerusalem."	וּבִזְרֹעַ נְטוּיָה. זוֹ הַחֶרֶב, כְּמָה שֶׁנֶּאֱמַר: וְחַרְבּוֹ שְׁלוּפָה בְּיָדוֹ, נְטוּיָה עַל־יְרוּשָׁלָיִם.

I was supposed to be making a condolence call.

The voice on the phone was surprisingly calm, even upbeat, and sounded genuinely glad to hear from me. The words that had formed in my head crumbled and I haltingly improvised on the spot.

"It's Dr. Weinkle. I'm calling . . . to check in . . . about your mother?"

The other sibling who had contacted me a week earlier was clear that Mom was on a ventilator, with severe COVID-19 pneumonia, and that the next day they'd be withdrawing support when the last members of the family arrived at the bedside. Could I please help them get through this awful time?

As often happens, the call I meant to make on Monday to learn the inevitable news and to share my sympathies turned into a to-do item for Tuesday that got moved to my Wednesday list and would *definitely* get done Thursday. My right hand was already about to close my laptop Friday afternoon when I determined that I couldn't put this off any longer.

"Oh, Dr. Weinkle, thanks for calling. She's doing so much better, and off the ventilator. We're actually supposed to be bringing her home tomorrow!"

SIGNS AND WONDERS

"And the Lord took us out of Egypt with a strong hand and with an outstretched forearm and with great awe and with signs and with wonders" (Deuteronomy 26:8). The Seder, and the whole holiday of Passover, commemorates this exact moment. By using this language, it also encapsulates the conceit of modern medicine (the age of medical miracles) that captivates healers and patients alike. For many professionals, these signs and wonders made us want to practice medicine in the first place. For people facing illness, modern medicine gave us hope where previous generations had none, and inspired pilgrimages from the developing world to the West. Patients moved from rural areas to the great cities and their academic medical centers, and from our simpleton family doctors to the shiny clinics of the world expert consultants to seek these wonders

The mother in the vignette above was in her late 80's. About a year before that story, in December 2020, I was conferring with my colleague and neighbor Ariella Reinherz, a pulmonary and critical care doctor who was actively engaged in trying to keep one of my patients alive and off the ventilator at her hospital. "If you're over 60 with COVID," she explained, based on what she and her team were seeing daily at the time, "your mortality rate if you get intubated is roughly equal to your age." The moment I heard that my patients' mother had been intubated, even before the contact where they said they'd be withdrawing support, my mind went to that statistic—perhaps a 10% chance of survival.

But to borrow from a different holiday tradition, a great miracle happened there[1], or several great miracles. When Ariella and I were struggling to save our patient, only a handful of intrepid volunteers for clinical trials and a smattering of healthcare workers and nursing home residents had been vaccinated—yet even this was a miracle, a working vaccine against a disease only *discovered* one year earlier. In February 2022, at the height of the Omicron wave, 95% of elderly Americans had received at least the primary series of COVID vaccinations, and many were boosted with a third dose. The difference in mortality was enormous, in some reports more than a 90% reduction in mortality compared to an unvaccinated person the same age and with the same health status.

Not only had this woman been vaccinated, but she had access to medicines invented to treat a disease that we didn't know existed three

---

1. This phrase refers to the miracles of Hanukkah, both the miracle of the oil and the miracle of defeating the mighty Greek army.

years ago. It was or repurposed from the last apocalyptic disease, Ebola, that thankfully never grew wings the way SARS-CoV-2 did, or was even pulled off the shelf of oldies-but-goodies and given a new chance to show it still had superpowers. Lost in the political arguments where COVID treatment is a matter of party instead of science is the fact that tremendous knowledge of both novel and existing treatments is piling up every day, at an almost unthinkable pace. The previous record for vaccine development was four years, for mumps—but mumps disease had been known for centuries before the virus was finally identified. A great miracle happened here, in our days.

Even the fact that she was on a ventilator to begin with is miraculous. It's a scant 60-odd years since the disciplines of emergency and critical care medicine began to emerge in my hometown of Pittsburgh. A doctor named Peter Safar started codifying the mass chaos of ambulances, well-meaning bystanders, and white-coated hospital staff rushing to the scene of a cardiac arrest into data-driven protocols, algorithms and nationally standardized classes on how to resuscitate, stabilize and sustain someone at death's door long enough for the rest of the system to figure out what happened and reverse it. Today's critical care teams are literally trained to operate like NASCAR pit crews[2] both in speed and communication. The protocols are so fine-tuned that a change like the ratio of chest compressions to rescue breaths requires a full re-write; and the success rates, at least outside the hospital in a witnessed arrest, are astounding.

For a hot minute, it felt like modern medicine had succeeded in finding a way out of Egypt.

STRONG ARMS AND STRONG MEDICINE

The quintessential event of Passover took place in a single night, overturning 210 years of enslavement in a few hours. Modern medicine's attempt to usher humanity out of the narrow place of disease and pestilence has taken centuries and is far from over. Yet the outward trappings are the same—with one notable exception.

In her biography *The Doctors Blackwell*, Janice P. Nimura gives a careful, sober account of the lives of Elizabeth and Emily Blackwell, respectively the first and the third women granted medical degrees by

---

2. When I did this training in residency we watched video of NASCAR races to see how efficiently they changed tires and refueled the cars.

established, theretofore all-male, medical schools in the United States. Part of Elizabeth Blackwell's journey to medicine took her through the "strong hand" of what Nimura and other medical historians term the "heroic era" of medicine. Determined to distinguish between its own remedies and the patent medicines, faith healing and other "quackery" of the time, established medicine in the 1800s often relied on dramatic cures, noxious odors, potent side effects and bringing the patient to the edge of death to create a theater of cure. Failure was excusable as a preordained tragedy, but cure a mark of true medical prowess, a feat of both courage and power.

Elizabeth Blackwell was horrified, though she wisely kept this aversion to herself. In attending to her own medical issues, she eschewed these extravaganzas, opting for rest, cold water, and exercise—until she contracted trachoma during a clinical placement and nearly lost her sight. Then it was the strong hand of a renowned French ophthalmologist that painstakingly restored her vision with the most potent treatment the era had to offer.[3]

The passage of 175 years has not diminished our taste for the extreme in trying to bring people back from the brink of death, dismemberment, or blindness. Cytotoxic chemotherapy, drastic surgeries and resuscitation protocols that leave the hospital room covered in blood, sweat and trash are still mainstays of 21st century medicine. We still prefer the strong hand and pulling out all the stops. These markers of our medical might are the signs and wonders of our profession, the very things that inspire great awe. They're the reason that people once tolerated the misery of a year of treatment with interferon for hepatitis C, willingly endure all their hair falling out on chemotherapy, or submit to having railroad maps of intersecting scars on their abdomens from multiple surgeries for Crohn's disease.

That strong hand is the might of a medical profession that believes it's made death optional. In exchange for that implied promise of eternal life, the profession came to expect a certain amount of awe, which it reinforced through the spectacle of cures and recoveries—a man rolling out of the hospital wearing a smile and harboring a beating piece of plastic in his chest, or a paralyzed football player standing up at a hockey game to an ovation.

---

3. Nimura, The Doctors Blackwell, 104–116.

OUT OF OUTSTRETCHED ARMS?

What has often been missing from medicine, especially in the United States and especially in recent years, is not the strong hand but the outstretched arm. I initially thought of the outstretched arm as proactively reaching out, moving toward those who couldn't benefit from the medical Exodus because there were insurmountable barriers to care. I read those two words in the same vein as the poem, "Where Will I Find You," by Yehudah HaLevi, in which the poet says to God, "And in my going out to meet you, I found you coming toward me."[4]

The Haggadah seems to tell a very different story. "'And with an outstretched forearm'"—this [refers to] the sword," says the Haggadah.[5] Multiple commentators agree that this refers to God's direct involvement in the final five plagues, smiting the Egyptians and in particular effecting the plague of the firstborn. A far cry from the compassionate outreach I envisioned.

Or perhaps it's the same. Just before the Israelites cross the Sea of Reeds, in Exodus 14:14, Moshe tells them, "God will battle for you; you keep silent," after which God commands Moshe to stretch out his arm over the sea to split it.

Susan Sontag, in *Illness as Metaphor*, firmly rejects the militarized language of modern, Western medicine, and particularly the treatment of cancer, on which President Nixon famously declared a "War" in 1971.[6] Following in Sontag's footsteps, healers (and especially those who work in caring for dying patients) have adopted more medically pacifist rhetoric in recent years. But just as pacifists in the political realm often find that they, too, must take up arms; healers who hate using violent metaphors must nevertheless engage in real fights, taking up the sword on behalf of their patients.

THE OUTSTRETCHED ARM THAT HOLDS THE SWORD

I'm not referring to the "strong hand . . . signs and wonders" that we're able to do, the medical magic and miracles I discussed above. The outstretched arm reaches out to those who can't access those miracles, often

---

4. Halevi, "Where Will I Find You."
5. I Chronicles 21:16.
6. Sontag, *Illness as Metaphor*, 64–71.

because something stands in their way. It's up to the outstretched arm of the healing professions to both pull in the person who remains apart, and to sweep away the obstacle.

In 2010, our health center invested in a mobile medical unit, a tricked-out RV equipped with running water, a wheelchair lift, and both a medical triage room and full exam room. The mobile unit goes wherever people need us but have trouble reaching us: Neighborhoods on hilltops and in cul-de-sacs where public transport rarely goes, rehabilitation facilities where the residents have limited freedom of movement to help facilitate their tenuous recovery, and communities where travel outside their immediate neighborhood exposes the residents to peril from immigration authorities. We bring care to health professional shortage areas and to individuals who are isolated on a lonely island in a sea of options they can't navigate. It's an outstretched arm on wheels, in the "coming toward me" sense.

Sometime around 2018, one of our regular sites suddenly became a minefield of excrement. Every Tuesday afternoon, we arrived to find fresh piles of animal droppings placed quite deliberately on the sidewalk next to our usual parking spot. For a couple of weeks, we stepped around it, assuming someone had forgotten to clean up after their dog. But it soon became clear that the piles were too big for any normal dog, and as far as we know no one in that neighborhood was out walking their horse, or their elephant, on a regular basis. There was also a clear intent—the mess was only on that stretch of sidewalk, not across the road or further up or down the road, and it was often in formed shapes that did not come out of any animal of any size looking like that. Someone was collecting these unwanted gifts on purpose and placing them on our sidewalk.

We contacted the municipal police force numerous times. The neighbor whose sidewalk was being defiled, himself a nurse practitioner and a member of that same immigrant community, placed surveillance cameras on the outside of his home to attempt to catch the offender. We even contemplated witty signs to post along the street to shame the individual into stopping. No luck so far. But we kept brandishing our sword until COVID put a stop to our trips.

Our guess is that anti-immigrant sentiment was behind this whole disgusting story. In an America that has become increasingly hostile to newcomers, we've felt increasingly like Shifra and Puah, the Egyptian midwives who refuse to carry out Pharaoh's genocidal order to murder the Hebrew babies on the birthstones. We've helped the so-called "uninsurable" get temporary insurance or affordable costs to access care that averted life-threatening illnesses or disabling pain. We've helped families attend their asylum hearings without having to simultaneously grapple with tending to their severely disabled children in the courtroom for 14 straight hours. And nearly weekly, we battle with a Kafkaesque citizenship office that routinely denies disabled, elderly, and demented members of that community a waiver from the citizenship examination on bureaucratic technicalities or by impugning our integrity as healers.

The battles don't end there, of course. We battle the stigma facing our patients in recovery from addictive disorders. We battle both public and private insurance companies who seem to think that their role is to prevent people from getting too many services instead of helping them afford care for their medical needs. And we battle the fragmentation, inflexibility and arbitrariness of the entire medical system that keeps our patients from accessing their own records, getting timely appointments and care, or keeping us in the loop of communication that would enable us to take proper care of them.

Often, we battle for the people whom all those signs and wonders have yet to bring out of Mitzrayim. People for whom no "real" diagnosis can be found, who don't "meet criteria" for the disease we believe they have, or who don't experience the "expected benefit" from the medications they receive. We battle for people who have the one-in-a-million side effect that "couldn't possibly" be from the medicine they're attributing it to, and for people whose excessive bleeding, numbness, disorientation, or other serious symptom has been dismissed as "that happens sometimes."

Occasionally, the battle is for those who've left Egypt—only to find themselves, like the Israelites, in an endless desert with a long way to go before they get home. These are the folks who survive one cancer to find that their treatment has caused another—a phenomenon so common in survivors of childhood cancer that many pediatric cancer centers have survivorship clinics dedicated to monitoring for those second cancers. Others grapple with loss of jobs, family, or identity that didn't survive their illness, even though their bodies survived. Sometimes when the scans are clear, the real work is just beginning.

FIGHTING FOR THE "FIGHTER JET"

Sometime in late summer of 2021 I lost my cool during a protracted attempt to get a simple wheelchair for a patient who could no longer appropriately use their walker without falling. It was rejected numerous times despite having a sympathetic person on the inside at the medical supply company who was spoon-feeding me language to add to my notes so they'd pass muster. The actual clinical need for the chair was never in doubt—it was all about getting the paperwork right. Finally, on the phone with my incredibly calm, gentle care navigator, I yelled, "It's not like I'm trying to justify getting this person a fighter jet!!!" A couple weeks later, having cooled down considerably, I was enjoying running a few late afternoon errands in the neighborhood when I received a text. "P.S. The fighter jet has landed at the patient's home! I thought you would be happy to know."

It's easy for healers in our time to feel like we're fighting these fights alone; that the system is content to let those who can't get themselves in the door remain shut out. It's helpful at times like these to pay close attention to the fact that, if we choose to stretch out our arms, and take up arms in defense of those who need it, that we're *not* alone. There are those who are our colleagues, and those who seem like part of the problem until we speak to them directly and make them our allies. I would text and email with that sympathetic ally at the DME supplier regularly; we would prop each other up when frustrated and provide each other insight that allowed us to do our jobs better and be of more help to the people we care for.

The final element of God's redemption of the Israelites in this passage is *mora gadol*, great awe. No one will be surprised to hear that the strong hand, the signs, and the wonders generate awe. But that awe is for technology, for the superpowers we suddenly possess after thousands of years of medicine being mere window-dressing for nature taking its course. Our outstretched arms, our willingness to advocate and strive on behalf of the people we care for, deserves a different kind of awe. That kind that has been lost in the past sixty years of corporatization and technologization of medicine—awe for the profession and for the healer as exceptional, and worthy of praise for their humanity and love of others.

The Haggadah says that "God brought us out of Egypt," means God *personally*, "not through an angel and not through a seraph and not through a messenger," promises to redeem the Israelites. I spend a lot of time figuring out what tasks of care I can delegate to others on my team (like landing fighter jets), but the *responsibility* can't be delegated, even if the individual task might be done by another person. When I train students, I ask them to "take ownership" of the patients they see: To "own" their responsibility for what happens, not treat the visit as an isolated learning experience where the relationship ends when they leave the exam room. Even though their roles in our health center only last four or five weeks, during that time they're the point person for tracking down test results, looking up treatment options, and making phone calls to reassure and educate. Whether we're stretching out an arm in outreach or in advocacy, "we and not an angel" must be invested in that stretching out. It's an integral part of keeping the promises we've been discussing to this point.

As we extend those arms to individuals yearning to leave their own narrow places, may we be deserving of such awe. At the same time, medical practitioners should learn to feel awe themselves. The word *mora*, awe, is a form of *yir'ah*, which really falls somewhere between awe and fear. We've talked extensively about the dangers of the medical heroics we employ. Both patients and their caregivers should remember not to be so cavalier about those "strong hands," because they can be as deadly as the diseases they treat. We need to hold them in fearful awe even as we're in worshipful awe of their miraculous achievements.

And finally, the "Israelites" themselves, those experiencing the illness, deserve awe. Never forget that a nurse in the hospital is with the patient perhaps half an hour to an hour out of a 24-hour day. A doctor may see a patient once a week, once a month, or more likely once or twice a year. The patient is with themselves continually, living with the illness and its consequences without a break. The fact that they find the strength to keep coming back, to keep living their lives, to keep crying out for help even when previous cries go ignored, displays a resilience that merits awe—from their healers, from their families, and from the person themselves. Few people realize their own strength, their own heroism; they ought to hold themselves in much higher regard. This "great awe" is every bit as important to a person getting out of their narrow place as the wonder drug or the activist physician.

Thoughts and Discussions

- What healing miracles have you been privileged to experience? Who did them and who received them? Were they "miracles of modern medicine" or something that defied medical explanation?
- Describe an "outstretched arm" moment you've been a part of.
- Who do you know that's deserving of "great awe?"
- When do you "take ownership," and why?

23

A Missing Midrash

The last line of the story is left out of most Haggadot—what can that teach us?

Deuteronomy 26:9	דברים כ״ו:ט׳
(9) bringing us to this place and giving us this land, a land flowing with milk and honey.	(ט) וַיְבִאֵנוּ אֶל־הַמָּקוֹם הַזֶּה וַיִּתֶּן־לָנוּ אֶת־הָאָרֶץ הַזֹּאת אֶרֶץ זָבַת חָלָב וּדְבָשׁ:

The declaration of first fruits in the Torah, Deuteronomy 26:5–9, concludes with the verse, "bringing us to this place and giving us this land, a land flowing with milk and honey." Yet the Haggadah contains no midrash, no homiletical explanation, on these lines. The interpretation of the declaration ends with the previous verse, the one that discusses the redemption of the Israelites from Egypt "by a mighty hand, by an outstretched arm and awesome power, and by signs and portents," and then proceeds directly to the ritual of recounting the ten plagues.

Most versions of the Haggadah don't even include Deuteronomy 26:9 at all. The only thing that prompted me to look for it was the fact that our family's regular Haggadah, Noam and Mishael Zion's *A Night to Remember*, does include that verse. They print the entire declaration *before* launching into the line-by-line analysis, an inclusion the rest of the Haggadot on my shelf don't bother with. Zion's intent is that some families may choose to read the passage in its entirety, as if they're arriving at the Temple with first fruits in hand, and then discuss what this passage means to them, in total and in pieces, without relying on the embedded midrash of the traditional Haggadah text.

My mentor Bob Arnold, one of the leading figures in palliative medicine, never failed to return to a few signature lines when speaking with families, or teaching students, about their decisions regarding a life-limiting illness. Invariably, someone would ask, "Dr. Arnold, is there any hope?" His signature answer to that question was, "Hope for what?"

Too often, as we strive to free someone from their narrow space–the destination, the goal for which they wish to be freed, never comes up. It ought to be the first question: "What are you hoping to achieve by asking for my help today? What do you want me to do?" Sure, we say, "what can I do for you?" but what we mean is, "tell me the problem." What they hope to achieve usually gets short shrift. I think we assume that everyone knows what "better" looks like, but as Bob points out specifically at end of life: Hope may be the thing with feathers, but not everyone agrees on what color feathers they're hoping for. One family member hopes for a peaceful end without suffering, another for a miracle cure, and a third for just a few more days so Uncle Barney can get in from Cleveland.

In the long game of primary care, it's no less important to make sure we all agree on the object of that long game. Over my dozen-plus years in practice, I've cared for many people who've opted to treat their obesity, and the secondary diseases that accompany it, by having some form of gastric bypass surgery. Here, too, Bob's question, "hope for what?" is appropriate. It may seem obvious that the answer would be, "to lose weight," but when a person undergoes a surgery that fundamentally changes the way their body works, those three words aren't enough. Some hope to never need insulin again, others to stop blood pressure medication, and others to feel beautiful again. But the surgery may not deliver those specific medical outcomes, even if a person cuts their insulin requirements by 90% or reduces from three blood pressure medications to one. A surgery can't change internalized feelings of being unsightly—or prepare a person for the visual shock of sudden weight loss that doesn't have the same effect as photoshopping off the unwanted curves but looks rather like rapidly melting a person like a burnt candle.

The shock and betrayal of finding oneself unable to swallow, or becoming dizzy and fainting every time one eats anything with sugar, or of suddenly developing a life-threatening bowel obstruction five years out from the initial surgery, is a consequence of not having that initial discussion of, "where are we going with this, and what will the journey be like?"

I often find myself caring for patients who seek care with me after feeling something has gone horribly awry elsewhere, hoping to puzzle out with me what that was. Many times, what went wrong was failing to clarify what "success" would mean before starting the process.

The missing discussion of Deuteronomy 26:9 is a powerful reminder of this problem in medicine of being so exquisitely powerful to do things, yet so bad at communicating what we're doing and why—and may also be an important clue on to how to address that problem.

The seder as we know it coalesced after the Second Temple had already been destroyed, the Pesach sacrifice could no longer be offered, and much of the Jewish people had been exiled from the land of Israel. Today we might call it ethnic cleansing, or erasure, with the Romans plowing salt into the fields to make agriculture nearly impossible, and renaming key Judaean cities with Latin, pagan names. Some of the seder texts are from Torah, but their arrangement into an order (a seder) is codified first in the Mishna, tractate Pesachim, completed sometime in the second century CE perhaps a hundred years after the Temple lay ruined and smoking. The Haggadah as a whole probably dates to 280–360 CE, two to three hundred years after the Romans laid waste to Jerusalem. Given the "present tense" language of the final line of the declaration, which is intended to be spoken in the Temple, I can understand the desire not to speak in present tense about a Temple that no longer exists—one which was still smoldering in the living memories of some of the rabbis who set down the Mishnaic text.

Exile was a strange sort of limbo—not slavery, so one could still celebrate the Exodus, but also not the promised land, so one had to celebrate an incomplete, ongoing redemption. Increasingly, people couched it in Messianic terms. "Someday" the redemption would be complete, and the final verse would be fulfilled in past tense just as the other four were.

This limbo is familiar to many who are chronically ill, especially those who have passed some sort of life-threatening experience to now find themselves living in its aftermath. They're alive and yet diminished in some way. This is the experience of cancer survivors who may spend the rest of their lives under surveillance, searching for the sign that perhaps they were not cured after all, or of people living with chronic auto-immune disease who spend their good days marking the time in between flares—catching up on everything that fell apart during the last hospitalization or bedridden episode.

It's hard to talk of a promised land in these situations when even a cure feels like no more than a temporary reprieve. "Someday" is too long a time, a promise delayed so long that it's meaningless. One recurring theme in the seder is an argument over four vs. five—like whether this passage should include four lines or all five. One of the other four vs. five debates is how many things God has promised the Israelites, with each promise corresponding to a glass of wine in the seder. The fifth promise is this one—the promise of a Promised Land, the one still unfulfilled. How long, say millions who continue to suffer with chronic pain, debility, or emotional illness, must we wait for You to keep this promise?

The years in the wilderness were years of thirst, warfare, calamitous turns into idolatry, crises of faith, rebellion against leadership, and ultimately the death of an entire generation. The disillusionment begins almost immediately, as soon as the waters of the Sea of Reeds have closed behind the Israelites, drowning the Egyptians, and they realize the truth of a verse that had yet to be written: "Water, water everywhere, but nary a drop to drink."

A person goes under anesthesia; the surgeon is finally going to set things right once and for all. Three hours later she emerges smiling from the OR, wiping her hands, and proclaiming success; the patient will be in the ICU in a little while so we can watch him until he wakes up. A day later he's died, of a complication that's known to happen 5% of the time but was pushed from the list of possible outcomes by that beaming surgeon in the family waiting room saying, "We made it."

After my oldest son's scoliosis surgery, he had the recovery nurses beside themselves with laughter, quoting *Borat* with a near perfect accent as he, too, proclaimed, "Great success, great success." In his room his camp friends called and kept him on the phone for an hour because he was the best entertainment they'd heard in weeks, still loopy from anesthesia. In surgical recovery, it's all fun and games until you realize you can't move your left leg. Only two more surgeries, several extra weeks of recovery, a blood transfusion and a custom-made polymer exoskeleton eventually got us to the promised land of a less crooked, but still incredibly twisted (at least where his sense of humor is concerned), teenager who could walk on his own and feel all ten of his toes.

The march of Exodus begins with an acknowledgement that we don't always follow the straightest, quickest path toward redemption. "God did not lead them by way of the land of the Philistines, although it was nearer (Exodus 13:17)." What's missing from that verse are the words, "And God said to Moshe, 'I will not lead them,'" or "and Moshe spoke to the people, saying, 'God will not lead you. . .'" The people were not aware of going the long way around—they found out as it was happening. Each obstacle they encountered felt like a journey gone horribly wrong.

Why is there so much unexpected suffering in 21st century medical care, though? Are we not living in the age of informed consent, where all the potential pitfalls are spelled out beforehand? Don't people have a legally-enshrined right to see their medical records whenever they want—often to the degree that they get uninterpreted test results immediately, even before the doctor that ordered them has a chance to figure out what they mean? How could anyone be taken by surprise?

Maybe because 21st century medical *practitioners* are expected to do ever more, everything possible, in the same amount of time. We've all seen direct-to-consumer advertisements for medications—and heard how fast the announcer talks when reaching the list of side effects. There are just so many to read in a 60 second commercial that no one can possibly slow down the conversation long enough to absorb them all. In the clinic, we all tend to revert to just "hitting the highlights" listing not every complication but the most common ones, and usually editorializing just how worried, or unworried, we're about them.

But under stress, no amount of time will be enough to allow patients to really internalize the information being dumped on them. Few clinicians really use effective teach-back techniques to gauge understanding; their goal is to deliver the information, and it's the patient's job to receive it. Or not. Think of it as the Amazon of health education—we make sure the package of knowledge arrives and notify you that it's there; it's up to you to worry about bad weather and porch pirates.

The cognitive bias of hope is strong, regardless of what color feathers it has. A colleague at the University of Pittsburgh Medical Center, Douglas White, demonstrated with his fellow researchers several years ago that even when we're explicit with patients or their families about a person's exact chances of survival or "success" in each situation, there's a wide range of how that information is interpreted. Patients often err in the direction of assuming a better chance of success than the data warrants.[1] As Dr. White explained it to me at that time, they've their own stories to tell that mean more to them than numbers: Dad is strong; Mom always ate right and exercised; Grandma went to church every week and now we're all praying for her; Aunt Minnie is a fighter. In every case

---

1. Lee Char, Evans, Malvar, and White. "A Randomized Trial of Two Methods to Disclose Prognosis to Surrogate Decision Makers in Intensive Care Units."

there's a belief that the data doesn't apply because the person in front of us has found the "secret sauce" to beating the odds.

Professionals are not immune to this bias. A procedure we believe in, or a medication we routinely use to good effect, seems benign and benevolent to us. We'll soft-pedal side effects or even explicitly dismiss them ("Theoretically . . . but I've never seen that happen."). Often this takes the form of ignoring, steamrolling over or otherwise belittling a person's concerns or questions, which we may take as antagonistic, insulting to our skills or just downright foolish. Speaking as a dyed-in-the-wool advocate for vaccination in general and for COVID-19 vaccination specifically, I can attest that this is the typical way that people like me handle conversations with vaccine skeptics.

Following a procedure, a dose of medication or an immunization, the opposite bias sets in. Negativity bias attunes people much more to the suffering than to the benefits, especially if the former hits as soon as they wake up and the latter are still weeks down the road. Once that starts, any negative feeling will tend to be piled onto whatever was actively done to the patient. Compounding negativity bias is recency bias; even if things went well overall, if the final phase of the surgery, the illness, or the recovery from the vaccine was bad, that negative memory will be much more vibrant than the relative ease of earlier phases. Again, speaking as a vaccine advocate, this mindset tends to be how vaccine skeptics operate—especially since the cases of disease that didn't happen, the people that didn't die, aren't something you can easily see.

All these biases played out in the wilderness. The hopeful enthusiasm of the night of the Exodus is quickly wiped away by fear of the Egyptian army. The relief of crossing the sea evaporates with the realization there's nothing to drink.

My teacher Erica Brown, in her book *Leadership in the Wilderness*, references the leadership model of technical challenges vs. adaptive challenges to address these issues. Moshe's leadership begins to falter when the challenges of leading the people become less about technical issues—where to find water—and more about adaptive ones—how to behave like free people instead of enslaved people.[2] I would argue that many healing professionals, especially MDs/DOs, advance practice providers, pharmacists, and bedside RNs, are often very adept at technical leadership but struggle with adaptive leadership. We can fix things that are broken, but

---

2. Brown, *Leadership in the Wilderness*.

we're not very good at frame shifting, interpretation or regrouping after disappointment. Our therapeutically oriented colleagues in the behavioral health world and the rehabilitative world excel at these latter challenges—but are rarely put in the driver's seat to help a person direct their care.

One of the errors in leadership Brown points out in her book is a failure to understand the depths of what's bothering the people; Moshe is likewise frequently brusque and dismissive. His attitude toward much of the complaining is "at-leastism," as I would call it in practice. You can readily imagine what I mean: "At least you're not mixing bricks for pyramids anymore!" A person can "at-least" themselves all they want; it's a primary adaptive skill and one of the building blocks of resistance (even if you must mix the mortar for it yourself). The trap is when an authority figure, like a healer or a teacher or a politician, tries to at-least someone else. Many have argued, among them Rabbi Jonathan Sacks in his final book, *Morality*, that right-wing populism in the 21st century grows directly out of a failure to address the real pain felt by deeply rooted working classes outside the urban centers, who are being bypassed by the growth and change taking place in those centers.[3] I'd have to imagine that no one came to them ahead of time and said, "Hey, what should progress look like?"

We repeat the same mistake with the people we care for at our own peril, and theirs. Not only do they suffer terribly when the "promised land" looks nothing like what they expected, but our relationship with them is damaged, maybe irreparably, for having led them astray. We can't afford to miss this midrash.

One of the many goals of the seder is to make meaning out of the text, and by extension out of our lives—which in the history of the ritual were often lived under threat, in pain, or at loose ends—not knowing what came next. While there are myriad tools for making meaning in a medical context, the gold standard for many is Arthur Kleinmann's "Illness Narrative" model. Central to this model are the eight "Kleinmann Questions." Fittingly, the last of these is, "What are the most important results you hope to receive from the treatment?" In other words, "What does your promised land look like?"

Thoughts and Discussions

- *What gets left out of our conversations about illness and wellness that needs to be there? How would talking about it change things?*

3. Sacks, Morality, 125.

24

Blood in the Water

After finishing the exploration of the story in the First Fruits Declaration, we recount the ten plagues and spill out some of our wine in empathy for the suffering of the Egyptians.

Pesach Haggadah, Magid, The Ten Plagues	הגדה של פסח, מגיד, עשר המכות
And when he says . . . the ten plagues . . . he should pour out a little wine from his cup.	כשאומר . . . עשר המכות . . . ישפוך מן הכוס מעט יין:
These are [the] ten plagues that the Holy One, blessed be He, brought on the Egyptians in Egypt and they are:	אֵלּוּ עֶשֶׂר מַכּוֹת שֶׁהֵבִיא הַקָּדוֹשׁ בָּרוּךְ הוּא עַל־הַמִּצְרִים בְּמִצְרַיִם, וְאֵלּוּ הֵן:
——-	——
Blood	דָּם
Frogs	צְפַרְדֵּעַ
Lice	כִּנִּים
[The] Mixture [of Wild Animals]	עָרוֹב
Pestilence	דֶּבֶר
Boils	שְׁחִין
Hail	בָּרָד
Locusts	אַרְבֶּה
Darkness	חֹשֶׁךְ
Slaying of [the] Firstborn	מַכַּת בְּכוֹרוֹת

...Rabbi Yose Hagelili says, "From where can you [derive] that the Egyptians were struck with ten plagues in Egypt and struck with fifty plagues at the Sea? ... You can say from here that in Egypt, they were struck with ten plagues and at the Sea, they were struck with fifty plagues." Rabbi Eliezer says, "From where [can you derive] that every plague that the Holy One, blessed be He, brought upon the Egyptians in Egypt was [composed] of four plagues? ... You can say from here that in Egypt, they were struck with forty plagues and at the Sea, they were struck with two hundred plagues." Rabbi Akiva says, says, "From where [can you derive] that every plague that the Holy One, blessed be He, brought upon the Egyptians in Egypt was [composed] of five plagues? ... You can say from here that in Egypt, they were struck with fifty plagues and at the Sea, they were struck with two hundred and fifty plagues."	...מִנַּיִן אַתָּה אוֹמֵר שֶׁלָּקוּ הַמִּצְרִים בְּמִצְרַיִם עֶשֶׂר מַכּוֹת וְעַל הַיָּם לָקוּ חֲמִשִּׁים מַכּוֹת? ...אֱמוֹר מֵעַתָּה: בְּמִצְרַיִם לָקוּ עֶשֶׂר מַכּוֹת וְעַל הַיָּם לָקוּ חֲמִשִּׁים מַכּוֹת. רַבִּי אֱלִיעֶזֶר אוֹמֵר: מִנַּיִן שֶׁכָּל־מַכָּה וּמַכָּה שֶׁהֵבִיא הַקָּדוֹשׁ בָּרוּךְ הוּא עַל הַמִּצְרִים בְּמִצְרַיִם הָיְתָה שֶׁל אַרְבַּע מַכּוֹת? ...אֱמוֹר מֵעַתָּה: בְּמִצְרַיִם לָקוּ אַרְבָּעִים מַכּוֹת וְעַל הַיָּם לָקוּ מָאתַיִם מַכּוֹת. רַבִּי עֲקִיבָא אוֹמֵר: מִנַּיִן שֶׁכָּל־מַכָּה וּמַכָּה שֶׁהֵבִיא הַקָּדוֹשׁ בָּרוּךְ הוּא עַל הַמִּצְרִים בְּמִצְרַיִם הָיְתָה שֶׁל חָמֵשׁ מַכּוֹת? ...אֱמוֹר מֵעַתָּה: בְּמִצְרַיִם לָקוּ חֲמִשִּׁים מַכּוֹת וְעַל הַיָּם לָקוּ חֲמִשִּׁים וּמָאתַיִם מַכּוֹת.

IT DOESN'T GO TO ELEVEN

Early in the COVID-19 pandemic, we said and did a lot of things that made little sense. Recommendations changed almost daily. We gravely took specific precautions that turned out to be useless, like hanging plexiglass shields and buying stores out of toilet paper. And we talked a lot about "silver linings," like how glad we were to take a break from working in offices or wearing dress clothes. Two years in, the recommendations were still changing faster than we could keep up with, precautions we thought we finally had figured out turned out (again) to be minimally effective, and the only silver lining I saw was in my hair.

According to Rabbi Schiff, one of the nonsensical things a lot of involved Jews did then was to compare the COVID-19 pandemic to one of the plagues visited upon Egypt. In a Facebook post dated April 1, 2020,[1] (but not intended as a joke) Rabbi Schiff implored his audience not to compare our present situation to the "Eleventh Plague" or to mention it

---

1. Schiff, https://www.facebook.com/dschiff.o/posts/10220070274441156

at seder. "This is the wrong parallel," he wrote. "Let's remember: The Ten Plagues were delivered by God deliberately as a punishment for Pharoah's obstinacy. Does anybody seriously believe that God deliberately delivered this current pandemic as a punishment? I don't. No thoughtful Jewish theology would support such an idea."

He went on to suggest that the better comparison would be to the plague that killed 24,000 of Rabbi Akiva's students, which the rabbis in tractate Yevamot[2] compared to diphtheria. It was a natural, infectious plague that caused loss and calamity which we still mourn in our own time during the period of the Omer.

Unfortunately, the parallel to the plague in Rabbi Akiva's time runs deeper than the analogy between diphtheria and COVID-19. In April 2020 we were only beginning to see the rifts that opened in our society, and indeed in most countries, around every aspect of the pandemic: Masks, lockdowns, vaccinations, treatments, and even whether the virus itself exists at all. These rifts mirror fundamental, cultural-political rifts that predate the pandemic and that appear, unfortunately, to be about the only thing that's wholly immune to COVID-19.

Yevamot explains the plague as follows: "They said by way of example that Rabbi Akiva had twelve thousand pairs of students in an area of land that stretched from Gevat to Antipatris in Judea, and they all died in one period of time, because they did not treat each other with respect." In other words, the plague was the result of baseless hatred between individuals.

SARS-CoV-2 is not a Divine punishment for baseless hatred.

But we know that the virus was not the only plague circulating during the pandemic it caused. I'm a seder fanatic, savoring each bit of the text over the objections of certain (okay, most) members of my family, but one thing I could reliably point to that I was skipping over was the section in which the rabbis play with words and numbers to argue that there were not just ten plagues, but fifty, or perhaps two hundred, or even two hundred fifty. I didn't see the point or the relevance of this little arithmetical exercise—until, twenty-one months into the pandemic, we came to reading the plagues in the cycle of Torah readings, and I understood that it wasn't the specific numbers that mattered, but the multiplication of maladies.

Secondary pandemics, and pre-existing ones, have been running in parallel to the coronavirus pandemic. Drug overdoses and addiction;

2. Talmud Yevamot 62b:9

Loneliness and other serious mental health crises; disruptions in our educational system, our judicial system, and other parts of our healthcare system; racial, gender, and economic inequality exacerbated by both the disease burden of the virus and its societal impacts. Woven through all of these is the plague of political tribalism, which in most cases stakes a person to a fixed position on each of these other pandemics, a position from which they're prone to view anyone who disagrees with them as not only wrong, but evil. And regarding these plagues, we're not blameless.

These plagues invite a new, different comparison to the plagues of Egypt. I'm not speaking of the theology of God punishing the Egyptian enslavers, but the symbolism of what happened to Egyptian society during the plagues, and how similar it's to what ails us now.

The plagues struck Egypt in the ways that hurt Egyptian society most, attacking the god-figures and the sustaining forces in Egyptian life—the animals, the crops, the Nile, and ultimately the first-born children including Pharaoh's own son, the incumbent godhead of all Egypt. They turned Egyptian society upside down, in one case literally turning day to night. And here, in pandemic-era America, our gregarious society known for its abundance, its never-ending activity, and its show-must-go-on spectacles became a place of empty streets, scarcity, cancellations and staffing shortages. We barely recognized ourselves.

The river, water, the sustaining force of all life, in Egypt and everywhere on the planet, turned to blood. This was not water you could drink: "The fish in the Nile died. The Nile stank so that the Egyptians could not drink water from the Nile; and there was blood throughout the land of Egypt."[3] In modern English, when we say there's "blood in the water," we mean it as a metaphor for "the sharks are circling." A fitting description of our time. It doesn't matter which side of the political divide you fall on; there are sharks circling, both ones that are angling to eat you, and ones you're hoping will eat the people you hate.

Nearing the two-year mark of the pandemic, I began to feel like the Burning Bush, perpetually on fire, and wondered how much longer I could burn, and push through pandemic life, before finally being charred beyond recognition. I needed water to drink to refresh me, to keep me from being consumed.

Like everyone else in America, I fell into the pattern of believing that water with blood in it was just fine to drink, that righteous, or

---

3. Exodus 7:21

self-righteous, anger, snark, vitriol, and acid wit was going to buoy me up. I bought into the fiction that not only was the pandemic a punishment, but it was a punishment that someone else deserved, that someone else was causing. I got angry—very angry—at people who wouldn't mask, wouldn't stay home despite Samuel L. Jackson reading them a vulgar bedtime story that instructed them to do so, wouldn't get vaccinated, or insisted on telling me that I didn't know anything about medicine. It made things worse.

Drinking this "bloody water" turns everything upside down. The hatred is so thorough that people turn themselves inside out in their criticism of the other side, espousing viewpoints they can't possibly agree with. People who once called the end-of-life provisions in the Affordable Care Act "death panels" and protested to keep Terry Schiavo on life support rallied behind a lieutenant governor who suggested it would be okay to sacrifice some grandparents' lives to get the economy going again. People who steadfastly serve in the US military, support our troops, and welcome strict security measures at our borders, in the airports, and on our city streets to guard against terrorism and crime cry that the government is infringing on their freedom when it asks individuals to wear masks, get vaccinated, or limit activity to protect thousands of vulnerable lives. People who support reducing government regulation on just about everything because "regulation stifles innovation and slows down progress" wouldn't use highly effective, efficiently developed vaccines. They felt vaccines were developed too fast without enough oversight and they don't trust what's in them—the same argument their opponents have made for years about chemicals that leach into the environment due to lack of regulation of their development or use. People who deny the existence of systemic racism and keep Confederate memorabilia are suddenly very concerned about the Tuskegee experiment and its relevance to vaccines.

On the other side of the political divide, people who marched in the streets to remove the stigma and victim-blaming around HIV, drug addiction and mental illness broadcast their schadenfreude whenever someone prominent contracts COVID after mocking the disease, publicly refusing vaccination, or touting disproven treatments. People who support universal, single-payor healthcare call on social media for hospitals to refuse care to unvaccinated individuals with COVID-19. People who support equity in education and are sensitive to issues of racial and economic inequalities in school resources support sudden, prolonged closure of schools and a move to digital platforms while most disadvantaged students had no reliable way to access those platforms.

On every side, people advocate for actions they normally despise, use language they'd normally despise, champion ideas they normally ridicule and undermine ideals they normally cherish for the sake of winning this debate, as if it can be won. The water gets bloodier, and the whole thing stinks like dead fish.

I've engaged in more than my share of this behavior myself, despite knowing better and even trying to write myself a different script[4] in the blog posts I put up during 2021 and 2022. It keeps happening, a plague no less contagious, no less persistent, than the pandemic virus itself. Worse, it keeps mutating; every new issue becomes a new battleground, every point of policy a new cause for fighting.

So no, the SARS-CoV-2 virus is not a Divine weapon of retribution. But the other societal illnesses swirling around it are undoubtedly due to our inability to treat each other with respect, and we're trapped in a darkness where a person can't recognize their fellow from mere inches away. There's most certainly blood in the water.

More telling still is the fact that the plague of the bloody Nile is never officially declared over. Moshe doesn't plunge his staff back into the blood and turn it back to water, nor does the text clearly state that it reverted on its own. We learn only that after seven days of the first plague, the plague of frogs begins. The river can sustain life again—but the kind of life that usually lives in a foul swamp. Pittsburgh's polluted rivers sustain life—but they're the type of mutant, heavy-metal-laden carp that don't belong on the dinner table. The hateful speech will not go away on its own, nor can it be forcibly contained. Only a slow, steady trickle of clean, fresh water, a stream of goodwill and compassion, brought forth from the ground by a sustained effort, can dilute away that blood and filth.

Tradition holds that the groundwater in Egypt was spared the plague of blood. In Exodus 7:24 we learn that "all the Egyptians had to dig round about the Nile for drinking water, because they could not drink the water of the Nile." Remember that feeling of being like the Burning Bush? Exodus 3:2, the verse that tells us about how the bush "was not consumed," is translated to Aramaic in Targum Yonatan to mean "remained moist." How does a bush growing in the desert stay hydrated? By tapping into the groundwater, deep underneath the bush, the only uncontaminated water left.

---

4. See a 2021 post on my Healers Who Listen blog, "Golden Guilt." https://healerswholisten.com/golden-guilt/

Brian Miller[5] describes the burning bush well when he contrasts people who burn out with people he describes as "on fire": The ones who seem to be lit up by the excitement of doing their healing work.[6] As we discussed earlier, he feels that the people in that second category are "leaning in," embracing instead of fleeing the emotionally challenging part of their work. The trick to surviving and thriving, whether as a healer in times of pandemic or a person whose troubles never seem to remit is to "lean in," or perhaps "dig deep" to find that source of clean water. This is the fuel that will keep you "moist" instead burning you up. The next sections of the seder are designed to help us dig.

Thoughts and Discussions

- *What other modern "plagues" do the ten listed in the Haggadah conjure up for you?*
- *When you think about these plagues, do you think of them as outside forces that are affecting you, punishments for societal ills, or things that you're doing that harm others?*
- *How, if at all, does an individual person's illness fit into this understanding?*

---

5. See Chapter 20, the section entitled "Leave the Light On."
6. Miller, Reducing Secondary Traumatic Stress, 5.

25

The Danger of *Dayenu*

After recounting the plagues, the seder participants sing the song Dayenu, "It would have been enough for us."

Dayenu	דיינו
How many degrees of good did the Place [of all bestow] upon us!	כַּמָה מַעֲלוֹת טוֹבוֹת לַמָקוֹם עָלֵינוּ!
If God had taken us out of Egypt and not made judgements on them; [it would have been] enough for us. . .	אִלּוּ הוֹצִיאָנוּ מִמִצְרַיִם וְלֹא עָשָׂה בָהֶם שְׁפָטִים, דַּיֵּנוּ.
If He had given us their money and had not split the Sea for us; [it would have been] enough for us.	אִלּוּ נָתַן לָנוּ אֶת־מָמוֹנָם וְלֹא קָרַע לָנוּ אֶת־הַיָּם, דַּיֵּנוּ.
If He had split the Sea for us and had not taken us through it on dry land; [it would have been] enough for us. . .	אִלּוּ הִכְנִיסָנוּ לְאֶרֶץ יִשְׂרָאֵל וְלֹא בָנָה לָנוּ, אֶת־בֵּית הַבְּחִירָה דַּיֵּנוּ.
If He had brought us into the land of Israel and had not built us the 'Chosen House' [the Temple; it would have been] enough for us.	

| How much more so is the good that is doubled and quadrupled that the Place [of all bestowed] upon us [enough for us]; since he took us out of Egypt, and made judgments with them, and made [them] with their gods, and killed their firstborn, and gave us their money, and split the Sea for us, and brought us through it on dry land, and pushed down our enemies in [the Sea], and supplied our needs in the wilderness for forty years, and fed us the manna, and gave us the Shabbat, and brought us close to Mount Sinai, and gave us the Torah, and brought us into the land of Israel and built us the 'Chosen House' [the Temple] to atone upon all of our sins. | עַל אַחַת, כַּמָּה וְכַמָּה, טוֹבָה כְפוּלָה וּמְכֻפֶּלֶת לַמָּקוֹם עָלֵינוּ: שֶׁהוֹצִיאָנוּ מִמִּצְרַיִם, וְעָשָׂה בָהֶם שְׁפָטִים, וְעָשָׂה בֵאלֹהֵיהֶם, וְהָרַג אֶת־בְּכוֹרֵיהֶם, וְנָתַן לָנוּ אֶת־מָמוֹנָם, וְקָרַע לָנוּ אֶת־הַיָּם, וְהֶעֱבִירָנוּ בְּתוֹכוֹ בֶּחָרָבָה, וְשִׁקַּע צָרֵנוּ בְּתוֹכוֹ, וְסִפֵּק צָרְכֵּנוּ בַּמִּדְבָּר אַרְבָּעִים שָׁנָה, וְהֶאֱכִילָנוּ אֶת־הַמָּן, וְנָתַן לָנוּ אֶת־הַשַּׁבָּת, וְקֵרְבָנוּ לִפְנֵי הַר סִינַי, וְנָתַן לָנוּ אֶת־הַתּוֹרָה, וְהִכְנִיסָנוּ לְאֶרֶץ יִשְׂרָאֵל, וּבָנָה לָנוּ אֶת־בֵּית הַבְּחִירָה לְכַפֵּר עַל־כָּל־עֲוֹנוֹתֵינוּ. |

PLATITUDES OF GRATITUDE

If you know one song from the Seder, chances are it's *Dayenu*. And if you know it like most American Jews, you know maybe three of the fifteen lines of the whole litany that's *Dayenu* in the Haggadah. Maybe just one:

> *Ilu hotzi- hotzianu, hotzianu mi-Mitzrayim*
> *Hotziyanu mi-Mitzrayim, Dayenu*
> *Day-Dayenu, Day-Dayenu, Day-Dayenu, Dayenu Dayenu!*
> "If God brought us out of Egypt
> It would have been enough for us!"

Chances are, if you've ever heard the word "*Dayenu*" uttered in conversation *outside* of seder, it wasn't an expression of gratitude. It was probably being used to mean, "Enough already! We can't take anymore!"

I'll give you an example:

From the time I started this project to the time it went to the publisher, we endured the pandemic, the massive reckoning around racial justice, the brutal election of 2020 and the aftermath that ended in an insurrection, the worst inflation in forty years, a major mental health crisis, a war in Ukraine, a devastating attack on Israel and an equally devastating war that followed, *another* brutal election, and even a (mercifully brief) cyber-catastrophe. Dayenu!

Uttered that way, the word calls to mind Carol Channing's appearance on *Free to Be You and Me*, where she speaks the famous line, "Some kinds of help are the kind of help that we all can do without." Or if you prefer, *Wall Street Journal* columnist Jason Reilly's book title *Please Stop Helping Us*. With that context, it's hard to get my head around *Dayenu* at seder every year, accustomed as I am to hear it as a term of exasperation.

Dayenu lists the fifteen "steps" of the redemption, meant to correspond to fifteen actual stairs leading from the women's courtyard of the Temple to the Israelite courtyard, or the fifteen psalms (120–134) that begin "A Song of Ascents." The message of the song is that each of the fifteen miracles that God wrought for the Israelites, beginning with taking them out of Egypt and ending with the building of the Temple with its fifteen steps, would have been enough to earn our gratitude on its own.

NO DAYENU IN THE DESERT

Unfortunately, the gratitude described in Dayenu is scarce in the generation that left Egypt. Take the transition from step five, giving us the wealth of the Egyptians (which occurred during the plague of darkness), to step six, splitting the Sea of Reeds. "If (God) had given us their money and not split the sea for us, it would have been enough." But at that moment, in Exodus 14:11–12, the Israelites cry to Moshe, "Was it for want of graves in Egypt that you brought us to die in the wilderness? What have you done to us, taking us out of Egypt? Is this not the very thing we told you in Egypt, saying, 'Let us be, and we will serve the Egyptians, for it is better for us to serve the Egyptians than to die in the wilderness'?" This doesn't sound much like gratitude to me; it sounds like, "Dayenu! Enough!" For all our talk of fulfilling promises, these are a people who have just seen promise after delayed promise finally kept, and they respond to that strong hand and outstretched arm by slapping the hand away.

Rabbi Joshua Kulp, in his commentary in *The Schechter Haggadah*,[1] brings in the parallel text of Psalm 78:

> He performed marvels in the sight of their fathers
> in the land of Egypt, the plain of Zoan.
> He split the sea and took them through it;
> He made the waters stand like a wall.
> He led them with a cloud by day,
> and throughout the night by the light of fire.
> He split rocks in the wilderness

---

1. Kulp, *The Schechter Haggadah*, 235.

and gave them drink as if from the great deep.
He brought forth streams from a rock
and made them flow down like a river.
But they went on sinning against Him,
defying the Most High in the parched land.
To test God was in their mind
when they demanded food for themselves.[2]

The Psalm, and the "response" that's Dayenu, is rich in "strong hand" imagery of the kind I described earlier, yet the response of the people is, "What have you done for me lately?" Healers, perhaps more so during the COVID-19 pandemic than ever before, recognize this feeling. Every healer I know has a story of a patient whose life they likely saved by diagnosing a deadly cancer and rushing them to treatment, only to have that person leave the practice because it took a little too long to return a phone call. Most patients I know have stories of the torture they've endured because of the "help" they got from their healers: The exorbitant bills, the dreadful side effects, and the "lost lifetime" of waiting, traveling to appointments, and repeating their story hundreds of times to strange new faces whose roles in their care were never clarified.

TAKING THE LONG VIEW

So how did that attitude morph into gratitude? According to Rabbi Kulp, the first appearance of *Dayenu* in a Haggadah is that of Rav Saadyah Gaon in 9th-10th century Iraq. More than two thousand years had passed since the Exodus, and 800 years since the end times of the Second Temple, when the concept of the seder first formed in the way we know now. In a time of relative peace, Rav Saadyah was able to have perspective on the events of the Exodus, much as the declaration of first fruits looks back over the whole arc of the narrative in a time of plenty. The message of both *Dayenu* and the first fruits declaration is, "Look how fortunate you are, look how far you've come and think about how much God has done for you. Even a fraction of this would deserve your praise and blessing." These texts aren't refrigerator magnets telling us to "Adopt an Attitude of Gratitude!" They're the product of hundreds of years of perspective in the case of *Dayenu*, or a text that "you'll understand when you get older" in the case of the First Fruits Declaration.

2. Psalms 78:12–18.

But for someone still in their narrow place, this message can sound *exactly* like a refrigerator magnet, a trite saying telling them to "look on the bright side." Rabbi Shai Held writes about a similar statement, "Blessed is the True Judge," which is supposed to be the first thing a religious Jew utters when they hear of a person's death, meaning, "Blessed is God who decides when each person's time is up." As a twelve-year-old boy in a religious school, he sat in a lesson about this phrase just months after his father had died suddenly of an aneurysm. Thinking he had to adopt an attitude of acceptance, young Shai had not even shared his loss with anyone who didn't already know, including his teacher. In this lesson, he finally had to protest, so he asked, "What happens when you hear something so bad and painful that you just can't bring yourself to say that?" The teacher's response nearly broke his faith: "For the true believer, that's *not* a question."[3] Teaching *Dayenu* to someone for whom everything that has happened so far is clearly *not* enough (the cancer's still growing; the source of the infection is still not identified) often has the same effect—one I see frequently in my own patients.

Viktor Frankl's most famous work, *Man's Search for Meaning*, is a fusion of his professional work in the psychotherapeutic approach he called "logotherapy" and his life experience as a survivor of Auschwitz. Modern literature on morality, resilience, and self-help abounds with references to Frankl's philosophy, which in his own words states that, "We can discover this meaning in life in three different ways: (1) by creating a work or doing a deed; (2) by experiencing something or encountering someone; and (3) *by the attitude we take toward unavoidable suffering* (emphasis mine).[4]

Lord Rabbi Jonathan Sacks, in his final book, *Morality*, observes, "Frankl's transforming insight was that, although the Nazis had taken away virtually every freedom and vestige of humanity from the camp inmates, there was one freedom they could not take away: The freedom to choose how to respond."[5] Rabbi Sacks also references another survivor, Edith Eger, and her book *The Choice*, in which she differentiates between victimization and victimhood, and makes much the same assertion as Frankl—one doesn't choose to be victimized (nor should we ever blame them for being victimized) but one does choose victimhood.[6]

---

3. Held, Judaism Is About Love, 67.
4. Frankl, *Man's Search for Meaning*, 133.
5. Sacks, *Morality*, 41.
6. Sacks, *Morality*, 203.

I read Frankl for the first time as a college freshman, still grappling with the murder of a grade-school classmate the year before. The message of a Shoah survivor telling me I have the power to choose the meaning my life will have felt like a superpower. As an adult dealing daily with people confronting unavoidable suffering after unavoidable suffering, I've come to recognize that Frankl, Eger, and indeed the survivors I've known personally were heroes; as were those like Natan Sharansky that stood strong in the face of Soviet oppression. We call them heroic precisely because they did something extraordinary; most of us don't have that much inner strength.

THE MINDSET MINEFIELD

Just before I began this section, one of my students sent me an article from the online magazine *Psyche* entitled, "Why We Shouldn't Push a Positive Mindset on Those in Poverty," by Professor Jennifer Sheehy-Skeffington of the London School of Economics.[7] Sheehy-Skeffington challenges the "positive mindset" theory, a direct descendant of Frankl's, by questioning its bedrock principle, "what I call the assumption of free-flowing mindsets." This is the idea that everyone can decide, as Frankl and Eger asserted, "how to perceive and respond to the unavoidable constraints and challenges they face." The problem, she continues, is that mindsets aren't free-floating. While it's true that there are mindsets that are more constructive than others, mindsets "are neither optional strategies that everyone can freely adopt nor value-neutral ways of enhancing wellbeing. Instead, they're embedded in life conditions that have material, social and ideological dimensions, and this is just as true for those of us living in poverty as it is for the rest of us living in financial comfort."[8]

The "bad" attitude of the Israelites leaving slavery, and all the catastrophe it created, was conditioned by 210 years of enslavement. Their years of trauma, of poverty in the shadow of the massive wealth of ancient Egypt, and even the nine-time false hope of the plagues, had taught them (as it did the author quoted in Sheehy-Skeffington's piece) "It's best not to hope." As Sheehy-Skeffington explains further, "The emerging picture is one of material adversity triggering social adversity, such that it is only

---

7. Many thanks to Mackenzie Kross for sharing this with me, and probably compelling me to write my *next* book about this thorny problem. You earned your "A."

8. Sheehy-Skeffington, " Why We Shouldn't Push a Positive Mindset on Those in Poverty."

wise to behave, and teach your children to behave, in ways that prevent you or them being exploited by a hostile world."

In discussing where the story of the Exodus begins, I mentioned my friend Deborah Gilboa's take on the 80% of Israelites who chose never to leave Egypt, whose "chosen attitude," if you can call it that, was that hope is futile.[9] But even those who left, the ones who made it into the desert, were still prisoners of that belief. It's not that it was impossible to believe they were headed toward redemption. It was just rare.

One-fifth of the Israelites had enough faith to choose to leave Egypt. Once they were in the desert, one-sixth had the courage to believe they could successfully enter the Promised Land of Israel and settle there— Yehoshua and Calev, alone among the twelve scouts who went in to tour the land. One person in thirty were able to leave enslavement and believe they'd reach their destination. One in thirty—very nearly the odds Frankl laid for himself (one in twenty, and elsewhere in the book one in twenty-eight based on actual survival statistics) to survive the camp in a speech he gave to fellow prisoners during his last months in Dachau, before the liberation.[10] Yehoshua and Calev, like Frankl and Eger thousands of years later, were heroes against long odds.

For the rest, it was simply not time. A few months of miraculous occurrences couldn't undo centuries of conditioning or convert resignation to rejuvenation. That generation had to die in the wilderness and be supplanted by a new generation of people born free—born with nothing but the clothes on their backs and the assurance that just enough food would fall from the sky each night to keep them alive for one more day. This new generation, born without resources but also without limitations, without preconceptions, could gaze at the miraculous skyfall each morning and say, "If God had just given us this manna, it would have been enough," knowing that they fully expected that more was on the way. They could see how far they had come—how much farther, indeed, they were even when they *started* than their parents had been. They could see the Promised Land growing closer—and they could see the obstacles fall before them one by one.

---

9. Chapter 13.

10. Frankl, *Man's Search for Meaning*, p. 103.

THE END OF HISTORY, OR THE BEGINNING OF THE END?

For many people living in 21st century America, it's easy to look at the Israelites leaving Egypt, or our immigrant grandparents, or the generation of the Great Depression, and think how much better *we* have it than them—sometimes to the point of having arrived at the "top step." If anything, *Dayenu* is there to remind *us* that we didn't get here on our own. Those previous generations were the ones who had to climb those difficult steps. Some of them climbed a lot farther than others, like those in *this* country who endured enslavement, then Jim Crow, then redlining, redistricting, and other structural remnants that serve as a perpetual reminder they still have a lot more steps to climb. For their present-day descendants, there's no illusion of having arrived, only awareness of still being on a long journey.

Even for those who imagine being on the top step, Rabbi Sacks reminds us that we're not, and never were, living what philosopher Francis Fukuyama called *The End of History*, a supposed triumph of liberal democracy and freedom over the chaos and turmoil of the rest of human existence. There have always been periods of peace and calm: From the "Pax Romana" of ancient history to the tranquility of Rav Saadia Gaon's Baghdad in the 10th century to the late 20th century in the US. During those times, it's easy to believe that it's always going to be like that, that the world is *supposed* to be like that.

For most of the world, however, the twenty-nine out of thirty people who never reach that promised land, Jennifer Sheehy-Skeffington's words ring much truer. To hope is to have your hopes dashed. To want is to waste your time. To dream is to be disappointed. To feel great when you wake up one morning is to know there's a cancer diagnosis or a heart attack or a death of a loved one coming to derail you. And when we encounter people who are in that place, the privileged encountering the powerless, *Dayenu* is dangerous. It's flaunting our privilege, dancing on the graves of those who have suffered and continue to suffer. It's, as I called it in the *Avadim hayyinu* chapter, "Atleastism" at its worst.

BOWLER AND BROOKS

I learned about atleastism from the Christian theologian Kate Bowler. Bowler's book, *Everything Happens for a Reason and Other Lies I've Loved* is her narrative of being diagnosed with metastatic colon cancer at age 35, and consequently exploding all the platitudes she had ever been handed about suffering. Topping her list (quite literally; it's number 1 on the list of things not to say in her appendix) is "At least. . ." "Whoa, hold up there," writes Bowler. "Were you about to make a comparison? At least it's not . . . what? Stage V cancer? Don't minimize."[11] Frankl addresses "atleastism" as well, writing, "suffering completely fills the human soul and mind, no matter whether the suffering is great or little. Therefore the 'size' of human suffering is absolutely relative."[12]

Bowler echoes Jennifer Sheehy-Skeffington about the dangers of believing that mindset is a free-floating choice. In a 2021 interview with columnist David Brooks, she describes herself as "lovingly homicidal" toward "the mindset people," she had encountered repeatedly during her illness. "Mindset is a whole thing. David, if you haven't heard about it, if you have the right mindset, this won't be happening to you. I don't know what this is, but it won't happen again. But the, you know, obsessive just be present. Make a gratitude list. A lot of chiding you on not having locked your mental framework into into like a life without desire somehow. Or your only desire is for today and I don't I don't think that's I don't think that's possible."[13]

Bowler is a scholar of the Prosperity Gospel, the Christian theological movement to which many of the 1980s televangelists belonged, which preaches the idea of "Name it and claim it." Pray fervently enough for the thing you most need, and it'll be yours. She admires the movement's faith, its belief that a better day is coming—and also felt personally hurt by the implication that she wasn't getting better because she, somehow, wasn't praying hard enough or didn't believe truly enough. Coming from the Mennonite tradition, where every family had a coffee table book entitled *The Martyr's Mirror* (where their focus on family and suffering made me certain they were just Jews who had gotten confused a few hundred years ago) the idea that one could just pray away the suffering seemed too easy to her. Kate had grown up believing that suffering was part of the fabric of life, and that the religious response to suffering was to keep suffering *together*.

Kate Bowler also helped me see that for all the danger of *Dayenu* becoming just another way of saying to the suffering, "Cheer up! See how

---

11. Bowler, *Everything Happens for a Reason and Other Lies I've Loved*, p. 169.
12. Frankl, *Man's Search for Meaning*, p. 64.
13. Bowler, The Everything Happens Podcast. "Kate Bowler and David Brooks: Never, Ever Enough."

much better you have it than Anne Frank?" *Dayenu* is not really about that at all. During her conversation with Brooks, she described asking a senior colleague, who was nearing retirement, "have you gotten there? Have you felt it?" The colleague shared his story and Bowler "realized that everything else was just crumbling. And he was like, Oh, Kate, but it comes undone. And then I thought, Oh my God. I suppose there isn't some kind of some kind of arrival gate like, I'm not going to stick this landing, I suppose."

Brooks' response to that story, "the idea that you never arrive," is embedded in the ending of *Dayenu*. The fifteen steps, conclude with, "and built us the 'Chosen House' (the Temple)," but the Haggadah adds one more line, "to atone upon all of our sins." Even once we "arrive" at the top step, we'll still be imperfect, still striving, and still be messed up enough to require atonement.

Consider the "step" of Shabbat. Shabbat is a miniature version of the World to Come, the Messianic time. *Dayenu* doesn't say, "God brought us into the World to Come." That hasn't happened yet. We can still only pray that someday we experience something like it. But we have Shabbat, what Abraham Joshua Heschel called "a sanctuary in time."[14] We have a little window into what the next world might be like, one we peer through every week and then must shutter again until the following week. But it's this glimpse through a window that sustains me through the next stretch of desert, as it has for a couple of my Christian colleagues for whom Heschel's vision also frames their Sabbath practice. We're still always, on the stairs, never at the top.

Dayenu isn't aimed at those who are still in their narrow places. It's a humbling reminder to those who have made it out to always remember that we didn't make it out alone. Bowler and Brooks both lament that they've regularly had their books end up in the self-help section. Rabbi Sacks devotes a whole chapter of *Morality* to the limits of self-help, paying particular mind to the story of the origins of the Paralympics. They were started by a typically-able physician who needed to recognize and encourage the potential in his paralyzed patients and free them from the narrow place that previous doctors had imposed on them before they could take over "climbing the stairs" on their own.[15]

---

14. Heschel, *The Sabbath*,
15. Sacks, *Morality*, 44–45.

The *Dayenu* message is that each of the steps God took us on was a gift. Even if we'd only one step, we might make something out of it, like feeding ourselves for one more day of crossing the wilderness or allowing ourselves a glimpse of a far future hope. People at all stages of life, in all sorts of distress, still find room for gratitude in their lives. *Dayenu* is a reminder that even something transient, even something partial, can still be meaningful and precious. Like our lives themselves, even though they're not eternal, they're the most precious thing we have. So too, these little steps, these small victories, may be incomplete, but they're cause for joy—the kind of joy that consists of saying, "Today was a good day" and not appending a "but" about what tomorrow will look like.

We should certainly be in awe of the resilience of those who survive and thrive in the thick of their illnesses, of those who resolved to leave Egypt, and never forget the role their strength plays in that Exodus. Conversely, no one "brings themselves out of Egypt" entirely on their own; in the words of the sages, "the prisoner cannot free himself from prison,"[16] even if he might have freed someone else in the past or be destined to do so in the future. God needed to help us take that first, and that next step. Likewise, for those who are still in their narrow places, we—all of us, not just doctors or nurses or political leaders—are the ones who must help them take *their* first step.

---

16. Talmud Berakhot 5b

26

The Pesaḥ Sacrifice

The first century sage Rabban Gamliel II mandated that every seder gathering discuss three items after reciting the plagues; the first is the Passover sacrifice, represented by a lamb shank.

Rabban Gamliel's Three Things	פסח מצה ומרור
Rabban Gamliel was accustomed to say, Anyone who has not said these three things on Pesach has not fulfilled his obligation, and these are them: The Pesach sacrifice, matzah and marror.	רַבָּן גַּמְלִיאֵל הָיָה אוֹמֵר: כָּל שֶׁלֹּא אָמַר שְׁלשָׁה דְּבָרִים אֵלּוּ בַּפֶּסַח, לֹא יָצָא יְדֵי חוֹבָתוֹ, וְאֵלּוּ הֵן: פֶּסַח, מַצָּה, וּמָרוֹר.
The Pesach [passover] sacrifice that our ancestors were accustomed to eating when the Temple existed, for the sake of what [was it]?	פֶּסַח שֶׁהָיוּ אֲבוֹתֵינוּ אוֹכְלִים בִּזְמַן שֶׁבֵּית הַמִּקְדָּשׁ הָיָה קַיָּם, עַל שׁוּם מָה?

In Chapter 11, "Insomniac Rabbis," I mentioned the lecture I watched online while the rest of the ICU was having Christmas dinner: "Is Harry Potter Good for the Jews?"

The lecturer concluded, quite enthusiastically, "Yes!" Despite the Torah's obvious discomfort with witchcraft, the contemporary characters of Harry, Hermione, Dumbledore, Neville, and McGonagall so clearly exemplified Jewish values that they could only serve as a positive point of departure for teaching our kids how to be *menschen*. While I can no longer locate the original lecture in the morass of Web 2.0, numerous other articles highlighting this connection have hit the internet since that time, many in 2014 when author J.K. Rowling confirmed what all of us already knew: Ravenclaw student Anthony Goldstein was Jewish.[1] One piece from that year, by Yvette Alt Miller, identified five of these messages: 1) our choices define us, 2) we have a crucial role to play, 3) work to develop your talents, 4) treat everyone with respect, 5) and choose your friends and your community for those that will remain steadfast with you through the years.[2]

One of the frequent contributors to this line of thinking is Rabbi Moshe Rosenberg, author of *Morality for Muggles: Ethics in the Bible and the World of Harry Potter*, who in 2019 released *The (Unofficial) Hogwarts Haggadah*. For Rosenberg, "the crux on which the entire Hogwarts epic rests" is self-sacrifice, starting with Lily Potter's all-important decision to place herself between Voldemort's curse and Harry, which imbues Harry with the ancient magic that renders him invulnerable to Voldemort until Harry himself decides to make a similar sacrifice to save his friends.

When Rabban Gamliel insists in the Haggadah that we must discuss the *Pesach* sacrifice, represented on the table by the *z'roa*, the shankbone of a lamb (or, for the punning vegetarians in my life, a sweet potato serving as the Paschal Yam), Rosenberg links it to that central theme of the novels. The Israelites were courting danger by sacrificing lambs in Egypt, as the lamb was an object of worship there, and so put themselves at great risk in making the first *Pesach* offering. "This explanation of *korban*, or sacrifice," continues Rosenberg, "fits well with the view of the Ramban (Nachmanides) that the symbolism of animal sacrifice is the self-sacrifice of the person who brings the offering."[3]

---

1. Over the ten years since, the author has drawn much criticism for her positions on gender identity, which don't appear explicitly in the novels. She has also come under fire for precisely this feature of the novels—naming her characters in heavy-handed, token fashion—and for using old, antisemitic stereotypes in the description of the goblins. I disagree with her on the first point and have mixed feelings about the second and third. Ben Zoma teaches, "Who is wise? One who learns from every human being (Avot 4:1)." Even those we disagree with vehemently. I've elsewhere in my writing quoted from Roald Dahl's moving letter about his daughter's death from measles for want of sufficient vaccine. Dahl was a virulent antisemite; the letter is a powerful message about the forgotten dangers of that disease. I learn from both without feeling any obligation to endorse either's beliefs.

2. Alt Miller, "Harry Potter and Jewish Values."

3. Rosenberg, *The (Unofficial) Hogwarts Haggadah*, p. 67.

My editor reminds me that the ram might disagree with this point of view, so let me offer (see what I did there) a few words of explanation. Prayer, the form of worship most of us engage in these days (if we worship at all) can literally be lip service. Our mouths make sounds, or sometimes just move silently, in words that are often empty—words we may not understand, especially for many Jews, Muslims, Catholics, and Orthodox Christians who may be praying in languages they don't speak. But even without a language barrier, there's no shortage of people who may understand what they're saying, but don't mean it or intend to follow through.

Animal sacrifice, as uncomfortable as it makes most people in the 21st century, means literal "skin in the game." Giving something of tangible value, an animal the person had invested in raising themselves and was necessarily of high quality, gave real weight to a person's connection. It symbolized their "coming close," to God, which is perhaps why the word *korban,* sacrifice, comes from *karov,* close.

The lamb shank on the seder plate is called *z'roa* for the *z'roa netuyah,* the outstretched arm of God, that reached out over Egypt at the exact moment that the Israelites were in their homes consuming the sacrifice. We spoke earlier about what that outstretched arm means in the context of our healing metaphor—the sword, ready to do battle on behalf of those stuck in the narrow place, to finally free them. Highlighting the *pesach* at the table is a way of drawing attention to the forward-looking part of the seder message: "Next year we shall be free," and not only us, but others who are not yet free.

To this point, the Haggaddah focuses on what *was.* It builds participants' identity with those who were enslaved, emphasizing both the parallel and the throughline between their story and ours. In naming the three essential symbols on the table, we focus on what *will be*—and on what we're asked to contribute to bring about that future.

The *z'roa* calls to mind the battles we fight in the quest to help people heal, not by invoking medical miracles, but by putting ourselves—our time, our resources, and our reputations—on the line on someone else's behalf. Traditionally, the *pesach* is the only one of the three symbols which we only point to, rather than lifting it up to show everyone. We want to be clear that our *z'roa* is only a remembrance of the real sacrifice we made when the Temple still stood. However, this reserved, understated way of calling out the symbol is also relevant to the healer.

Self-sacrifice can be tricky. Many of the people I care for have disabling conditions that require them to have some amount of attendant care. They can't drive themselves to appointments, may not know the language, and in many cases need help with some of the most basic activities of daily living, like bathing and dressing. Often, the caregiver is a spouse, a child (or a child-in-law), or a sibling. Providing the care, even if there's some state funding coming in, means that person may need to sacrifice a career, a chance at marriage, or the time they need to rest and rejuvenate. We talked (in Chapter 22) about the limited slice of a patient's life that a doctor or a nurse might see, and the great awe we should have for these caregivers who are "on" for seven, ten, even twenty-four hours a day, sometimes even sleeping in the same room. A best-selling book on the topic many years ago went even further: *The 36-Hour Day*.

Some of these caregivers are, to use Brian Miller's description, "on fire." They cajole the person they care for into exercising, going out to family gatherings and community outings, and engaging in conversation about things beyond basic needs. They help re-create, in many cases, a life that was lost to illness, trauma, or displacement. They're "burning bushes," tapping into some deep reservoir of water they get from the very act of caring and seeing the results to keep going at this task.

Others, however, are burnt out. Caregiving is one of the many forms of labor that's historically underpaid and underappreciated; in fact, when Moshe is taken into the palace by Pharaoh's daughter, his caregiving is entrusted to an enslaved woman—who happens to be his own biological mother.[4] It could certainly have been one of the types of work included in the description of *avodah b'farekh*, backbreaking, demoralizing labor.

Alongside the caregivers I described in the last paragraph are those who drop their charges off at my office and take off, taking with them their critical knowledge of what the person is eating, how hard it's to bathe them, and whether they're taking their medicine. Others come in but won't give the person room to speak, bark orders at them, or treat them roughly when helping with shoes or clothing. Still others are dutiful and kind, but radiate depression and defeat, which often morph into illness in their own right—illness which the caregiver frequently neglects until something catastrophic happens and they find themselves no longer able to provide care. I see many of those caregivers as patients, too; they teeter between sacrifice and martyrdom, and many do suffer life-threatening

---

4. Exodus 2:8

events of their own because of how badly they've exhausted themselves. Maybe that's why we point to the bone instead of lifting it—it can be hazardous to your health. There's a reason it was a *burnt* offering, back in the day.

It's shameful, with people quietly pouring out their souls in sacrifice for their loved ones, to see the institutions that are supposed to be doing the "signs and wonders" engaged in so much lip service. They pay lip service to being "welcoming" by placing a multilingual banner over the front entrance but fail to offer interpretation services where they're really needed or call themselves "patient-centered" but make it nearly impossible to obtain a full copy of one's own health record. On a personal level, I know I see myself as having "sacrificed"—being at work late, getting frustrated with bureaucracy, or doing a visit I know I won't get paid for—but fail to fight the fight that might really take a "piece of my flesh" on someone else's behalf. By not raising the plate with the *z'roa* we can remind ourselves not to say *Dayenu* about our own sacrifices. Instead we can ask, "What else might we be doing to realize the dream of "next year"?

Thoughts and Discussions

- *What have you sacrificed in the past year? What have others sacrificed for you? Was it worth it? Was it enough?*

27

Matzah (again?)

The second of Rabban Gamliel's three symbols is the Matzah.

| This matzah that we are eating, for the sake of what [is it]? | ?מַצָּה זוֹ שֶׁאָנוּ אוֹכְלִים, עַל שׁוּם מַה |

DISAPPOINTING DINNER

My teacher, Erica Brown, may be a bit sheepish about serving seder. In her Haggadah, *Seder Talk*, she writes, "There is something sad about the matzah lying flat on the table, as if it speaks to those who are about to eat it with an apology: I'm sorry for providing so little by way of satisfaction."[1] Yet this disappointing piece of flatbread is apparently critical to our story, for Rabban Gamliel includes it as his second of three obligatory explanations in the seder.

Brown contrasts matzah with challah, the usual star of the holiday or Shabbat table. "The Shabbat *after* Passover (italics mine), we look at the contours of the *halla* cover, and it is high and rounded."[2] It reminds me a little of a meme that circulated a few years ago, the week of Pesach and Easter, with a photo of the Pillsbury Doughboy that proclaimed, "He is Risen!" and a second photo of a flat "matzah man" wearing a baker's hat

1. Brown, *Seder Talk*, 85.
2. Brown, *Seder Talk*, 85.

emblazoned with a *magen David*, answering, "He is NOT!"[3] There are times when we feel full, flush, almost overflowing with goodness. We're bursting at the seams, like one of those cardboard tubes of Pillsbury rolls that has just been given a little twist. But at Pesach, we're meant to remember the times we feel, well, flat.

We might ask, "Why do we need to discuss the *matzah* here? Haven't we covered this already—three times?" We've broken the middle *matzah* in half and spoken of brokenness, perforations, and Humpty Dumpty. We've spoken of the hubris of *hametz* and the humility of *matzah* as we try to make tonight just a little different from all other nights. And we've held the *matzah*, broken and whole together, over our heads as we issued an invitation to those in need of food and those in need of a *Pesach* to join our table. What else could there be to say?

HUMBLE BRAG, HUMBLE BREAD

For a food with no flavor that binds both jaws and bowels, *matzah* has a lot to say. Contrast Erica Brown's characterization of placing the *matzah* on the seder plate with the feast that Avraham sets out for the three travelers (angels) that come to announce Sarah will soon conceive a child. He says, "Let a little water be brought . . . And let me fetch a morsel of bread that you may refresh yourselves. . .," then goes and has Sarah bake cakes and fetches a calf for her to prepare. Avraham's "humble brag" about a little water and a morsel turns into a full meal fit for, well, an angel.[4]

Despite Avraham's humility, the very *absence* of him feeling full of himself, we as readers get the feeling of fullness and plenty from this scene. It's a feeling I experience in my work when I walk into a room and suddenly know a diagnosis beyond the shadow of a doubt; and know with equal certainty that I can treat it and make it better. I think of the preschooler with the swollen knee who lives in the suburbs and has woods in his backyard. Six weeks earlier, on an unseasonably warm January day he was playing in the woods and didn't do a tick check before bed. I'll treat his Lyme arthritis, he'll make a full recovery, and he'll go on to play in those woods again.

---

3. One year Ramadan also coincided with Passover and Easter. A version of the meme that year included a Pillsbury crescent roll in the third panel and read, "He can only be eaten after dark."

4. Genesis 18: 3–4.

It's a rare treat, but it's the type of satisfaction we live for in primary care. We feel smart, we feel powerful, and most importantly, our patients feel cared for and well again. Everyone wins. It deserves a fatted calf and some fresh baked bread. But for so many people I see, those who suffer from chronic pain, or lingering depression, or the ubiquitous triad of heart-attack causing diseases—high cholesterol, blood pressure, and blood sugar—I've little to offer. I enter and leave the encounter feeling like Erica Brown forced to serve her guests *matzah*.

With all our "strong hand" maneuvers, our "signs" and "wonders,"; modern physicians often gloss over this moment in our training. Yet it's the defining posture of most of what we do. Countless patients suffer without a diagnosis, by which I mean they've no name to call their illness, only, "my sickness." Others suffer without a prognosis, not knowing whether they'll ever feel better, or when. Patients with a terminal diagnosis are sometimes easier to face; at least (there's that phrase I hate) we can provide some certainty about how things will end. Still others have a sickness that should be getting better but isn't. They're the unlucky 10% that don't benefit from that 90% cure rate or have the most severe form of a disease that "usually isn't this bad" and we've exhausted all our usual maneuvers. All we can offer is a flat, "I'm sorry you're going through this," and another medicament we know probably won't work any better than the last one, or else will make things worse with a new side effect.

We could ask ourselves, "Why is this night different from all other nights?" What gives us any confidence that we'll walk into the room and things will somehow be different than they've been every other time? If you live on the patient's side of this encounter, you could be asking the same question. "I've seen this yutz three times a year for the last decade and I still have high blood sugar. Why do I think he's somehow going to find the magic bullet today? All he has to offer is the same words, the same medications I'm already taking that don't work."

But the humility to admit these limitations, the humility that *matzah* symbolizes, is the way into real relationships and real caring between healer and patient. I can think of a handful of patients with whom I've enduring connections because of the dumb luck of making the right rare diagnosis or providing a cure for something that ailed them. But most of my longest and deepest therapeutic relationships are with people to whom I've had to repeatedly say, "I've no idea what comes next. I'm not even sure what happened last."

SHE STOOPS TO SANCTIFY

Lord Rabbi Jonathan Sacks, in an essay on Parashat Pekudei (the last section of the book of Exodus) comments on the reciprocity between *kiddush*, separating and elevating something that was common into something holy, and *tzimtzum*, contracting the holy into less than its previous space to make room for the common and profane. God creates the universe through *tzimtzum*, contracting the Infinite, Divine holiness to create finite space for there to be, well, *everything else*. Contraction requires humility, the ability to say, "I don't need to take up this much space. I'll make room for someone or something else." When that "something else" is a relationship with another human being, it allows that person to expand to fill the vacated space, to be sanctified. In marriage, specifically, we call that sanctification by the same word, *kiddushin*, but other relationships like friendships, mentorship, and parenting are just as holy and elevated.

Having that degree of humility in the clinical setting requires *tzimtzum*, a recognition that all that acquired knowledge is less-than total, and a creation of space for the other person's suffering to reside. Enough space, in fact, for both the suffering and the person experiencing it, so that their very existence isn't subsumed in that space by the enormity of their suffering. The Physician's Prayer by Dr. Marcus Herz asks God, "In the sufferer, let me see only the human being."[5] In other words, don't allow me to reduce the sufferer to his disease or her symptoms, but allow me the humility to create enough space for them to be a person in full who also happens to be ill. Let me be flat, so that others can reach their fullness.

Thoughts and Discussions

- *Talk about the times you feel full and the times you feel flat.*
- *How do we make our time with someone worthwhile—even when there's nothing new to offer?*
- *When and why have you "flattened" yourself?*

---

5. Herz, "Daily Prayer of a Physician," https://www.jewishvirtuallibrary.org/daily-prayer-of-a-physician.

28

Biting Bitter Herbs

The third of Rabban Gamliel's symbols is the maror, the bitter herbs.

| This marror [bitter greens] that we are eating, for the sake of what [is it]? For the sake [to commemorate] that the Egyptians embittered the lives of our ancestors in Egypt... | מָרוֹר זֶה שֶׁאָנוּ אוֹכְלִים, עַל שׁוּם מַה? עַל שׁוּם שֶׁמֵּרְרוּ הַמִּצְרִים אֶת־חַיֵּי אֲבוֹתֵינוּ בְּמִצְרָיִם... |

HORSING AROUND

My grandfather and his friend Sid Baker were both shiny bald on the tops of their heads. Their other friend, Merv Binstock, whom I loved dearly even though he was my dentist and orthodontist throughout my childhood, had plenty of hair and an interesting hobby: Preparing his own horseradish from scratch. It was Merv's freshly grated horseradish, perfectly colored with beet juice, that graced our seder table in the enormous dining room with the bay window, the cushioned window seat, and the "Pittsburgh" stained glass. When the time came to eat the *maror*, Gramp and Sid would each take a heaping spoonful on a piece of matzah and pop it into their mouths. Neither would say anything, nor move a muscle of their faces, but the bald pates would glow bright red.

I've so far been fortunate to defy the *bubbemeises* that says male-pattern baldness is inherited on your mother's side. Gramp was totally bald save for a fringe by the time he was forty, and I still have most of my hair (don't you dare peek under my *kippah*) past fifty. My own reaction to horseradish is somewhat less respectable, however. For several years in my teens and twenties, I spent second seder with my dear friend Dan Vogel (sorry, Commander Daniel Vogel, USN, Ret.) and his family. In 1994, I brought my girlfriend (now wife) to the midnight madness that was the Vogel seder for the first time, introducing her to my closest high school friends. Perhaps I was subconsciously trying to impress her, but I quite literally bit off more than I could chew; a piece of raw horseradish root the circumference of a quarter and the thickness of a Hershey bar. I gnawed on it for perhaps thirty seconds, feeling the heat rise, until I suddenly felt myself nearly asphyxiate. I was unwilling to admit defeat by spitting the mess out, and determined that I would succeed in swallowing it. Apparently, I looked so ridiculous that no one remembers whether I succeeded. Korach '94, as it'll forever be known, will be remembered for my ludicrous appearance and behavior, and not for whether I ultimately triumphed over that slice of root vegetable.

MEANING IN UNAVOIDABLE SUFFERING

Rabban Gamliel's purpose in obligating us to discuss these three symbols is to ensure we walk away understanding the meaning of gathering for seder. The symbols anticipate Viktor Frankl's three paths to discovering meaning in life. The *pesach*, the shank bone, represents the outstretched arm of God and the tangible sacrifice made by each household in anticipation of the night of the last plague. It parallels "creating a work or doing a deed," the first possible way to discover meaning. The *matzah* symbolizes humility, making space for another person or people in our lives, analogous to Frankl's second way to discover meaning: "Experiencing something or encountering someone," love. And *maror*? As my silly stories above are meant to suggest, *maror*, both the abstract symbolism of it on the seder plate and the concrete act of eating it, is about Frankl's third path, "the attitude we take toward unavoidable suffering." Some suffer in silent dignity; others make dramatic fools of themselves (OK, me).

Earlier, I referred to Frankl and his fellow survivor Edith Eger as heroes because what they did defied incredibly long odds and required a fortitude that most people don't have—certainly not me. But I missed something the first time I read *Man's Search for Meaning* thirty years ago, and I think many modern readers also miss it: Frankl *knows* the odds are long and that maintaining hope and dignity is heroic. "It is true that only a few people are capable . . . Of the prisoners, only a few kept their full inner liberty and obtained those values which their suffering afforded, *but even one such example is sufficient proof that man's inner strength may raise him above his outward fate.* Such men are not only in concentration camps. Everywhere man is confronted with fate, with the chance of achieving something through his own suffering."[1]

In 2022 the world witnessed a tremendous example of this: Ukranian civilians literally pushing back invading Russian tanks with their bare hands. Ukranian president Volodymyr Zelenskyy, grandson of a Holocaust survivor, walked into his office with television cameras following him and said defiantly, "Here I am, I'm not hiding. Come get me!"

Yet as Frankl readily acknowledged, we're not all Frankl, we're not all Zelenskyy, we're not all Edith Eger. In holding up the *maror*, we're admitting something that Western liberalism has often ignored: Suffering is everywhere. The inexorable march of progress has not eliminated it, only created progressively more new kinds of suffering. Not only that, but the gap between those who suffer and those who can avoid it has grown. And not everyone will succeed in finding the meaning in that new suffering, that senseless death.

What both Frankl and the seder offer is a declaration that hope and meaning are *possible*, even in the worst of circumstances, while at the same time exhorting us only to choose the route of finding meaning in suffering that's *unavoidable*. "In no way is suffering *necessary* to find meaning. I only insist that meaning is possible even despite suffering—provided, certainly, that the suffering is unavoidable. If it *were* avoidable, however, the meaningful thing to do would be to remove its cause, be it psychological, biological, or political. To suffer unnecessarily is masochistic rather than heroic."[2] Something I should perhaps have considered that night in 1994.

Think of Greenberg's assertion that the Exodus narrative teaches that we're not meant to be enslaved. For 210 years, the Israelites did find meaning in their suffering: They maintained their Hebrew names instead

---

1. Frankl, *Man's Search for Meaning*, pp. 88–9.
2. Frankl, *Man's Search for Meaning*, 136

of assimilating and they cried out to their God instead of abandoning monotheism in despair. The midwives Shifrah and Puah found clever ways to keep Hebrew babies alive under a death decree.[3] Miriam, according to midrash, convinced her father and the other men not to resort to celibacy and doom both the girls and the boys when Pharaoh had decreed against only the boys.[4] And her mother Yocheved floated Moshe down the river so he could survive[5]—a defiant act of sacrifice, like the ones we highlighted in our discussion of the *pesach*, which was the starting point of the entire redemption.

LAUGHTER IN THE FACE OF DEATH

Once God heard the Israelites' cry, the time to suffer meaningfully ended.[6] Now was the time to devote all energies to realizing the dream of redemption—which may in turn have brought unavoidable suffering of a different sort, but the goal now had to be release, not resignation. Yet Frankl points out that it would *not* have been reasonable if, during the prior 200 years, the Israelites had said to themselves, "If we're not released from enslavement one day, all of this will have been for naught." He writes on several occasions about prisoners who lived for the day of liberation from the camp, only to lose the will to live when their specific day of hope passed without it coming to pass.[7]

Frankl's speech was designed to help his companions find meaning, then and there, not tied to a future that might crumble and take their meaning, and all hope with it. He talked of hope just for the next small thing—an easier work detail or an extra ration—and the meaning that comes from choosing one's attitude. He also spoke of meaning from the past—from all the experiences already lived, experiences that were fixed and permanent and couldn't be taken away.[8] In the film version of that same war, perhaps on that same day hundreds of miles away in Morocco, one would-be lover said to another, "we'll always have Paris."

---

3. Exodus 1:15–20.
4. Ramban (Nachmanides) and others on Exodus 2:1.
5. Exodus 2:3.
6. See the discussion about suffering and the view of bioethicist Laurie Zoloth in Chapter 44, about Psalm 118.
7. Frankl, *Man's Search for Meaning*, 96.
8. Frankl, *Man's Search for Meaning*, 104.

These treasured moments from the past came up in a conversation I had with my friend Rabbi Mark Asher Goodman. In his book, *Life Lessons from Recently Dead Rabbis: Hasidut for the People*, he relates a teaching of the Ba'al Shem Tov. ll blessings are meaningless without peace, because without peace, all the other blessings can be taken away.[9] I pushed back. Not all blessings can be taken away, and even in the absence of peace it's possible to have real, meaningful blessings, even if they only last a moment. Otherwise, what meaning can there be for the person dying young of inexorable disease; what joy can there be for people living through crisis after crisis?

This realization also allows us to make more sense, belatedly, of Dayenu. Throughout his memoir Frankl recalls the miniscule but real pleasures of things that would happen in the camp that were unexpectedly not horrible—even including moments of comedy. In a universe where the first substance created was chaos, the existence of any order at all is cause for joy and praise to God. *Maror* is here, right after Dayenu, to help us understand that it *would* have been enough just to be released from bondage. That moment can never be taken from our people, or from the world. Jews have continued to commemorate it in our worst moments thereafter, including during the Shoah.

I've had this same conversation with people whose cancer has returned, and individuals who have entered a relapse of their substance use disorder. The recurrence doesn't invalidate what went before; they'll always have those well-lived years free of cancer, those nine months of peaceful sobriety. Those took strength and courage to achieve, and they can never be taken away. Even if we never reach the "top step," it's enough to know that we have, at least for a time, risen even the tiniest bit from the lowest depths of suffering.

9.. Goodman. Life Lessons from Recently Dead Rabbis, 140–142.

29

In Every Generation

Rabban Gamliel's three things are followed by a powerful message—don't just remember the Exodus. Act as if you've experienced it yourself, and be changed by it.

| In each and every generation, a person is obligated to see himself as if he left Egypt . . . Not only our ancestors did the Holy One, blessed be He, redeem, but rather also us [together] with them did He redeem, as it is stated (Deuteronomy 6:23); "And He took us out from there, in order to bring us in, to give us the land which He swore unto our fathers." | בְּכָל־דּוֹר וָדוֹר חַיָּב אָדָם לִרְאוֹת אֶת־עַצְמוֹ כְּאִלּוּ הוּא יָצָא מִמִּצְרָיִם . . . שֶׁנֶּאֱמַר: לֹא אֶת־אֲבוֹתֵינוּ בִּלְבָד גָּאַל הַקָּדוֹשׁ בָּרוּךְ הוּא, אֶלָּא אַף אוֹתָנוּ גָּאַל עִמָּהֶם, שֶׁנֶּאֱמַר: וְאוֹתָנוּ הוֹצִיא מִשָּׁם, לְמַעַן הָבִיא אוֹתָנוּ, לָתֶת לָנוּ אֶת־הָאָרֶץ אֲשֶׁר נִשְׁבַּע לַאֲבֹתֵינוּ. |

One enduring message of a lifetime of sedarim and half a lifetime of medical training and practice is that the real conversations happen at night. I spent a lot of nights in the neonatal ICU during my residency, and on one of those nights happened to be working with one of the veteran nurses who saw working with residents as an opportunity to teach us to be better doctors. What she taught me that night, however, had nothing to do with neonatology.

In subtle violation of the hospital dress code, the edge of a tattoo extended above the V-neck of her scrubs on the left side. I don't remember how the conversation started or what the tattoo depicted. But as Dana and

I worked delicately through the process of inspecting, injecting, detecting and protecting a tiny newborn, she explained that she was a breast cancer survivor. The original "tattoo" on her left breast was four tiny crosses, like "x" marks on a pirate treasure map, used by the radiation oncologist to line up the beams they used to shrink her tumor before surgery. The final product was her way of transforming the experience of cancer into a permanent visual reminder of what she was capable of enduring, and of beautifying something which initially seemed to be disfiguring her body. Minute to minute, day to day, the experience of surviving cancer was with her.

IDENTITY AND EMPATHY

What Dana did in her lifetime with her tattoo is what Jews do throughout history with the seder. We've arrived at what the Minchat Ani calls "the central statement of the Passover seder."[1] *Bekhol dor vador hayyav ha adam lir'ot et 'atzmo k'ilu hu yatza miMitzrayim.* "In every generation a (the) person is obligated to see themselves as if they came forth from Mitzrayim." Dana's narrow place was breast cancer, and she made sure she would not only recall that place at every point but transformed it into a mark of hope and defiance. The "take-home point" of calling out the three symbolic objects in the seder is to "see" ourselves, and others, in light of the narrow places we've been.

The seder is a dual-purpose exercise. On the one hand, it's an exercise in identity. "Those enslaved people, thousands of years ago? They were us. We descend from them, and without the redemption that happened to them, we ourselves would be slaves." Exodus 13:5–8 tells the Israelites leaving Egypt what they should do to mark the Exodus once they *enter* Israel and settle there, and the conclusion of this commandment is, "And you shall explain to your child on that day, 'It is because of what Hashem did for me when I went free from Egypt.'"

Does this verse address the adults leaving Egypt (all of whom except two will die in the desert) their children who are destined to be old when they finally cross into the Promised Land, the desert-born generation who are born free and enter the land as adults, or the children yet to be born who will live their entire lives on the soil of the land of Israel? Rabbi Ya'akov Lorberbaum, in his commentary Ma'aseh Nissim, looks past all

---

1. Ettlinger, Minchat Ani, "Rabban Gamliel's Three Things."

of that, to his own generation in 18th century Ukraine, and acknowledges that this is not a literal commandment anchored in history, but rather explained by the word *k'ilu*, "as if."

Ma'aseh Nissim references a phrase, "for our ancestors and for us," that we see in the Haggadah in the *V'hi she'amdah* text.[2] What God did for them, says Ma'aseh Nissim, was done so that we could have the privilege we have today, of remaining Jews and living by the Torah. We weren't *in* the actual Mitzrayim, but we recognize our debt and our obligation to God for effecting that redemption which shaped our identity.

But if this is all figurative, why bother with this statement at all? Avadim Hayyinu already taught us, in interpreting Deuteronomy 6:23, that we owe this debt to God for ensuring that we ourselves are not still enslaved in Egypt. Why add another passage? No verse of Torah is supposed to be redundant or superfluous. Exodus 13:8 and Deuteronomy 6:23 can't amount to the same thing, even though the whole book of Deuteronomy is Moses' retelling of the story of the Israelites from the Exodus until just before he dies. Hence the name "Deuteronomy," second telling.

There are two verses in the statement because identity formation is only *one* of the goals of seder. The second goal is the development of empathy. Deuteronomy 6:23 suggests that this goal is "in order to take us and give us the land promised on oath to our fathers." This is an identity goal, taking a people out of enslavement so they can be brought into the place where they were meant to live together as a nation. But there's another, broader goal to redemption, and so to seder.

"Who brought you out of the land of Egypt to be your God," reads Numbers 15:41. That verse is read twice daily in the last paragraph of the Shema prayer—the one our insomniac rabbis had to be reminded to recite because their discussion went on so long. Deuteronomy 6:24, the verse after the one that Avadim Hayyinu interprets, says that taking on God's commandments is a goal of the Exodus. The Israelites, as a "people that dwells apart, not reckoned among the nations,"[3] further define and separate themselves through the observance of laws which don't apply to other nations. But these laws have more to them than just peculiar folkways to maintain that separate identity.

Those observances are meant from the inception to be kept *in the company of other nations*. In the aftermath of the near sacrifice of Yitzhak,

---

2. See Chapter 15.
3. Numbers 23:9

the angel tells Avraham, "All the nations of the earth will be blessed by your descendants." The presence of Avraham's descendants, through the line of Yitzhak, Ya'akov and beyond, in the world is supposed to be a positive for the whole world.

How this benefit is to be realized becomes clear after the Exodus, and after the smoke and thunder of the revelation at Mount Sinai. Exodus 22:20 prohibits us from wronging or oppressing a stranger, "for you were strangers in the land of Egypt." This is the first of at least thirty-six mentions of this prohibition in the Torah.[4] Therefore: Avraham made a covenant with God, on multiple occasions, and was warned that in the process of fulfilling that covenant, his descendants would be enslaved in a land not their own. The end goal of that covenant was that the nations of the world would be blessed by those descendants. For that to happen, they needed to be redeemed from that narrow place, brought to their own place, and given their own laws. The commandment not to wrong the stranger, whose observance is inextricably linked to remembering what it was like to have been strangers themselves, appears in those laws more often than any other. In other words, *the most heavily emphasized consequence of being liberated from Mitzrayim* is empathy with, and aid for, those who are still there.

In this context it's easy to understand why American Jews in the seventies held Soviet Jewry seders to raise awareness for their fellow Jews living under communism. It explains the existence of women's seders that focus participants' attention on domestic violence, restriction of women's access to education in many countries, and gender inequity in the workplace. And it explains the attempts at each year's seder to make sense of that year's looming crisis and what it means to the lives of our neighbors: COVID-19, the Russian invasion of Ukraine, or the plight of Darfuri, Uighur, or Rohingya minorities under oppressive and violent rulers. It's why there's a Human Rights Haggadah, and why a thoroughly Ashkenazi Jew like me owns a copy of the Israeli Black Panther Haggadah. And it explains why, even as sedarim in 2024 commemorated the attacks of October 7, 2023, and the literal captivity of many of its victims, other sedarim—and sometimes *those same sedarim* (including mine)—turned their attention to the suffering of the residents of Gaza in the war that followed those attacks. The identity formed in the first part of the seder is supposed to pay off in the empathy we develop in its second part.

---

4. Talmud Bava Metzia 59b

FOUR QUESTIONS, FOUR CUPS, FOUR KINDS OF . . . EMPATHY?

But if empathy for others, rather than identity with our own group, is the purpose of the Exodus and ultimately the purpose of the seder ritual, doesn't the Ma'aseh Nissim undercut that purpose by dismissing our attempts to feel as if we were "actually there?" Wouldn't our empathy be stronger if we were able to viscerally imagine the pain of enslavement, the degradation of bondage and the exuberance of liberation?

About ten years ago, a team of physician-researchers at Nagoya University medical school in Japan, led by Muneyoshi Aomatsu, attempted to answer that exact question.[5] They were concerned with existing research that showed, on the one hand, the importance of empathy as a clinical skill in medicine and, on the other hand, declining levels of empathy in medical trainees as they moved up the medical hierarchy. In response, they gathered focus groups of their medical students and residents[6] to ask how each of them viewed empathy—and more importantly, how they displayed empathy to others.

Aomatsu's group built on an older framework by Morse and colleagues that identified four forms of empathy: Emotive, moral, cognitive, and behavioral.[7] Emotive empathy is the plain meaning of the *Bekhol dor vador* verse: One should be able to feel oneself as a formerly enslaved person who's been freed in their lifetime, is subjectively reliving the experience, and understanding what it *feels like*. Aomatsu's students exhibited high levels of emotive empathy. The students and residents alike in Aomatsu's group identified moral empathy as their obligation to understand people's suffering and help them with it. It's the equivalent of the word *hayyav*, required or obligated, in the verse. We *must* empathize; it's our duty.[8]

---

5. Aomatsu et al, "Medical Students' and Residents' Conceptual Structure of Empathy."

6. Medical students are learning to be doctors. Residents are licensed doctors undergoing additional training before they can practice completely independently. In teaching hospitals, more senior residents are often primarily responsible for most of the care their patients receive, with the attending physician serving as a kind of ground control while the resident is the pilot.

7. Aomatsu et al, "Medical Students' and Residents' Conceptual Structure of Empathy," 5.

8. Aomatsu et al, "Medical Students' and Residents' Conceptual Structure of Empathy," 6.

Then the study got interesting. The decline in empathy that previous researchers had identified wasn't as clear-cut as it seemed. Rather, Aomatsu's group realized, that residents, as they grew in clinical experience, didn't feel they could keep up the *emotive* empathy any longer. They'd witnessed too much suffering and felt they ran the risk of emotional burnout themselves if they leaned forward into it too much.[9] They bought into the truism about "compassion fatigue" that Brian Miller has argued is a myth.

However, these residents did not just put up walls against emotionally charged situations. Instead, they developed a much stronger degree of *cognitive* empathy, the intellectual ability to identify and understand the sources and significance of another person's suffering from a more detached point of view. Then, they recognized the correct, useful response— a response not unlike the Ma'aseh Nissim's response to the Exodus. This response acknowledges he didn't experience the event firsthand but can understand the debt he owes. Similarly, the residents knew they couldn't live through the emotions that every patient was experiencing, but they could recognize what those emotions must mean to the patient and respond even without feeling them personally.

This cognitive empathy led in turn to a high degree of *behavioral* empathy, the ability to communicate a response to a person's suffering that resonates positively with them in a time of suffering. Trzeciak and Mazzarelli, in *Compassionomics*, argue that behavioral empathy isn't empathy at all, but compassion. They define compassion as concrete behaviors, including ones we might refer to as "outstretched arm" behaviors, while empathy is defined as primarily emotional and cognitive, something we feel instead of something we *do*.[10] So, the residents weren't avoiding compassion fatigue—they were electing to get off the emotional roller-coaster so they could *engage* in compassion more effectively.[11]

I (if you'll forgive me) feel them. In the beginning, in 2008 when I was a new attending physician, I wanted to cry with everyone. There are too many tears shed in my office for that to be possible. But as I grew in experience, and learned how far my outstretched arm could reach, my empathy would just as often take the form of transportation assistance as of tears. Emotional empathy can often lead to lots of "thoughts and

---

9. Aomatsu et al, "Medical Students' and Residents' Conceptual Structure of Empathy," 6–7.

10. Trzeciak and Mazzarelli, *Compassionomics*, 3.

11. Aomatsu et al, "Medical Students' and Residents' Conceptual Structure of Empathy," 6–8.

prayers." Maybe my behavioral empathy, my compassion, comes in the form of paperwork instead of prayers, but it means someone gets their citizenship, or their accessible housing.

FAKE IT 'TIL YOU MAKE IT

The growth and change of empathic responses of the Japanese students and residents raises an interesting question: What is "real" empathy? Is it empathic behavior, the part that the patient sees and responds to, or is it the inner mental state? Is it a problem if the clinician "Walks the walk" but doesn't "feel the feel" inside? In 21st century America, we devalue people who "aren't genuine" or who are "fake," not saying what they mean all the time. Is the person exhibiting behavioral empathy "fake" if they lack the emotive component?

Rabbi Chaim Josef David Azulay, in his 18th century Haggadah commentary "Simchat HaRegel," made a word choice which caught my eye in this section. He wrote, *she-hayyav* l'har'ot *atzmo*, "that is obligated to *show (or present)* himself," instead of "lir'ot *atzmo*," "to *see* himself."[12] The commentary Safa Echat explains that this means, "(he) will get very excited and make preparations as if this night the holiday will be sanctified and he is willing and ready to leave Egypt."[13] Safa Echat is describing behavioral empathy, *acting* in a manner that shows others that the person making the seder really means it, that he really believes he's about to be redeemed from enslavement.

I care for a couple of people who have worked as "simulated patients." They were specially trained to play the role of a patient for the purpose of training medical students, nursing students, PA students, or some other trainee in the health professions. The students might practice doing an exam, conducting an interview, or some other skill requiring interacting with a live person whose well-being doesn't depend on the outcome of that interaction. In my first meeting with one of them, we ventured into some difficult topics, and I gave a brief response to encourage the person to continue. "Boy, doc," they remarked, "you're really knocking that empathetic language out of the park."

I was momentarily flustered, but eventually responded, somewhat hesitantly, "Sorry, that's actually how I speak. Is it a problem?" They

---

12. Azulay, *Simchat HaRegel*. "In Every Generation."
13. Azulai, *Safa Echat*, "In Every Generation."

reassured me that it wasn't, and that despite their tone it was meant as a compliment. They had just heard so many others try, and stumble over the words, that hearing them used in the normal flow of conversation was a surprise.

EMPATHIZING SLOWLY

Remember that many of those who flub their attempts at validating language are among those most likely to have a high degree of emotive empathy—people in their early years of training. I watch it happen all the time with students. I know they're concerned, compassionate human beings, but they turn stiff and awkward when they need to express their concern and compassion to the person to whom it's directed. This is especially true if that person is somehow "other" than them for reasons of race, culture, language—or a teenager, because teenagers can be cynical about absolutely *everything*.

The exhortation we're discussing comes only after we've heard the narrative in two different forms, asked questions, sung songs about recurring persecutions, praised God for all the blessings of Dayenu, and spilled wine to remember the suffering of the Egyptians. Now, and only now, have we internalized enough of the story to *act* the part of one who has themselves gone forth from Egypt. Only now have we performed enough parts of the ritual that it's becoming natural for us to *behave* like people who have been redeemed from slavery ourselves. Perhaps this is why the Maaseh Nissim thinks this command isn't meant for the generation that left Egypt, the generation of the desert, or even the first generation born in the land. Centuries of telling and refining the story had to pass before we really understood what we were being told.

Similarly, behavioral empathy that we effect on the first flush of emotion for someone's sad plight is in danger of feeling more like pity than empathy, or ends up being misplaced, awkward, or inadvertently hurtful. It takes a tremendous amount of listening, holding space and processing a story—what physician-author Victoria Sweet calls "slow medicine"—to get to a place where one can behave empathetically in a way that's both genuine and genuinely helpful to the person we're caring for. I got to hear Dr. Sweet speak about her time at Laguna Honda hospital in San Francisco, documented in her book, *God's Hotel*, during a 2022 conference. She cared for patients there whom society had mostly given up on. That care was facilitated by ample, beautiful physical space and protected time to go deep with patients, both in collecting the details of their medical history and in learning their stories, which were often inextricably tangled together.[14]

Laguna Honda made space for conversations and interactions like the ones I had with my nurse friend years ago in the NICU, and like the ones we have around the seder table. The consultants inevitably came and wrecked Laguna Honda with their concerns about "efficiency," and it's no surprise to anyone who's attended a seder that people always complain it's taking too long, even the short ones. Empathy can't be generated, internalized and practiced quickly, any more than knot-tying or heart surgery. Only at the end, after careful listening, completion of all the steps of the process, and free-ranging questions and answers, can a new healer truly say, "now I feel you."

NO NEED FOR "AS IF"

If you've read this far in this book, you know that I, too, have spent a lot of time with my foot in my mouth, and not just in clinic. Many years ago, when I'd just started providing a lot of refugee healthcare, I got the idea to invite one of the refugee families I was working with to our seder, to make the whole experience more tangible for the other guests. I took the plan to my wife with great enthusiasm, which immediately evaporated when she looked at me blankly and replied, "A family of refugees? You mean, like me and my parents?"

Not everyone needs to be taught to empathize or exercise their imagination to understand what another person's going through. Some people do it effortlessly, because they *have* been there. They say, "this is because of what God did for me when I came out of Egypt," and mean it literally. People like Dana, whose story I told at the beginning of this chapter.

They're the people who organize the races for cures, the support groups, and the Facebook forums so that the next person who faces the same sickness won't go through it alone. They pass on the medical equipment they no longer need and the knowledge they learned the hard way. They help healers learn from the mistakes they had to endure so that others won't have to walk the same road—like the family who endowed

14. Sweet, "Slow Medicine."

the death and dying workshop for my pediatric residency in memory of their own child who died at our hospital years before. Sometimes, they become healers themselves, like several of the residents I trained under—and several of the students I've trained—whose own struggles with illness compelled them to be there for others experiencing the same thing.

I've been very clear that I don't know why we're faced with monumental challenges. Our world is chaos, and chaos hurts like hell. But this turning point in the seder tells me what to do with those challenges—turn around and help others with theirs. And I'm definitely feeling that.

Thoughts and Discussions

- *What kind of empathy are you best at? What kind do you find helps you the most?*
- *Is it enough to say the right thing without feeling it—or to say the wrong thing with the right emotion?*
- *What have you endured in your own "narrow place" that makes you able to be there for others?*

30

A Happy Mother of Children

Hallel is a collection of six psalms (113–118) of effusive praise recited in synagogues on the mornings of the major holidays, new months, and Hanukkah. Only on Passover do we recite Hallel at night: Psalms 113–114 before dinner, and Psalms 115–118 after dinner. , The music and poetry of these special Psalms help us achieve the feeling of "being there" at the Exodus.

Psalm 113	תהילים קיג
Halleluyah! Praise, servants of the Lord, praise the name of the Lord. May the Name of the Lord be blessed from now and forever. From the rising of the sun in the East to its setting, the name of the Lord is praised. Above all nations is the Lord, His honor is above the heavens. Who is like the Lord, our God, Who sits on high; Who looks down upon the heavens and the earth? He brings up the poor out of the dirt; from the refuse piles, He raises the destitute. To seat him with the nobles, with the nobles of his people. He seats a barren woman in a home, a happy mother of children. Halleluyah!	הַלְלוּיָהּ הַלְלוּ עַבְדֵי ה', הַלְלוּ אֶת־שֵׁם ה'. יְהִי שֵׁם ה' מְבֹרָךְ מֵעַתָּה וְעַד עוֹלָם. מִמִּזְרַח שֶׁמֶשׁ עַד מְבוֹאוֹ מְהֻלָּל שֵׁם ה'. רָם עַל־כָּל־גּוֹיִם ה', עַל הַשָּׁמַיִם כְּבוֹדוֹ. מִי כַּיי אֱלֹהֵינוּ הַמַּגְבִּיהִי לָשָׁבֶת, הַמַּשְׁפִּילִי לִרְאוֹת בַּשָּׁמַיִם וּבָאָרֶץ? מְקִימִי מֵעָפָר דָּל, מֵאַשְׁפֹּת יָרִים אֶבְיוֹן, לְהוֹשִׁיבִי עִם־נְדִיבִים, עִם נְדִיבֵי עַמּוֹ. מוֹשִׁיבִי עֲקֶרֶת הַבַּיִת, אֵם הַבָּנִים שְׂמֵחָה. הַלְלוּיָהּ.

I spent Pesach in Israel in 1993. It was a giddy time by Israeli standards, flush with the first real prospect of peace with the Palestinians. That, in turn, came on the heels of having survived both the Gulf War and the epochal winter of 1991–92, where the heavy snow did more damage to the roofs in Petah Tikvah than the Scud missiles. No less important, in 1991 the remainder of the Jewish community of Ethiopia arrived in a coordinated military action called Operation Solomon.

While visiting a friend in Even Yehudah just days before the holiday, I caught a program on television featuring the singer Shlomo Gronich, singing with a choir composed of children and teens from Ethiopia. They were called "Makhelat Sh'va," the Sheba Choir, after the biblical queen of Sheba who supposedly wed King Solomon (Shlomo!), and with him had offspring who were purported to be the ancestors of the very children singing in that choir. Before they could stand on that stage in front of that camera, they had walked hundreds of miles across desolate country into hostile Sudan so they could board stripped down 747s carrying nearly a thousand people each.

Their song moved me to the kind of joyous, lump-in-the-throat tears that I never see coming.

'Od m'at, 'od k'tzat, l'harim raglayim, ma'amatz aharon lifnei Yerushalayim

"A little longer, a little further. Lift your feet, one last effort before Jerusalem!"

Nineteen Pesachs later, I was cleaning closets to prepare the holiday when I noticed something wrong with *my* foot. I'd done a little more walking that weekend than I was accustomed to, though certainly not walking from Ethiopia to Sudan, and developed what one of my colleagues initially thought was a stress fracture. I limped through one day of work before the pain subsided, but during that day of work I mused on how my being hobbled just as I was preparing to "leave Egypt" put me in mind of the much greater suffering a patient who's been in my care for years.

Like the children of the Sheba choir, this person also had to march for miles to get to the nearest city with the airport, and the US consulate, to get safely to the United States to begin a new life. She undertook the journey in shoes no sturdier than dollar-store flip-flops, and the damage to her feet was so pervasive that my first three years of working with her consisted of little more than referrals back and forth to a foot and ankle surgeon.

There was one thing more. She still hoped for another child, an American-born child in celebration of her new home. The worry that she might no longer be able to realize that dream hung over everything that happened afterward.

I've learned not to underestimate the powerful pull of having children. So many of my most moving stories from practice revolve around fertility and infertility—with couples that can't conceive and those who finally do. Even with would-be grandparents who pine for the grandchildren that those couples have not yet gifted them. Infertility struggles are well-represented in Biblical texts, with Sarah and Rivkah, Rahel and Hannah, and the archetypal childless ones in Isaiah 57. And they're represented here, in the Haggadah, as we begin to sing the Hallel.

Psalm 113 begins as the introduction of Hallel says it should: By heaping praise on Hashem, the Incomparable One. But when the psalmist asks the question, "Who is like the Lord, our God, Who sits on high; Who looks down upon the heavens and the earth?" it's not the 'rising of the sun in the East (and) its setting' that makes Hashem Incomparable. Rather, "He brings up the poor out of the dirt; from the refuse piles, He raises the destitute. To seat him with the nobles, with the nobles of his people. He seats a barren woman in a home, a happy mother of children."

All the work of creation, ordering the heavens and dwelling on high, is the stuff of every mythology and cosmology ever told. It's also entirely out of reach of the human beings who are told at the outset of the Torah that we're created in God's image. But the *end* of Psalm 113 is entirely within our grasp, to bring the poor out of the dirt, raise the destitute, and seat them with the nobles—including here, with us, on this very night as we offered to do back in *Ha Lahma 'Anya*. And yes, to seat a barren woman in a home as a happy mother of children.

My friend with the sore feet didn't end up requiring my intervention. Her American daughter was born about three years after her arrival in the US, and she now sits in her home as a happy mother of five children. The Sheba Choir still brings me to tears, and you, readers, have not heard the last of Shlomo Gronich.

Thoughts and Discussions

- *What seemingly "miraculous" things are within your power to accomplish?*
- *What is not in your power?*

31

Taunting the Sea

Psalm 114 celebrates the Israelites crossing the Sea of Reeds, the moment they are truly free from Egypt.

Psalm 114	תהילים קי״ד
In Israel's going out from Egypt... What is happening to you, O Sea, that you are fleeing, O Jordan that you turn to the rear; O mountains that you dance like rams, O hills like young sheep? From before the Master, tremble O earth, from before the Lord of Ya'akov. He who turns the boulder into a pond of water, the flint into a spring of water.	בְּצֵאת יִשְׂרָאֵל מִמִּצְרָיִם... מַה לְּךָ הַיָּם כִּי תָנוּס, הַיַּרְדֵּן—תִּסֹּב לְאָחוֹר, הֶהָרִים—תִּרְקְדוּ כְאֵילִים, גְּבָעוֹת כִּבְנֵי־צֹאן. מִלִּפְנֵי אָדוֹן חוּלִי אָרֶץ, מִלִּפְנֵי אֱלוֹהַּ יַעֲקֹב. הַהֹפְכִי הַצּוּר אֲגַם־מָיִם, חַלָּמִישׁ לְמַעְיְנוֹ־מָיִם.

Reeeeeeed Sea, Reeeeeeed Sea....

Don't mess with the tune for B'tzeit Yisrael.

There are synagogue tunes so old, so well known, that cantors refer to them as "mi-Sinai," handed down on Mt. Sinai with the Torah. We've been singing them forever and they're the tunes that God Personally intended to be used with these songs. This theory is iron-clad, so long as you don't visit another synagogue and hear them sing their mi-Sinai tune—which is totally different from your heretical version.

The canonical tune I've grown up with for B'tzeit Yisrael, the 114th Psalm that appears at this point in the seder, is the one where the latter four verses are a call and response that begins with the words, Mah l'kha, ha-yam? "What's your issue, sea?" What's wrong with you that you're fleeing? What's wrong with you, Jordan River, that you're turning around?

It sounds like a taunt, and a triumphant one at that, with the third "response" line soaring to hit a gut punch of a high note (ha ^{Yaaaar}den) that calls out the Jordan River, and later returns to call out the flint which melts into a puddle of water. It reminds me of hockey fans razzing a goaltender whose luck has suddenly left him. I was watching from home one night as Dan Vogel and his daughter used their prime seats at the Penguin game to chant "Eeee-gor! Eeee-gor!" at New York Rangers' netminder Igor Shesterkin as he surrendered five goals in about 12 minutes.

Pittsburgh sports legend has us believe that such taunts hold the power to change a game. On October 1, 2013, a playoff-starved Pirates fan base showed up 40,000 strong and in full throat. After Cincinnati Reds' ace pitcher Johnny Cueto served up a home run to Marlon Byrd, he appeared a little rattled. After getting the next batter out, he gave the fans all the provocation they needed to heckle him mercilessly—he dropped the ball on the mound.

"Cueeeee-toooo! Cueeeee-toooo!" They sang. It was a gift to Pirate catcher Russell Martin, who hit yet another home run, causing pundits on Twitter to proclaim, "the fans at PNC Park just hit that home run. Cueto is a mess."

But why on earth would the Israelites at the shores of the sea, 3,000 years before the invention of ice hockey or baseball, be thumbing their noses at the Sea of Reeds? To understand that we must examine their relationship to water across the whole book of Exodus.

AT THE WATER'S EDGE

The moment before the mockery breaks out, the water appears to be a fatal obstacle. With the pursuing army of Mitzrayim hot on their heels, the water before them appears to spell their doom. They face Hobson's choice of drowning or dismemberment. At the last moment, after God has told them to keep quiet while a Divine miracle saves them from the hand of Pharaoh, the waters part to provide an escape route, then reunite to trap their pursuers. In time, these same waters will become a wall behind us, preventing us from taking the easy way back to Mitzrayim, back to the illusory comfort of enslavement when the burdens of freedom become too much to bear.

After the crossing, it's not the presence of water but the absence of water that fills the Israelites with despair. At Marah, the water is too bitter to drink, until God directs Moshe to throw in a piece of wood to sweeten it. At Rephidim, there's no water to be had at all, until the same staff that rendered the waters of the Nile (indeed, throughout Mitzrayim) undrinkable as they turned to blood now strikes the rock and turns "the flint into a pool of water," the final image of this psalm.

How could we not sing at such a time? It's the great illusion of modern, Western life that we can control every circumstance and that our default state in life should be one of material contentment and absence of want. Human history is a quest for fuel and water, protein and shelter (it's been suggested that intoxicating beverages may be on that list as well). The 21st century ethos seems to be that the quest is at an end. It's a version of the naturalistic fallacy, believing that we're supposed to have these objects of striving in hand, in abundance, always. Water is supposed to be the source of life. And yet. . .

Our ancestors knew otherwise. They'd seen their infant sons and brothers drowned in water and been forced to fetch water (and straw) to make the very bricks they'd then be forced to stack into pyramids. Seeing the waters of the Sea of Reeds, the flow of the Jordan River, and the gushing rock suddenly obey God's command to their benefit, they couldn't help but rejoice. For once, things were going their way. They were, for the moment, getting the better of the water. Like John Donne, mocking Death in his poem "Death, Be Not Proud" for being subject to the whims of kings and keeping the company of sickness and poison, so the Israelites needle the sea for not being so tough after all.

The second year of the COVID-19 pandemic taught a similar lesson. Year two was very different than year one. For the first year of the pandemic (it seemed, at least in my private experience) as though everything had been frozen in amber, time standing still until some future date when things would resume as they had been before. In year two, however, just as we began emerging from that suspended animation, things began to fall apart. Supply chains, technology, workforce—how many times did I scream in frustration that year, "Why doesn't anything $#%#^% work anymore?!?"

When Hashem began to create the heavens and the earth, the earth was in chaos . . . The natural state of things is not order, but chaos, wildness, entropy. Only through sheer effort or genuine miracle is it otherwise. Water runs downhill, is often brackish and dangerous to drink, and people drown in it if they don't know how to swim. We have no right to get angry at the water for being water, and we have no right to get angry at an inherently chaotic world for being chaotic. But when we can cross water on dry land, or drink it in the desert, or draw it forth from a well at Beit HaSho'eva,[1] that's cause for gratitude. And after a long series of tantrums, I can say that when I can seamlessly access my patients' records, or when I can purchase exactly what I'm looking for in the store, or when I'm introduced to the person we just hired to do a job that's gone undone for 27 months, that's also cause for joy.

That moment of joy and triumph, even if it's the exception to the rule, is also the end of fear. Water still has the capacity to drown, or dry up, and yet having crossed the sea and struck the rock we know beyond a doubt of the possibility that things can turn out differently. In the second year of the pandemic, the paralyzing fear of the virus subsided, at least somewhat, as vaccination, repurposed medications, and ultimately specific treatment turned an unchecked, deadly scourge into more of a smoldering nuisance. It continues to disrupt lives and Life, and not all our attempts to control it have such wonderful or sustainable results. As Edison remarked during his drive to create the light bulb, "Now we know 99 things that don't work."

But when one of them does, we should sing.

---

1. According to Mishnah Sukkah 5:1, the rejoicing in this place was the greatest joy anyone had ever seen. Ovadia Bartinoro explains in his commentary that the water they were drawing was water for the libation offering in the Temple, not just simple drinking water. The joy is linked, both by Bartinoro and Maimonides, to Isaiah 12:3, *u'sh'avtem mayim b'sasson*, you shall draw water in joy.

32

Four Cups of Coffee

The Magid section of the seder concludes with the second cup of wine, which is blessed with its own blessing.

Second Cup of Wine	כוס שניה
. . . we shall thank You with a new song upon our redemption and upon the restoration of our souls. Blessed are you, Lord, who redeemed Israel.	וְנוֹדֶה לְךָ שִׁיר חָדָשׁ עַל גְּאֻלָּתֵנוּ וְעַל פְּדוּת נַפְשֵׁנוּ. בָּרוּךְ אַתָּה ה', גָּאַל יִשְׂרָאֵל.
Blessed are You, Lord our God, who creates the fruit of the vine.	בָּרוּךְ אַתָּה ה', אֱלֹהֵינוּ מֶלֶךְ הָעוֹלָם בּוֹרֵא פְּרִי הַגָּפֶן.

If my current trend keeps up, I'll soon be having four cups every day, including one right in this spot, just before my meal.

Coffee. I mean four cups of coffee. What did you think I meant?

That steaming elixir that my teacher Shekar Venkataraman used to refer to as "hot, brown liquid" as he corralled us to go tank up on the stuff at the Pop Stop before PICU rounds is as inextricably linked to the practice of medicine as wine is to the conduct of the seder. Many of us mark the passage of our days with at least four cups, sometimes far more, sometimes continuing through the night and into another day like the sages at B'nai B'rak.

But to what end?

When we drink a cup of wine at the seder, we're, to paraphrase Lin-Manuel Miranda, raising a glass to freedom. Each cup is linked, in the Talmud Yerushalmi, to one of Hashem's four promises to Israel in Exodus 6:6–7:

1) "I will free you from the labors of the Egyptians and deliver you from their bondage." 2) "I will redeem you with an outstretched arm and through extraordinary chastisements." 3) "and I will take you to be My people," 4) "and I will be your God." We can dither about whether there should be a fifth cup, representing the promise of verse 6:8, "I will bring you into the land which I swore to give to Abraham, Isaac, and Jacob, and I will give it to you for a possession,"[1] or whether, in the opinion of the Maharal of Prague and of Rabbi Isaiah Horowitz, the cups actually represent our four matriarchs, but the fact remains that the cups of wine are laden with significance.

In contrast, I think of the T-shirt I once bought my friend Mort. It depicted an old man with a fez and a long-handled *finjan*, the kind of

---

1. See Chapter 22.

coffee pot you use to boil Turkish coffee. The caption read, "First coffee kept me alert. Then it kept me awake. Now it keeps me alive."

It's a double-edged sword, this witches brew of methylxanthine alkaloids, sugar, and cream, with its intoxicating aroma that clings to our clothes as tenaciously as the stains of the liquid itself. It brings wakefulness and focus, but also tremor and panic. It puts our brains back online but tears our stomachs apart. It powers the tremendous feats of medical skill and, yes, of human caring that we aspire to, even as I sense a direct correlation between a healer's coffee consumption and their score on the Maslach burnout index.

The legal, generally safe nature of coffee makes it easy to forget that for many of us, coffee is an addiction. Frankly, my relationship with coffee is one of the best reminders I have of how blurry the line is between my own behavior and my patients'. When I hear myself constantly clearing my throat, feel my hands shaking, or wince at the pains in my stomach, it's hard to get on my high horse about *anything* my patient is doing. It's also a window into the anxiety and dread many of them feel. I had a pain management doctor, usually called in to deal with addictions to opioid pain medicines, go on a tirade about the addictive drug his patients were all on. Turns out he was talking about caffeine. And I've known some impressive "super-users": People who can drink an entire pot of black coffee and go straight to bed, and one woman with a visible tremor whose daily Starbucks intake calculated out to about 144 ounces of regular coffee.

Whether our coffee consumption will resemble an addiction or an elevation on any given day is entirely up to us, and how we choose to frame our caffeination. Any other meal in which a person consumed four glasses of wine *outside* the bounds of the meal itself, plus however much free-flowing beverage they knocked back to wash down the brisket, would be a self-indulgent, drunken embarrassment. Only the ritual of *seder* imbues that intoxicating liquid with such meaning that consuming it's no longer gluttonous (and definitely not glutinous!). It's sacred.

POP STOP PROMISES

What promise does the second cup of coffee hold for the lunchtime parade of white coats heading to the Pop Stop (not, God forbid, on Pesach, but any other time of year)? What pledge do I recall as I sip my midday cup of Zotz Blend? The second cup is the cup of rescue, and frankly by lunchtime it's rescuing me from collapsing face-first on my desk in the stolen moment between visits. It's a necessity for me to keep working. But this is a Mitzrayim mentality, not the mentality of someone who's just rejoiced at the crossing of the Sea of Reeds and blown raspberries at the receding waters.

The body of the *b'rachah* over the second cup brims, overflows if you will, with a special kind of gratitude. Not only are we grateful that Hashem has brought us to this moment by rescuing us from the waters, but we're *so* grateful that we pray that Hashem will bring us back to this moment again and again in the future, and eventually to a future where we can celebrate fully.

We're not finished with our journey. It's approaching halftime, but as any sports fan knows the second half is fraught, even when we think we're winning. When we stop to utter blessings and praises at the midpoint, whether over wine or coffee, it must be for more than just to power through to the end. We have to pause and reflect on what we want the end to look like. If the cup is just to wake us up to keep going, or just to drown our sorrows, then it's meaningless.

There's a popular bumper sticker among shelter pet owners that reads, "Who Rescued Who?" The promise of rescue, as we've learned, is that we'll be rescued *so that someday we may rescue others*. We're being saved for a purpose. And the gift of that purpose, so much more so the possibility of fulfilling it again in the future, is worthy of our thanks indeed.

Thoughts and Discussions

- *What stories do we tell ourselves about our bad habits to justify them to ourselves? How might we reframe them to make them holier?*
- *What does rescue or redemption look like?*
- Who have you rescued? Who has rescued *you*?

33

A Clean Break?

After Magid, seder participants wash their hands a second time, this time saying the traditional blessing when washing before all meals.

Rachtzah	רחצה
We wash the hands and make the blessing.	:נוטלים את הידים ומברכים
Blessed are You, Lord our God, King of the Universe, who has sanctified us with His commandments and has commanded us on the washing (lit. "raising up") of the hands.	בָּרוּךְ אַתָּה ה׳, אֱלֹהֵינוּ מֶלֶךְ הָעוֹלָם, אֲשֶׁר קִדְּשָׁנוּ בְּמִצְוֹתָיו וְצִוָּנוּ עַל נְטִילַת יָדָיִם.

What's the difference between washing and washing?

It's neither a Zen *koan* nor a bad pun (When is a door not a door? When it's ajar). It's a legitimate question, one that Elisha Waldman's six-year-old son asked at the seder. Why wash twice? What's the difference between the one without the blessing, *ur'hatz*, at the beginning of the seder, and this one, *rahtzah,* just before the meal?

Ever the rabbi's son, Elisha tried explaining the origins of the pre-*karpas* washing and the washing before bread, to which his son responded, "I'm not sure I really heard an answer."

Well, young Waldman, let your dad and me try this again to see if we do better together.

GO WASH YOUR HANDS AGAIN!

As Elisha and I batted around this question of two washings, we thought of the role of handwashing pre- and post-COVID. What was remarkable was that washing itself didn't change. COVID followed years of attention to hand hygiene occasioned by rampant healthcare-acquired infections with such nasty organisms as methicillin-resistant *staph aureus* (MRSA), vancomycin-resistant *enterococcus* (VRE), *clostridium difficile* (c. diff), and extended-spectrum beta-lactamase (ESBL) producing gram negative bacteria (and no, medical professionals don't pronounce those names with any less difficulty than you do). These antibiotic-indifferent bugs hitchhike on medical personnel's hands, clothing and equipment from one patient to another. Only hand hygiene and separation stand in the way of us making patients sicker than they were when they arrived. It reminds me a little of when my *own* kids were six and my wife and I used to send them back to the sink before they could come to the table, saying, "go wash your hands again—and use *soap* this time!"

Instead, the behavior and the mindset around washing changed. Every patient, and every *colleague*, was now a hazard that demanded not just clean hands, but a facemask, goggles, gloves and gown. The behavior of clinicians in the room changed; even clinicians like Elisha and me, who treat sitting down with the patient as a sacred obligation and insist on unhurried, thorough discussion, remained standing and watched the clock so we didn't spend too long in the room, especially if the patient was known to have COVID. Even our body language, the proffered handshake or the gentle touch on the shoulder, had to be discarded in favor of standing rigid in the corner or next to the door, afraid to even graze the tray table.

Washing in the "before times" created sterility, in the positive sense. It delineated a sacred space, one where unhealthy germs were banished so healing could get underway. But as Elisha observed in our conversation, washing (and gearing up) during COVID-19 created a sterile space in the negative sense of that word. Devoid of emotion, warmth, or humanity. Bland, antiseptic, stark.

Washing created a sacred space, but was it a bridge too far to attempt to create a sacred space when everything was so colored by fear and panic? Perhaps not.

BE AFRAID. BE VERY AFRAID. BUT ALSO, IN AWE.

There's a word in Hebrew that crosses that far bridge between fear and sanctity. The word is *yir'ah*, most often rendered as "awe" to which the English expression "God-fearing" refers. Its descendant words are widespread in Jewish liturgy and practice, even naming our most sacred days. In English, the High Holy Days, the *Yamim Noraim* are days of *yir'ah*.

Importantly, the point of feeling *yir'ah* is not to be *afraid* of God, but rather to stand in awe of God's power. My friend Ira and I have a running argument over whether *yir'ah* is the emotion which Rabbi Abraham Joshua Heschel referred to when he used the term "radical amazement." I think they're equivalent, and Ira—well, Ira isn't the one writing this book, now, is he?

But *yir'ah* does contain an element of danger, if not outright fear (fear in Hebrew is *pahad* or *haradah*). We've seen this earlier in the Haggadah itself, when God leads the people out of Egypt *b'mora gadol*, with "great radically amazing awesomeness." (My translation; *mora* is some sort of concrete noun from the same root, while *yir'ah* is the noun referring to that internal feeling of, well, radical amazement). This means that the plagues that strike, well, fear and a sense of danger into the Egyptians fill the Israelites with awe for their God. I missed the 2024 solar eclipse, but both recently and historically, an eclipse was an event that carried both of these emotions—the fear of the darkness and the awe of the divine power that made it possible. Fittingly, the 2024 event fell on the first day of the Hebrew month of Nissan, exactly two weeks before Pesach—the moment when some scholars believe the plague of darkness occurred. Was this eclipse repeating itself just like the washing?

God, and the world God created, is dangerous. God is our intimate friend, and yet when we get too close God can destroy us merely by being that close. Nadav and Avihu, the two sons of Aaron, are burnt from the inside out after approaching the altar with strange fire.[1] The event is sometimes interpreted as punishment for their deviance from the prescribed ceremony. However, others see it as a reminder that God created a universe with fire and whirlwinds and tectonic upheaval, and that we shouldn't imagine such a Deity to be easily, casually approached without great trepidation. Without *yir'ah*.

So, too, with medicine. Human bodies, and the invisible, ineffable life which both sustains and attacks them, are to be held in awe. The

---

1. Leviticus 10:1–2

process of washing is awesome. *Kal va'homer* (that's Hebrew for *a fortiori*, which is Latin for "so much the moreso") if there's a pandemic going on and washing is only the first step of a multi-step process. It creates the space in which we can encounter the process of illness and healing with the proper amount of *yir'ah*.

(*The little Waldman kid still doesn't think he's gotten his answer. He doesn't realize we're not done yet—that'll teach him to ask two doctors, one who's a rabbi's son and the other who has a philosophy degree—anything at all.*)

So again, why two washings? And why a blessing the second time but not the first?

The first wash, Elisha speculates, gets you ready to *really* wash. In the *Dayenu* section we learned that the steps of *Dayenu*, the *simanim* (sections) of the seder, the "Songs of Ascent" in the book of Psalms and the steps in the Temple all numbered fifteen, symbolizing fifteen stops on the climb from enslavement to true, law-governed freedom. The first wash creates a space that's sacred—ready for the new life and hope of the *karpas*, breaking a matzah in half, and hearing the story. The story, in all its non-linear detail and richness, is what awakens the *yir'ah*, the awe and respect that we need to really be able to enter the sacred space of healing. Aware of this *yir'ah*, we now have the proper intention to wash and bless the act:

Baruch atah Hashem, elo-keinu melekh ha'olam, asher kid'shanu b'mitzvotav v'tzivanu 'al n'tilat yadayim. "Blessed are you Hashem, our God who rules the universe, that sanctified us with God's mitzvot and commanded us concerning raising up our hands."

Not washing, *raising up*. Bringing our hands up before our eyes, using the same verb that we use at the opposite pole of the year for *taking up* the four species of Sukkot and shaking them around. We raise up our hands so we can see their cleanliness, their purity—and hold our hands, too, in *yir'ah*. Because as God's instruments, our hands are also worthy of awe. They're powerful, beautiful, kind and yes, dangerous all at once, depending on what we do with them.

Raising up our hands is also demonstrative. We're preparing to *do* something with them. The story we've been retelling to create empathy in us works on the first three types of empathy that Aomatsu and colleagues described—the emotive, the moral, and the cognitive. It makes us feel and think the things we're supposed to feel and think. Raising the hands as we wash and dry them is a reminder that we're supposed to *act*, to engage in behavioral empathy, in compassion.

Armed with the stories we've heard throughout our *Maggid* section (some of them very private, vulnerable stories) we're poised to either effect great healing, or do great damage, with these pure, divinely created hands. What did Hashem command concerning raising up these hands? To use them for deeds of loving-kindness, to emulate the aspects of God that create and not consume.[2]

The first wash got us ready to wash. The second wash, and its blessing, prepares us to get out of the classroom, the nursery of Maggid. It gets us into the serious business of healing that we begin by, quite literally, breaking bread.

---

2. Talmud Sotah 14a

34

Breakable Bread

The final three rituals before the meal are: Blessing the matzah (both as bread and as matzah), blessing the bitter herbs and eating them dipped in haroset, and making a special sandwich of the two things to commemorate the missing sacrifice.

Motzi Matzah	מוציא מצה
Blessed are You, Lord our God, King of the Universe, who brings forth bread from the ground.	בָּרוּךְ אַתָּה ה', אֱלֹהֵינוּ מֶלֶךְ הָעוֹלָם הַמּוֹצִיא לֶחֶם מִן הָאָרֶץ.
Blessed are You, Lord our God, King of the Universe, who has sanctified us with His commandments and has commanded us on the eating of matzah.	בָּרוּךְ אַתָּה ה', אֱלֹהֵינוּ מֶלֶךְ הָעוֹלָם, אֲשֶׁר קִדְּשָׁנוּ בְּמִצְוֹתָיו וְצִוָּנוּ עַל אֲכִילַת מַצָּה.

Maror	מרור
Blessed are You, Lord our God, King of the Universe, who has sanctified us with His commandments and has commanded us on the eating of *marror*.	בָּרוּךְ אַתָּה ה', אֱלֹהֵינוּ מֶלֶךְ הָעוֹלָם, אֲשֶׁר קִדְּשָׁנוּ בְּמִצְוֹתָיו וְצִוָּנוּ עַל אֲכִילַת מָרוֹר.

Korech All present take matzah and *marror*, wrap them together and eat them saying . . . In memory of the Temple according to Hillel . . . when the Temple existed, He would wrap the Matzah and *marror* and eat them together, in order to fulfill what is stated, (Numbers 9:11): "You should eat it upon matsot and *marrorim*."	כּוֹרֵךְ כל אחד מהמסבים לוקח כזית מן המצה השלישית עם כזית מרור, כורכים יחד, אוכלים בהסבה ובלי ברכה. לפני אכלו אומר. זֵכֶר לְמִקְדָּשׁ כְּהִלֵּל. כֵּן עָשָׂה הִלֵּל בִּזְמַן שֶׁבֵּית הַמִּקְדָּשׁ הָיָה קַיָּם: הָיָה כּוֹרֵךְ מַצָּה וּמָרוֹר וְאוֹכֵל בְּיַחַד, לְקַיֵּם מַה שֶּׁנֶּאֱמַר: עַל מַצּוֹת וּמְרוֹרִים יֹאכְלֻהוּ.

BREAD?

Spring in Jerusalem is incomparable. There's a certain winding boulevard you can walk where, if you head south, you have a gently sloping valley to your right the entire time, and parallel arcs of limestone houses and apartments climbing the hillside to your left. Just after noon on an April day, the light, the temperature, the breeze and the exact shades of cream-colored stones, maroon roofs, and forest green leaves are all perfect.

One such perfect day, I had lunch to celebrate the seventh day of Pesach, as one does, with my roommate's girlfriend's parents. Their living room window overlooked the same panorama as the path I'd walked, and the apartment filled with the scent of Persian food. The whole afternoon felt like one continuous sigh of contentment.

Except the beginning of the meal. In Persian Jewish custom, even at the non-seder meals during Pesach, the person saying the *bracha* over the matzah raises it in their hands and says, "*Al akhilat matzah, Baruch Atah Hashem, Elokeinu Melekh Ha'olam, Hamotzi lehem min ha-aretz.*" "On eating matzah, Blessed are you Hashem, our God, ruler of the universe who brings forth bread from the earth." They announce, just in case anyone missed it, "hey, this isn't actually bread, we're having matzah today." Years later, when I first read Erica Brown's essay about apologetically serving matzah (see Chapter 27), this is the episode I thought of.

Being exactly 0% Persian, I of course immediately adopted this custom and have maintained it to this day, muttering '*al akhilat matzah* under my breath every time I'm about to say Hamotzi over a piece of matzah. Another friend has his own custom: When blessing matzah, he stops at the word *lehem*, bread, and appends a question mark in mid-sentence,

"Who brings forth bread (?) from the earth." Could this really be bread? Surely there's been a mistake.

IT'S WHAT WE HAVE TO WORK WITH

Here we are, the climactic point of the seder, about to eat the meal (climactic because, let's face it, it's what most of the guests have been waiting for since they walked in the door), and we're registering—disappointment.

These three *simanim* of the seder—Motzi/Matzah, Maror, and Korekh—are seemingly here to do something astounding: To bless that which is less than ideal, unpleasant, a diminished version of what could have been.

Matzah we've already discussed. That poor substitute for bread is the sticking point that keeps joyous, springtime, sensory-overload, four-cups-of-wine Pesach from being hands-down the best holiday of the year. No amount of chocolate covered cashew bark, Manischewitz imitations of Fruit Loops and graham crackers made with tapioca starch, or even the sweet-and-sour brisket can dissuade my children from counting down until the dishes are packed away again and we can make pasta at the end of the eighth day.

We go straight from that experience to blessing and eating Maror, the bitter herbs. It's the quintessential bitter pill to swallow. Yet again, we thank God for sanctifying us by *commanding* that we eat the stuff. Thank you, Hashem, may I have another?

HILLEL THE ELDER, THE ORIGINAL EARL OF SANDWICH

Why, yes, you may, because just in case we didn't get our fill on the first try of Maror, we take more of it, or a different type (most traditional seder plates have a leafy green bitter herb, which is the actual maror, and also *hazeret*, which is usually horseradish or some other bitter root) and make Korekh—the "Hillel sandwich."

Hillel's sandwich (invented 1800 years before a certain compulsive gambler slapped some roasted meat between two slabs of bread so he wouldn't have to interrupt his card game) was his interpretation of how the Pesach sacrifice should be eaten, like the book says, "on matzah and bitter herbs you should eat it." But less than 50 years after he created the custom, there was no more sacrifice. The sandwich we eat for Korekh today has no Pesach offering—just more maror, some matzah and some *haroset*, which is of course supposed to represent, you know, mortar. Yum (although our *haroset* is so tasty my wife has it for breakfast every day during Pesach).

All of which is to say, we're giving thanks that we're here at all. Imitations, substitutes, bitter pills—all of it's from God, and it sure beats the alternative. I work in a resource-challenged environment. Our health center exists because our patients don't have insurance, or because they have insurance, but some other barrier prevents them from accessing the space-age medical care our city has to offer. We practice excellent medicine, but often in a way that feels like matzah: Prescribing generic drugs instead of fancy brands, doing procedures ourselves instead of referring out to a fancy specialist, or reframing from ordering every test in the book when one will do. We know what we're doing works, but it doesn't stop folks from looking down their noses a bit at us. We also know what we're doing is exhausting, like that back-breaking labor we discussed in Chapter 20.

Perhaps we're even reveling in the suffering a little bit—a practice I recommend avoiding. Otherwise, you may end up either as crispy as a piece of matzah, or literally biting off more than you can chew as I did during Korekh '94. You remember: When I may possibly have sliced off a round of raw horseradish that may possibly have been the size of four US quarters stacked one atop the other. I may possibly never have lived this down with any of the people present. Yet I may possibly, secretly, enjoy this memory so much that I'm now telling it to you for the second time in this Haggadah.

Possibly. But I'll definitely never try that again.

B'te-avon—that's Hebrew for *bon appetit!*

35

Soup's On

The Shulchan Orekh section of the seder is a festive meal—and chicken soup with matzah balls often features prominently in that meal.

| Shulchan Orech | שולחן עורך |
| We eat and drink. | .אוכלים ושותים |

No one buys a Haggadah hoping for fascinating insight on Shulchan Orech, the part where dinner is served. So, I'll provide my recipe for matzah balls and my wife's chicken soup, and if somewhere in the recipe I say something profound, no one will object.

NANA'S MATZAH BALLS

Truthfully, Nana never shared the ingredients for her matzah balls, only the secret to making them perfect. Neither cannonball-hard "sinkers" nor fall-apart fluffy floaters, her matzah balls were perfectly firm, yet light and airy. The trick was a Pesach-cooking version of the Marshmallow Experiment—no peeking! Once the last matzah ball went in the pot, the lid went on, with just a tiny crack left for enough steam to escape so they wouldn't boil over, and no touching, no peeking, no disturbing for 30 minutes. The ingredients I figured out from the back of the Streit's Matzah Meal box, then tinkered with substitutions and proportions until they were perfect. The result is far enough from what I originally read off the box that I feel safe calling it my own. Or if you prefer, it's my midrash, my d'var Torah, spoken in the name of my teachers Elinor Goodman and Aron Streit.

Ingredients—Matzah balls (Pareve, vegetarian but definitely not vegan)

This is the single recipe (probably feeds some people, but I'm used to feeding more) so if you think you have a lot of folks attending seder, or plan to host both, double it. Or quadruple it. Just keep the proportions the same *and don't peek!*

- 4 eggs, beaten
- 2 tablespoons olive oil (or whatever kosher for Pesach oil you have handy, but I promise you this tastes better)
- 2 tablespoons seltzer (try to use a brand-new bottle—and open it carefully, would you, please?)
- 1 cup matzah meal
- Salt and pepper to taste (don't over-salt—remember that the whole point of this is texture, and that each matzah ball will absorb the taste of the soup once they're combined)

1. In a large glass bowl, beat together the eggs and olive oil.
2. Season with salt and pepper and mix.
3. Add the seltzer and whisk together.

4. Immediately begin adding matzah meal a little at a time, whisking with a fork more or less continually to keep the matzah meal from clumping.

5. Keep the seltzer bottle handy; if the mixture appears too dry as you're adding the last of the matzah meal, add a few additional drops of seltzer (and I do mean a few drops, just enough to dampen the mixture so everything mixes together).

6. Once everything is evenly mixed into a thick, moist paste, cover with plastic wrap or foil and place in the refrigerator for 30 minutes. If you're hosting seder, I'm certain you have other things to do in the meantime.

7. Set a very large pot of salted water to boil on the stove.

While waiting for the mixture to be ready, consider the following: There are communities in which it's not Pesach without matzah balls, and others where matzah balls aren't even permitted on Pesach because of an issue called *gebrokts* (Yiddish for broken). The problem with *gebrokts* is that, in theory, even the most strictly prepared matzah might have a little flour left in it that was never wet. If that flour were to then get wet in the process of preparing, say, matzah balls, it would, after 18 minutes of that wait time in the fridge, begin to rise, and my matzah balls would become *hametz*!

The debate over *gebrokts* reminds me of how we deal with diet in medicine. There are so many restrictions: Cardiac diets with limited salt, diabetic diets with no sugar and very limited starch, renal (kidney) diets with low potassium and Celiac diets with no gluten. Individuals may choose to be vegetarian or vegan, have food allergies, or have migraines which react poorly to the tyramines in things like cheese, cured meat and red wine. They may get gout from too much meat, cancer from nitrosamines, or ulcers from too much coffee. And we haven't even gotten to people with more than one dietary restriction—or with conflicting ones.

Two schools of thought usually emerge. The strict school (we'd call them *mahmir* in the Jewish world) equates tighter adherence to the diet to better healing. They're not without merit. I once had dinner out with a friend who has celiac, and she ordered a very attractive platter of meats, cheeses, and nuts with not a single gluten-containing item among them. The following morning, she was so ill that she missed the next day of our conference. The wooden board that held her meal had previously been used to serve dry bread and was just wiped clean with a dry cloth before being reused. Even the tiniest bit, like that little theoretical lump of dry flour, was enough to cause calamity.

But after years of trying to abstain strictly from coffee for a month or two at a time to get my reflux, my hoarse voice, or my sore stomach to calm down, I see the limits of the *mahmir* school. Absence makes the heart grow fonder, and abstinence makes the heart desire the forbidden thing more intensely. The lenient (in Hebrew *meikel*) school recognizes that strict adherence to a diet may be great for some, but for most it has a time limit. When that time limit is up, they go "off the wagon" so spectacularly that it often undoes any progress they may have made in their illness, whether that illness is ulcers, diabetes, or migraines. Instead, we (yep, I'm in this school) encourage people to try their best, maybe even plan "off days" or "cheat days" into their health promotion plan. Back when eggs were forbidden to people with high cholesterol, Bernard Lown used to prescribe omelets for his cardiac patients on Sunday morning so they'd be more likely to stay away from eggs the rest of the week.[1]

Matzah balls are the concession. Pesach is a holiday of restrictions, a narrow place to help us commemorate the narrow place we escaped. Matzah balls are the recognition that no matter how spiritually aware we are, or how intensely we *want* to feel compelled to follow those restrictions, we need to find ways to actually *live* within those restrictions, not just exist. Whether you're living with illness, or caring for someone else who is, think of ways for life to continue and joy to exist, even in the narrow space among all the limitations.

Well, the mix should be ready by now, go check the fridge! What are you waiting for?

8. When 30 minutes are up, and the cookbook author is done pontificating, take the batter out of the fridge.
9. Fill a smaller glass bowl with cold water, and make sure your hands are squeaky clean. Wet your fingertips.
10. Take the lid off the pot of boiling water.
11. With your fingertips, pick up a small amount of batter and form it into a ball about 1 inch in diameter (don't worry if you like larger matzah balls, it'll expand in the pot). You may prefer rolling them

---

1. Lown, *Lost Art of Healing*.

between your palms instead of free form shaping with your fingers; either is fine.
12. Drop each ball straight into the boiling water as soon as you make it.
13. Every few balls, re-wet your fingers in the small bowl, shaking off excess water so the batter doesn't get too wet.
14. As soon as the last matzah ball goes into the pot, cover with the lid angled ever-so-slightly to ensure it doesn't boil over.
15. Watch for a few minutes until the pot is back at a rolling boil, then lower the heat to a simmer *without touching the lid* (I know you were thinking you'd just peek to see what was happening, don't do it).
16. Let simmer for 30 minutes and *don't touch the lid* (oy, some people, they just can't leave well enough alone)!
17. When 30 minutes are up, you can actually touch the lid. If you were a good listener and this was the first time you touched it, reward yourself with two marshmallows. Well, reward might be a strong word. They're kosher for Pesach marshmallows, after all. But have some marshmallows.
18. With a slotted nylon spoon, remove the matzah balls carefully one at a time, let the water drip back into the pot, and place in a single layer in a large baking pan. Cover and set aside for later.
19. At mealtime, either add the matzah balls to the soup pot, or keep separate as we do (there are always a couple vegetarians, so we keep them pareve[2] and have chicken soup and vegetarian soup) and add the matzah balls to each bowl as the soup is served.

---

2. "Pareve" means neutral, neither meat nor milk, and applies to all fruits, vegetables, and grains, as well as eggs and fish. Any animal that must be (kosher) slaughtered is meat, including poultry, beef, lamb, and goat. Any dairy product from the milk of a (kosher) animal is dairy, whether liquid milk, butter, or cheese. Pareve foods can be consumed with either meat or dairy foods. Note that "pareve" doesn't mean "vegan," since eggs and fish are pareve, but our pareve soup is fish-free. The matzah balls have eggs, though, as you know if you read the recipe, so they're vegetarian but not vegan. There's only so many things a person can be *mahmir* about at once.

Vita's Chicken Soup (Fleischig—meat—but feel free to use a meatless soup instead if you wish/must)

This is a much less fussy recipe. In the largest stock pot you have, combine:

One whole kosher chicken, separated into parts, and including the parts you might not serve otherwise (neck, back, etc.).

Several whole carrots

1 whole very large onion (preferably yellow—the flavor is better than white, and red onions turn a really sketchy color when boiled for hours)

1 whole parsnip

1 bunch of celery, broken into stalks

1 large bunch of parsley

1 large bunch of dill

Salt, pepper, and cinnamon to taste (you read that right; the cinnamon brings out all sorts of flavors in the chicken).

Enough stock and/or water (chicken stock or vegetable stock, or a mixture, or just water) to fill the pot most of the way to the top.

1. Put all the solid ingredients in at once, cover with whatever liquid you're using, and bring to a boil. Lower the heat so it remains at a simmer and let it go for a few hours. If you used stock, the soup will be ready sooner and likely need less seasoning; if you used water let it go longer and use a much freer hand with the seasonings.
2. When the soup tastes ready, take it off the fire. Use a spork, tongs, or other useful utensil to remove all the solid parts from the soup and separate them into the stuff you're keeping and the stuff you're tossing:
3. Keep: Chicken parts, carrots
4. Toss: Celery, onion, herbs, parsnip
5. Let the soup cool for a bit and skim some of the extra fat from the top (but not all of it! Fat is flavor!).
6. After the skimming is done, cut the carrots into bite-sized round slices and return them to the soup.

7. Take the chicken pieces and strip as much of the meat as possible from the bones (tongs are really good for this) and return to the soup. No need to chop; this recipe is best when the chicken has sort of a "pulled" quality to it.[3]

8. Dragoon a guest who has been to your house enough times that they're family to help you dish and serve soup or you'll never get to sit and eat—you've earned it! After all, this is the holiday of freedom!

---

3. I can also highly recommend using the chicken to make chicken fried rice, if you eat *kitniyot* (non-biblical grains like rice and corn and legumes, eaten by Sephardic and Mizrahi Jews on Passover but avoided by Ashkenazi Jews) on Pesach, or if you want to just freeze and save for after the holiday so you can use real soy sauce (most soy sauce has wheat in it).

36

The Missing Piece

Tzafun (hidden, the name of this part of seder): Time to find that hidden piece of matzah, called the Afikomen. Believe it or not, it's dessert.

You may know the phenomenon that happens in high school where, just as teens are about to launch into the wider world, they suddenly discover the profound, hidden truths in what they ditched in their pre-teen and early high school years as being "childish." The animated movies, lullabies, and children's books sometimes bring them exactly the comfort they need just as everything is about to change. They had hidden away parts of themselves, things they dearly loved, and broken themselves a bit in the process, so they could look cooler, more grown-up. Then they found, as they were about to become actual grownups, that they needed those pieces.

When I was in high school, one of those hidden parts that I had broken off was the Shel Silverstein book, *The Missing Piece*. I'm not sure I had ever read it when I was actually a small child, though I was certainly raised on his other classic poetry like *Where the Sidewalk Ends*, *A Light in the Attic*, and *The Giving Tree*. But *The Missing Piece* was the one that resurfaced in senior year. It was the way to signal that you were confident enough in your maturity not to be embarrassed by reading a children's book—and the gift you might give the right someone to tell them that they were *your* missing piece.

When we go to look for the *afikomen* at the end of seder, we're doing the same thing—finding pieces that we broke off and squirreled away, sometimes deliberately hoping that no one would ever find them. *Sach ha-kol*, after all, they're just crumbly pieces of matzah, of which we've already had more than our fill, and our kids have stashed them so perfectly that we haven't a prayer of locating them. Over the years, the *afikomen* has been under the mattress of a crib (with a baby asleep in it), in a huge bronze mortar and pestle on top of the breakfront in my grandparents' dining room, and in the matting behind a picture frame.

Those hidden pieces are priceless, though. Without them, we traditionally can't finish the seder, because those crumbly bits are supposed to be our "dessert," the final thing we consume before blessing the end of the meal and moving on to the singing. They're so valuable that in my family we ransom them back from our children who have done the hiding, and they drive a hard bargain. In 2019 they conspired to pull a classic negotiating move, asking for a helicopter and then, feigning disappointment when we refused, saying, "Fine, a puppy," and extending a hand for me to shake before I realized what I had agreed to.

The puppy finally arrived at Hanukah 2020, and he was my emotional support animal during the worst stretch of the pandemic, not an *afikomen* gift. But he—and his wingman—are now part of our family.

That's not my favorite *afikomen* story, though, nor is it the most telling. One year we shared our seder with several other families, all with children under 12, an 11-year-old boy named Shachar, was the ringleader for a pack of about 10 kids who cooked up an elaborate hiding scheme—then proceeded to all fall asleep before we got to *Tzafun*. Only my middle son, Akiva, who at the time was still our youngest and was about four years old, was still awake, but being four, couldn't quite remember where the *afikomen* was hidden. After about 30 minutes of searching, a light-bulb suddenly went on.

"Abba, it's in here!" he said excitedly, and pointed at a cabinet in the kitchen.

My heart sank. The cabinet he indicated was one below counter level where we'd stowed all the year-round dishes—the ones with *hametz* on them that weren't kosher for Pesach.

Fortunately, we had a rabbinic opinion on site, who assured me that, as long as the *afikomen* was wrapped well (it was) and the dishes had not been disturbed (they had not), we could proceed with the seder.

Those hidden pieces of us: The Shel Silverstein books and the imaginary friends (think Pixar's *Inside Out*) and the bedtime songs, are priceless. When we're not feeling well, reconnecting with them is a powerful way to heal—whether from cynicism or from disease. Sometimes, however, the pieces are more than just memories—they're pieces of a story that needs to be told, pieces that no one remembers how to find, and it's up to the healer to search high and low to find them. And sometimes that means going into places where the rules say we're not supposed to go—but if we don't go there, we can't help someone move forward.

This is the art of medicine, or of healing more generally: Going into the hidden spaces, the dark corners, to find the missing pieces and put the puzzle back together. Sometimes it requires paying dearly with time, or emotional resources, or breaking taboos. It can demand that a person confronts parts of themselves that they're not prepared to encounter or acknowledge truths they'd rather deny. We could see this placement of *Tzafun* as the final piece of the seder meal as a fulfillment of the purpose of seder that I discussed at the outset. This is an exercise in transforming trauma into memory so we may finally leave our narrow place, mentally and emotionally as well as physically. By handing over our hidden, broken bits and allowing someone to ransom them from us if necessary, we can take that final step. We walk into the glorious crescendo of blessing, praise and song that awaits in the coming pages, the coming days, the coming years. We can experience joy and wholeness again.

37

Satisfaction

Barekh—Birkat HaMazon, the blessing after a meal, comprises multiple blessings—Over the food, the land that produced it, and various other goodness we've enjoyed in our lives. It's a long prayer, usually sung joyously together at the seder. Its joy is felt rather than discussed, but there's some deep theology in there. Here are three especially important passages.

Birkat HaMazon	ברכת המזון
. . .Those that sow with tears will reap with joyful song. He who surely goes and cries, he carries the measure of seed, he will surely come in joyful song and carry his sheaves. (Psalms 126)	. . . הַזֹּרְעִים בְּדִמְעָה, בְּרִנָּה יִקְצֹרוּ. הָלוֹךְ יֵלֵךְ וּבָכֹה נֹשֵׂא מֶשֶׁךְ הַזָּרַע, בֹּא יָבֹא בְרִנָּה נֹשֵׂא אֲלֻמֹּתָיו.
. . .And you shall eat and you shall be satiated and you shall bless the Lord your God for the good land that He has given you." Blessed are You, Lord, for the land and for the nourishment.	. . . וְאָכַלְתָּ וְשָׂבָעְתָּ וּבֵרַכְתָּ אֶת ה' אֱלֹהֶיךָ עַל הָאָרֶץ הַטּוֹבָה אֲשֶׁר נָתַן לָךְ. בָּרוּךְ אַתָּה ה', עַל הָאָרֶץ וְעַל הַמָּזוֹן:
. . .I was a youth, and I have also aged, and I have not seen a righteous man forsaken and his offspring seeking bread (Psalms 37:25). The Lord will give courage to His people. The Lord will bless His people with peace (Psalms 29:11).	. . . נַעַר הָיִיתִי גַם זָקַנְתִּי, וְלֹא רָאִיתִי צַדִּיק נֶעֱזָב, וְזַרְעוֹ מְבַקֶּשׁ לָחֶם. יי עֹז לְעַמּוֹ יִתֵּן, ה' יְבָרֵךְ אֶת עַמּוֹ בַשָּׁלוֹם.

The Zevach Pesach, Rabbi Isaac Abarbanel's 1496 commentary published in the wake of the Inquisition and the resulting expulsions of Jews first from Spain, then from Portugal, contains the following stark passage that we've referenced several times now:

> What have we gained, living in exile, from the fact that our ancestors went forth from Egypt that we should say, "If God had not taken our ancestors out of Egypt, we, our children, and the children of our children would still be subjugated to Pharaoh in Egypt?" It might have been better for us to live peacefully in Egypt than to live in exile of Edom and Ishmael. After all, our ancestors said, "It would have been better for us to serve the Egyptians than die in the wilderness." (Ex.14:12) Living among the nations had made us victims to pogroms and expulsions; some were subject to the sword and others to famine and still others to captivity. Worst of all, we have been forced to abandon our faith because of the severity of our misfortunes.[1]

Abarbanel's words are a chilling challenge to us throughout the seder experience, but especially as we say *Birkat HaMazon*, the blessing after meals, which contains the verse from Deuteronomy 8:10, "When you have eaten and are satisfied, you will bless Hashem, your God, for the good land which He has given to you." God commands the Israelites to keep in mind the abundance of the land they're about to enter, including its characteristic seven species of fruit and grain but also its mineral wealth and general richness, as they bless their food. The verses that follow—in the Bible, not in the prayer—warn of dire consequences to follow if, surrounded by this bounty, the people don't give thanks, but rather say to themselves, "my own power and the might of my own hand have won this wealth for me."[2]

All well and good to warn those who are "satisfied" or "wealthy" against arrogance and self-satisfaction. But the Zevach Pesach is asking us how we can demand gratitude from those who are unable to savor the abundance, or feel the joy that's "supposed" to follow from these blessings, or aren't privy to the blessings at all.

I'm reminded of a running debate from my young adult years, generated purely due to a quirk in the tune most American Jews use to sing *Birkat HaMazon*. Toward the end, the music doesn't line up well with the text when we reach the line, *Na'ar hayiti v'gam zakanti, ve'lo ra'iti tzadik*

---

1. Abarbanel, *Zevach Pesach*, Tenth gate.
2. Deuteronomy 8:17

ne'ezav v'zar'o m'vakesh lahem—"I was young, and I have grown old, yet I have never seen a righteous man forsaken, nor his children begging for bread."³ The usual musical solution was to repeat the last phrase, *v'zar'o m'vakesh lahem*, "nor his children begging for bread."

How could we repeat, seemingly for emphasis, this line that suggested the children of the righteous never go hungry when it's so obviously not true? The socially conscious folks at the table couldn't countenance a version of the tune that so callously ignored reality, so they changed the phrasing to remove the repetition.

But for the Zevach Pesach, the whole verse is a problem. Surely, both in youth and old age, *all* of us have seen righteous people forsaken, and their children going hungry. How can we sing the line at all, even once?

The verse sounds like a version of what modern philosophers call the moralistic fallacy: A statement that something is a certain way because it *ought* to be that way. Righteous people shouldn't be abandoned, and their families shouldn't lack anything, because righteousness should be rewarded with security. They *ought* to be able to count on eating, being satisfied, and giving thanks—but they can't. So why are we joyously singing about it as if they can?

Birkat HaMazon is the seder in microcosm. The reason the seder exists, the reason you're on this journey with me, is twofold. At the same time as we remember and rejoice in past triumphs and miracles, we learn about present challenges to which we must respond—challenges facing us and challenges facing others. We've fulfilled the commandment to give credit where credit is due for our abundance, but there's one more task—to recognize the scarcity that others face. Perhaps that repetition is aimed at those who believe the moralistic fallacy. "You think the righteous are cared for, but they're not—what are you going to do about it?"

Or perhaps *na'ar hayiti* is an unfinished sentence, one which *should* read in full, "I was young, and I have grown old, yet I have never seen a righteous man forsaken, nor his children begging for bread, [and not rushed to help]." It's a call to action, to compassion, yet the tune taunts us, "you say you're doing all you can, and perhaps you've done much. So let me repeat: His children are begging for bread!"

In this finite life, blessing is never complete. In trying to answer the Zevach Pesach's question, I think not about the figurative cancer of persecution, but the literal cancers so many of my patients endure. Many

---

3. Psalm 37:25

of them, during treatment, have enjoyed remissions of many months or even several years, followed by a relapse that ultimately proves fatal. My late cousin Ann Gould received her initial diagnosis of breast cancer in 1984 and died of its complications in 2020—a thirty-six-year-long fatal illness. Surely, we would not have told Ann, who was contagiously energetic throughout those years and continued to heal others as a nurse for much of the duration of that illness, that she shouldn't have been thankful for those remissions.

Another answer to the question is embedded in the prayer itself. On holidays and Shabbat, including on Pesach, we add Psalm 126 to the beginning of *Birkat HaMazon*. The final lines of that psalm speak to the dark times that Abarbanel was living in when he wrote the Zevach Pesach—so much so that at the founding of the State of Israel in 1948, from the ashes of the Shoah, some suggested that this psalm, not *Hatikvah*, should be the national anthem:

> *Hazor'im b'dim'ah b'rinah yiktzoru*
> *Halokh yelekh uvakho, nosei meshekh hazara*
> *Bo yavo b'rinah nosei alumotav*
> Those who sow in tears will reap in joy.
> He goes out crying, carrying his seed-bag.
> He returns in joy, carrying his sheaves.

Rabbi Shai Held, writing on Pesach 5783 (2023), observes, "The second half of the Psalm is still hopeful, but it's also plaintive and weary. The exhaustion is real: So much waiting is asked of us, so much living in the perpetual not yet. But weariness is not equivalent to despair. God has acted in the past. Just when things seemed darkest, God brought glimmers of light. And as hard as it can be for so many of us to believe, the psalm reminds us—insistently and joyfully—that God will act similarly in the future."[4]

We eat, we're satisfied, and we bless, even when the blessing we received is fading into memory, or barely visible on a horizon. Better that we should have enjoyed it than it never was, or that we despair of the blessing ever coming to pass. Yes, there are still hungry children with righteous parents, and there always will be. Yes, we may, in fact, *be* those righteous parents. We can never stop struggling with what's not right in this world—but neither can we stop blessing the things that *are* right. In the words of the conclusion of the *Birkat HaMazon*, may Hashem give

---

4. Held, "Between Memory and Anticipation,." 43.

strength to God's people—strength to carry out the work still ahead of us—may Hashem bless God's people with peace—peace of mind and contentment to enjoy the blessings that have already come—and to continue hoping for those yet to be.

Thoughts and Discussions

- *Give thanks for a blessing you enjoyed in the past that no longer is. What lasting mark has it left even in its absence?*

- *Look ahead to a blessing that may yet arrive. What seeds of that blessing are you carrying with you right now?*

- *When you're satisfied and feeling well, do you remember to acknowledge that blessing?*

38

A Cup of Survival

The third of the cups of wine follows Birkat HaMazon, and consists only of the simple blessing over wine.

Third Cup of Wine	כוס שלישית
Blessed are You, Lord our God, King of the universe, who creates the fruit of the vine.	בָּרוּךְ אַתָּה ה', אֱלֹהֵינוּ מֶלֶךְ הָעוֹלָם בּוֹרֵא פְּרִי הַגָּפֶן.

What is there to say about the wine the third time we do it? When we do a ritual so often it can become *pro forma*, losing much of its significance. In my first book I told the story of Lawrence Weed, a physician whose career spanned from the 1940s into the 21st century, and his creation of the modern standard for interviewing a patient in a medical setting. Among his innovations were sections of the interview known as the review of systems (ROS for short) and the social history.

The ROS was born out of Weed's realization that the medical trainees he worked with often didn't know answers to questions that could have settled their patient's diagnosis because they hadn't asked them. An ROS provided a detailed checklist of things to ask nearly every patient, and often resulted in valuable clues that together formed an unmistakable pattern. Social history, meanwhile, fleshed out the patient into a person, telling the physician what they did for a living, who their "people" were, and what kind of lifestyle they were subjecting their body to.

Weed's inventions were revolutionary, but over decades of practice and habituation, they've turned into mindless rituals that many trainees (and seasoned veterans) in my day "phone in," using boilerplate language or a cut-and-pasted template. During training some people would literally phone it in. The real veteran attendings would sit at the nurses station dictating their notes into the phone so fast you could barely understand them. They spoke in a rapid-fire monotone and repeated whole segments of the note exactly as I had heard them do the day before; the only way the transcriptionist (this was before AI voice recognition) knew where to end a sentence was because the dictating doc would say "period" in the same flat voice as the rest of the words.

As a result, all the clues we were supposed to uncover with this ritual sit there in plain view, often ignored, or dismissed, by providers hoping that whatever item has come up positive (meaning abnormal), is not significant. Yet when people tell me that another provider wasn't listening to them, it's often these items, mentioned in social history or on ROS, that are the details we've bypassed.

Patient education, where a person is supposed to learn all about how to keep themselves healthy, or how to take their medicine, often becomes just as rote as the ROS. Suddenly, it's the patient tuning out. Sure, we *said* the medicine might cause cough, or that it was important that they not stop suddenly, but were they listening? There was such a long information dump that no one could absorb everything—especially not after their eyes glaze over...

What are we missing due to our "kiddush fatigue" by the time we get to the third cup? Most of my seder guests barely even raise this cup to their lips, they're so tired of wine. Is there a message here that we're not listening to? Remember the t-shirt that read, "First coffee kept me alert. Then it kept me awake. Now it keeps me alive?" Are we at the point where our blessings are no longer bringing us awareness or joy, but merely keeping us going? Even my favorite sources on the Haggadah, Rabbi Sacks, Erica Brown, and the Shechter Haggadah have literally nothing to say on the topic. Was there really nothing more to be said?

Rabbi Naftali Silberberg, writing for askMoses.org,[1] has something for us. The four cups symbolize four evils decreed by Pharaoh: 1) slavery, 2) the command for the midwives to commit infanticide when a male child was born to an Israelite mother, 3) the command to drown the

---

1. Silberberg, "Why Four Cups of Wine?"

Hebrew boys in the Nile (after the midwives would not follow the previous command), and 4) the decree that the enslaved Israelites would not be given straw to make brick but would have to get it themselves.

The third cup, then, is the liberation from the command of drowning—the very command from which Moshe was rescued by Pharaoh's daughter. It's the cup we raise, however belatedly, to the victory over the water we sang about in Psalm 114 before the meal, a cup symbolizing turning the tables on the Egyptians who tried to drown us. Silberberg points out that when people link the cups to God's promises to the Israelites, the third promise is the promise of redemption—the promise that he says is fulfilled when the waters close behind the Israelites and put a definite end to the power the Egyptians held over them.

This seder experience, the seder of healing, is part of a long, winding road back from a narrow place. Each stop along the way, whether it's a text, a food, or a cup of wine is a part of that process of stepping out into the open. With this third cup we're attempting to close the door on that part where we're nearly swept under the waves for the last time. As we'll see, however, we have to think carefully about whether we close the door silently and slip away, or slam it shut.

Raise a glass to the things that you have survived.

39

Eliyahus, Every One

Tradition holds that Eliyahu (Elijah) visits every seder table just after the meal. We set aside a cup of wine for him, filled with wine from every person at the table, and sing: Eliyahu the Prophet, Eliyahu the Tishbite, Eliyahu the Gileadite— speedily in our days he will come to us with the Messiah, descendant of David

אליהו הנביא, אליהו התשבי, אליהו, אליהו הגלעדי
במהרה בימינו יבוא אלינו עם משיח בן דוד

Remember the chilling story from Chapter 21 about the man who jumped from a bridge because no one saw his cry for help?

If that story had taken place in the Talmud, or in Hasidic literature, the man would undoubtedly have lived. A stranger, a beggar, a wagon driver, or a porter, dressed in grubby rags or soiled work clothes, would have gazed kindly into his eyes, or grasped his hand firmly in greeting. And that humble figure would have been the prophet Eliyahu.

The harbinger of the Messiah, the messenger of salvation, Eliyahu bides his time until the end of days by showing up wherever he's needed, giving just the right nudge to events to ensure that the deserving succeed and the arrogant get their comeuppance. He brings tidings of pregnancy to barren couples and treasure maps to poor men digging for lost coins under their floorboards. And once a year, at Pesach, he visits every home in the Jewish world, stepping through an open door to the strains of people singing his song. Santa Claus must drop down chimneys to get his cookies; Eliyahu waltzes right in the guest entrance and is rewarded with wine.

Not just any wine, though. Wine that we've already said we may not really need or want at this point—so we pool it together in a single cup to share with this mystical being.

Mazzarelli and Trzciak tell their story to make the point that any of us can be the Eliyahu in that story. One of the lessons of this seder experience is that "healer" is a title that doesn't always come with an expensive degree or years of preparation, but rather with doing the right thing in the singular moment when we're called to. For that man on his way to the bridge and countless others who suffer, any beggar in rags with friendly eyes will do. We can all aspire to be that beggar, that Eliyahu. All we need to do is pour out a little bit of ourselves and see who drinks it in.

40

Neither In Your Name Nor Mine?

After opening the door for Eliyahu, many communities ask God to pour out Divine wrath on those who have harmed the Jews. Other communities single out the positive and ask God to pour out love on those who have been friends. The tension between these two sheds light on dealing with anger and trauma.

ROAD TO NOWHERE

Not everyone who finds themselves back in the same narrow place where they once escaped can be so hopeful. It's hard to recognize the "winding road out of the narrow place" when it's in the process of winding up right back where it started. Rev. Martin Luther King, Jr. is often quoted as saying, "The moral arc of the universe is long, but it bends toward justice," but it takes a special kind of resilience not to wonder if the arc has bent so far the other way that it's irreparably broken.

In observance of Dr. King's birthday in 2023, my congregation was graced by a visitor, Rev. Gavin Walton of Grace Memorial Presbyterian Church in Pittsburgh's Hill District, once simultaneously the center of Black and Jewish Pittsburgh. Rev. Walton spoke about Exodus 6:9, just after Moshe tells the Israelites about God's promise of deliverance. "*V'lo sham'u el Moshe mi-kotzer ruah u-me-'avodah kashah*—when Moses told this to the Israelites, they wouldn't listen to Moses, their spirits crushed by cruel bondage."

Rev. Walton spoke from a place not unlike Abarbanel. He looked at the journey of Black Americans since the Emancipation Proclamation, and wondered aloud if, after 160 years, his community was traversing the desert on the way to the long-promised land, or was in fact still in *Mitzrayim*, in different guise. He spoke of the dual meaning of the word *ruah*, translated above as "spirits," but also meaning, "breath." Instead of "spirits crushed," *kotzer ruah* can mean, "out of breath." Those who continue to struggle to escape from the narrow place they're in—illness, oppression, abuse, loss upon loss—feel like they can barely breathe, like all they can do is gulp air to stay alive while they're practically drowning. Especially having just raised a glass to being *saved* from drowning, the idea of continuing to gasp for breath is crushing.

Just as I tried to do above, however, Rev. Walton found a *nehemta*, a comfort, that he could share with our congregation. "Just show up," he said, "and don't worry about whether you're reaching the goal that's set for you. Just don't quit trying. Just keep breathing."

ROAD RAGE

Not everyone can be so determined. For everyone who responds with dogged persistence and patient hope, there's another person who responds with anger.

Immediately after the *Birkat HaMazon* ends and the third cup of wine has been blessed, after we pour Elijah's cup and invite him in, we declare through the open door:

> Pour your wrath upon the nations that did not know You and upon the kingdoms that did not call upon Your Name! Since they've consumed Ya'akov and laid waste his habitation (Psalms 79:6–7). Pour out Your fury upon them and the fierceness of Your anger shall reach them (Psalms 69:25)! You shall pursue them with anger and eradicate them from under the skies of the Lord (Lamentations 3:66).

The Exodus, and in particular the night of watchfulness, when the blood-painted doorposts of the Israelite homes served as a powerful barrier to harm, serves here as a template for everything we hope will befall our enemies. These are the ones who've put us in the position of having to ask the question Abarbanel asks, including the Inquisitors of the fifteenth-century Church that drove him into exile. Hashem did it once, Hashem will do it again, this time in our name.

In our name. It's a frightening parallel to the violence committed by humans in God's name—including the very Inquisition that Abarbanel fled in the years before he published the Zevach Pesach. Violence that Rabbi Sacks argues, in his 2012 book *Not in God's Name*, is fundamentally antithetical not just to Jewish teaching, but to all Abrahamic religion.

It's also a fundamentally human response to being wronged or to the perception of being wronged. I spend substantial time in conversation with trauma victims, and their fury at their abusers, persecutors, and tormentors often either consumes them or motivates them to their own horrible acts. It drives mass shootings and underlies the generational trauma of domestic violence.

In response to this potential for ugliness, many twentieth-century Haggadot from the liberal-progressive spectrum of Judaism have supplemented or replaced *Shfokh Hamtkha*, Pour Out Your Wrath, with a passage called *Shfokh Ahavatkha*, Pour Out Your Love. Instead of seeking vengeance, participants in these sedarim call on Hashem to pour out love on the good guys, the so-called "righteous gentiles" who have been, to use a 21st century term, allies to the Jews over the millenia; sheltering us, standing by our sides, and speaking out on our behalf in dark times.

IN THE NAME OF MY FRIENDS AND NEIGHBORS?

At Pesach 2019, my own community in Squirrel Hill found itself on the horns of this suddenly real dilemma. In the wake of the terrorist attack on three of our holy congregations, how should we channel our fury, our tears, and our pain? Into love for the police, fire, and paramedics who undoubtedly saved lives, and the neighbors, friends, and total strangers who reached out to provide comfort? Or into anger at the terrorist, the white supremacist social media culture that created him, or the gun culture that enabled him to carry out his plan?

I lost friends, neighbors and colleagues that day. I've no idea what Cecil and David Rosenthal, Jerry Rabinowitz, or Rich Gottfried might say if I asked them this question; they and seven others are no longer here to answer.

Ultimately, I turned to a dear friend who's one of several survivors of the event I'm fortunate enough to know, a healer in his own right who was very nearly the twelfth person lost that day. My friend Dan Leger attributes his life today to having just enough strength left to grab the leg of a first responder who ran past him on the steps into the building as he lay there bleeding. He suspects the first responder thought him already dead until Dan's hand closed around his ankle.

Dan's recovery lasted months, but he was finally well enough to be out in public again a month or so before Pesach, when our burial society (the New Community Chevra Kadisha) gathered for our annual dinner on Adar 7, the traditional anniversary of the death of Moshe. The NCCK had been integral in the community response to the tragedy, preparing several of the victims for burial and assisting in the cleanup of the site, since any additional remains found at the scene would also require proper burial.

The secondary trauma of that process would have been quite enough, but there was more. Jerry Rabinowitz had been one of our most stalwart members. In the months since his murder, members had invoked his name at every turn, often saying without irony, "what would Jerry do?" when we encountered a situation that would have required his medical knowledge, or just his humor and calm. One member even changed the way he wore his gloves, "in memory of Jerry's custom."

In that already raw moment, our leadership invited Dan to speak at the dinner. Dan has always been one of my heroes, a devotee of Fred Rogers whose gentleness and insight equals that of our late Neighbor-in-Chief (yes, Squirrel Hill is Mister Rogers' Neighborhood; his house was perhaps six blocks from where I live now). That evening, however, he spoke some of the most moving words I've ever heard.

Dan described the moment he regained consciousness in the hospital, looking up into a gauzy white "sky" and seeing four silhouettes of figures bent over him. Not fully clear if he was alive or dead, he says, he thought calmly to himself, "my friends! My friends (from the NCCK) have come to accompany me on my journey to burial." God will bless his people with peace, indeed.

Nearly two years later, I approached Dan about the question of pouring out wrath. I wasn't satisfied with the Pour Out Your Love passage, written by American Jews with fading memories of what it was like to be persecuted. I needed to hear from a man whose entire life's work was grounded in love who had nevertheless just experienced raw hatred—one who could easily be described in the words of the psalm as a *tzadik ne'ezav*—a righteous person seemingly abandoned.

We took a walk: Me, Dan, and my puppy, through the tranquil woods that sit just moments away from his front door. He described for me how disturbing he found the roiling anger he was encountering in the community as people began the work of healing—and how he found that anger detrimental to the healing process. Perhaps, said Dan, we needed something different. The following is what he shared:

SHFOCH CHAMATKHA

A suggested ritual: Each person pours some of their wine (and water from Miriam's Cup if it's part of your tradition) into Elijah's cup. Or the contents of Elijah's cup and some of each person's (or all the remainders) into Miriam's cup. The door is opened. Suggested Reading:

Now we have thanked HaShem for our food. And for our evolving freedom.
And we ask again. But for what in the face of all we have had to bear?

Not for us . . . but for You, our God.
Please HaShem,
Don't let this warmth we've made together
Find its way back to fire
Destroying itself and all in its path,
Trying to correct what never can be
By such a means as wrath.
Let us pour it out together.
Let's carry it in one cup
To the open door of our hearts,
And let the earth
Soak it in instead of the very hearts
We hold so dearly tonight
Having found one another again this year.

Eliyahu and Miriam, now hand in hand,
Rising from this table, walking in embrace
Through our open door
Having tasted matzah with us
And allowed the bitter herbs to warm our lips –
The korbanot now fully slaughtered, eaten, the
Leftovers burned completely with
Not a broken bone.

And we, so awfully aware of
Blood spilled somewhere else—
But not here. Not tonight.

Pour out Your warmth on us
And let it stand and glow
Before the nations as an eternal light.
Let there be no longer a furnace—
But a crucible of love
Making our faces radiant
Like that of your servant Moses
And his sister Miriam,
Shining on one another until next year,
And again, and again, and again.

One or all take the cup through the open door and pour it onto the earth.
We come back and sit around the table again to complete the Hallel.

Daniel Leger
Pesach, 5781

THE RIGHT AMOUNT OF WRATH?

Dan is one of the wisest people I know. I wish I could give him the last word, but as we learned in Chapter 15, *terrible things keep happening*. Literally the day after I dove headlong into my second draft of this book was October 7, 2023. On this terrible day, Hamas carried out an enormous pogrom in Southern Israel, murdering over 1,000 people, raping and disfiguring women, burning entire communities to the ground, and kidnapping over 200 people (from pregnant women and infants as young as 10 months old to frail elders in their 80s).

I've avoided discussion of this tragedy because both the event and its aftermath have rendered people so angry that we're no longer able to speak to one another, let alone sit at the table together. I'm angry, but so are millions of Gazans who have had no reliable water, electricity, shelter, or food since October 8th, and millions more who are understandably heartbroken on their behalf. Are they not praying to God (because let's remember, while the forms of prayer are different, Jews, Muslims and Christians are all fundamentally praying to the same Almighty God of

Avraham) to pour out wrath as well? Isn't anger the source of the destruction—in fact, the very anger that led someone to decide they should carry out a pogrom? Doesn't anger transform righteous indignation into all-consuming fire?

"One type of man is wrathful," wrote Maimonides, "he is constantly angry. [In contrast,] there is the calm individual who's never moved to anger, or, if at all, he will be slightly angry, [perhaps once] during a period of several years."[1] Both of these individuals were mistaken, it would seem. The proper way with every character trait, in Maimonides' opinion, was the middle path, the exact balance between two extremes. As for anger, "he should not be wrathful, easily angered; nor be like the dead, without feeling, rather he should [adopt] an intermediate course, i.e., he should display anger only when the matter is serious enough to warrant it, in order to prevent the matter from recurring."[2]

Those who, in horrible times such as these, feel no anger are like the dead. In my own practice I've seen it, among those abused or tortured so badly they can't feel, registering only shock and numbness. Faced with the same situation again, they make excuses for the very people who have hurt them, fall into the same pattern that allowed the hurt to take place, and accumulate more trauma. A little anger might do them good, "in order to prevent the matter from recurring."

There are also those so angry that the rage can't be contained. Their explosive outbursts are directed at no one in particular—me, the staff in my front office, their employers and co-workers, or random strangers on the road or in a movie theater. They make headlines for all the wrong reasons. They're the abused who in the next generation become the abusers, the perpetuators of the cycle. Neither these, nor those, are the words of the living God.

Anger has a place—but we must be careful about how much *pride* of place we give it. Erica Brown explains that balance as follows:

In reciting this passage, we say to ourselves that we'll not remain neutral and ask God not to remain neutral when others suffer. We recite a verse that asks God to spill divine wrath as a way of also placing the burden of this anger on God *and taking it away from us* (italics mine). We may judge too harshly or misunderstand the motives behind an action. We ask that God, rather than human beings, bring about ultimate justice.

---

1. Maimonides, Mishneh Torah Human Dispositions (Hilkhot De'ot) 1:1.
2. Maimonides, Mishneh Torah Hilkhot Deot,1:4.

In fact, it is remarkable that we limit our anger in this whole story to a tame collection of three verses that seek more to validate the emotional cost of victimhood than to express violence.[3]

A DIFFERENT POURING OUT

The text asks God to "pour out God's wrath," and Erica Brown's assessment of the text as a whole reminds me of a different part of the text, a ritual we skipped over when discussing the plagues that involves another, literal, "pouring out." When reciting the ten plagues, seder participants pour out ten drops of the wine in their cups at that moment (most people do this by dipping a finger in the wine and wiping it on a napkin or their plate, and most seder leaders yell "Don't lick your finger!" as they're doing so).

Wine is joy. Spilling out wine diminishes our joy a little. As angry as we might have been at the Egyptians, we shouldn't rejoice at their suffering. Even God, the one to whom we entrust this anger, "rejoices not in the downfall of the wicked" according to Rabbi Jacob ibn Habib in his work Ein Ya'akov. Ibn Habib, remarkably, was a contemporary of Abarbanel, also exiled from Spain in 1492, yet he shares this story, attributed to Rabbi Yohanan. "What is the meaning of the passage (Ex. 14, 20) And the one came not unto the other all the night?[4] This means that the angels of Heaven wanted to sing the usual song, when the Holy One, praised be He! said unto them: 'My creatures are drowning in the sea, and you want to sing songs!'"[5] Would we prefer that the Egyptians not have drowned and caught up to us on the far shore? Of course not. But we're a little diminished because it had to happen that way.[6]

So, what do we do with our own anger? What if we can't manage to give it back to God, and continue to harbor it? Anger, and the associated traits of hostility and aggressiveness, take their toll not only on the targets of that anger, in the form of outbursts and destructiveness, but on the person feeling the anger—in the form of heart disease, chronic migraine, eating disorders, and a host of other chronic conditions.[7]

---

3. Brown, *Seder Talk*, 116–119.

4. A part of the story of the parting of the Sea of Reeds, allowing the Israelites to cross on dry land then drowning the Egyptian soldiers who tried to pursue them.

5. Glick, *Ein Ya'akov*, Megillah 1:11.

6 See also Chapter 45.

7. Staicu and Cutov, "Anger and health risk behaviors," .372-375.

Brown addresses this issue indirectly in another of her books, *Happier Endings*, a look at death and dying. She reexamines the "stages" of grief from Elisabeth Kubler-Ross's *On Death and Dying*,[8] one of which is anger. The key innovation of Brown's own stages is the final one. Where Kubler-Ross ends with "acceptance," coming to terms with the fact that death is real and will occur, Brown goes one step further. Acceptance she calls, "resignation," a stage in which we recognize that nothing will change the fact that death is approaching or has already happened. But there's a stage beyond resignation that Brown calls "inspiration," a stage in which a person forges a new life with its own meaning in the face of the loss.[9]

It's a measure of inspiration to spill wine even over the death of someone who was trying to kill you. It's a measure of inspiration, to try to get out of the narrow place that anger itself creates for us, a place where our own well-being is imperiled. To view even necessary anger and violence undertaken in self-preservation, as tragedies. In the time since October 7, even as I continue to pray for the safety of my friends and family and a safe return for the hostages, I've begun spilling my Shabbat wine as well, for the terrible cost people on the opposite side are paying to secure those prayers.

Spilled wine is a symbolic gesture, though. Like the old fifties sitcom joke where the mother says, "Clean your plate, there are children starving in China," and the kid says, "maybe we can send them this." No one can sustain themselves with it. It's "thoughts and prayers." When I shared this new ritual with my congregation, my fellow Haggadah enthusiast Dr. Murray Gordon sent me something incredible. He shared an illustration from the 1609 Venice Haggadah, depicting Israelites on the far shore of the Red Sea *reaching into the water to rescue the drowning Egyptians!* Imagine that: A ghettoized Jewish community (ever wonder why ghetto is spelled that way? It's an Italian word *first used in Venice* to refer to the place the Jews were confined in!) that envisioned their ancestors rushing to the aid of the oppressor when they realized they couldn't swim. So too, even during this war, there are groups like World Central Kitchen that have fed displaced civilians on both sides, and Israeli groups like Rabbis

---

8. These stages are long misunderstood, both because Kubler-Ross was describing people facing their own deaths, not in grief over losing a loved one, and because Kubler-Ross never meant to describe them as sequential, fixed steps that everyone experiences in the same way. https://www.ekrfoundation.org/5-stages-of-grief/5-stages-grief/

9. Brown, *Happier Endings*, 149–175.

for Human Rights providing "protective presence" to West Bank towns fearing violent reprisals.

Which brings me to the donkey.

Imagine that one of those Egyptian soldiers survived the drowning in the Sea of Reeds. Imagine that his pack animal survived with him. Imagine that he was trekking through the Sinai desert with everything he could salvage piled on the donkey's back. Finally, imagine the donkey gave out in the springtime heat and collapsed under the weight of his load. Just weeks after the drowning of the Egyptian army, the Israelites, encamped at Sinai, get instructions on what to do if they encounter this hypothetical lost Egyptian. "When you see the donkey of one who hates you crouching under its burden, restrain from abandoning it to him—unbind, yes, unbind it together with him."[10]

More than once in my career, I've had to care both for an abuser and their victim, for people I know are on opposite sides of the same conflict, and for people who think I killed Jesus and control the banks and have the tattoos to attest to it. I have a colleague who spent five years of their career providing psychological support for convicted sex offenders. I have another long-time friend who practices primary care medicine in the jail and a former co-worker who's the psychiatrist there. Certainly, there's plenty of room for anger—and instead we pour out . . . ourselves.

RAGE AGAINST THE WRATHFUL ONE

And finally, what if our anger is *at* God? Kubler-Ross's anger stage encompasses a lot of "why me?" thoughts. Thoughts which often turn a believer against a God they thought was on their side. Does the anger over getting metastatic cancer at 35, having a heart attack at 45, losing a child to a drunk driver at 15, get poured out against God's Divine Self? Perhaps it does. As Avraham asked, rhetorically, in the negotiation over Sodom and Gomorrah, ""Will You sweep away the innocent along with the guilty? . . . Far be it from You! Shall not the Judge of all the Earth deal justly?"[11] I'm angry, God. You ought to be ashamed of Yourself for letting this happen to me.

So perhaps this section is about what my friends in the American Black church call, "Letting go and letting God," a phrase I've never

---

10. Exodus 23:5.
11. Genesis 18:23–25.

understood well in the context of Jewish law that keeps placing the burden for action back on us. But the burden of the burning emotion of anger? Maybe God is better equipped to handle it than we are. Rabbi Hama bar Rabbi Hanina warns in the Talmud against trying to emulate God in all ways because "God is like a consuming fire." Better to just embody the gentle, positive Divine qualities.[12]

For our part, let us remember the lessons of Maimonides, Erica Brown, Rabbi Yohanan, and the overloaded donkey: Get angry enough to stand up for yourself, but no more. Get angry enough that you don't accept oppression or hatred, then hand off the wrath to God. Don't forget that even your enemies are human; and find something constructive to do with that anger, even if it means doing a favor for that enemy. And if we find ourselves drifting back into the cycle of being taken advantage of again, repeat from the beginning. It's a long road.

Thoughts and Discussions

- *When is your anger productive, and when is it destructive?*
- *If you're reading this as a person dealing with your own illness, who are you angry at? What about? How would you like to see that anger resolved?*
- *If you're reading this as a healer, who are you angry about? Is it on behalf of the people you care for, or at them, and why? Is it the people you work for? The system?*

---

12. Talmud Sotah 14a:3–4.

41

Nerves of Silver

After Eliyahu, the seder returns to the remaining parts of Hallel—Psalms 115–118, followed by Psalm 136, which recaps many of the same themes, and portions of the early morning prayers, perhaps in memory of the Rabbis who stayed up so late . . .

| ... Their idols are silver and gold, the work of men's hands. They have a mouth but do not speak; they have eyes but do not see. They have ears but do not hear; they have a nose but do not smell. Hands, but they do not feel; feet, but do not walk; they do not make a peep from their throat. Like them will be their makers, all those that trust in them . . . He will bless those that fear the Lord, the small ones with the great ones . . . It is not the dead that will praise the Lord, and not those that go down to silence. (Psalms 115) | .... עֲצַבֵּיהֶם כֶּסֶף וְזָהָב מַעֲשֵׂה יְדֵי אָדָם. פֶּה לָהֶם וְלֹא יְדַבֵּרוּ, עֵינַיִם לָהֶם וְלֹא יִרְאוּ. אָזְנַיִם לָהֶם וְלֹא יִשְׁמָעוּ, אַף לָהֶם וְלֹא יְרִיחוּן. יְדֵיהֶם וְלֹא יְמִישׁוּן, רַגְלֵיהֶם וְלֹא יְהַלֵּכוּ, לֹא יֶהְגּוּ בִּגְרוֹנָם. כְּמוֹהֶם יִהְיוּ עֹשֵׂיהֶם, כֹּל אֲשֶׁר בֹּטֵחַ בָּהֶם . . . יְיָ זְכָרָנוּ יְבָרֵךְ. יְבָרֵךְ אֶת בֵּית יִשְׂרָאֵל, יְבָרֵךְ אֶת בֵּית אַהֲרֹן, יְבָרֵךְ יִרְאֵי ה', הַקְּטַנִּים עִם הַגְּדֹלִים . . . לֹא הַמֵּתִים יְהַלְלוּ יָהּ, וְלֹא כָּל יֹרְדֵי דוּמָה . . . (תהילים קט״ו) |

Kurt Vonnegut's play, "Fortitude," depicts an ambitious doctor endowed with millions of dollars and tasked with keeping his only patient, a wealthy but aging woman, alive beyond all natural limits. By the time the play opens, the original patient is all but gone, a human Ship of Theseus[1]

---

1. Worley, "The Ship of Theseus."

where all that remains of the flesh-and-blood person is her head. Every limb and internal organ has been replaced with robotics and chemical apparati filling an entire laboratory beneath her "living" quarters. By the time the play ends . . . well, no spoilers.[2]

Psalm 115 says of the pagans, "Their idols are silver and gold, the work of men's hands."[3] The word for "idols" is *atzabeihem*, from the root word *etzev*, which in modern Hebrew means, "nerve." I always hear the line as "their nerves are silver and gold." Just like the patient in Fortitude, the idols are a representation of the human, or of the divine, but with the life taken out of them and replaced with things that are temporally precious but spiritually worthless.

Certainly, it's tempting to go after the nerves of silver. It's a form of immortality. If the highest good in the world is to praise God, we should seek immortality—because in the words of this very same psalm, "The dead will not praise God, nor will those who go down in silence."[4] If we must be alive to fulfill that destiny, shouldn't we do whatever it takes to keep it going?

Nor is the cyborgification of the human body so terrible either. Nancy Eiesland, in her 1993 book, *The Disabled God*, lays out a Christian theological rejection of the ableist notions of the Divine. In one narrative, she tells the story of a woman named Nancy Mairs, who learns to embrace what she refers to as her "braces and bones body," the fusion of her assistive devices and the limbs she was born with that no longer obey her intentions. This combination allows her re-entry into the world from which she felt cast out when she became ill.[5] So why shy from Vonnegut's dystopian vision?

Not only do the idols in Psalm 115 have nerves of precious metal, but "they have mouths, but cannot speak, eyes, but cannot see; they have ears, but cannot hear, noses, but cannot smell; they have hands, but cannot touch, feet, but cannot walk; they can make no sound in their throats."[6] These reconstructions of flesh from metal and stone only mimic life; they don't live it. And what's more, "Those who fashion them will become like them."[7] Once motivated by love, Vonnegut's doctor is now in thrall to

2. Vonnegut, "Fortitude."
3. Psalms 115:4.
4. Psalms 115:17.
5. Eiesland, *The Disabled God*, 43.
6. Psalms 115:5–7.
7. Psalms 115:8.

the vast sums of money that flow through him while his patron remains "alive." As he worships gold, her nerves become silver...

Eiesland's book represents a triumph of the living taking inanimate parts into themselves to live even more fully. Vonnegut's work shows the machinery supplanting the biological until she survives but no longer lives, until the worship of immortality drains away all the life. She's beyond praising God; she would rather "go down to silence." But she can't end her own life; she tried that before, so the doctor rigged her arms to prevent her from being able to harm herself. It never occurred to him to stop her from harming *him*...

No, it's for those who are fully human to do the work of praise; to fill this earth with real life. No matter what condition we might be in—we must do the impossible every day, "the small with the great,"[8] We must hold in our minds simultaneously that our lives are infinitely precious, and vanishingly finite. Accept our inevitable end while always fighting to cling to one more moment of middle, and striving for ever more new beginnings.

---

8. Psalms 115:13.

42

How Can I Repay You for Disappointing Me?

AKA *The Baklava of Redemption*

Psalm 116 asks us to think about trust, disappointment,
and repaying debts of gratitude.

| ... I have trusted, when I speak—I am very afflicted. I said in my haste, all men are hypocritical. What can I give back to the Lord for all that He has favored me? A cup of salvations I will raise up and I will call out in the name of the Lord... | ... אֲנִי אָמַרְתִּי בְחָפְזִי כָּל הָאָדָם כֹּזֵב. מָה אָשִׁיב לַי־יָ כָּל תַּגְמוּלוֹהִי עָלָי. כּוֹס יְשׁוּעוֹת אֶשָּׂא וּבְשֵׁם ה' אֶקְרָא... |

I have a lot of quirky socks.

I don't buy them myself, the way my middle son does. They come as gifts from people I care for, usually but not always around Hanukkah. Because of the way socks tend to behave kind of like Frodo's ring and leave their owner whenever they choose, I almost always have need of more. Plus, now that our dress code at work is a little more casual, I can sport almost any design I like.

So, I have a lot of quirky socks. Hanukkah accoutrements. A few shirts, a custom-tailored suit, and a purple knit hat. Fond memories of a whole lot of baklava, candied apples, and homemade cookies and muffins. And cards pinned to my bulletin board, some with original artwork by very talented children I've watched grow up.

Psalm 116:12 reads, "how can I repay all the gracious acts Hashem has done for me?" I recognize these gifts not just as a kindness I receive from generous patients, but as a gesture that says, "I don't know how to repay you for what you've done for me—so here's some socks." I feel nothing but warmth; the connection I sense during the moment someone hands me a gift bag or a card just might be the pinnacle of emotional fulfillment for my entire career in medicine. Inevitably, though, by the time I return to my desk, another feeling has attached itself: Guilt.

It's not guilt at the expense; I recognize the need for people even in desperate circumstances to show that they, too, can honor and thank someone. While American culture has squeezed the desire to force-feed people out of most folks, I'm steeped enough in other cultures to know that when someone offers you food or gives you a gift, it's not the time to say, "you shouldn't have," or, "thanks, I'm not really that hungry."

No, the guilt is because I know the rest of the Psalm, especially the line right before, Psalms 116:11: "All men (humans) are false." False, as in liars, sure, but the Hebrew *kozev* goes to a place beyond that. It means "disappointing." A *nahal k'ziv* is a stream that runs dry much of the year—one you can't depend on for water. I feel guilty because no matter what I may legitimately have done for someone in the past, I've almost certainly let them down as well—and if I've not let them down yet I'm sure to do so in the future.

The ways in which I've disappointed the people I treat in my practice could be its own Yom Kippur confessional, one which I'll reuse without shame if I ever write a "Medical Mahzor" for the High Holidays. I've forgotten promises, I've been in a hurry, I haven't been in *enough* of a hurry, I've succumbed to unconscious bias, I've been hard to get a hold of, I've lost my temper, I've used unkind words, I've embarrassed you, I've failed to ask permission before asking sensitive questions or doing parts of the exam, and I've perpetuated the flaws in the system instead of correcting them.

And that was just last week.

Not that I think people haven't noticed. Some of the people with whom I've the best relationships have called me out on these behaviors.

Others looked at me knowingly and kept quiet. Still others have left the practice. And a whole different group *begin* their relationship with me *expecting* that I'll disappoint them—just like "all those other doctors who can't figure out what's wrong with me and tell me I'm crazy."

I know that as healers, we have a similarly low view of what our patients will do. I know I've gone through my schedule at the beginning of a busy day and said, "Well, at least I'll be able to catch up here; Richard never shows for his appointment." A faculty member I worked with in residency told me he never waited more than three months after a first abnormal cholesterol reading to put someone on medication, "because no one ever succeeds at keeping up with the lifestyle changes we recommend." Emergency physicians I know don't even bother to hope that people who regularly turn up in their departments due to chronic homelessness, addiction, or lack of access to primary care will have a better outcome after *this* discharge. We've met this last story a couple of times already—in the vignette about Dr. Abdul Al-Sayed's decision to enter public health, and in James Groves' description of the self-destructive "hateful patient," Old George.

It's a low expectation that's ripe for confirmation bias—and fraught with bad outcomes. Much of the time the negative predictions come through, reinforcing our confidence the next time we predict the same thing. But what if Richard does show up? Now, I'm likely to be annoyed with him for being there because I'd hoped to use the time to review lab results and get my second cup of coffee.

I certainly won't bother with the effort it takes to promote diet change if I'm convinced they won't follow through; I'll just click through the prescribing module. If lifestyle change is hard, societal change is impossible, and the ER can't break the cycle, they can only participate in it. Yet I know—we all know, because I talked about it in Chapter 8—that there *are* doctors, and institutions, and even whole cities and states, that believe it could be otherwise, and are doing something about it. That second cup of coffee that Richard made me miss was supposed to be the one that reminded me I'm here to help other people out of their narrow places, even if it's hard. What's stopping me?

Despite my inadequate action, there are still gifts. Sometimes I can't even think of what I've done to earn an outpouring of gratitude; outwardly, to me, the person seems just as unwell as they were when I first met them. But something must have happened for someone to say, "You saved my life," or "I owe it all to you." Why?

Because of the *first* part of Psalm 116:11, "I said *in my haste*, all men are false." We rush to judgment, patients and healers alike, seeing the worst in each other—and in ourselves—due to our deep negativity bias. When we do so, we miss the actual miracles and the genuine reasons for hope. We miss the things that point us to the answer to "how can I repay" in verse 13:

"I will lift a cup of redemption and call on the name of Hashem."

Don't get me wrong, I love the socks. But the best repayment is seeing the genuine gratitude and sense of wonder in someone who realizes they may finally be well again.

Second best would be raising a baklava of redemption. I like pistachio.

43

Hesed Forever!

Psalm 117, 118, and 136 address a common theme—hesed, tangible acts of kindness that people do for others and that Jews believe God does for all of us.

Praise the name of the Lord, all nations; extol Him all peoples. Since His kindness has overwhelmed us and the truth of the Lord is forever. Halleluyah! Thank the Lord, since He is good, since His kindness is forever. Let Israel now say, "Thank the Lord, since He is good, since His kindness is forever." Let the House of Aharon now say, "Thank the Lord, since He is good, since His kindness is forever." Let those that fear the Lord now say, "Thank the Lord, since He is good, since His kindness is forever." (Psalms 117:1–118:4)	הַלְלוּ אֶת ה' כָּל גּוֹיִם, שַׁבְּחוּהוּ כָּל הָאֻמִּים. כִּי גָבַר עָלֵינוּ חַסְדּוֹ, וֶאֱמֶת ה' לְעוֹלָם. הַלְלוּיָהּ. הוֹדוּ לַיי כִּי טוֹב כִּי לְעוֹלָם חַסְדּוֹ. יֹאמַר נָא יִשְׂרָאֵל כִּי לְעוֹלָם חַסְדּוֹ. יֹאמְרוּ נָא בֵית אַהֲרֹן כִּי לְעוֹלָם חַסְדּוֹ. יֹאמְרוּ נָא יִרְאֵי ה' כִּי לְעוֹלָם חַסְדּוֹ.

In the space between disappointment and gratitude, lies *hesed*.

It's become fashionable among liberal Jews to invoke "the Jewish value of *tikkun olam*, repairing a broken world." The phrase often gets stretched to the breaking point, applied to every imaginable action of a socially engaged nature, and almost never used in its original Talmudic or later mystical meanings.[1]

1.. Krasner, "The World is Broken, So Humans Must Repair It: The History and Evolution of Tikkun Olam."

No, the real Jewish values are *Tzedek* and *Hesed*, justice and a kindness suffused with love of one's fellow creations.

Psalm 117 and the beginning of Psalm 118, form a call-and-response chorus during the Hallel service, featuring the response line, *Ki l'olam hasdo*, "For His[2] (Hashem's) *hesed* is eternal."

What's *hesed*? Better I should give you some examples. Burying the dead, giving their eulogy, and attending *shiva* to comfort the mourners is *hesed*, in fact *hesed shel emet*, true *hesed*, because we can never expect repayment from the dead, so we must be doing a kindness to them purely of love and duty. But we're certainly allowed to receive thanks for our

---

2. I usually use avoid using gendered pronouns for God, to recognize both God's uniqueness and God's transcendence of any single gender. Keep reading and understand why I needed a singular pronoun here, and stuck with the nominally male one implied by the Hebrew *hasdo*.

hesed—even purple hats[3]—when we do things like welcoming guests, helping bring a couple under the wedding canopy, providing provisions like wine and candles for religious observances, or countless other acts.

And yes, healing the sick, keeping faith with the downtrodden and making happy mothers of barren women are on that list—Hashem's *hesed* is exactly what we read about at the end of Psalm 113 (Chapter 30, "A Happy Mother of Children"). Hashem's *hesed* is exactly the part of the "Divine Image" in which we were made. We can't arrange the stars in their heavens, create light and darkness, or cause the wind to blow and the rain to fall, but we *can* heal the sick, comfort the bereaved and free the captive—even a proverbial captive in a proverbial narrow place.

When this psalm calls out three different groups to say *Ki l'olam hasdo*, it's calling them to action. In turn, Israel as a people, the house of Aaron (the priests), and the *yir'ei Hashem*, those who are in awe of Hashem, are called on to respond. When it says, "Hashem's *hesed* is eternal," it's exhorting each of those groups to make it so. Even those who aren't part of the Israelite nation can take part: "Praise the LORD, all you nations; extol Him, all you peoples, for great is His *hesed* (here translated as 'steadfast love') toward us."[4] This is a job for all of humanity—yes, some of us are priests, some extremely pious, but even the common folk, of any nationality, can perform acts of *hesed*. Maybe "His" doesn't refer to Hashem (there are, after all, no capital letters in Hebrew, so we only assume this refers to Hashem)—it refers to each of these groups. "Israel's *hesed* is forever! The House of Aaron's *hesed* is forever! The God-revering ones' *hesed* is forever!"

I write through the lens of a primary care doctor. This book (and the sedarim I hope it inspires) is often an exercise in forcing myself to understand, deeply, the narrow places people are stuck in when I encounter them, so that I and people in my position can do them whatever *hesed* we can. But of course, that isn't the only way to read it. Healing, like *hesed*, is not just the province of primary care doctors, or doctors in general, or even health professionals more generally.

There's a woman I know only as Debbie, and the only reason I know her is because every time I see one of my older patients, Debbie is sitting in the room with her. She only ever makes small talk, doesn't interfere with the conversation, or offer unwanted advice. She's just there because

---

3. Weinkle, "Purple Hats."
4. Psalms 117:1.

she is the ride to the doctor's office—and the entertainment to bide the time while I run chronically late.

There are several young men in one of our refugee communities that I've seen repeatedly at other people's doctor visits—and not always the same people. At first, I assumed they were sons bringing their mothers and fathers to see me—until I realized they couldn't possibly have that many parents and grandparents. They're not dutiful sons—they're the glue that holds their community together and makes certain the elders who *don't* have someone looking out for them don't fall through the cracks.

There are parents of children with special needs, many of them continuing to provide round-the-clock care well into the child's adult years. There are grandchildren barely out of high school, putting careers and relationships of their own on hold to ensure, in the words of another psalm, that their grandparents are not cast out in the time of their old age.[5]

All of them, from Debbie on through, are healers because of the *hesed* that they do for others. Indeed, in a system as fractured as ours, in a time where a global pandemic and absurd working conditions have left the professional ranks of that system woefully depleted, these informal, unpaid, underappreciated healers are often the only ones keeping things together. *Ki l'olam hasdam*, their *hesed* is eternal, for they'll never stop doing it, never get bored, never find something more "meaningful" to do.

---

5 Psalm 71:9

44

Psalm 118—The Narrow and the Wide

After opening with four lines about God's hesed,
Psalm 118 turns to a cry for help getting out of a narrow place.

From the strait I have called, Lord; He answered me from the wide space, the Lord. The Lord is for me, I will not fear, what will man do to me? . . . It is better to take refuge with the Lord than to trust in man. It is better to take refuge with the Lord than to trust in nobles . . . They surrounded me like bees, they were extinguished like a fire of thorns— in the name of the Lord, as I will chop them off . . . I will not die but rather I will live and tell over the acts of the Lord. The Lord has surely chastised me, but He has not given me over to death.	מִן הַמֵּצַר קָרָאתִי יָהּ, עָנָנִי בַמֶּרְחָב יָהּ. ה' לִי, לֹא אִירָא—מַה יַּעֲשֶׂה לִי אָדָם, ה' לִי בְּעֹזְרָי וַאֲנִי אֶרְאֶה בְשֹׂנְאָי . . . טוֹב לַחֲסוֹת בַּיי מִבְּטֹחַ בָּאָדָם. טוֹב לַחֲסוֹת בַּיי מִבְּטֹחַ בִּנְדִיבִים . . . סַבּוּנִי כִדְבֹרִים, דֹּעֲכוּ כְּאֵשׁ קוֹצִים, בְּשֵׁם ה' כִּי אֲמִילַם . . . לֹא אָמוּת כִּי אֶחְיֶה, וַאֲסַפֵּר מַעֲשֵׂי יָהּ . . .

Sometimes, with aging and with complex chronic illness, the narrow place just keeps getting narrower. Imagine a Jew who keeps kosher, avoiding pork and shellfish, buying only properly slaughtered kosher meat, strictly separating it from dairy products, and checking each package for the *hekhsher* that verifies its fitness for consumption. They do all of this with pride and joy in their adherence to a venerable tradition, their fulfillment of God's will.

A protracted period of intestinal distress leads to a diagnosis of celiac disease, and suddenly gluten joins the list of forbidden foods. Sometime later, despite strict adherence to not only *kashrut*, but to the gluten-free diet, the discomfort returns, and the doctors determine them to be lactose intolerant as well. With time, the chronic conditions of hypertension, diabetes, and high cholesterol creep in (perhaps also gout) and eventually there remains almost nothing permissible to eat. The restrictions are also not cheap; kosher food is expensive enough, but food that meets all these requirements comes in packages so small, with price tags so large, that a simple breakfast feels extravagant. The joy of the *mitzvah* of *kashrut* is replaced by a longing to escape from the restriction, to lose the chains of this diet and barge into a restaurant and order one of everything.

As a medical resident, one of the most sobering experiences was working in the adult intensive care units, trying to maintain what we call "homeostasis." The balance of processes that keep key elements of human life, like blood sugar, oxygen levels, pH, electrolyte balance, and hydration status in the narrow ranges that enable that life to continue. When it works, which it does every day for the vast majority of people, it's an ongoing miracle. When it fails, as it does every minute in the ICU, it's a nightmare.

What drives a lot of that failure is the successive abdication of responsibility by one organ system after another. Often the heart or the lungs are the first to quit; inevitably the kidneys almost always join the general strike. The end of the line is usually when the brain hands in its resignation, though sometimes the brain will do some "quiet quitting" well before actually walking off the job, in the form of seizures, altered mental status, or hallucinations. With each system that goes down, the narrow space in which life can exist gets narrower and narrower, and the options for holding things there become fewer and fewer.

Well before the ICU, however, the homeostasis that exists in our lives in the wide world is easily lost as we age. Atul Gawande, in his book, *Being Mortal*, spends four chapters on the slow progression of aging: The loss of strength, sensory acuity, mental focus and social capital. The eventual shrinking of a person's world, often against their will, that almost inevitably follows as they move through a series of "total institutions" walls them into increasingly narrow places.[1]

---

1. Gawande, *Being Mortal*, Chapters 2–5.

I've often watched people who have not yet hit "aging" experience the same contraction of their worlds. Injured, they find their mobility limited. Concussed, they find their tolerance for activity reduced to the point of crushing boredom. Traumatized, they find their trust in the world beyond their door, or even within their walls, shattered. Alone, they find even simple daily activities impossible without needed support that never materializes. Addressing one of these seemingly insurmountable challenges requires steps that they can't take because of the other challenges. Joseph Heller made his name describing the Catch 22—the situation from which any escape was impossible, because the escape plan deposited you right back into the same situation.

This may be the first Haggadah about the Exodus from illness to health, but the Hallel Psalms, especially Psalm 118, have been read by some rabbis as a narrative of one person's illness and recovery for nearly 2,000 years.

In the Babylonian Talmud, Pesachim 117a, the rabbis debate who first recited Hallel. Rabbi Elazar ben Azarya (one of the insomniac rabbis from Chapter 11) declares, "Hezekiah and his company recited it when Sennacherib stood against them." Hezekiah was king of Judah during the time when King Sennacherib's Assyrian empire destroyed the kingdom of Israel, and all of the 8th century BCE pundits were certain that Judah would be next to fall. The Assyrian emissaries taunted the Judahites, mocking their reliance on Egypt, their small numbers, and their lack of resources like horses. Yet God wrought a miracle on their behalf—a plague decimated the Assyrian troops before they could attack, and Judah was saved.[2]

Hezekiah was not just a king saved from military disaster—he also survived an illness which he was predicted to die from. If these 6 psalms of Hallel which bookend our seder meal are the words of Hezekiah, then this ritual has been one of healing since its inception in the Mishnah.[3]

Psalm 118, verse 5 says, *Min ha meitzar karati.* "I called to Hashem from the narrow place. Hashem answered me in the wide-open space." *Meitzar*—the singular of *Mitzrayim*.

---

2. Which, after what we discussed in chapter 39, should make us at least a little uncomfortable. Makes me wonder if I need to spill out some of the fourth cup to mourn the Assyrian soldiers who died in the plague.

3. Many of the seder texts have been added much later, but reciting Hallel is mandated in Mishnah Pesachim 10:6–7, and we know precisely which psalms are included from quotations in Mishnah 6 and in the Gemara on 117a and elsewhere. It's been there since the very beginning.

The Malbim (Meir Leibush ben Yehiel Michel, a 19th century commentator from Volhynia, Ukraine) teaches, "'I called to Hashem from the narrow place' because he was ill and like to die, 'Hashem answered me in the wide-open space' for then the danger had already passed, and he took it as a sign that (Hashem) would also save him from the king of Assyria."[4] The text in Isaiah describes Hezekiah in his moment of most severe illness as lying in bed, turning his face to the wall as if to further narrow his place. Isaiah himself lacked even the basics of bedside manner, telling the king, "Thus said the LORD: Set your affairs in order, for you are going to die; you will not get well."[5]

I knew someone whose doctor told him (or actually, told his wife) to "get his affairs in order." He lived another twenty years. One of the most enduring urban legends in medicine is the doctor who hands such a grim prognosis to a patient only to have that patient attend that doctor's funeral.

There are a variety of ways to respond to such a bombshell, ranging from despair to defiance. In Isaiah, Hezekiah seems to despair, turning his face to the wall (38:2) and weeping profusely (38:3). But in Psalm 118, he's defiant: "I will not die, but I will live and tell of the deeds of Hashem." The link between the two is the prayer he utters in the first half of 38:3, "Please, O LORD," he said, "remember how I have walked before You sincerely and wholeheartedly and have done what is pleasing to You." As a reward for this, Hashem calls again to Isaiah and reverses course, saying, "Go and tell Hezekiah: Thus said the LORD, the God of your father David: I have heard your prayer, I have seen your tears. I hereby add fifteen years to your life."[6]

Psalm 118 encompasses the whole range of experiences of serious illness. "Beset by bees," whether they be ancient bloodletters or modern lab technicians, penetrating the skin again and again, purportedly in the name of healing. "Nearly falling," saved only by the grace of God (or by the conscientious physician who remembers to do a fall-risk assessment during their Medicare Wellness Visit). "Being severely afflicted," perhaps believing that these afflictions are sent by God, yet not dying—even when death might have been more welcome than this afflicted life.

One aspect of the illness narrative captured starkly in Psalm 118 is "distrust." After all the beestings, all those afflictions, all those dour

---

4. Malbim on Psalm 118:5:1.
5. Isaiah 38:1
6. Isaiah 38:5

predictions of death, a person readily loses confidence in the promises of doctors and nurses. When Hezekiah declares, "It is better to shelter with Hashem than to trust a human being; better to shelter with Hashem than to trust the generous," he echoes the feelings of so many people I've cared for, who have eyed me suspiciously, and long since abandoned faith in the treatment they were receiving. When Malbim explains that we have doubts about whether a human being will fulfill our request for help, he reminds me of my failure to follow through on good intentions like I described in Chapter 42. When he continues to point out that even the generous, though they may be inclined to see things through, may find themselves powerless to do so, I remember the times I've found myself overpromising something that was out of my control to deliver.

Hezekiah is passing through the stages of coming to terms with his illness. His distrust is one manifestation of the anger stage, which we see again when he keeps promising to "cut down" his enemies.[7] He passes through denial, declaring, "I will not die, but live, and proclaim the works of Hashem!"[8] He bargains, declaring, "Open the gates of righteousness, and I will enter them and thank Hashem; this is the gate of Hashem, the righteous will enter it."[9]

Musically, this psalm is the ecstatic peak of the Hallel service, whether around the seder table or in synagogue, and the previous line is the beginning of a sequence that, when I sing it, is my favorite moment in the entire synagogue liturgy:

> Open the gates of righteousness for me
> that I may enter them and praise the LORD.
> This is the gateway to the LORD—
> the righteous shall enter through it.
> I praise You, for You have answered me,
> and have become my deliverance.
> The stone that the builders rejected
> has become the chief cornerstone.
> This is the LORD's doing;
> it is marvelous in our sight.
> This is the day that the LORD has made—
> let us exult and rejoice on it.[10]

---

7. Psalm 118:10–12
8. Psalm 118:17
9. Psalm 118:19–20
10. Psalm 118:19–24

It speaks of a reversal, made possible by devotion and repentance, where the defeated triumph, the downtrodden stand tall, and the distraught can feel joy again.

Musically, this passage also whitewashes a lot of the suffering. I've attended Hallel services in many synagogues, and sung these psalms at many sedarim, and the verses from 6 through 18 are often skipped—the verses with the bee stings, the cutting down of surrounding enemies, the falling and the severe punishment. We hear one plaintive line about calling out from the narrow place, and the answer from the wide-open space, and then mumble until we burst forth in exultation.

When we pick up the tune again, we're bargaining. We're righteous. We'll ask to enter the gate of the righteous, and we'll be rewarded with a reversal of fortune that we so richly deserve. Right?

Wrong. Psalm 118 works theologically only as a whole, when we acknowledge the suffering out loud. When we recognize that we can bargain all we want, come out on the short end of the bargain, and still be able to reach that final stage of processing. Kubler-Ross calls it acceptance, Erica Brown calls it inspiration, and the Kubler-Ross Foundation labels it integration.[11] Those are the places where we recognize that a loss, a setback, or a defeat, are real. Instead of trudging through life in their aftermath, or becoming so depressed that we're barely living at all, we decide to live, anew, in a world in which those things have happened.

Verses 19 and 20 echo a common sentiment in the Abrahamic religions—and among secular believers in medical science. Even if we're aware of the inherent dangers of being alive, we tend to think in absolutes: "If I do this, everything will be fine. If I do the other thing, I will die." Or, flipped on their heads, "if I fail to do the good thing, I'll die, and if I avoid doing the bad thing, nothing bad will happen to me." It's a recipe for a crisis of faith, whether you're praying or getting a medical checkup. Risk and reward don't operate that way, in the spiritual or the physical spheres. Believing that they do can only lead to disappointment.

And yet the righteous die, and the wicked perish, every year. And every time someone with wavering faith thinks about that reality, they become less convinced that the Judge is Just.[12] In the medical realm, over the past three years, we've at times elevated our pandemic mitigation strategies to a holy liturgy of public health policy, to similar effect. Every

---

11. See Chapter 39.
12. Chapter 39, the reference to Genesis 18:23–25.

time a fully vaccinated person becomes critically ill, or a person wearing an N95 mask while jogging outdoors alone contracts COVID anyway, resolve weakens, and skepticism grows.

Think of all the times you've joked about the Guinness record holder for world's oldest living person attributing their longevity to, well, Guinness (the beer that spawned the book). More tragically, think of James Fixx, the running guru who died of a heart attack in his forties, the non-smokers you know who succumbed to lung cancer, or the young adults who grew up having family meals and open conversations with their parents every night and still developed substance use disorders. It's no wonder that well-funded accusers from the tobacco, chemical and anti-vaccine industries have found it so easy to sow doubt in the medical profession; to create the equivalent of science atheists.

Whether in prayer or public health, there's no room for absolute certainty. Remember that the first thing God created was chaos, and the whole rest of the Creation process is an ongoing effort to create and maintain separation in that chaos. This effort fails frequently and dramatically, like the post-COVID attempts to get things "back to normal" we talked about in Chapter 31.

There are things that we can do to maintain the separation, reverse the slide back to chaos, or postpone the inevitable—sometimes. The great fallacy of Western medicine is that we're in control of the body; the great fallacy of pagan religion is that we're in control of God. Even as the Abrahamic faiths turned from the worship of many to the worship of one all-powerful God, they couldn't uproot the deep-seated belief that there was some way to game the Great One, whether according to the recipe of one's own creed, or by following the latest science or pseudo-science.

Let's acknowledge that chaos is always going to be there. The science that describes the impact of changing any single risk factor is complex and dreadfully boring to read, so it's no use trying to catch the public's attention that way. And the impact of spiritual change and growth is one of the universe's eternal mysteries, one we may be fortunate enough to understand after it's already too late to keep us alive in this world.

It's easy to feel powerless in the face of chaos, but we aren't. How much power do we have? Who knows. But we have agency, which is better than nothing. We have repentance, prayer, righteous action, seat belts, vaccines, strong relationships, home care for the elderly, cholesterol medicine, exercise, suboxone, compassion, defibrillators, and emergency surgery, and we hope (no, pray) that it'll be enough.

According to bioethicist Laurie Zoloth, the exercise of that power is the only meaningful thing about suffering. Suffering, she quotes Franz Rosenzweig, is ordinary and essential. It's nothing to write home about—and certainly not to be accepted. She argues (basing herself on philosopher and Shoah survivor Emmanuel Levinas) that theodicy to prove Hashem innocent of human suffering is a scandal.

Theodicy is one of those words that contains whole worlds. It's the philosophical term for, essentially, "getting God off the hook for the existence of evil." There are many flavors of theodicy; philosopher Richard Rice catalogued what he felt were the seven major arguments in his 2014 book *Suffering and the Search for Meaning*. But more interesting to me is the Hebrew term for theodicy (you knew this was coming): *Tziduk ha Din*.

The term uses two different Hebrew roots for justice, *tz-d-k* and *d-y-n*, and if you take it at its surface meaning, it means "justification of the judgement." But *tz-d-k* words, like *tzedakah*, the obligation to helping the poor not be so poor, imply equity or fairness—what we sometimes call "distributive justice." *D-y-n* words, like *dayan*, judge, or *beit din*, court, are about application of the law, including crime and punishment and settling lawsuits. These are about, if you like, "retributive justice." And God is the *Dayan*, the Judge. If the Judge's Judgments (*din*) are not fair (*tzodek*), then how can the Judge be the True Judge? I'm not going to answer that question here—you'll have to wait for the next book (when I still won't answer it, but I'll talk about it for a *lot* longer).

Suffering happens in this world, says Zoloth and Levinas before her. It's sad, and it *should* make us angry.[13] Hezekiah's protest that he will not die, but live, may be a manifestation of a stage of coping and struggle with his illness, but it's a noble protest, an act of justice. Declaring that he will live, and not die, and enter the gates and rejoice there, is the only reasonable response to suffering—and if to his own suffering, how much the more so to the suffering of others?

So, in the face of such suffering, how can Hallel sound so triumphant? We learned from Rabbi Yitz Greenberg, way back in the introduction, that the Exodus teaches us that God cares that human beings should be free and not suffer enslavement. Hallel is *supposed* to be triumphant,

---

13. Zoloth, "Suffering and its Uselessness."

because we're *supposed* to refuse to turn our faces to the wall, refuse to put our affairs in order, refuse to allow our people to be subjugated or our loved ones to suffer. We're *supposed* to be angry, and we're *supposed* to rejoice when the evil decree is altered. Today is the day Hashem has made, let us be glad and rejoice in it.

45

Hesed Forever—For Everyone?

Psalm 136 returns to the theme of hesed, but some of the divine acts described here don't seem so kind—to the other guy.

Thank the Lord, since He is good, since His kindness is forever . . . To the one who made the Heavens with discernment, since His kindness is forever . . . To the One that smote Egypt through their firstborn, since His kindness is forever. And He took Israel out from among them, since His kindness is forever . . . And He jolted Pharaoh and his troop in the Reed Sea, since His kindness is forever . . . And he killed mighty kings, since His kindness is forever. Sichon, king of the Amorite, since His kindness is forever. And Og, king of the Bashan, since His kindness is forever . . . (from Psalm 136)	הוֹדוּ לַיי כִּי טוֹב כִּי לְעוֹלָם חַסְדּוֹ . . . לְעֹשֵׂה הַשָּׁמַיִם בִּתְבוּנָה כִּי לְעוֹלָם חַסְדּוֹ . . . לְמַכֵּה מִצְרַיִם בִּבְכוֹרֵיהֶם כִּי לְעוֹלָם חַסְדּוֹ. וַיּוֹצֵא יִשְׂרָאֵל מִתּוֹכָם כִּי לְעוֹלָם חַסְדּוֹ . . . וְנִעֵר פַּרְעֹה וְחֵילוֹ בְיַם סוּף כִּי לְעוֹלָם חַסְדּוֹ . . . לְמַכֵּה מְלָכִים גְּדֹלִים כִּי לְעוֹלָם חַסְדּוֹ. וַיַּהֲרֹג מְלָכִים אַדִּירִים כִּי לְעוֹלָם חַסְדּוֹ. לְסִיחוֹן מֶלֶךְ הָאֱמֹרִי כִּי לְעוֹלָם חַסְדּוֹ. וּלְעוֹג מֶלֶךְ הַבָּשָׁן כִּי לְעוֹלָם חַסְדּוֹ . . .

About three-quarters of the way through the movie, we realize the narrator is dead, and he's not happy about it.

The movie in question is *Vice*, the 2018 film starring Christian Bale as Vice President Dick Cheney. The narrator whose voice we've been hearing throughout the film turns out to be the man whose heart was transplanted into Cheney's chest. The thing he's not happy about is that Cheney keeps referring to it as "my new heart."

"That's *my* heart," the narrator fumes, from beyond the veil.

Psalm 136 picks up where Psalms 117 and 118 left off, repeating, "For (God's) *hesed*, lovingkindness, is eternal." But in 136 we learn that God has a funny way of showing it. The psalm tells the story of God's *hesed* toward the Israelites, going all the way back to creation. Somewhere along the line, though, it gets pretty dark. "Who smote the firstborn of the Egyptians, his *hesed* is forever! Who jolted Pharaoh and his army in the Sea of Reeds! Who killed mighty kings!" It seems to me that neither the firstborn Egyptians, nor the charioteers in Pharaoh's army, nor Kings Og and Sihon were feeling much *hesed* in those moments.

Every cop or superhero show you've ever seen ends with a scene of the protagonists hugging against a backdrop of devastation. We're supposed to be elated that our heroes survived, but what about the people whose houses were destroyed, or the ones that the monster got before the heroes showed up on the scene? What about the real-life people whose livelihoods were ruined, or who lost children, in the war that "our side" won—or is still fighting? What about the people on the "other side" of the conflict who are thanking God (yes, we're usually praying to the same God; see chapter 40) for *our* misfortune and calling it *hesed* for them? Where is the *hesed* there? What price was paid so that we could stand safely on the far shore of our Sea of Reeds?

I'm a doctor, not a statesman, so I'll bring the question to a more personal level. The truth is that there are a lot of Dick Cheneys out there, and for every one of them there's a faceless narrator—or ten, or a hundred. For every life saved with a deceased donor organ, there is a deceased donor whose life ended abruptly, inexplicably, tragically. Many more lives depend on research performed on bodies, or body parts, whose former owners willed their bodies to research, knowing that they were too ill to have organs that would be usable for transplant. And every physician, as well as most PA and nurse practitioner clinicians, began their training standing over a cadaver that was donated to science in similar fashion.

We could look at this and say, "yes, but that's exactly where the *hesed* is—the lovingkindness of that organ donor, making a final gift for which they can never be repaid." It's the reverse of the *Chevra Kadisha* work I talked about in Chapter 33, work that's called *hesed shel emet*, true *hesed*, because there can be no expectation of thanks for a kindness you do for someone who's already dead. Here, the kindness is being *done* by someone who's already dead, so while the recipient may be thankful, the giver can't *accept* that thanks anymore.

But a lot of our miracles don't depend on the lovingkindness of a willing donor. The *Vice* narrator checked the organ donor box on his driver's license application. Tens of thousands of people in many countries around the world, including but not limited to China, have never been given the option to check a box. Instead, they had their organs harvested involuntarily.[1] Others unknowingly become research subjects, like the now-famous Henrietta Lacks whom I mentioned in Chapter 14. Like Lacks, they die and disappear into obscurity while others, often of greater privilege and less "other" status, build both their fame and fortune on that person's genetic material or medical history.

Even when the offense isn't as egregious as stealing an organ from a political prisoner, our own perception of *hesed* often depends on the desperation of others who weren't so lucky. Margaret Edson's 1993 play, *W;t*, follows Professor Vivian Bearing from the moment of her stage IV ovarian cancer diagnosis to the moments after her death. Vivian enters treatment through a research protocol run by Dr. Harvey Kelekian and his brilliant but obnoxious fellow, Dr. Jason Posner. As Vivian gets sicker, she and her nurse, Susie, decide she's to be "no code," and to let her heart stay stopped, with no CPR, if it stops. When that moment finally arrives, however, Jason calls a code anyway. When Susie yells at him, "She's DNR!" Jason retorts, "She's RESEARCH!"[2]

Just like there are a lot of Dick Cheneys roaming around with other people's hearts, there are a lot of Vivian Bearings who have entered research protocols, not out of a selfless desire to help humanity, but out of desperation to maybe earn a little *hesed*, a tiny miracle, of their own. Faced with a terminal diagnosis like stage IV ovarian cancer, ALS, or advanced heart failure, people will submit to a lot, even if the disclaimer on the study consent clearly promises them nothing. But there are people who I see today surviving with ovarian cancer, thirty years after the fictional Vivian died. These real-life Vivians enrolled in real studies just like hers. My patients often survive long-term and lead full, rich lives—and owe it all to the memories of the Vivians that went before.

Of course, people should rejoice in what they've been blessed with. I won't take that away from them. Nonetheless, Psalm 136 challenges us:

---

1. Nguyen, " Forced Organ Harvesting: A Decades-long Injustice in Need of International Accountability and Action."

2. Edson, *W:t*, 82.

Find a way to not only make *hesed* forever, but to make *hesed for everyone*. May we live to see the day when no one's salvation needs to be built on someone else's suffering.

46

Body and Soul and Spirit

Nishmat Kol Hai is the final part of the early morning prayers, and the final part of the Hallel section of the seder.

The soul of every living being shall bless Your Name, Lord our God; the spirit of all flesh shall glorify and exalt Your remembrance always, our King . . . The Lord neither slumbers nor sleeps. He who rouses the sleepers and awakens the dozers; He who makes the mute speak, and frees the captives, and supports the falling, and straightens the bent . . . Were our mouth as full of song as the sea, and our tongue as full of joyous song as its multitude of waves, and our lips as full of praise as the breadth of the heavens, and our eyes as sparkling as the sun and the moon, and our hands as outspread as the eagles of the sky and our feet as swift as deers—we still could not thank You sufficiently . . . Bless the Lord, O my soul; and all that is within me, His holy name. . .	נִשְׁמַת כָּל חַי תְּבָרֵךְ אֶת שִׁמְךָ, ה' אֱלֹהֵינוּ, וְרוּחַ כָּל בָּשָׂר תְּפָאֵר וּתְרוֹמֵם זִכְרְךָ, מַלְכֵּנוּ, תָּמִיד . . . וַיי לֹא יָנוּם וְלֹא יִישָׁן—הַמְּעוֹרֵר יְשֵׁנִים וְהַמֵּקִיץ נִרְדָּמִים, וְהַמֵּשִׂיחַ אִלְּמִים וְהַמַּתִּיר אֲסוּרִים וְהַסּוֹמֵךְ נוֹפְלִים וְהַזּוֹקֵף כְּפוּפִים . . . אִלּוּ פִינוּ מָלֵא שִׁירָה כַיָּם, וּלְשׁוֹנֵנוּ רִנָּה כַּהֲמוֹן גַּלָּיו, וְשִׂפְתוֹתֵינוּ שֶׁבַח כְּמֶרְחֲבֵי רָקִיעַ, וְעֵינֵינוּ מְאִירוֹת כַּשֶּׁמֶשׁ וְכַיָּרֵחַ, וְיָדֵינוּ פְרוּשׂוֹת כְּנִשְׁרֵי שָׁמַיִם, וְרַגְלֵינוּ קַלּוֹת כָּאַיָּלוֹת—אֵין אֲנַחְנוּ מַסְפִּיקִים לְהוֹדוֹת לָךְ . . . בָּרְכִי נַפְשִׁי אֶת ה' וְכָל קְרָבַי אֶת שֵׁם קָדְשׁוֹ. . .

After the ecstasy, the sun rises.

The period of the Omer, covering the forty-nine days from Pesach to Shavuot, is bookended by classic mystical experiences that barrel on through the night until dawn—immersed in the sea of Torah, trying to break free from the narrow place of this world and achieve redemption in one single night. On Pesach we sit around the seder table and dine at midnight, reliving the legend of the five sleepless Rabbis who dined in B'nei B'rak and had to be interrupted at dawn to say Sh'ma Yisrael.[1] On Shavuot, we engage in the *Tikkun Leil Shavuot*, the Kabbalist innovation of studying text to keep us up until dawn to relive the singular event of Jewish history: The revelation of the Torah at Sinai.

The world looks different after an all-night Shavuot event. There's at once a mental clarity that allowed me one year to articulate a sudden insight into the nature of revelation to my friend Maya Rosen, and a desperate fatigue that longs only for a pillow. I could float on the sea of Torah forever—or for just long enough to make it home to bed.

I recognize that feeling. I had it drilled into me for six years, as an upper-year medical student and resident, and for another eight or nine years as a parent to children under three (some of those years overlapped—that was a special kind of torment indeed). I learned to diagnose while barely keeping my eyes open; solve complex treatment dilemmas while unable to maintain an upright posture.

In those years I learned the truth of the words of the *Nishmat Kol Hai* prayer that appears at the end of Hallel. "Hashem will neither slumber nor sleep, who wakes the sleepers and startles the nappers, who gives voice to the mute and frees the captive, who supports the fallen and straightens the bent." In shul it always feels like this language is directed at those who need our care, but at awful o'clock in the morning on call, it's Hashem who's animating the corpse-like overnight physician to be able to be there for others.

Overnight call is a special kind of torture. I'm not at all sure it's any less tortuous for the patient than for the doctor, and less sure it should even exist, but it's been a fixture of Western medicine for a hundred years or more—maybe far longer as I think about it. Only since 2003 has there been serious consideration to change to shift work, the way nurses have done forever. But in my training, just after that watershed year and still very much the time of 30-hour shifts, it was me who was mute, bent,

---

1. Chapter 15.

fallen, and held captive, and Hashem who restored me to the status of a human being in time to care for others.

Nishmat reminds us of our limits. "If our mouths were as full of song as the sea is of water, and our tongues with joy. . .our hands spread out like the eagles of the sky, our legs as light as rams. . .we would not suffice to thank you." It reminds us that while we're creatures of Divine spirit, the *neshamah*, the Breath of God in every living thing, we're also flesh. While Hashem is in us, Hashem is spirit or soul animating flesh, *ruah*[2] *kol basar*. Hashem animates our exhausted, half-dead forms so that we can keep people alive through the night; just as Hashem animates our lifeless bodies for whatever time we're allotted on this earth.

Yet it's we, not angels or some other immortal being who were redeemed, and who are now entrusted with redeeming others from their own narrow places. We who are tasked with keeping our eyes open, propped with toothpicks if needed, splashing water in our faces, and forbidden to sit—like they did in my medic's course in the army. We who chronicle the torment our patients go through in long technical notes, only to have them end in an illegible scrawl trailing down the page (or in 2024, a string of random characters entered when our faces finally fell on the keyboard). We who are privileged to have access to some of the power Hashem has placed in the world to extend and enrich life, and therefore burdened by putting it to use without regard to our own comfort or convenience.

And yet *Nishmat* also reminds us that we're not alone, and that amazing things are possible. That's why it ends, "I command my soul to bless Hashem and all that is in me to praise Hashem's holy name." Exhausted though we may be, this is an awesome responsibility. Not everyone gets to do this. It's a cause for humility and a cause to rejoice all at once. And I mean both healing and being a part of a seder, of course.

Nishmat ushers us out of the dark and into the dawn, welcoming the day as I used to welcome my colleagues on the day shift. Do we have stories to tell! Glad to see you—finally! You'll never believe what happened overnight!

---

2. Also, breath, see Chapter 39.

47

A Cup of Kindness

The final cup of wine at the seder is followed by a last blessing for finishing the wine and blessing the land it came from. We pray for mercy and kindness from Hashem.

Blessed are You, Lord our God, King of the universe, who creates the fruit of the vine.	בָּרוּךְ אַתָּה ה', אֱלֹהֵינוּ מֶלֶךְ הָעוֹלָם בּוֹרֵא פְּרִי הַגָּפֶן.
Blessed are You, Lord our God, King of the universe, for the vine and for the fruit of the vine; and for the bounty of the field . . . build Jerusalem Your holy city quickly in our days, and bring us up into it and gladden us in its building; and we shall eat from its fruit, and be satiated from its goodness . . . Blessed are You, Lord, for the land and for the fruit of the vine	בָּרוּךְ אַתָּה ה' אֱלֹהֵינוּ מֶלֶךְ הָעוֹלָם, עַל הַגֶּפֶן וְעַל פְּרִי הַגֶּפֶן, עַל תְּנוּבַת הַשָּׂדֶה . . . וּבְנֵה יְרוּשָׁלַיִם עִיר הַקֹּדֶשׁ בִּמְהֵרָה בְיָמֵינוּ וְהַעֲלֵנוּ לְתוֹכָהּ וְשַׂמְּחֵנוּ בְּבִנְיָנָהּ וְנֹאכַל מִפִּרְיָהּ וְנִשְׂבַּע מִטּוּבָהּ . . . בָּרוּךְ אַתָּה ה', עַל הָאָרֶץ וְעַל פְּרִי הַגָּפֶן.

If you're in any way involved with American secular culture, you know the old Scottish song, "Auld Lang Syne." Robert Burns' poem is *the* song sung and played at midnight, as one year passes into the next. Each chorus ends with the line, "We'll tak a cup o' kindness yet, for auld lang syne."

This fourth cup of wine, the final one of the seder, is the cup we held during Hallel, when we sang Psalm 116, "I will raise a cup of redemption," as a thanks to Hashem for all of Hashem's gracious acts. That psalm, as we saw, walks the line between gratitude and disillusionment, between our thanks to God and our disappointment with our fellow humans. But I urged, in reading Psalm 117, that in the space between those extremes is *hesed*, lovingkindness. *Hesed* is a path anyone can follow, a grace any person can bestow on any other—rich or poor, sick or healthy, living or dead. And it's the only path by which a human being can bring about redemption on their own—the only way in which a person can extricate another from their narrow place.

Therefore, let this be the cup o' kindness Burns wrote about—because through *hesed*, kindness, we'll achieve *yeshuah*, redemption.

48

Get Up and Do It Again

The Nirtzah, "satisfied," section is the final part of the seder. We say a brief prayer formally ending the festivities—and already wishing to repeat them next year.

Completed is the Seder of Pesach according to its law, according to all its judgement and statute. Just as we have merited to arrange it, so too, may we merit to do [its sacrifice]...	חֲסַל סִדּוּר פֶּסַח כְּהִלְכָתוֹ, כְּכָל מִשְׁפָּטוֹ וְחֻקָּתוֹ. כַּאֲשֶׁר זָכִינוּ לְסַדֵּר אוֹתוֹ כֵּן נִזְכֶּה לַעֲשׂוֹתוֹ...

I listened to Jackson Browne's song, "The Pretender," hundreds of times when I was in college, thinking about how I wanted to find a life that wasn't made up of endlessly repetitive, middle class routine. Browne touchingly described the aching, not-quite-there yearning of the average 1970s American, trapped in the monotony, lulled into submission by the sameness, oppressed by being a cog in the wheel of the capitalist machine. Yet after a night's sleep, they would wake and do the whole thing all over the next day.[1] Not unlike the Israelites that kept the machinery of ancient Mitzrayim humming until they just couldn't take the routine anymore.

Truthfully, there isn't much distance between routine and ritual. The same acts, repeated in the same order—what is a seder, after all? It's the meaning with which we imbue it that makes the difference. That bears

---

1. Browne, "The Pretender."

repeating—and so does a ritual. It bears repeating day after day, or week after week, or year after year.

The Pretender in the song is probably not unlike most of the people our healers care for—struggling for legal tender and getting injured, or chronically ill, or emotionally damaged in the process.[2] Or perhaps slow-walking through the same daily routine of pills, exercises, appointments and burdensome symptoms and side effects until they can lay down. Or, as Browne and many of his fellow musicians did in the seventies (and in pretty much any other decade), turning to self-medication with drugs to feel something different, a process Browne sings about in another of his Seventies hits, "Cocaine."[3]

For that matter, many of the healers themselves may feel that way, caught between the longing to provide real care for their panel of Pretenders and the harsh financial and temporal constraints that frustrate those efforts. They're fighting other people's battles, and even if they win, they feel empty. Their souls have been sucked out of them. And sleep doesn't provide much of a respite—either bed becomes a place to lay awake for hours and brood, or sleep is wracked with disturbing dreams.

Contrast that with how we feel about rituals. The final paragraph of the seder proper declares that the ritual has been completed according to custom and law, and proclaims, "we have merited to arrange it." Merited—the ritual was our privilege to perform. We wish we could do more. And next year we even hope to take the show on the road, to a rebuilt Jerusalem. In fact, some of the Rabbis, as we heard all the way back before dinner (if you came to my house, it would have been a long time ago indeed), believed we'll keep celebrating this ritual in the World to Come.[4]

We might not sleep. Because as the first of many songs that follow this paragraph tells us, all the good stuff comes to pass at midnight. Certainly, that's true in medicine—the daring rescues and the deep conversations, the moments when you learn who really has your back and realize how much you really know, or how much strength you really have—but didn't have the confidence to believe. And that's true regardless of which side of the bed you're on. As we learned in the last chapter about Nishmat, we're expecting to just barrel on until morning.

But it's all good. The all-nighter, the endlessly repeating ritual—because it's ritual, not routine. It's a privilege. It means something.

2. See Chapter 20.
3. Browne, "Cocaine."
4. See Chapter 15.

It's not that we'll stop suffering because of one healing seder. After all, one Exodus didn't bring about the final redemption of the universe. A song for the second seder, V'Amartem Zevah Pesah, talks about how all sorts of other redemptions—the beginning of the end of Haman, the toppling of the walls of Jericho, or the handwriting on the wall in Daniel—happened on Pesach, but the fact that these redemptions were necessary meant that bad stuff kept happening!

Are we okay with this? NO! Laurie Zoloth, whom I referenced in Chapter 44, called her talk, "Suffering and its Uselessness." The only thing it's good for is inspiring us to fight against it; whether you're the one suffering or the person "standing them up," as it's described in Berachot 5b.[5] This Talmudic story, which formed the basis of Zoloth's argument, is the same one Ruhama Weiss refers to when she describes the Underground Against Suffering.[6]

Healing, on the other hand, is a privilege. Refusing to accept your own suffering is a right. And reaching out to the person who will extend their hand to "stand you up" is like the cry of the Israelites that Hashem heard,[7] the cry of protest without which there would never have been an Exodus to begin with. Suffering is no privilege—it's a fact of life, and a lousy one at that. But crying out to Hashem, or to another human being even more so, is a privilege. It's the first step that all healing depends on. No miracle, no act of "heroism" by a medical practitioner, no "covenant of healing" is possible without that cry.

That cry is also the difference between the routine of the Pretender and the ritual of the seder. We may recline at seder, but we don't "lay down." We stand up, we cry out, we weep tears, we sing songs, we rejoice and redouble our efforts, we pour out our wrath and we pour more wine. When we imbue our days of encountering illness with this kind of energy—equal parts joy, fury, regret, and reflection—we're no longer pretending. We're no longer trudging. And when we reach the end, we thank Hashem for the privilege of having won the day, the privilege of the connection, of the breakthrough, of the right to be in this world and do for one another. And we can't wait to get up and do it again.

---

5. Chapter 10 and elsewhere.
6. Weiss, "Neither Suffering nor Its Rewards," 107–128.
7. See Chapter 21.

49

I Love to Count

The second night of Pesach commences the seven weeks of the Omer that run until the holiday of Shavuot. We count each day after sundown, saying the blessing below before we do so.

| Blessed are You, Lord our God, King of the Universe, who has sanctified us with His commandments and has commanded us on the counting of the *omer*. Today is the first day of the *omer*. | בָּרוּךְ אַתָּה ה׳, אֱלֹהֵינוּ מֶלֶךְ הָעוֹלָם, אֲשֶׁר קִדְּשָׁנוּ בְּמִצְוֹתָיו וְצִוָּנוּ עַל סְפִירַת הָעֹמֶר. הַיּוֹם יוֹם אֶחָד בָּעֹמֶר. |

At God-oh-no-clock in the morning, I woke for no reason. I rolled over to go back to sleep, head still heavy, eyelids still drooping, but my heart was having none of it.

Flop. Thump. Run like a rabbit.

I knew this story. This gripping feeling of dread in the middle of the chest, this disobedient heartbeat. It was a common thread linking my clinic days together; binding my patients in commonality across ethnic boundaries, socioeconomic status, gender and age.

I also knew this story in men my age occasionally meant we'd spontaneously developed a serious heart arrhythmia called atrial fibrillation. The thought of being featured in a commercial for Eliquis[1] did not appeal

---

1. Generic name apixaban, a blood thinner we put people on when they have atrial fibrillation, so they don't have a stroke.

to me. And of course, a little knowledge being a dangerous thing, this only added to the inability to ignore the *avant garde* jazz drummer in my ribcage, unable to decide between Dave Brubeck in five or a Balkan rhythm in thirteen.

It was time to follow my own advice, to do the thing I always told people to do in this situation. The "poor man's Holter monitor."

I took my right wrist in my left hand and planted my left index and middle fingers squarely but gently over my radial artery and counted.

One heartbeat! Two heartbeats! Three heartbeats! Four! Four wonderful heartbeats!

No Brubeck, no Balkans. Steady and boring as an analog clock ticking in an empty room. The flopping and thumping stopped. The Eliquis logo evaporated before my closed eyelids. I fell back asleep.

Every night for the previous four and a half weeks I'd been counting. Not heartbeats, but days. The second night of Passover, at the seder table, begins the counting of a period known as the Omer—named for the sheaf of barley brought to the Temple as a "wave-offering" on that day. We count forty-nine days (about one and a half months). We count these, seven weeks, until the next harvest, the festival of first fruits, which falls on the fiftieth day of Shavuot.

With the drift of time and the historic upheavals that the Jews have endured, the Omer's meaning has morphed from an agricultural one into a spiritual one. It's the forty-nine rung spiritual ladder we climb from leaving slavery in the "narrow place," Egypt, to the heights of Mount Sinai where we received the precious words of Torah. Ironically, according to midrash, Mount Sinai is the lowliest of the mountains, chosen for this purpose precisely because of its humility.

As Rabbi Schiff reminded us in Chapter 24 ("Blood in the Water"), it's the remembrance of a plague which nearly wiped out civilization as we know it, or at least Jewish civilization. The plague struck the students of Rabbi Akiva, the great sage who helped define the Judaism that we're discussing here. It was the post-Temple, post-agricultural Judaism that most of us recognize even though we may adhere to either more Orthodox or more liberal forms of it. At a time less than 60 years after the Romans destroyed the Temple, the survival of such a Judaism, of any Judaism, was by no means assured. A plague ravaging the disciples who were being counted on to perpetuate that knowledge and those behaviors could spell the end.

As a result, our counting is one of the most spiritually confusing times of the year. It's spring, midway between two of our greatest holidays and with the world in full rebirth and bloom. We're anticipating the greatest gift of all, the gift of Torah. We climb a mystical, spiritual ladder, one that the Chasidic tradition labels with the names of seven of the emanations of the Divine. One emanation is assigned to each week, and then we repeat these seven for each day within the week—giving each day a unique name like, "Strength that is in Lovingkindness." And at the same time of the Omer, we're in mourning for those lost in the plague, and many Jews refrain from behaviors like cutting their hair or going out to engage in entertainment. We've been rehearsing for a pandemic year, or a war year, or a mourning year, it seems, for nearly two millennia.

And each evening, to keep ourselves on track, we recite an intention, a *Kavanah* (from the word for "direction" or "aim"), that says, "I'm ready to fulfill the mitzvah of counting the Omer, as it's written in the Torah: *U's'fartem lachem*—and you shall count for yourselves. . ."

The chanting of this *Kavanah* was what I heard as the Balkan Brubeck faded away. *U's'fartem lachem*. Count for yourselves. After all, wasn't that what I was doing? Counting for myself?

Counting has power. It allows us to take stock of time that has passed, and to anticipate time that has yet to come. Power to take a catastrophic event and put walls around it, drag it into perspective—or to appreciate the outsized significance of an event we've seemingly overlooked.

When I count heartbeats, it allows me to take stock of what's really going on inside my chest, to uncouple the feeling from the phenomenon. The dreadfully out-of-date novel *The House of God* popularized many rules that I would never follow, but one that retains its power is, "In a code (a cardiac arrest) the first pulse you take should be your own." We "take the pulse" of a situation. When we count, we can control, at least a little bit.

Even the teachings about counting itself are ambivalent. The Torah tells of a huge census of all the tribes, giving exact numbers—yet another relevant parallel to this strange year we're living through. Elsewhere in Jewish tradition, we're discouraged from counting heads of Jews at all, lest we discover that we're not "as numerous as the grains of sand on the seashore," as God promised Abraham. And what of the modern truth that when we count, the numbers mean nothing unless we agree on what exactly we're counting? Numbers proliferated in the news during spring 2020, but many of them were a primer in how *not* to understand statistics.

None of these matters to me in the middle of the night. Nor does it matter to me just after dark each night, when I stand to recite, "From the day you bring the wave offering, seven complete weeks, until the day after the seventh week count fifty days." I, along with my palpitating patients, am counting to reassure myself I'm OK, that I'm still here. Or they're counting to say, "I've had two migraines this week—that's better than four last week, but maybe I can have a week with none." Or "this piece of bread is my third serving of carbs for the day—I'll stop now so my blood sugar doesn't rise."

Thirty-one! Thirty-two! Thirty-three!

I was counting toward the end of a plague that I "knew" would end, that with every passing day was one day longer, but also one day closer to being "over." I reached day 33, called Lag B'Omer after the letters *lamed* and *gimel* whose numerical values are thirty and three. This historically was the day that the plague of Akiva stopped. Would that be the day that *our* plague stops? There's a debate as to whether "stop" means the plague ended, or that it paused, only to resume until Shavuot when it finally ended for good. Some Jews pause their mourning rituals on Lag Ba'Omer only to resume them the next day, others finish and move on. Would our "end" be the end, or just a pause?

The chronically ill, and those that care for them, know this feeling. We call it "remission." With every remission comes the sense that one shouldn't celebrate too hard or rejoice too fully. Remission could be the early recognition of "cure"—or it could just be a one-day reprieve before a return to illness. A flare of lupus. A relapse of the addiction. A new metastasis. Editing this chapter nearly four years after my heart went thump in the night, the whole world is chronically ill, with COVID-19 and all sorts of other diseases ebbing and flowing, hospital numbers rising and falling; nowhere near the finish line that we've only ever reached once, with smallpox.

Still, I'm counting toward Sinai. I'm counting because I know there's a high point coming. I also know that Tisha B'Av, the lowest of the low points, will come exactly two months later. I know that one day, my heartbeat counting trick may not work, that the palpitations may be real. But in the middle of a long night, counting reminds me of where I am, of what's coming next, of the approach of something worth keeping track of. I'm counting to regain a measure of control over a world that I know is fundamentally out of my control.

Forty-eight! Forty-nine! Fifty! Fifty wonderful days! AH-HA-HA—I love to count!

50

The House of Hashem

Not content to leave the seder table just yet, we conclude with singing. These final three chapters explore the "greatest hits" of seder songs. We begin with Adir Hu, "Mighty is (God)," a song about building the House of God.

Adir Hu	אדיר הוא
Mighty is He, may He build His house soon. Quickly, quickly, in our days, soon. God build, God build, build Your house soon. Chosen is He, great is He, noted is He. Quickly, quickly, in our days, soon. God build, God build, build Your house soon . . .	אַדִּיר הוּא יִבְנֶה בֵיתוֹ בְּקָרוֹב. בִּמְהֵרָה, בִּמְהֵרָה, בְּיָמֵינוּ בְּקָרוֹב. אֵל בְּנֵה, אֵל בְּנֵה, בְּנֵה בֵיתְךָ בְּקָרוֹב. בָּחוּר הוּא, גָּדוֹל הוּא, דָּגוּל הוּא יִבְנֶה בֵיתוֹ בְּקָרוֹב. בִּמְהֵרָה, בִּמְהֵרָה, בְּיָמֵינוּ בְּקָרוֹב. אֵל בְּנֵה, אֵל בְּנֵה, בְּנֵה בֵיתְךָ בְּקָרוֹב. . .

"The jackhammers of the Wing of Zock had been wiggling my ossicles for twelve hours." These are the words of the sleep-deprived, overworked intern, Dr. Roy Basch, in Samuel Shem's classic, raunchy, bitingly critical 1978 novel, *The House of God*—the house, as it were, of Ha-Shem.[1]

Medicine has been described as having an edifice complex. Go to any major city in the US and you're just as likely to see hospitals as you are to see skyscrapers featured in the skyline. My hometown behemoth of a university medical center is the largest employer in the state, and the pediatric hospital is a funky, multi-colored ode to childhood creativity

---

1. Shem, *The House of God*, 41.

perched on a bluff over a river so it can be seen from miles around, whether you're kayaking on the water or commuting on the highway.

Even the holy city of Jerusalem is crowned by hospitals overlooking the holiest spot in the world. Hadassah is on Mt. Scopus, just to the northeast, and Augusta Victoria is on the Mount of Olives, almost due east. They're just above the cemetery where the Resurrection is supposed to take place someday. The Beth Israel in Boston may be the model for *The House of God*, but these hotels-Dieu[2] pretty much take the cake.

Therefore, it shouldn't surprise you that when I hear the words of *Adir Hu* imploring Hashem to build God's house speedily, in our days, I can't help thinking of hospitals and, well, Samuel Shem. Elisha Waldman's speculation that medicine had taken on the trappings of being its own religion didn't shock me at all—between the vestments, the dietary restrictions, the rites of initiation and passage, the confessional conversations and the bodily mortifications—it's honestly hard to tell them apart. Little wonder, then, that medicine's complex edifices (I've gotten lost in more of them than I can count) take on the status of Temples.

My entire medical training has had a soundtrack of jackhammers, going back to the demolition of Pitt Stadium I wrote about in Chapter 14. That same year there was constant construction going on *inside* the med school as well. We even did a bit on it in the talent show. It started with Brad Sobolewski, now a pediatric ER physician in Cincinnati, doing his best impression of an electrician with a stepladder and saggy pants, and ended with me storming off stage and coming back in a Kermit the Frog costume. But that's for another time.

In the first week of the COVID-19 pandemic, a new "neighborhood hospital" opened down the road from one of my offices. It was touted as a new idea. Never mind that from the eighties through the early 2000s, probably a dozen small hospitals around town that probably qualified as "neighborhood hospitals" shut their doors. Some of them were not too far from this new one. Some were the main employer and primary source of healthcare in majority-minority neighborhoods, and when they closed, the jobs, and the care moved out of the valley and into the richer, whiter suburbs. I fear for the lives of the few that remain.

---

2. The Hotel-Dieu de Paris—"God-Shelter of Paris"—is possibly the oldest continually operating hospital in the world, dating to somewhere between 651 and 826 CE and the only hospital in Paris before the 17th century (https://www.solosophie.com/hotel-dieu-paris/). It's likely Shem/Bergman was alluding to this hospital, as well as the various Jewish hospitals like Beth Israel in the US, when he chose his title.

As I write, the behemoth is in the midst of construction projects that are snarling traffic in two of the major urban centers in Pittsburgh. They're expanding further on two of the flagship hospitals that already boast Level I trauma centers, regional specialty centers, and loyal patient bases. These projects were undertaken while good friends of mine were getting arrested protesting that many health system employees were not earning a living wage.[3]

So, what are we singing about when we belt out *Adir Hu*? Do we need another house like the *House of God*? Another place where bright minds are brutally broken by the un-Godly amount of work they're asked to do? Where wealth, rather than wisdom, makes the real choices? Where people of means get care they don't need, and people who are needy find that means nobody cares? And why are we asking Hashem to build it, when clearly, it's *us* who need to have such big buildings?

All houses of God, from the very first one, were built by human hands. When we sing *Adir Hu*, we aren't asking Hashem to pick up a hammer. We're asking Hashem to come home.

That very first house, the portable one in the wilderness, was built because Hashem said, "*Ya'asu li Mikdash v'shakhanti be'tokham.*"[4] "They will make me a holy place, and I will dwell among them." Not "in it," but "among them," as numerous commentators point out.[5] Hashem didn't need a fancy golden building to live in. The Divine Presence, the *Shekhinah* (root *sh-k-n*), needed a golden-hearted people to live among; *lishkon* (root *sh-k-n*) *be'tokham*. Three thousand years later, the Kotzker rebbe rebuked his students, who facilely answered him that God was everywhere, saying, "NO! God is wherever we let Him in!"[6]

And if Hashem is the still, small voice that spoke to Elijah, we're going to have an awfully hard time hearing it over the jackhammers of the Wing of Zock. We have enough buildings. We need to let holiness into the work we do inside those buildings, and outside those buildings.[7]

---

3. In fairness, the system *has* since made it system-wide policy to raise their minimum hourly wage to $15, in large part *because* of these protests. On the opposite foot, it's actively undermined the formation of employee unions. Progress is slow. . .

4. Exodus 25:8.

5. Or HaChaim on Exodus 25:8.

6. Levin, Dan, "Where We Let God In."

7. See Chapters 8 and 42.

51

Who *Really* Knows One?

The song Ehad Mi Yode'a, "Who Knows One," recounts thirteen key items in Jewish tradition—but it's the Oneness that counts.

Who knows one? I know one: One is our God in the heavens and the earth . . . Who knows thirteen? I know thirteen: Thirteen are the characteristics, twelve are the tribes, eleven are the stars, ten are the statements, nine are the months of birth, eight are the days of circumcision, seven are the days of the week, six are the orders of the Mishnah, five are the books of the Torah, four are the mothers, three are the fathers, two are the tablets of the covenant, One is our God in the heavens and the earth.	אֶחָד מִי יוֹדֵעַ? אֶחָד אֲנִי יוֹדֵעַ: אֶחָד אֱלֹהֵינוּ שֶׁבַּשָּׁמַיִם וּבָאָרֶץ . . . שְׁלֹשָׁה עָשָׂר מִי יוֹדֵעַ? שְׁלֹשָׁה עָשָׂר אֲנִי יוֹדֵעַ: שְׁלֹשָׁה עָשָׂר מִדַּיָּא, שְׁנֵים עָשָׂר שִׁבְטַיָּא, אַחַד עָשָׂר כּוֹכְבַיָּא, עֲשָׂרָה דִבְּרַיָּא, תִּשְׁעָה יַרְחֵי לֵדָה, שְׁמוֹנָה יְמֵי מִילָה, שִׁבְעָה יְמֵי שַׁבַּתָּא, שִׁשָּׁה סִדְרֵי מִשְׁנָה, חֲמִשָּׁה חוּמְשֵׁי תוֹרָה, אַרְבַּע אִמָּהוֹת, שְׁלֹשָׁה אָבוֹת, שְׁנֵי לֻחוֹת הַבְּרִית, אֶחָד אֱלֹהֵינוּ שֶׁבַּשָּׁמַיִם וּבָאָרֶץ.

If a doctor had written "Who Knows One?" it might go something like this:

Who knows one? I know one. One is the diagnosis, one is the diagnosis, one is the diagnosis, according to Occam's Razor.

Who knows two? I know two. Two are the knots you tie in a suture.

Who knows three? I know three. Three are the layers of the meninges (the membrane that covers the brain. Insane!).

Who knows four? I know four. Four are the markers of inflammation (backup singers: "Rubor, calor, tumor, dolor")

Who knows five? I know five. Five are the fingers on the hand.

Who knows six? I know six. Six are the hours that Lasix lasts.

Who knows seven? I know seven. Seven are the causes of hypercoagulability I memorized for the USMLE.

Who knows eight? I know eight. Eight are the markers of cognitive decline we ask about when we screen for dementia.

Who knows nine? I know nine. Nine are still the months of pregnancy (some things never change).

Who knows ten? I know ten. Ten are the days we prescribe antibiotics for strep throat.

Who knows eleven? I know eleven. Eleven are the diagnostic criteria for lupus.

Who knows twelve? I know twelve. Twelve are the seconds your heart stops when I administer adenosine to cardiovert you back to sinus rhythm.

Who knows thirteen? I know thirteen. Thirteen is the floor missing from the hospital elevators because all the "scientific" hospitals think it's an unlucky number.

Could this raucous, late-night song be more than a mnemonic device for all the important things in Judaism, as if we didn't already know the length of a pregnancy, or how many matriarchs there were (although in some liberal circles we list six, counting Zilpah and Bilhah)? Do we need these verses to remind us what's in the AD-8 (there's a clue in the name) or what covers our brains? Even this late in the seder, are we striving for something more?

Yes, we are.

I imagined this essay was going to be a throwaway little coda to this whole exercise of the Healer's Haggadah. It was a chance to write the cute little litany above and maybe challenge my friends and colleagues to do the same, maybe even stump each other in a Passover-themed version of the medical hazing ritual called, I'm ashamed to report, "pimping." It worked something like this: "Dr. Weinkle! I'm sure you'd be happy to share with us this morning what pentad (that means five, the attending is showing off their knowledge of ancient languages, just like I've been doing throughout this book) of signs indicates a patient has thrombotic thrombocytopenic purpura." I know five—I'd better, or it's going to be a very long day.

WHO REALLY KNOWS ONE?

At most seders I've been to that make it to the end, this song is a kind of "pimping" as well. The leader yells out, or sings out, in English or Hebrew, "Who knows ten?" Someone at the table, usually one of the kids who hasn't gone to sleep, yells or sings back, "I know ten! Ten are the *teeeennnn* commandments," then sings their way backward through the previous verses to "One is Hashem, One is Hashem, in the heaven and the earth!" (Oooh, aaaah, ooh aah aah . . .). Extra points for doing it all in one breath, especially thirteen.

The *Marbeh Lesaper*, however, thought there was more to it.

> The question "Who knows one" implies something else as well. Rabbi Bahya Ibn Pakuda in his philosophical work teaches that there are two types of "Oneness:" There's a numerical One—as in not two, not three, etc; and there's a qualitative One—as in the uniqueness and unity of God. The question then, is "Who knows the real one"—not the numerical but the qualitative meaning of God's oneness. The real One is OUR GOD. And how do we know the unity and uniqueness of God—we know God not by His essence (which is unknowable) but by his creations in Heaven above and on Earth. We know God through God's deeds.[1]

This song isn't meant to be a feat of respiratory fortitude. It's the cornerstone. There's that word again, like in Psalm 118, where the thing we thought was a throwaway turns out to be the most important part. This song is the cornerstone of the Healer's Seder and of my whole philosophy of healing and Judaism.

No one wants a doctor, or nurse, or pharmacist, who *doesn't* "know one"—or four or eleven or ninety-eight-point-six degrees or one-hundred-twenty-over-eighty or whatever number the correct dose of your chemotherapy is. Ninety-five percent of medical training (training in all the related professions) is spent cramming people's heads full of those numbers and the knowledge they purport to represent. Even the mental health professions have their bulleted diagnostic criteria, formalized protocols, and numerically scored validated structured interviews.

But I don't want to be a healer who "knows one" in that sense but doesn't know Oneness—and I don't want someone like that caring for me, either. I don't mean someone who doesn't know God's Oneness—I've worked with perfectly compassionate physicians who identify as atheists.

---

1. Weil, *Marbeh Lesaper,* Nirtzah, Echad Mi Yodea 1

I mean not knowing the Oneness, the Divinity, the Uniqueness, of the person they're caring for.

What really matters is not just the data the healer has managed to memorize, but the degree to which they take the time to learn about the deeds, the defining features, the uniqueness of the person we hope to heal by means of that data. Otherwise, how do we explain the person we met in Chapter 23, who undergoes gastric bypass surgery only to look in the mirror a year after a "successful" operation and get angry because they don't recognize themselves? How much of the essence, the uniqueness of that person, was bound up in their pre-surgical body image, and who was the "successful" surgeon who didn't recognize that about them before irreversibly altering their metabolism?

That's an odd critique, since the Exodus narrative in the Torah doesn't seem to privilege this kind of data at all. Exodus likes, well, Numbers: Multiple censuses, chapter upon chapter spent on the intricate details of the building of the *mishkan*, the sacrifices, and the priestly garments. The Israelites are always referred to in the collective, both in their redemption and in their falling short of God's expectations. They're both rewarded and punished as a faceless crowd. If God, bringing the Israelites out of their national narrow place, didn't stop to consider the individuality of each enslaved Judahite or Ephraimite, how can we demand of human healers that they stop curing "cancer" and start focusing on curing Judy and Effie, who happen to have the same kind of cancer but are as different as night and day?

The song itself gives us the answer. Hashem is unique, One not just in the sense of not being two, but of being unlike anything else in the universe. Yet at the final verse, we learn that Hashem is, in fact, thirteen—characterized by the thirteen attributes of God which "pass before Moshe" while he hid in the rock during his second trip up to Sinai. Each of these aspects forms a different way that Hashem relates to humans, and two humans relating to the same God may find themselves having entirely different experiences. One God, but a multitude of ways of connecting with the Divine.

With humans it's the reverse. Each human being is one of a multitude, and subsets of that multitude are held together by some binding similarity, or perhaps many binding similarities: A national identity, patronage of the same sports franchise, or yes, the symptoms of the same disease. We must, as healers, relate to and take account of those similarities—and those who are suffering may actually benefit from knowing that they don't suffer alone. It's comforting to know that someone else has been through this before, that there's even research being done on their precise condition at this very moment (or even better) that the research has concluded and there's a new treatment that could cure them.

We remember three patriarchs. Four matriarchs. Nine months of pregnancy and eleven stars in Joseph's dream. They matter collectively, bound together by their group identity. Yet each one stood out alone— Avraham was not Ya'akov, Rivka was not Rahel, and the third month of pregnancy is vastly different from the eighth. No two of the eleven "stars" was quite the same as the others when the aftermath of the dream unfolded. Each one, as it moved from being one of the eleven stars to one of the twelve tribes, had a different fate and destiny unfold. On his deathbed, Ya'akov blesses each of his sons according to their character; at the end of the Torah Moshe does the same for each of the tribes. The same, but different.

I remember those folks whose gastric bypass surgery went awry—as a group they serve as a collective warning to be very hesitant to refer anyone else for that procedure. But I also remember each story in its uniqueness: For one person a perpetual struggle to swallow without pain, another a battle to eat without their blood pressure plummeting. One died by suicide, another nearly died—twice—from a late surgical complication years later. Each brought their own set of emotions, their own process of relearning who they were and what their newly reconstructed body was—and was not—able to handle.

"Who Knows One?" is a reminder that no matter how good we're at counting; at regurgitating learned facts, at deep breathing, we always return to the uniqueness of the person before us. God is unique, we're in God's image, so *we* are unique—and as Mishna Sanhedrin reminds us, we're unique *from one another* even though we're like coins stamped by God from the same "mold" (God's own likeness).[2] If we tried the same thing ourselves, we'd make eight billion clones, like the armies in *Star Wars*. But when God does it, God gets eight billion *unique* souls. "Who Know One?" tells the person who's stuck in a narrow place, "You're unique, and yet you're not alone. Your suffering matters because you're you; and your redemption will come because of what you share with others." Finding the balance between the two is the whole healing enterprise.

---

2. Mishnah Sanhedrin 4:5.

52

Priceless at Any Price

The final song is Had Gadya, "An Only Kid," which seems to describe a dog-eat-dog world. Or perhaps it describes something very different indeed.

Chad Gadya	חד גדיא
One kid, one kid that my father bought for two *zuzim*, one kid, one kid . . . Then came the Holy One, blessed be He and slaughtered the angel of death, who slaughtered the *schochet*, who slaughtered the bull, that drank the water, that extinguished the fire, that burnt the stick, that hit the dog, that bit the cat, that ate the kid that my father bought for two *zuzim*, one kid, one kid.	חַד גַּדְיָא, חַד גַּדְיָא דְּזַבִּין אַבָּא בִּתְרֵי זוּזֵי, חַד גַּדְיָא, חַד גַּדְיָא. . . וְאָתָא הַקָּדוֹשׁ בָּרוּךְ הוּא וְשָׁחַט לְמַלְאַךְ הַמָּוֶת, דְּשָׁחַט לְשׁוֹחֵט, דְּשָׁחַט לְתוֹרָא, דְּשָׁתָה לְמַיָּא, דְּכָבָה לְנוּרָא, דְּשָׂרַף לְחוּטְרָא, דְּהִכָּה לְכַלְבָּא, דְּנָשַׁךְ לְשׁוּנְרָא, דְּאָכְלָה לְגַדְיָא, דְּזַבִּין אַבָּא בִּתְרֵי זוּזֵי. חַד גַּדְיָא, חַד גַּדְיָא.

Not every memory of my beloved seders with the Vogels involves me choking on horseradish. . .

Dan's mother, Eva, was born in Germany and got out in the nick of time in the 1930s as a child—but she retained much of the German Jewish culture she was born to. It came out in her cooking, the use of little metal sidecars for the plates to put bones in when she served fish, and delightfully, at the end of the seder, when we sang *Had Gadya*.[1]

Or, rather, when she sang *Ein Lambschen*.

---

1. "One kid goat," in Aramaic.

That used to fill me with inexplicable joy. There were many elements in that joy: The giddiness of it being 2:45 in the morning, the twinkle in her eye as she sang the words playfully and delicately, and the memory of my own childhood seders. There, the vernacular rendition of *Had Gadya* involved my grandfather, my cousin Richard, and several of the other adult men chanting in English, "an only kid, an only kid, my father bought for two zuzim," at breakneck speed out of tiny, gray, cloth-bound Union Haggadahs.

When Eva passed in 2021, Dan and his sister Miriam Fenster invited their friends and family to engage in the tradition of studying Mishna (the first written collection of the Jewish oral traditions) in memory of the deceased during the *shloshim*, the thirty days after her funeral. The aim of this practice is to divvy up the entire Mishna among the participants, and thereby complete study of the whole breadth of Jewish law (and a lot of its lore) in just one month. This is followed by a festive *siyyum Shas*, a small celebration of completion, on the day marking the end of *shloshim*. In Eva's case, it was planned for the Sunday of *Chol HaMoed Sukkot*, so that we could honor our learning and honor her precious memory at the same moment.

Eva's siyyum was beautiful, of course. Miriam and Dan loved their mother deeply, and both their teaching of Torah and their touching stories made her memory for a blessing. But what returns to me now, as I complete this Haggadah, is the learning I did in support of this effort—the one pole of the sukkah, if you will, that I helped erect.

My assignment was the tractate *Arakhin*, valuations, which explores the legal and monetary ramifications of Chapter 27 of Leviticus, beginning with verse 2: "When any party explicitly vows to *Hashem* the equivalent for a human being. . ."

It was possible, in biblical and Temple times, to make a vow to God to pay the value of a person, a home, or of livestock; and different values are assigned in the chapter to different types of people.

None of us have a problem even today, surely, with valuing an animal or a home. One of my wife's favorite hobbies is surfing the real estate web, which prominently displays both the asking price and the website's valuation of homes for sale (and which will gladly tell you the value of your own home as an enticement to get you to consider selling, too). Charities now routinely ask us to consider donating property or used vehicles to them, rather than trading them in or selling them. And even a shelter pet comes with fees attached, so much more so a pet acquired at a pet shop or from a breeder (especially if one is careful to go to a reputable breeder and not a "puppy mill").

What bothers us is the idea that *human beings* have a monetary value. The first Mishna in *Arakhin* states that anyone can take a vow of valuation, be valuated, vow to donate or be the object of a vow to donate (i.e. "I vow to donate the value of my dog Harry to the Temple treasury.") This is widely understood to mean, "everyone vows to donate to the Temple treasury the amount corresponding to their market value, if they were assessed to be sold as a slave."

Slavery didn't disappear from the world when the Israelites left Mitzrayim, nor for that matter after the American Civil War. Some organizations combatting slavery in modern times estimate that, worldwide, there may be more people enslaved today than ever before.[2] Closer to our text, slavery did not disappear from Israelite society when they left Mitzrayim. While the biblical texts seem to describe post-Exodus slavery as more of a time-bound indentured servitude (except in cases where the slave, against the advice of the text, chose to remain in the possession of the owner) there's still a hierarchy that allows for some human beings to be the property of others, and to be valued and sold as such.

---

2. Levin, Shlomo, *The Human Rights Haggadah*, 17–19.

We're not the first generation to find this whole system problematic. Jewish thought beginning with the prophets, through the rabbis of the Talmud and the writings of the Hassidic masters into our own time, has taken exception to the idea that a people whose foundational myth is about their liberation from slavery could condone any form of human bondage. Like the death penalty or the punishment of the rebellious son, it's been qualified out of any practical existence. What, then, could I learn, after steeping myself in learning about the value of freeing ourselves and others from the narrowness of Mitzrayim, from a tractate that (from its inception) assumes that a human being can be valued as property?

I can begin with *Had Gadya*. This is no nursery rhyme, at least not when we sing it at the seder. One popular interpretation is that the kid, the goat, is the Jewish people, and the "Father" is *Hashem*. The two *zuzim* are the two tablets that Moshe brought down from the mountain, and the "buying," I would propose, is the redemption of the Israelites from enslavement in Mitzrayim.

In the musical, *A Funny Thing Happened on the Way to the Forum*, a slave in ancient Rome spends the entire show trying to earn enough cash to buy his freedom. The practice of purchasing one's way out of slavery existed in a lot of slave-holding societies, including the American South, and in biblical times. Perhaps the system in Leviticus, expanded and codified in *Arakhin*, is a way of acknowledging that Hashem purchased our freedom, and voluntarily offered to (in a sense) *redeem* ourselves from the Redeemer. Freedom, after all, is tenuous. Our history proves that, the seder makes a very clear point of reminding us, and there are myriad examples in our own time demonstrating how fragile freedom is. By making a vow of valuation, we say, "I'm pledging to repay my own value that you, Hashem, paid to redeem me from Mitzrayim, toward the preservation of our freedom to serve You and not a human master."

However, that understanding doesn't wipe away the disparities in how an individual is valued—by gender (including complicated language around how someone of indeterminate gender is to be valued, or not), by slave vs. free status, and by level of disability or intellect. In very Orwellian fashion, while Mishna Sanhedrin may tell us that Hashem created Adam alone to teach that each life is worth an entire world; some lives are worth more valuable worlds than others.

While this, too, offends our sensibilities, it seems to fit perfectly with our practices in the 21st century. A fictional president asks his new speechwriter, "why is a Kundunese life worth less to me than an

American life," and the speechwriter replies, "I don't know, sir, but it is."[3] Life imitates art, and when the real-world United States withdraws from a military commitment to protect the lives of its own soldiers, or refrains from getting involved in another for fear of what it might do to a fragile economy, or underfunds public health and disease-fighting capabilities at home and abroad due to a high price-tag, that fictional president's words seem quite apt.

This doesn't only happen at the government level. These valuations take place throughout the healthcare system, a kind of cold calculus of human worth. In more centralized systems, meaning much of the Western world outside the US, these valuations are explicit. Resources are limited even in the best of times. Providing unlimited value to one individual means taking away from someone else, or more likely many others. Costly intensive care and experimental treatments cut into the budget for vaccines, sanitation, and prenatal care—which contribute disproportionately to increases in life expectancy. Age and ability are often at the forefront of these calculations.

The US seems to believe itself to have unlimited resources, and to be the bulwark against healthcare "rationing" that takes place elsewhere. Yet that freedom from rationing is an illusion. Those who are worth more financially are also the ones more worth saving, because they have better health insurance—or so much cash on hand that insurance isn't necessary. They have so much influence that the "best" doctors and hospitals are a phone call away. Those individuals and institutions will drop everything else, including a less "valuable" patient, to provide care when that call comes.

That same system makes valuations when they say we have too much hospital capacity and closes neighborhood hospitals in poorer areas of cities—or even in poorer counties—often leaving no provider at all in the wake of the closing. It values the insured over the uninsured, and both over the "uninsurable." It makes calculations about the cost-effectiveness of a treatment based on metrics like DALYs (Disability Adjusted Life-Years) or QALYs (Quality Adjusted Life-Years) to decide whether to offer a treatment or not.

In the most tragic, yet the most forgivable circumstances, these decisions are made at moments of extreme crisis. The decisions are almost always wrong from at least one perspective; there are no right answers

3. *The West Wing*, Season 4, Episode 14, "Inauguration, Part 1." Spoken by Martin Sheen as President Josiah Bartlet and Joshua Malina as Will Bailey

when Hurricane Katrina rages outside, or when the COVID tsunami washes over the hospital. In reverse-Orwellian fashion, some answers are more wrong than others, but at least here each decision is personal; made with agony in the heart and mourned afterward. In the worst case, these decisions are lines in a ledger of a hospital's profits and losses, representing a human being the accountant making the decision has never met.

I think the reason the idea of valuation so offends our sensibilities is because our experience overwhelmingly supports one conclusion: That human beings attempting to place a value on other human beings invariably get it *wrong*. We're wrong to think we can commodify human beings at all, and even more wrong to think we can know how much any one individual is worth (though most of us would happily tell anyone who wants to know what *our* hourly rate is). *Had Gadya* teaches us that, too.

An only kid, an only kid, my father bought for two zuzim. Two zuzim was a tiny fraction—one one-hundredth—of the standard bride price outlined in the traditional *ketubah*. This Jewish marriage contract was revolutionary in its day for ensuring that a widowed or divorced woman would not be destitute or dependent. At a minimum, she'd have 100 baby goats-worth of equity to venture out in the world (and this was way before Heifer International). But one of those goats on its own? Not worth much.

And yet that goat ended up being important enough, when all was said and done, that the Creator of the Universe needed to get involved to put a stop to things. We have no idea what someone is worth, or what they can set in motion, when we attach value to them according to some "system." As we read in Hallel (see Chapters 45 and 51), "The stone cast away by the builders has become the cornerstone."[4] Only the person themself can show us what they're truly worth—by their deeds and how deeply they're treasured by others. We have only one choice: Treat every kid as if they were the Only Kid, every life as if it were the entire world. If we're not up to the task, then we find someone who is—even if we have to appeal all the way to the Top.

At least, those are my two *zuzim* on the subject. Good night, everyone.

---

4. Psalm 118:22.

Appendix

Not Quite 100 Gates—
Themes and Recurring Stories

I've invited a wide audience to read this book, knowing that different parts of it will appeal to different needs and sensibilities. Some will prefer the exploration of Jewish texts, others the stories of my experiences as a physician, still others the words of inspiration and comfort. Here is a far-from-complete list of many recurring themes and favorite stories that appear in different parts of this Haggadah, to help you find what you need at any particular moment.

Theme	Chapters
Mitzrayim – The Narrow Space	1 - Everyone Needs a Seder, 18 - Brought Down to the Narrow Place, 33 - A Clean Break, and throughout
COVID 19 (Isolation, Politics, Danny Schiff on the Plagues)	1 - Everyone Needs a Seder, 20 - Broken Backs, 24 - Blood in the Water, 49 – I Love to Count
I Am Nowhere, Bhutan	3 – Signposts, 18- Brought Down to the Narrow Place, 19 – Wicked Wisdom
Accompanying In Good and Bad Times	3 - Signposts
Afikomen In the Hametz Cabinet	2 – Searching for Hametz, 36 - Missing Piece
Mussar and Humility	2 – Searching for Hametz, 15 – Promises that Stand the Test of Time
Race	1 – Everyone Needs a Seder, 2 – Search for Hametz, 8 – Poor Bread, 24 – Blood in the Water

Theme	Chapters
Mundane Work That Is Holy	1 - Everyone Needs a Seder, 4 – Sanctifying the Moment, 22 – The Outstretched Arm of the Healer, 29 – In Every Generation, 43 – *Hesed* Forever!
The System Is Broken	4 – Sanctifying the Moment, 22 – The Outstretched Arm of the Healer, 24 – Blood in the Water, 29 – In Every Generation
Paradoxical God	5 – Waldman on Washing Part 1
Mixing Sadness And Joy	6 – Of Spring and Salt,
Brokenness	7 – We Are the King's Horses,
Boundaries and Silos	1 – Everyone Needs a Seder, 4 – Sanctifying the Moment, 8 - Poor Bread, 14 – From the Beginning, 20 – Broken Backs, 32 – Four Cups of Coffee, 40 – Eliyahus Every One, 43 – *Hesed* Forever!
My Family's 2001 Seder	9 – So What Else Is New? 12 – Four Feelings,
Nana	9 – So What Else Is New?
Abarbanel – What Good Did It Do Us That Our Ancestors Were Freed From Egypt?	10 – We Were Slaves, 25 – The Danger of Dayenu, 37 – Satisfaction
Moses the Upstander	4 - Sanctifying the Moment, 10 – We Were Slaves
Sharansky's Seder	1 - Everyone Needs a Seder, 10 – We Were Slaves
The Prisoner Cannot Free Himself From Prison	10 – We Were Slaves, 25 – The Danger of Dayenu
Sleeplessness/Late Nights	11 – Insomniac Rabbis, 13 – Where Shall I Begin, 29 – In Every Generation, 32 – Four Cups of Coffee, 46 – Body and Soul and Spirit, 48- Get Up and Do It Again, 49 – I Love to Count!
Sacred Space and Time	4 – Sanctifying the Moment, 13 – Where Shall I Begin?,
Graven Images	14 – From the Beginning, 41 – Nerves of Silver, 50 – House of Hashem
"Calculating The End"	1 - Everyone Needs a Seder, 15 – Promises that Stand the Test of Time

Theme	Chapters
Fickle Promises	15 – Promises that Stand the Test of Time, 22 – The Outstretched Arm of the Healer, 29 – In Every Generation, 42 – How Can I Repay You for Disappointing Me?
Importance of Language and Idiom	17 - An Aramean Told My Father to Get Lost . . . or Something Like That. . ., 21 – Idioms of Distress
Synagogue Shooting	22 – The Outstretched Arm of the Healer, 39 - Neither in Your Name Nor in Ours?
Not Recognizing Ourselves	23 – Missing Midrash, 51 – Who Really Knows One?
Limbo Of Chronic Illness	23 – Missing Midrash
At-Leastism	23 – Missing Midrash, 25 – the Danger of Dayenu,
Jonathan Sacks, *Morality*	23 – Missing Midrash, 25 – The Danger of Dayenu
Victor Frankl, *Man's Search For Meaning*	25 – The Danger of Dayenu, 28 – Biting Bitter Herbs, 48- Get Up and Do It Again,
Physician's Prayer	15 – Promises that Stand the Test of Time, 27 - Matzah (again?)
Vogel Seder	28 – Biting Bitter Herbs, 34 - Breakable Bread, 52 – Priceless at Any Price
Chaotic Universe	28 – Biting Bitter Herbs, 31 – Taunting the Sea
Shlomo Gronich and The Sheba Choir	30 – A Happy Mother of Children, 44 – Psalm 118: the Narrow and the Wide
Ritualization of Behavior	34 – Breakable Bread, 47 – Get Up and Do It Again
Restricted Diets	33 – A Clean Break?, 34 – Breakable Bread
Trauma Becomes Memory	1 - Everyone Needs a Seder, 10 – We Were Slaves, 36 – The Missing Piece
No Day But Today	28 – Biting Bitter Herbs, 37 – Satisfaction, 38 – A Cup of Survival, 49 – I Love to Count
Laurie Zoloth On Suffering	44 – Psalm 118: the Narrow and the Wide, 47 – Get Up and Do It Again
House Of God	48 – House of Hashem, 49 – I Love to Count

Bibliography

Abarbanel, Isaac. *Zevach Pesach*. Monopoli, Italy: 1496.
Alt Miller, Yvette. "Harry Potter and Jewish Values." https://aish.com/harry-potter-and-jewish-values/.
Aomatsu M et al. "Medical Students' and Residents' Conceptual Structure of Empathy: A Qualitative Study." *Education for Health* 26.1 (April 2013).
Azulay, Chaim Joseph David. *Geulat Olam*. Publication date est. 1792. https://www.sefaria.org/Geulat_Olam_on_Pesach_Haggadah?tab=contents.
——. *Safa Echat*. Publication date est. 1792. https://www.sefaria.org/Safa_Echat_on_Pesach_Haggadah?tab=contents.
——. *Simchat HaRegel*. Publication date est. 1782. https://www.sefaria.org/Simchat_HaRegel_on_Pesach_Haggadah?tab=contents.
Behzad, Nasir and Qarizadah, Daud. "The man who helped blow up the Bamiyan Buddhas." BBC Afghan, 12 March 2015.
Bingham, Emily. *My Old Kentucky Home: The Astonishing Life and Reckoning of an Iconic American Song*. New York: Knopf, 2022.
Block, Bradley. Interview with Megan Gerber. Physician's Guide to Doctoring, podcast audio. "The Physician's Guide to Trauma-Informed Healthcare Approaches with Dr. Megan Gerber." August 13, 2019. https://www.physiciansguidetodoctoring.com/podcast/episode/4e529538/physicians-guide-to-trauma-informed-healthcare-approaches-with-dr-megan-gerber.
Bondi, Tevele. *Maarechet Heidenheim on Haggadah*. Frankfurt am Main: 1898.
Bowler, Kate. *Everything Happens for a Reason and Other Lies I've Loved*. New York: Random House, 2018.
——. *The Everything Happens Podcast*, podcast audio. "Kate Bowler and David Brooks: Never, Ever Enough." November 30, 2021. https://katebowler.com/podcasts/david-brooks-kate-bowler-never-ever-enough/.
Brown, Erica. *Happier Endings: A Meditation on Life and Death*. New York: Simon and Schuster, 2013.
——. *Leadership in the Wilderness*. Jerusalem: Toby Press, 2013.
——. *Seder Talk: The Conversational Haggadah*. New Milford, CT: Maggid, 2015.
Browne, Jackson. "Cocaine." Track 5. *Running on Empty*. Asylum, 1977. Cassette.
——. "The Pretender." Track 8. *The Pretender*. Asylum/Elektra, 1976. Cassette.
Charon, Rita. *Narrative Medicine: Honoring the Stories of Illness*. London: Oxford University Press, 2006.
Children's Hospital of Pittsburgh. https://www.chp.edu/about/donate/albert-lexie.

Christakis, Nicholas. *Death Foretold: Prophecy and Prognosis in Medical Care*. Chicago: University of Chicago Press, 1997.

Dick, Phillip, Spotnitz, Frank, and Oleson, Erik. *The Man in the High Castle*. Season 2, Episode 3. "Travelers." Daniel Sackheim, director. Amazon Prime Video, streaming. December 16, 2016.

Drzymalski, Emily. "Scott Stern discusses American Plan legacy." *The Pitt News*, January 11, 2019.

Edson, Margaret. *W;t*. New York: Faber and Faber, 1993.

Eiesland, Nancy L. *The Disabled God: Toward a Liberatory Theology of Disability*. Nashville, TN: Abingdon, 1994.

El Sayed, Abdul. 2019 University of Michigan School of Medicine Commencement Address. https://www.youtube.com/watch?v=EQ7LnzP1QmU.

Epstein, Barukh HaLevi. *Barukh SheAmar on Haggadah*. Tel Aviv: National Library of Israel, 1968. Translated by Mark Greenspan. https://www.sefaria.org/Barukh_SheAmar_on_Pesach_Haggadah?tab=contents.

Ettlinger, Jacob. *Minchat Ani*. Altona, Germany: 1874.

Fortin, Jacey. "The Statue at the Center of Charlottesville's Storm." *New York Times*, August 13, 2017.

Fox, Andrea, Gurung, Ashok, Kurek, Kimberley, Thompson, Kenneth, and Weinkle, Jonathan. "Meeting the psychiatric challenges facing the Bhutanese refugee community in Pittsburgh: How one Community Health Center is doing it." Presentation at North American Refugee Health Conference (virtual), September 21, 2020.

Frankl, Viktor. *Man's Search for Meaning*. New York: Pocket Books, 1984.

Gawande, Atul. *Being Mortal*. New York: Metropolitan Books, 2014.

———. "The Hot Spotters." *New Yorker*, January 16, 2011. https://www.newyorker.com/magazine/2011/01/24/the-hot-spotters.

Glick, Shmuel Tzvi-Hirsch. *Ein Ya'akov*. Chicago: 1921.

Goelet, Ogden. "Moses' Egyptian Name." *Bible Review* 19:3 (2003). https://library.biblicalarchaeology.org/article/moses-egyptian-name/.

Goodman, Mark Asher. *Life Lessons from Recently Dead Rabbis:Hasidut for the People*. Middletown, DE: Bayit, 2023.

Gorfinkel, Jordan and Zadok, Erez. *Passover Haggadah Graphic Novel*. New Milford, CT: Koren, 2019.

Gormley, Ken. Public remarks at the ribbon-cutting of the Duquesne University College of Medicine, Pittsburgh, PA, January 17, 2024.

Greenberg, Rabbi Irving. "Judaism as an Exodus Religion." *The Jewish Way: Living the Holidays*. New York: Simon and Schuster, 1988.

Groves, James. "Taking Care of the Hateful Patient." *New England Journal of Medicine*, 298:16 (1978). 883–887.

Halevi, Yehuda. "Where Will I Find You?" Translation by Peter Cole, 2012. At https://www.poetryfoundation.org/poetrymagazine/poems/55427/where-will-i-find-you#:~:text=Where%2C%20Lord%2C%20will%20I%20find,place%20is%20high%20and%20obscured.&text=won't%20I%20find%20you,your%20glory%2-ofills%20the%20world.

Haza, Ofra. "HaKotel." Track 13. *Shirei Moledet 3*. Hed Arzi, 1998. CD.

Held, Shai. *Judaism Is About Love: Recovering the Heart of Jewish Life*. New York: Farrar, Straus, and Giroux, 2024.

———. "Between Memory and Anticipation: An Exploration of Psalm 126." *L'Or HaNer: The Light of Discovery*. New York: The Hadar Institute, 2023.

Hepps, Tammy. "The Jews of Homestead and the 1892 Strike." https://homesteadhebrews.com/articles/the-jews-of-homestead-and-the-1892-strike/.

Herz, Marcus. "Daily Prayer of a Physician." https://www.jewishvirtuallibrary.org/daily-prayer-of-a-physician.

Heschel, Abraham Joshua. *The Sabbath*. New York: Farrar, Strauss, and Giroux, 2005.

Ibn Pakuda, Bahya. *Duties of the Heart*. Zaragoza, Spain: 1080. https://www.sefaria.org/Duties_of_the_Heart?tab=contents.

Kinot for Tisha B'Av Day (Ashkenaz). https://www.sefaria.org/Kinnot_for_Tisha_B'Av_(Ashkenaz)?tab=contents.

Kleinman, Arthur. *The Illness Narratives: Suffering, Healing, and the Human Condition*. New York: Basic Books, 1988.

Kohrt BA and Hruschka DJ. "Nepali Concepts of Psychological Trauma: The Role of Idioms of Distress, Ethnopsychology, and Ethnophysiology in Alleviating Suffering and Preventing Stigma." *Cult Med Psychiatry*. 2010 June ; 34(2): doi:10.1007/s11013-010-9170-2.

Krasner, Jonathan. "The World Is Broken, So Humans Must Repair It: The History and Evolution of Tikkun Olam." Brandeis University, May 22, 2023. https://www.brandeis.edu/jewish-experience/history-culture/2023/may/tikkun-olam-history.html#:~:text=How%20can%20humanity%20restore%20the,world%2C%20which%20was%20intrinsically%20evil.

Kubler-Ross Foundation. "5 Stages of Grief." https://www.ekrfoundation.org/5-stages-of-grief/5-stages-grief/.

Kulp, Joshua. *The Schechter Haggadah*. Jerusalem: Schechter Institute of Jewish Studies, 2009.

Laskas, Jean Marie. *Concussion*. New York: Random House Group, 2015.

Lee Char SJ, Evans LR, Malvar GL, and White DB. "A Randomized Trial of Two Methods to Disclose Prognosis to Surrogate Decision Makers in Intensive Care Units." *Am J Respir Crit Care Med*. 2010 Oct 1;182(7):905–9. DOI: 10.1164/rccm.201002-0262OC.

Lentz, Laura. Facebook post. August 30, 2019. https://www.facebook.com/Laura.Lentz.6/posts/10220635357142590.

Levin, Dan. "Where We Let God In." https://reformjudaism.org/learning/torah-study/torah-commentary/where-we-let-god.

Levin, Shlomo. *The Human Rights Haggadah*. Middletown, DE: 2023. www.haggadahsrus.com.

Lewittes, Adina. "Smashing the Tablets: Disassembling and Reassembling the Torah for a New Generation." 19th Chevra Kadisha and Jewish Cemetery Conference (virtual), June 14, 2021.

Liebowitz, Liel, interview with Natan Sharansky. *Unorthodox*, podcast audio, Ep. 240, "Respect Your Elders," August 13, 2020. https://www.tabletmag.com/podcasts/unorthodox/episode-240-esther-povitsky-comedy-special-natan-sharansky-memoir.

Liebowitz, Liel, interview with Ethan Tucker. *Take One*, podcast audio, December 28, 2020. https://www.tabletmag.com/podcasts/take-one/pesachim-36-and-37.

Lockhart, PR. "New York just removed a statue of a surgeon who experimented on enslaved women." *Vox*, April 18, 2018. https://www.vox.com/identities

/2018/4/18/17254234/j-marion-sims-experiments-slaves-women-gynecology-statue-removal.

Lown, Bernard. *The Lost Art of Healing*. Boston: Houghton Mifflin, 1996.

Luzzatto, Samuel David. *Shadal on Exodus*. Padua: 1871. https://www.sefaria.org/Shadal_on_Exodus?tab=contents.

Mahler, Ari. "I Am the Jewish Nurse." Facebook post, November 3, 2018. No longer publicly available.

Maimonides, Moses. Mishneh Torah Human Dispositions (*Hilkhot De'ot*). https://www.sefaria.org/texts/Halakhah/Mishneh%20Torah.

Miller, Brian C. *Reducing Secondary Traumatic Stress: Skills for Sustaining a Career in the Helping Professions*. New York: Routledge, 2022.

Miranda, Lin-Manuel. "Take a Break." Act 2, Track 3. *Hamilton (Original Broadway Cast Soundtrack)*. Atlantic, 2015. CD

Morinis, Alan. *Everyday Holiness: The Jewish Spiritual Path of Mussar*. Boulder: Trumpeter, 2007.

Nguyen, Michael. "Forced Organ Harvesting: A Decades-long Injustice in Need of International Accountability and Action." Markkula Center for Applied Ethics, Santa Clara University. https://www.scu.edu/ethics/healthcare-ethics-blog/forced-organ-harvesting-a-decades-long-injustice-in-need-of-international-accountability-and-action/.

Nimura, Janice P. *The Doctors Blackwell*. New York: Norton, 2021.

Ochs, Vanessa. *The Passover Haggadah: A Biography*. Princeton, NJ: Princeton University Press, 2020.

Parnell, Peter and Sorkin, Aaron. *The West Wing*, S2:E10, "Noel." Directed by Thomas Schlamme. Aired December 20, 2000, NBC-TV.

"Parran Hall Name Disappears After Board of Trustees Agrees with Chancellor's Recommendation." *University Times*, 50:22 (2018).

Rabinowitz, David. *Ephod Bad*. Warsaw: 1872.

Reddick, Bonzo. "Implementation of a Health Equity Curriculum Into Undergraduate and Graduate Medical Education." Society for Teachers of Family Medicine Conference on Medical Student Education (held virtually). February 1, 2021.

———. "The Intersection of Racism & Race-based Medical Decision Making in Medical Education." Society for Teachers of Family Medicine Conference on Medical Student Education (held virtually). February 1, 2021.

Rogers, Stan. "McDonnell on the Heights." Track 7. *From Fresh Water*. Fogarty's Cove Music, 1984, CD.

Rogers, Tom. "Murray State Coach Asks for Lee Statue to be Removed." WKDZ Radio. June 1, 2020. https://www.wkdzradio.com/2020/06/01/murray-state-coach-asks-for-lee-statue-to-be-removed/.

Rosenberg, Moshe. *The (Unofficial) Hogwarts Haggadah*. Lexington, KY: Moshe Rosenberg, 2017.

Rosenberg, Yudel. *Divrei Negidim*. Publication date and location uncertain. https://www.sefaria.org/Divrei_Negidim_on_Pesach_Haggadah?tab=contents.

Sacks, Jonathan. *Morality: Restoring the Common Good in Divided Times*. New York: Basic Books, 2020.

Schiff, Danny. Facebook post, April 1, 2020. https://www.facebook.com/dschiff.o/posts/10220070274441156.

Sheehy-Skeffington, Jennifer. "Why We Shouldn't Push a Positive Mindset on Those in Poverty." *Psyche.* 16 February 2022. https://psyche.co/ideas/why-we-shouldnt-push-a-positive-mindset-on-those-in-poverty.

Shem, Samuel. *The House of God.* Richard Marek Publishers: New York, 1978.

Silberberg, Naftali. "Why Four Cups of Wine?" https://www.chabad.org/holidays/passover/pesach_cdo/aid/658549/jewish/Why-four-cups-of-wine.htm .

Skloot, Rebecca. *The Immortal Life of Henrietta Lacks.* New York: Crown, 2010.

Sontag, Susan. *Illness as Metaphor* and *AIDS and Its Metaphors.* New York: Picador, 1988.

Staicu M-L and Cutov M. Anger and health risk behaviors. *Journal of Medicine and Life* Vol. 3, No.4, October-December 2010, pp.372-375. https://www.ncbi.nlm.nih.gov/pmc/articles/PMC3019061/.

Sweet, Victoria. "Slow Medicine." Plenary address. Conference on Medicine and Religion, Portland, OR, March 14, 2022.

Tolkien, JRR. *The Two Towers.* New York: Ballantine, 1965.

Treves, Johanan. *Kimcha Davshuna.* Bologna, 1540.

University of Colorado School of Medicine, Center for Bioethics and Humanities. "What Worries You Most?" https://www.cuanschutz.edu/centers/bioethicshumanities/arts-and-humanities/past-exhibits/what-worries-you-most.

Van Der Kolk, Bessel. *The Body Keeps the Score: Brain, Mind, and Body in the Healing of Trauma.* New York: Penguin, 2014.

Vonnegut, Kurt. "Fortitude." *Wampeters, Foma, and Granfalloons (Opinions).* Delacorte Press: New York, 1974. TV version from the series *Kurt Vonnegut's Monkey House.* https://www.youtube.com/watch?v=JNNSQWw81rk.

Weil, Yedidiah Tiah. *Marbeh Lesaper.* Publication date and location uncertain. https://www.sefaria.org/Marbeh_Lesaper_on_Pesach_Haggadah?tab=contents.

Weinkle, Jonathan. "Dire Straits." Healers Who Listen blog. https://healerswholisten.com/dire-straits/.

———. "Don't Be an Adler." Healers Who Listen blog. https://healerswholisten.com/dont-be-an-adler/.

———. "Golden Guilt." Healers Who Listen blog. https://healerswholisten.com/golden-guilt/.

———. *Healing People, Not Patients: Creating Authentic Relationships in Modern Healthcare.* Monterey, CA: Healthy Learning, 2019.

———. "Purple Hats." Healers Who Listen blog. https://healerswholisten.com/purple-hats/.

———. "Try to Be a Man." Healers Who Listen blog. https://healerswholisten.com/try-to-be-a-man/.

———. "What Goes Up When the Idols Come Down?" Pittsburgh Jewish Chronicle/Times of Israel blog. https://blogs.timesofisrael.com/what-goes-up-when-the-idols-come-down/.

Weiss, Ruhama. "Neither Suffering nor its Rewards: A Story about Intimacy and Dealing with Suffering and with Death." *Midrash and Medicine: Healing Body and Soul in the Jewish Tradition.* Cutter, William ed. Woodstock, VT: Jewish Lights, 2011.

Wen, Leana and Kosowsky, Joshua. *When Doctors Don't Listen.* New York: St. Martin's, 2012.

White Coats for Black Lives. *Racial Justice Report Card, 2019.* http://whitecoatsforblacklives.org/rjrc.

Wible, Pamela. "What I've Learned from 547 Doctor Suicides (Now 2000+)." October 28, 2017. https://www.idealmedicalcare.org/.

Worley, Peter. "The Ship of Theseus." *The If Machine*. https://www.philosophy-foundation.org/enquiries/view/the-ship-of-theseus.

Zion, Noam and Zion, Mishael. *A Night to Remember: The Haggadah of Contemporary Voices*. Jerusalem: Zion Holiday Publications, 2007.

Zoloth, Laurie. "Suffering and its Uselessness." Plenary Session, Conference on Medicine and Religion. Ohio State University, Columbus, OH, March 13, 2023.

www.ingramcontent.com/pod-product-compliance
Lightning Source LLC
Chambersburg PA
CBHW071227230426
43668CB00011B/1337